ROBERT CREELEY'S LIFE AND WORK

UNDER DISCUSSION
Donald Hall, General Editor

Robert Creeley's Life and Work
A Sense of Increment

Edited by John Wilson

Ann Arbor
THE UNIVERSITY OF MICHIGAN PRESS

1990   1989   1988   1987   4   3   2   1

Poems from *Hello, Later,* and *Mirrors* copyright © 1975, 1976, 1977,
1978, 1979, 1981, 1982, 1983 by Robert Creeley; reprinted by
permission of New Directions Publishing Corporation.

Library of Congress Cataloging-in-Publication Data

Robert Creeley's life and work.

   (Under discussion)
   Includes index.
   1. Creeley, Robert, 1926–   —Criticism and
interpretation.   I. Wilson, John, 1947–   .
II. Title.   III. Series.
PS3505.R43Z88   1988   811'.54   87-19079
ISBN 0-472-09374-6 (alk. paper)
ISBN 0-472-06374-X (pbk. : alk. paper)

Contents

Part Two   The 1960s: Into a Present, a Presence

Part Three   The 1970s: A Life Tracking Itself

Introduction

"There is a sense of increment, of accumulation, in these poems that is very dear to me," Robert Creeley says in the preface to his *Collected Poems* to explain why he did not "decorously omit" a single poem that found its way into print between 1945 and 1975. Criticism of Creeley has been equally incremental and accumulative, making this volume of selected writings on his life and work as inevitable as his own collected works. Few American poets since 1950 have received so much persistent attention, in part because few have written with such steady perseverance. During the more than thirty-five years that have passed since *Le Fou* came out in 1952, Creeley's writing has issued in a steady stream of books and chapbooks—poetry, fiction, essays, letters, journals, interviews, a play—over eighty titles in all. And the responses to these works have amassed, ranging from the high praise of William Carlos Williams in his letter to Creeley dated January 18, 1960—"You have the subtlest feeling for the measure that I encounter anywhere except in the verses of Ezra Pound whom I cannot equal" (see Williams in this volume)—to the deprecation of an unnamed reviewer of *Poems 1950–1965:* "the effect [of Creeley's "numb repetition of colourless words"] is that of wading interminably through some unfamiliar shorthand or of listening to a glazed monotone, as of some drear party guest one has to watch because his boringness is hypnotic and girls are apt to fall under his greyly malign influence."[1]

The contention implicit in Williams's and this reviewer's remarks has been a central fact of Creeley's career as a poet. Two early and often-quoted critical judgments, those of Hugh Kenner and John Simon, have served as flags for the opposing camps: Kenner calls Creeley "one of the very few contemporaries with whom it is necessary to keep current," while Simon says, "There are two things to be said about Creeley's poems: they are short; they are not short enough." It should come as no surprise that Kenner, who shaped his very notion of a poem on the works of Ezra Pound and William Carlos Williams, would admire a younger poet who had schooled himself so much on their work; nor should we expect a man with Simon's conservative taste for tradition to be anything but displeased with Creeley's departures from it. But Creeley has not thrown off tradition, nor did Williams, notwithstanding his ardent appeals to American poets to turn their backs on England and Europe.

Many of Creeley's admirers share the view that his poems reaffirm tradition, and they variously trace him back to Provençal lyric, English Metaphysical, and American Puritan poetry. More often and fittingly his poetry is considered to be a part of the Whitman-Pound-Williams-Zukofsky strain of nonmetrical verse, which by now should also be considered a tradition. As early as 1950, after reading the first poems that Creeley sent to him in a letter dated May 27 of that year, Charles Olson wrote back, "say I (dictum): this man can . . . truly return us to the antient anglo-saxon heart" (see Olson's letter in this volume). Ten years later Williams expressed a similar opinion in another letter to Creeley: "the way the [w]ords fall into place . . . bespeaks your craft, your artistic ability just as [it did for] the poets of the Elizabethan era—whom you are destined to follow" (see Williams in this volume). And Robert Duncan, Cid Corman, George Butterick, and others also believe that Creeley is, in some sense or another, quite traditional. Especially before he found his way into a central place among the avant-garde in the 1960s, he was clearly working from the tradition in several ways.

Creeley is fond of ready-made language, and in his early poems it often comes from the works of earlier poets. That is, tradition comes into the poems as it has come into poetry for centuries, by way of allusion or the retrospective line. Many of these early poems are sharply ironic, and sometimes the lines he echoes are imbued with ironies aimed at himself. The best-known instance is his modification of Sir Edward Dyer's "My mind to me a kingdom is" to "My mind / to me a mangle is."

With the self-directed irony blunted, he also changes Byron's "She walks in Beauty, like the night" to "She walks in beauty like a lake," and Whitman's "Out of the cradle endlessly rocking" to "Out of the table endlessly rocking." This device would soon grow tedious, and fortunately Creeley abandoned it before it became banal. More often he is plainly stimulated by the language of a former poet: by Dante's vernacular, for example, in "*Guido, i' vorrei che tu e Lape ed io,*" which he renders, "Guido, / I would that you, me & Lapo"; or Campion's "follow thy fair sunne unhappie shadow," which attunes him to "another air, melody," when his love speaks; or Nashe's "Brightness falls from the air," which echoes in his mind equally with the simple words "flower, stream" in a poem beginning, "I'm almost / done, the hour / echoes"; or the two lines by Williams, "the stain of love / is upon the world!" which he has worked into two of his poems, "Love" in *The Charm* and "The Edge" in *In London*.

Creeley has also written in (and often played with) traditional forms, especially in his early versions of the ballad, the alba, and the song; and he has long relied on that most common of English stanzas, the quatrain, although he places his own asymmetrical, contemporary stamp on it. "Kore," one of Creeley's best-known poems, is written in such quatrains, which retain a faint trace of the traditional symmetry of metrical quatrains, though his are not measured uniformly by either accents or syllables. But the old balance shows through in the heavily stressed accents of the lines in iambic dimeter: "I came upon," "by chance to move," "and what I saw," "her eyes were dark," etc. The lack of variation in the stress of his accented and unaccented syllables would lead to a deadly monotony if he did not break away from the iambic dimeter. This is Creeley's way of achieving movement in the lines of "Kore" and many other poems, even if the movement is a jolting progress, or what Creeley has termed "stumbling" through a poem. "Kore" is even further removed from rhyme than from meter. In the six stanzas there is only one true rhyme (*green / seen*) and one slant rhyme (*move / love*).[2] In short, "Kore" only seems to be written in a traditional form. Even the inversion in that memorable first stanza—

> As I was walking
> I came upon
> chance walking
> the same road upon

—is not like the inversions in Sydney or Herbert or Pope. According to Robert Peters, "Creeley risks the sort of inversion Hardy liked to include as part of his poetic carpentry" (see Peters in this volume), but the severe wrenching of natural English word order in his placement of the second "upon" is closer to Emily Dickinson than to Hardy, and it resembles Cummings even more: a restrained version of the distorted syntax in "anyone lived in a pretty how town." Though the connection here between Hardy and Creeley seems improbable, Peters is not wrong to find in Creeley an affinity with Hardy, who, I should add, probably brought more of the English tradition into the twentieth century than any other poet. In *Mirrors* (1983), Creeley makes his own poem of Hardy's "The Voice" by adopting the echoing sounds, by establishing a stanza and then abruptly shifting from it, and most important, by sharing the grief that Hardy expresses because the happiness of his first days with Emma haunts him across a gulf of unhappiness (see "Versions" in this volume).

However much Creeley may make use of tradition in his poems, he is far more often and accurately associated with the new art movements of the 1950s and 1960s—in particular with Charles Olson and Projective Verse (Creeley's dictum, "FORM IS NEVER MORE THAN AN EXTENSION OF CONTENT," has been the most remembered assertion in Olson's "Projective Verse" essay); with the jazz of Charlie Parker, Miles Davis, and Thelonious Monk; and with Abstract Expressionism and Minimalism. Anyone who would say, as Creeley does in *Pieces*, "the damn function of *simile*, always a displacement of what *is* happening," certainly belongs more among mid-twentieth-century writers than the Metaphysicals, with whom Creeley has been compared in numerous reviews. Creeley's place among the new writers of the 1950s and his interest in the new art movements of that decade, then, provide a necessary

4

background for the experimental side of his poetry and how it developed.

As early as the 1940s, while still at Harvard, Creeley was spending hour upon hour day after day listening to jazz. (He was still doing so with his friend Dan Rice, an Abstract Expressionist, at Black Mountain College almost ten years later.) While he was absorbed in jazz and the possibilities of its rhythms in his poetry, he also became interested in the Abstract Expressionists. After Creeley moved to France in 1951, he met René Laubiès who ran the Galerie Fachetti in Paris, and it was Laubiès who introduced him to Abstract Expressionism. The first show of Jackson Pollock's paintings that Creeley saw was at the Galerie Fachetti, where he also saw paintings by Sam Francis and perhaps Gene Davis. "But at Black Mountain," Creeley said in an interview with Kevin Power, "I literally came into all the energy of and all the interest in the so-called Abstract Expressionists. They were very much a part of the college, although at that point they weren't physically present" (see Power in this volume). Dan Rice, of course, "the chosen of Kline, de Kooning and Rothko" was physically present. John Chamberlain, whose sculptures share a good deal with Abstract Expressionist painting, was also there and became a close friend of Creeley.

Despite Creeley's sustained interest, it wasn't until the mid-1960s that the methods of jazz and Abstract Expressionism became distinctly visible in his poetry. During this early period of excitement about the new jazz and art, Creeley was actually working more on fiction than on poetry. "Initially," he says in his introduction to *The Collected Prose,* "I had thought that my work as a writer would be primarily in prose and so *The Gold Diggers,* published by my wife then and myself as The Divers Press in 1954, is the first book of my own imagination despite three small collections of poems preceding it." This is not to say that the earliest poems are imitative or unimaginative, though some of them are, but simply that the stories came first. The stories drew critical attention to Creeley before his poems did and, for the impression they made on Charles Olson, helped ally the founders of one of the most prominent poetry movements since World War II. In his "Introduction to Robert Creeley," which appeared with several of Creeley's stories in *New Directions XIII* (1951), Olson says nothing of Creeley as a poet. Considering him as a fiction writer, Olson claims that "we are here in the presence of a man putting his hands directly and responsibly to experience which is also our own. It is his presence that matters, for it rids us of artifice. . . . He is time, he is now, the force" (see Olson's "Introduction to Robert Creeley" in this volume). Olson's sense of Creeley's stature as a fiction writer was grandiose ("the push beyond Lawrence," he wrote in a letter for *Origin*), but the point here is not the accuracy of Olson's estimation but what kind of writer Creeley was in his eyes.

It may be that Olson's excitement over the stories lay in "the perfect consistency between the principles [Olson] brings to bear upon and sees exemplified in [the] stories and the basic tenets of his own Projectivist poetics," as Nathaniel Mackey claims.[3] In brief, Mackey finds Creeley's stories more projective than his poems before *Pieces,* and for this reason, Mackey claims, Olson favored the stories. But the poetry and fiction on the whole, contrary to Mackey's distinctions, share a great deal from the beginning. Just as Creeley dispenses with a fictive narrator, he avoids personae in the poems. In both Creeley's poems and fiction, man, as Linda W. Wagner says, "is nearly always alone, frighteningly alone" (see Wagner's "Review of *The Gold Diggers*" in this volume). The stories and the poems are intensely focused on the details of domestic life as, one assumes, Creeley has lived it. Even the sentences in the stories, broken into tiny phrases by commas, resemble the "stumbling" narrow lines in the poems. The main difference between the fiction and poems is simply the expected one between lyric and story: that of duration. Creeley takes us with him longer in the fiction than in the poems. The sources of the feelings and the materials of the perceptions, however, are very similar, often the same. The single fact of a painful first marriage is the hub around which many of the poems in *For Love* and the stories in *The Gold Diggers* and *The Island* revolve.

Olson's early admiration for Creeley's stories and Creeley's proportionate admiration for Olson's poems led to an exchange of letters lasting two decades that has recently come to light in the Black Sparrow edition of *The Complete Correspondence*.[4] Creeley and Olson wrote at a furious pace during the first couple of years (the most important years of the correspondence), sounding each other's ideas and exchanging poems, stories, and essays. These letters were extremely consequential to both men and to the course of American poetry for years to come, because in them Olson and Creeley were working out their own poetics. Sherman Paul, an admirer of both Olson and Creeley and an apologist for their work, calls the exchange of letters "unquestionably one of the great correspondences of the twentieth century" (see Paul in this volume). It is doubtless one of the most intense and enthusiastic, although Olson's eccentric, telegraphic prose often seems affected and exasperating rather than comic or pithy, or simply irascible, as Pound's letters are.

The correspondence has more than a merely retrospective literary value (in how, for example, it contributed to Olson's "Projective Verse" and to Creeley's early poetry); it was also instrumental in the development of Creeley's career. On the basis of Creeley's letters as much as his stories and poems, Olson, who had become rector of Black Mountain College in the early 1950s, made Creeley editor of *Black Mountain Review* and a lecturer at the college. *Black Mountain Review* lasted only two years and its circulation remained small. But it was extremely important to the younger poets who embraced an open poetics developing out of Pound and Williams, and who consequently were ignored by the literary magazines then dominated by metrical verse and New Criticism (see Gilbert Sorrentino's "Black Mountaineering," in this volume). Creeley's reputation at the time did not extend far beyond the writers connected with his magazine and with Cid Corman's *Origin*. During the 1950s, only one established literary magazine, *Poetry,* consistently reviewed Creeley's books, which were being brought out by small publishers like Golden Goose Press, the Creeleys' Divers Press, and Jonathan Williams's Jargon Press. Even when Robert Bly drew attention to Creeley in 1959 by writing his seminal essay on "The Work of Robert Creeley," he was doing something quite eccentric. And this essay, published in the second issue of Bly's embattled new magazine, the *Fifties,* which was just starting to foster a new American Surrealism that would flourish in the next decade, attracted to Creeley a limited readership from a different circle of poets. But when Creeley gained recognition in the 1960s, Black Mountain College and *Black Mountain Review* were almost inseparable from his name.

Several key events helped Creeley toward renown. First, William Carlos Williams gradually rose to fame during the 1950s, which slowly opened a way for poets writing non-metrical verse (and no one had worked from Williams's lyrical poems into his own with more success than Creeley). Then, Allen Ginsberg rocketed into international notoriety after he read "Howl" at the Six Gallery in San Francisco in 1956, and the City Lights Books publication of *Howl and Other Poems* that same year resulted in the celebrated obscenity trial of 1957. By 1957 there was already something of an alliance between Ginsberg and Creeley. After he left Black Mountain in 1956, Creeley moved to San Francisco, and there he met Ginsberg, Michael McClure, Philip Whalen, and other Beat poets. And in the most famous issue of *Black Mountain Review,* number 7, which came out in the autumn of 1957, Creeley linked the Black Mountain writers with the Beat poets. A few years later Donald Allen's anthology *The New American Poetry* (1960) again placed the Beat and Black Mountain poets side by side and helped Creeley to attract the national attention that would increase during the 1960s, the decade that witnessed the emergence of his current critical reputation.

That Ginsberg became a hero (or archetype) to the alternative society in the 1960s is easy to understand. He shared its adherents' attraction to Eastern religions, chanted at his poetry readings, used and advocated that others use "mind-expanding" drugs, protested U.S. involvement in Vietnam, blew the whistle on the CIA, and so on. Ginsberg was almost an embodiment of the late 1960s. That the angry political poems of Robert Bly had a wide appeal to a growing mass of protestors against the Vietnam War is equally understandable. But how a poet as personal and as silent on politics and as "austere and demanding" as Creeley could attract a wide readership and large audiences at his readings is perplexing. Robert Hass, who uses those fitting adjectives "austere and demanding" to describe Creeley's poems, believes that Creeley became popular because his readers and audiences were "extraordinarily sensitive to language" and clearly sensed that Creeley had gone beyond the false assumptions commonly made in language (see Hass in this volume). Creeley does not assume as writers commonly do that he, in his conscious mind, is in control. Rather, he registers in his syntax and conveys in his subjects a "world manifestly and wildly out of control." According to Hass, Creeley's readers and audiences sensed this, that he above all the others was the poet of "a world gone out of control and the crazy assumption of control that the ego makes." "I Know a Man," Hass says, was "the poem of the decade" on that subject. Bly, Kenner, Duncan, and most others who admire Creeley agree with Hass, at least insofar as they all attribute much of Creeley's appeal to his use of language. But people probably were equally or even more attracted to something as obvious as the prominence of love in Creeley's poems. It is not, of course, the traditional ideal love, but a troubled, intense love that often leaves him feeling isolated rather than united. In this respect, he has been the poet of the strained, difficult love relationships that appear so often in contemporary American novels. Whatever its condition, love, even before language, has been Creeley's concern as a poet (*For Love,* after all, preceded *Words*). Through the politics and Eastern religions and "tribalism" of the 1960s, Creeley's "maid and her wight / Come whispering by"; and though Creeley's lovers are rarely as romantic as these two from Hardy's "In Time of 'The Breaking of Nations,'" their story, too, attracts us and will go on when the surrounding commotion of the 1960s has become a dim corner in history.

At this time, when Creeley's reputation was being made on the merits of *For Love,* his poems began to change. *Words* (1967) was the turning point, and *Pieces* (1969) and *In London* (1972) followed in relatively quick succession. The poems in these books are more open than those in *For Love* and are closely aligned with the paintings and jazz that had begun to impress him so much years earlier at Harvard, in Europe, and at Black Mountain College.

Words is far more abstract than *For Love,* more concerned with acts of thinking and writing than with thoughts or finished products. When Creeley was writing the poems in *Words,* he didn't want to get a thought down but to be "In- / side the / thinking" as he is in "The Circle." Eventually, in *In London,* this desire becomes artlessly literal: "He wants to sleep in a bed / he keeps in his head." But in *Words* it is not so simple and unmistakably resembles Pollock's desire to be *in* his paintings while in the act of painting them. Just as Pollock made paintings by focusing on the action of putting paint on a canvas independent of anything represented, Creeley makes the action of words falling into place the subject of a poem:

> Patterns
> of sounds, endless
> discretions, whole
> pauses of nouns,
>
> clusters. This
> and that, that
> one, this
> and that. Looking,
>
> seeing, some
> thing, being
> some. . . .
>
> ("A Method")

Creeley's recurrent metaphorical walking in his poems, walking with words, is as close as a poet can come to Pollock's literal walking on an unstretched canvas on the floor—across it and around it and in all directions—while he applied the paint. The poem in *Words* that best conveys Creeley's corresponding method is "Walking":

> In my head I am
> walking but I am not
> in my head, where

```
is there to walk,
not thought of, is
the road itself more

than seen. I think
it might be, feel
as my feet do, and

continue, and
at last reach, slowly,
one end of my intention.
```

Here as elsewhere in *Words,* Creeley focuses on the process of his thinking rather than on any object of his thought. The "music" in *Words*—the "Patterns / of sounds," "pauses of nouns, // clusters. This / and that, that / one, this / and that"—so clipped and tense and heavily punctuated, also seems at last to have captured the rhythms of jazz that had held Creeley's attention for so long. To my ear this music most resembles Thelonius Monk's ingenious pauses, splintering melodic lines, and reduction of notes struck, like "This / and that, that / one, this / and that." *This* and *that* lack referents here, as they do often in the poems since *Words,* and bring nothing to mind other than their sounds, their pattern of sounds. Here Creeley is writing purely with an ear that has been trained on jazz for years.

Like Williams in *Paterson,* Creeley begins *Pieces* (published two years after *Words*) by announcing his method, and the method is unequivocally indebted to Abstract Expressionism, or to use Harold Rosenberg's more accurate term, Action Painting:

```
A period
at the end of a sentence
which

began it was
into a present,
a presence
```

saying
something
as it goes.

•

No forms less
than activity.

But Creeley has no framework, no direction, no preconceived course that he will follow as Williams does in his quest for a language; rather Creeley builds his book with

Nothing but
comes and goes
in a moment.

At least he proposes to do so, and the plan carries him a good distance away from the familiar reflection on the past that has dominated poetry since Wordsworth. A few poems are situated in the past—"The Moon" is a beautiful meditation on the simple domestic activities of Creeley and his wife on a moonlit night and, at the same time, on being alone in the universe—but most of them attend to what is going on in an ongoing present that consists of both concrete things,

Cup.
Bowl.
Saucer.
Full.

and abstract thoughts. The abstractness of *Pieces,* according to Louis Martz, simultaneously vitalizes and threatens to ruin the poetry: "It is impossible, I believe, to become more abstract without destroying the very presence of poetry. Yet Creeley manages to hold himself at the taut edge of poetic existence. It is a dangerous technique, impossible, I imagine, to imitate successfully, but a unique and worthy achievement in its own right" (see Martz in this volume). Besides breaking away from the past time of most lyric poetry, Creeley also breaks down the boundaries of individual poems so that one often does not readily notice where a poem ends and another begins—as if a line in a Kline painting went off the edge of a canvas, onto the wall, and into the next canvas. Creeley no longer wanted to perfect the isolate poem, but to sustain the writing from day to day. This at once suggests what Creeley called Zukofsky's "continuing *song*," which a poet writes all his life, and a poetic journal in which the poems run on from entry to entry, as they literally do in *Hello: A Journal, February 29–May 3, 1976*.

A new development in *Pieces* and the books that extend from it for nearly ten years is the so-called Minimalism that actually began with "A Piece" in *Words:*

> One and
> one, two,
> three.

None of the Imagists ever reduced a poem so much, and even haiku are expansive by comparison.[5] In one important respect, however, this poem is not new at all. It thwarts our expectations as Mozart's music does. We hear an established melody coming back and expect it to be repeated, but instead it takes a surprising turn, and this brings us pleasure. Similarly, as soon as we hear "One and / one," we jump ahead of Creeley to complete the equation with "make two"; but Creeley meanwhile has pivoted in the second line, or dovetailed the first half of that simplest equation with the simplest sequence (one, two, three). Our expectation is unfulfilled and our pleasure increased, unless readers find such joinery in isolation too slight to enjoy (Mozart, after all, did not cut away all the furniture for the sake of a joint). Whether it occurs within a poem or is the poem itself, this pivoting in midclause or even midphrase fascinates Creeley and reappears in succeeding books. The way he pivots in the third line of "Here Again" from *Away* (1976)—

> After we
> were all
> a bed,

                                        a door, two
                                        windows
                                        and a chair

—results in a swing from narrative to objectivity, a swing away
from the perceiver toward the things perceived. A different kind
of pivot occurs within the entry of April 13 in *Hello:*

                                        Down and
                                        down, over
                                        and out.

In two three-word phrases consisting of four of the simplest
words in English, Creeley moves by suggestion from a foreboding doom to a simple signing off. There is no actor, no action,
nothing acted upon, no situation—and yet, because of the ordinary contexts of these phrases, we sense the fear and then the
relief, as if Creeley has had a sudden change of heart about death
itself: what at first seems threatening becomes the mere cessation
of activity.

   These poems are unarguably minimal. How much can I trim
without shearing away the poem altogether? Creeley seems to
have asked himself. What he sometimes ends up with is the
slightest trace, "And Ebbe / with love," or just the border of
something we cannot fathom, like the bit of blue or red streaking the edge of an otherwise empty Sam Francis painting.
Creeley gives us a phrase from a maxim without the maxim, one
from a narrative that he doesn't supply: "Those out for. / From
then on." In one poem in *In London,* he shows us how his
reductions may take place:

                                        Mouths nuzz-
                                        ling, "seeking
                                        in blind
                                        love," mouths nuzz-

                                        ling, "seek-
                                        ing in

<pre>
                    blind

                    love . . ."
</pre>

First there is at least a bit of flesh to embody a passion, but even that Creeley purposefully strips away to isolate the emotion that concerns him. Again, this impulse to abstract an emotion from any recognizable situation bears a strong resemblance to Abstract Expressionism, especially Pollock's "concrete pictorial sensations" freed from any images in the memory.

The impulse to abstract, reduce, and isolate leads Creeley not only to sever thinking and feeling from subject and object, but also to set an image apart from any surrounding images, as "The head / of a / pin on . . ." in *Pieces* serves to illustrate. Behind these isolated moments, images, phrases, and emotions lies the most extreme (and unrealizable) desire of any verbal reductionist. In an interview with Terry R. Bacon, Creeley spoke of his admiration for Samuel Beckett and indicated that he shares the desire that Beckett expressed to him one night in 1968 for "one word that would be autonomous, that would depend upon no other situation either in existence or in creation for its actuality."[6]

Creeley's most recent poems, contrary to this desire for one autonomous word, appear to be lengthening again, growing less jagged, less fragmentary, more balanced, and more complete. In a perceptive review of *The Collected Poems,* Thom Gunn remarks, "In the collections of the 1970s . . . poem leads into poem, group leads into group, and the book rather than the individual poem becomes the meaningful unit" (see Gunn in this volume). But in *Later* (1979) and *Mirrors* (1983), Creeley's attention returns to the discrete poem. And in these poems he is more reflective, more engaged with his past, with growing old, and with dying. For twenty-five years, Creeley's principal subject was, in Thom Gunn's words, "the intensely apprehended detail of the heterosexual private life" (X. J. Kennedy, less inclusively, has called it "the horrors of marriage"). In *Mirrors,* the earlier preoccupation with marriage and sex does not just diminish, it nearly vanishes. In its place come memories of childhood and reflections on his mother, his sister, his grandmother, and his father's death. The subject matter naturally leads Creeley into a more descriptive poetry, richer in images and more situational, as the conclusion to the initial poem, "First Rain," indicates:

> I
>
> walk quickly. The wind
> drives the rain, drenching
>
> my coat, pants, blurs
> my glasses, as I pass.

Poem after poem depicts a concrete scene, and the images suggest meaning in a traditional way:

> Wind lifts lightly
> the leaves, a flower,
> a black bird
>
> hops up to the bowl
> to drink. The sun
> brightens the leaves, back
>
> of them darker branches,
> tree's trunk. Night is still
> far from us.
>
> ("Wind Lifts")

Instead of making a poem of two phrases dovetailed together, he makes one of similes (that figure of speech he had so detested earlier), which fasten the little sound "oh" to appropriate visual images, ones that might evoke a small sigh. The latter of the two images expands beyond just a feeling of loss, caught in the fleeting moment, into an essential metaphor for life's brevity:

> Oh like a bird
> falls down

> out of air,
> oh like a disparate
>
> small snowflake
> melts momently.
>
> ("Oh")

Fred Moramarco finds "Prospect" (a poem on the color green and the memories it arouses in Creeley) to be "one of the most memorable and resonant poems in *Mirrors*" and yet, at the same time, "a completely atypical Creeley poem . . . because it utilizes conventional elements of poetry—symbolism, metaphor, and imagery—in a surprisingly typical manner" (see Moramarco in this volume). But "Prospect" is not an atypical poem in *Mirrors*. It is almost as if Creeley has begun to look in that essential mirror in which poets have reflected the world for ages, where night is death, green is the color of life, a melting snowflake is life's brevity, and so on—a far cry from "The head / of a / pin on. . . ." The moods, too, have changed. Death frequents the poems, but the intense loneliness of the earlier poetry has subsided. Loss of his own past concerns him more now, though even that he can half-recover, as he does in his "Mother's Voice":

> In these few years
> since her death I hear
> mother's voice say
> under my own, I won't
>
> want any more of that.
> My cheekbones resonate
> with her emphasis. . . .

The recent poems are rarely edged with the sharp irony of the early ones, and the sadness and fear and tenderness are at times soft, not "dreadfully soft," as Thom Gunn asserts, but openly soft. As he grows older and death comes closer, Creeley notices it more now in the plain details of his daily life, and his poems show us the man struggling to find the right attitude toward it:

Go down obscurely,
seem to falter

as if walking into water
slowly. Be of good cheer

and go as if indifferent,
even if not. . . .

("Be of Good Cheer")

In this brief directive, once again action and feeling absorb him. In this respect Creeley has not changed. His recent poems, in fact, offer no breakthrough, but—in the figures of speech, in the focus on activity, in the abstractness of some poems and concreteness of others, and in the "instances of feeling"—rather, a convergence of all that has gone before. *Mirrors,* after all, is a book of reflections.

Above all else, Creeley is a poet. The large body of stories and essays, the novel, the play, the literary diaries, his letters, and all else that he has written evince that he is also a writer in the larger sense; but fundamentally he is a poet because his mind turns first and last to words and the feelings locked up in and released by words. He has worked out of the tradition and in the vanguard, has been praised and panned for his performances in both, but when all is said, his place in the third quarter of twentieth-century American poetry will be central. His critics have called him narrow, but he has lived in so many places (Massachusetts, New Hampshire, France, Mallorca, Black Mountain, Vancouver, Guatemala, Buffalo, Bolinas, Maine . . .) and written so many books in various forms that include so much of his life, the word beside his name seems paradoxical. Within his slender poems there is range, and I hope that some sense of this range is conveyed in the selections in this volume. My first concern has been to include the best and most revealing responses to Creeley's work over the forty years he has been writing. This means that I have also included the criticism of insightful writers who dislike his work to give a voice to those who belong to countercurrents in modern American poetry. Suffice it to say that the essays, reviews, letters, and comments that follow bring out the variety of responses over the last four decades to Creeley's life and work, which, compared with most writers, are inseparable.

Acknowledgments

I am indebted to David Hamilton, who suggested me to Donald Hall when he was searching for someone to edit a volume on Robert Creeley, and to Donald Hall for offering me the task and for discerning advice along the way. Timothy Murray searched through letters to Robert Creeley held at Washington University and answered my every question with great care. The editorial advice of Lewis Hyde, Steve Allaback, and Beth Witherall has saved me time and kept me from regrettable errors. I thank all the authors who put me in touch with other authors of essays on Robert Creeley, none more than Robert Creeley himself, who has led me to works that I never would have found otherwise.

I also thank all the authors, publishers, and institutions that have granted permissions to reprint published material. Every effort has been made to secure permissions for all copyrighted work in this volume.

John Wilson

NOTES

1. John Berryman quotes this reviewer's final judgment, that Creeley's poems make "crushingly dull reading," in his poem "In & Out" and adds his own censure on apparently moral grounds when he says to Creeley, "Pray do not write to me again. Pitch defileth." Berryman appears to be speaking without irony even though "Pitch defileth" echoes Falstaff's mock-righteousness in the tavern scene of *Henry IV*, Part One, in which he plays King Henry in order to prepare Hal to meet with his father the next day.

2. This was, of course, a true rhyme and an extremely frequent one in Elizabethan and seventeenth-century English poetry.

3. Nathaniel Mackey, "*The Gold Diggers:* Projective Prose," *boundary 2* 6, no. 3; 7, no. 1 (Spring/Fall 1978): 471.

4. The selection of Olson's letters to Creeley that was published as the *Mayan Letters* (sixty pages written over a period of six months in 1951 when Olson was living in Lerma on the Yucatan peninsula) made readers aware of the correspondence, but few could have guessed its full scope before the publication of *Charles Olson and Robert Creeley: The Complete Correspondence*, 6 vols. (Santa Barbara, Calif.: Black Sparrow Press, 1980–85).

5. Creeley's Minimalism somewhat resembles Aram Saroyan's one-word poems like "Blod" and "*oxygen*," and Richard Brautigan's poems that are titles only (e.g., "8 Millimeter [mm]" in *Rommel Drives on Deep into Egypt*); but Creeley's Minimalist poems always retain at least some engagement in the movement of words strung together.

6. Terry R. Bacon, "How He Knows When to Stop: Creeley on Closure; A Conversation with the Poet," *American Poetry Review* 5, no. 6 (1976): 5–7.

Chronology

1926   Robert White Creeley born May 21 in Arlington,
            Massachusetts, to physician Oscar Slate Creeley and
            the former Genevieve Jules. One sister, Helen, born
            1922.

1928   Accident causes laceration to left eye and loss of the
            eye three years later.

1930   Father dies. Mother moves family to farm in West
            Acton where she works as public health nurse.

1940–43   On a scholarship attends Holderness School, a
            small boys' boarding school in Plymouth, New
            Hampshire. Publishes articles and stories in the
            Holderness literary magazine the *Dial,* of which he
            is editor-in-chief during his senior year.

1943   Enters Harvard.

1944–45   Drives an ambulance for the American Field Service
            in India.

1945   Returns to Harvard in the fall.

1946   Helps to edit Harvard *Wake,* no. 5, a special E. E.
            Cummings issue, in which Creeley's first published
            poem, "Return," appears. Marries Ann McKinnon
            and they move to Truro, Massachusetts.

1947   Drops out of Harvard during last semester of his
            senior year.

1948   Son David born in October.

1948–51   Lives at Rock Pool Farm near Littleton, New
            Hampshire, supplementing Ann's small income

from a trust fund by subsistence farming. Breeds pigeons and chickens, which he shows in Boston.

1949   Hears Cid Corman's Boston radio program "This Is Poetry" in December and begins correspondence with Corman that lasts until 1955.

1950   First public reading of poems on Corman's "This Is Poetry." In December son Thomas born. Gathers manuscripts from contemporary writers for an alternative magazine to be called the *Lititz Review*, which he and Jacob Leed attempt but fail to publish. Begins correspondence with Charles Olson. Becomes American editor for Rainer Gerhardt's German magazine *Fragmente*.

1951–52   Lives with family in Fontrousse and later Lambesc, both near Aix-en-Provence, France.

1951   Much of the material gathered for the *Lititz Review* goes into *Origin* I, the Olson issue, in which Creeley's "Hart Crane" appears. *Origin* II, "Featuring Robert Creeley," publishes four poems, three stories, the essay "Notes for a New Prose," and excerpts from letters by Creeley to Corman.

1952–55   Lives with family on Mallorca.

1952   In July daughter Charlotte born. Creeley serves briefly as American editor of Martin Seymour-Smith's Roebuck Press at Mallorca. *Le Fou*, his first book of poems, published by Golden Goose Press.

1953   Starts the Divers Press with his wife and, after printing *Origin* VIII and Paul Blackburn's *Proensa*, publishes his second book, *The Kind of Act Of* (poems), under the Divers Press imprint. *The Immoral Proposition* (poems) (Karlsruhe-Durlach, Germany: Jonathan Williams).* In December Olson asks Creeley to edit the *Black Mountain Review*.

---

*To distinguish them from American editions, the place of publication is given for English and European editions.

1954	*The Gold Diggers* (short stories) (Divers Press). In March first issue of *Black Mountain Review* comes out just before he leaves Mallorca without family to teach at Black Mountain College. In July returns to Mallorca to try to repair troubled marriage. Stays on quarterly schedule for *Black Mountain Review* with Summer, Fall, and Winter issues. Only three more issues appear, in 1955, 1956, and 1957. Anonymous pamphlet *A Snarling Garland of Xmas Verses* (Divers Press).
1955	In July returns to Black Mountain College. Divorced from Ann. *All That Is Lovely in Men* (poems) (Jonathan Williams).
1956	Resigns Black Mountain College. Visits San Francisco, where he meets Ginsberg, Kerouac, and other writers of the San Francisco renaissance. *If You* (poems) (Porpoise Bookshop). Moves to Albuquerque, where he teaches Latin, French, English, and later history, grades seven through nine, at the Academy for Boys (presently the Albuquerque Academy). "Given" a B.A. by Olson from Black Mountain College.
1957	In January meets and within two weeks marries Bobbie Louise Hoeck. *The Whip* (poems) (Worcester, England: Migrant Books). Begins work on M.A. at the University of New Mexico. In November daughter Sarah born.
1959	In February daughter Katherine Williams born. By July turns in M.A. thesis, a collection of poems. Moves with family to San Geronimo Miramar, near Patalul, Such., Guatemala, where he tutors the children of two *finca* owners over a two-year period. *A Form of Women* (poems) (Jargon Books in association with Corinth Books).
1960	M.A., University of New Mexico. Levinson Prize for ten poems in *Poetry,* vol. 96 (May issue). Included in Donald Allen's anthology *The New*

American Poetry: 1945–1960. In September begins writing *The Island*.

1961–62   Visiting lecturer at University of New Mexico.

1962   *For Love: Poems 1950–1960* (Charles Scribner's Sons). Given contract for *The Island* by Scribner's.

1962–63   Lecturer at University of British Columbia.

1963–66   Lecturer at University of New Mexico.

1963   Reads and lectures with Olson, Duncan, Ginsberg, Levertov, and others at the Vancouver Poetry Festival from late July to early August. *The Island* (novel) (Charles Scribner's Sons).

1964   Guggenheim Fellow. Levinton-Blumenthal Prize for thirteen poems in *Poetry,* vol. 104 (June issue).

1965   Participant in Buffalo Arts Festival and Berkeley Poetry Conference. *The Gold Diggers and Other Stories* (Charles Scribner's Sons). Edits with Donald Allen *New American Short Story* (Grove Press). Rockefeller Grantee.

1966–67   Visiting professor at State University of New York at Buffalo.

1966   Subject of National Education Television film *Poetry USA: Robert Creeley. Poems 1950–1965* (London: Calder and Boyars). Edits and writes an introduction to *Selected Writings of Charles Olson* (New Directions).

1967–78   Professor of English at State University of New York at Buffalo.

1967   Participates in the World Poetry Conference in Montreal. *Words* (poems) (Charles Scribner's Sons). Edits with Donald Allen *The New Writing in the U.S.A.* (Penguin).

1968–69   Visiting professor at University of New Mexico.

1969   *Pieces* (poems) (Charles Scribner's Sons). *The*

Charm: Early and Uncollected Poems (Four Seasons Foundation). Readings by Creeley issued on two records: *Today's Poets,* vol. 3, and *The Spoken Arts Treasury of 100 Modern American Poets,* vol. 16.

1970–71   Visiting professor at San Francisco State College.

1970   Participant in International Poetry Festival at the University of Texas and Neuvième Biennale Internationale de Poèsie at Knokke-le-Zoute, Belgium. *A Quick Graph: Collected Notes and Essays* (Four Seasons Foundation). *The Finger: Poems 1966–1969* (London: Calder and Boyars). Moves with family to Bolinas, California.

1971   Guggenheim Fellow. Radio play *Listen* broadcast in Germany.

1972   *A Day Book* (journal and poems) (Charles Scribner's Sons). *A Sense of Measure* (essays and an interview) (London: Calder and Boyars). *Listen* (radio play) produced in London and published by Black Sparrow Press.

1973   *Contexts of Poetry: Interviews 1961–1971* (Four Seasons Foundation). Selects and introduces poems in *Whitman* (Penguin's Poet to Poet series). Establishes permanent residence in Buffalo.

1974   *Thirty Things* (poems) (Black Sparrow Press).

1975   Participant in International Festival of Poetry, University of Toronto.

1976   In spring goes on extensive reading tour of Fiji, New Zealand, Australia, Singapore, the Philippines, Malaysia, Hong Kong, Japan, and Korea, sponsored by USIA. *Away* (poems) (Black Sparrow Press). *Selected Poems* (Charles Scribner's Sons). *Mabel: A Story and Other Prose* (London: Marion Boyars). *Presences: A Text for Marisol* (Charles Scribner's Sons). Divorced from second wife, Bobbie.

1977	Marries Penelope Highton.
1978– present	David Gray Professor of Poetry and Letters at State University of New York at Buffalo.
1978	*Hello: A Journal, February 29–May 3, 1976* (poems) (New Directions; also London: Marion Boyars).
1979	*Later* (poems) (New Directions). *Was That a Real Poem and Other Essays* (Four Seasons Foundation). Visiting professor at University of New Mexico (also in 1980 and 1981).
1980	*Charles Olson and Robert Creeley: The Complete Correspondence,* vols. 1–2, edited by George Butterick (Black Sparrow Press); vol. 3 comes out in 1981, vol. 4 in 1982, vol. 5 in 1983, and vol. 6 in 1985. Record *Home,* music by Steve Swallow set to poems by Robert Creeley (ECM), third in *Downbeat* poll.
1981	In January son William Gabriel born. Shelley Memorial Award, Poetry Society of America.
1982	*The Collected Poems of Robert Creeley, 1945–1975* (University of California Press). National Endowment for the Arts Grantee.
1983	*Mirrors* (poems) (New Directions). DAAD, Berlin Artists Program Grantee. In December daughter Hannah Highton born.
1984	*The Collected Prose of Robert Creeley* (London: Marion Boyars). On NEA Literature Fellowship Panel. Establishes a residence in Waldoboro, Maine, behind sister Helen's house.
1985	Premio Speciale, Leone d'Oro, Venice, 1985, for publication of *Poi* (*Later*). Record *Futurities,* music by Steve Lacy set to Creeley poems sung by Irene Aebi (Hat Hut Records).
1986	*Memory Gardens* (poems) (New Directions).

PART ONE   *The 1950s: Beginnings*

WILLIAM CARLOS WILLIAMS

Excerpts from Letters to Robert Creeley

10/8/53

Dear Bob:

 . . . As far as your work is concerned, though you too* are
difficult, I feel that with everything new I read of yours I am
coming to like it better. You are becoming much more coherent
with the improvement in the (I take it) . . . physical conditions
surrounding you. At least you are getting more used to the life
you lead and it shows in your work. You are more at ease. You
are no longer so jumpy as you were when you were having a
harder time (with the language?), your mind is more at rest, your
thinking is much improved. The poem you wrote in my honor
and which came out in ORIGIN is one of your good ones, I like
it, thank you.** (I think it is one of your poems! Anyhow I like
it, it is the one with my initials as part of the title which is due to
come out in the next ORIGIN.) I am going to look up the books
you sent me and read them again. Whatever happens what I have
said of you above, stands. . . .

Best luck
Bill

Robert Creeley Papers, Washington University Library, St. Louis, Missouri.
Excerpts from previously unpublished letters of William Carlos Williams,
Copyright © 1988 by William Eric Williams and Paul H. Williams; used by
permission of New Directions Publishing Corp., agents.

*In the previous paragraph Williams describes the difficulty he has with Charles
Olson's poetry. —Ed.

**"For W.C.W." —Ed.

Dear Bob:

. . . you are at the head of the list [of poets in *The New American Poetry,* edited by Donald M. Allen].

. . . It is particularly interesting to me that the structural elements of your [poetry have] been featured and not necessarily the moral elements of your poems which can be ignored. But the way the [w]ords fall into place, the vocabulary, the words, the words with their modern accretions are of prime importance. It bespeaks your craft, your artistic ability just as [it did for] the poets of the Elizabethan era—whom you are destined to follow. It's wonderful to be still alive in such an era.

. . . The loss of an eye has been important for you[,] and for us all[,] concentrating your attention on the singl[e]ness of your purpose to see, see, see to the fullest extent. I have thought much in the past about this. . . .

Affectionately yours
Bill

[P]. [S]. Thank you for *A Form of Women.* The 4th poem* in the little book astonishes me[,] it is so able and beautiful—it gave that inner conviction that I always seek in a poem and so seldom find.

W.

Dear Bob:

. . . You have the subtlest feeling for the measure that I encounter anywhere except in the verses of Ezra Pound whom I cannot equal. At your best, rarely, you perhaps surpass me with a passage that leaves me flat on my back but there is never much of

---

*"The Friend."—ED.

that. As you yourself say it is mostly unconscious when
something of that sort appears on the page. . . .

Affectionately yours
Bill

LOUIS ZUKOFSKY

A Letter to Robert Creeley

Oct. 11/55

Dear Bob:

Thanks for *The Gold Diggers* and the dedication. If I
"criticize," I should be repeating only what the Preface says
perfectly, and what you know yourself—obviously if one finds no
self-satisfaction in the moralist one's left with the compelling in
what follows: the accomplishment. The newness of it: the
metaphysics that takes on a "shape"—not the running argument
that's found in most "literature" that accompanies a form. That is
new—and along with it, the *thoughtfulness* that makes the shape—
the metaphysics of loneliness—you scrap a lot of 19c
"symbolism." And so the style. For me most compelling in A
Death, Fate Tales 2, 3, The Party (especially the beg. & end), the
last ¶ of In the Summer, The Boat and The Gold Diggers.* I'm
pleased that the last two escape the lulling rhythm of some of the
rest of it, so the "shape" is accepted by this blood wherever it
would rather flow off to let's say the lightness of Tale 2. All thru
"tradition" is beautifully *sealed*.**

But what pleases this moralist most is that you think and
don't think—so for a guy approaching 52 there's this kinship, and
the hope that at 52 you'll have done exactly what you say in the
Preface with a lightness—because loneliness will somehow have

Robert Creeley Papers, Washington University, St. Louis, Missouri. Permission
to quote Louis Zukofsky material given by Paul Zukofsky. No one may use this
material without obtaining the express permission of Paul Zukofsky, who now
owns the copyrights.

*In the left margin, Zukofsky adds, "These tell the *story* as of today."—ED.
**In the right margin, Zukofsky adds, "i.e. there, but never aped."—ED.

distilled itself into it—and my ghost will somehow be there as witness to no obsession.

It's pretty involved? i.e. this. By the way, Celia was charmed and impressed by the Preface.

Yes,

All our love,
Louis

CHARLES OLSON

A Letter to Robert Creeley*

[Washington, D.C.]
thurs. june 8 50

my excellent friend:

been tied up for three days (& is it not of
yr doin'?) on a thing now called "Story: Olson, & Bad Thing,"
which is verse rasslin out of prose, and prose winnin, and then,
verse emergin

otherwise you'd have heard sooner abt
Creeley: Packet of Verse for O, Ringlet, which, right off the bat
provoked: o wonderful, he, has two strings to his bow!

& now yr letter with at least one sentence
to make me, to, create this cit. for this day plus:

FORM IS NEVER MORE THAN AN EXTENSION OF
CONTENT,
&, try this on,

right form

From *Charles Olson and Robert Creeley: The Complete Correspondence,* vols. 1–2,
edited by George F. Butterick (Santa Barbara, Calif.: Black Sparrow Press,
1980), 85–89, copyright © 1980 by the University of Connecticut.

*After Olson had asked, "Tell me, Creeley, do you not, yourself, make with
verse?" (letter of May 27, 1950), Creeley included under the title "A Ringlet O'
Verse" seven poems for Charles Olson in his letter of June 1, 1950. The poems
were ": . . . So temptings green assail thee," "Still Life Or," "Ira," "The Epic
Expands," "The Primitives," "A Local Celebration," and "Song: 'Rough
Winds Doe Shake The Darling Of My Heart.'" These were the first poems by
Creeley that Olson had seen and the ones that gave rise to his response in this
letter.—ED.

is the precise & correct [*typed above:* (only possible)] extension of
content under hand

Anyhow, yrs
is beautiful, and most USABLE. . . .

Next: the verse of, my poultry man:

two strings, and the joint
was jumpin over "So temptings green assail thee" becoz, this
string I didn't know, tho the other I knew fr passage in letter
some time ago (to which I will come back)

now, two days later, i have to undo this nice
little leader and talk abt three—if, as I think, EPIC EXPANDS, is
diffrunt, at base, fr the YET UNDONE (the letter)

anyhow, let's go in ((remembering, as you'll
see, if I send you STORY, olson males (me, and the old man are
all i know) are weak (fr softness of the heart, i'm told—that is,
me, because of the irish) in in-work!)):

lets go in, as I was sayin, let's
make a picture of CREELEY, shall we?

say I (dictum): this man can
I.) truly return us to the antient anglo-saxon heart (it is a
   form, a form!)—because? he's got a head with a long stride
   in it (like they used to talk abt long legs as a sign of,
   distinction? anyhow, he thinks good, and the cadence of
   his thot is long & intricate, & thus he must continue, or
   show me more of

> . . . .So temptings green assail thee
> while all sweet voices wail thee,
> that they & thee
> do not agree,
> because thy head dont fail thee,—   [*Added in
> margin:* (beautiful!)]

> & let thee have such pleasure,
> the reason or the measure,

that short you'll make
the woman take
what shed have at her leisure . . .

[*Added in margin:* (here's a problem: at 1st I thot it was, a come
down fr the heavy of pleasure-measure; but no: obviously you
pronounce "leisure" the same.

It is, I think, that, a *negative* formulation is, in this last line,
required: to "rime" with last line of 1—the syntax has to be
like backed up.)]

II.) but just as his head is long, his breath is quick & short,
AND (which is, of course, in a way, the same thing: any
man who goes fast can't go without, *etcs,* which are
shorthand for the fastest sort of juxtapositions:
it's JUXTAPOSITIONS, that I mean by
quick breath, and that you are not yet getting in [*added in
margin:* Etcs. *have to be got in*], at least in the verse: possibly
exception THE EPIC EXpands; certain exception, the
LETTER (which I shall return to you, but want back).

the negative of it: "The Primitives"—where the shortness
comes
acropper (to me, that is)
(the negative of (I): "A Local Celebration"—which needs the
ANTIENT of "so temptings
green," the ARTIFICE, to
give the heart the fine
mind's wit)

THE POSITIVE IS, in these things, (ABSOLUTE) in the
use of the parentheses in THE EPIC EXPANDS—wow,
they are wonderful, AND ARE TO BE LEARNED
FROM, by Creeley as well as by me, and whoever else has
got an ear to hear with: exs.:

(or be
expanded by)

                    (throw up)
                         (will use)

                              &, above all, *too(too)*

((figure, myself, you lose the care in (say): but all the others,
 especially (*he could not*
 stop there)   or   (*put back into*
 quiet)

               These things make the poem, and, if I were an
editor, I'd print it instantly for their reason, even tho I do
not, I admit, and I think this is yr fault, (tho one is willing,
dealing with you, to throw in my own stupidities (of a day))
understand exactly what's going on:
                    it is the three coke bottles
                              (& the poets?)

that seem to be insufficient ambiguities, no?
                              (Aw, shit, exkuse
the fingers, only, just becoz we're on the mat, here's two
holes this citizen finds)

ROUGHWINDS DOE SHAKE THE DARLING OF MY
HEART is
confirmation of,
how antient is the heart of
Robert Creeley . . .

                                        love,
                                           Olson

CELIA ZUKOFSKY, ALLEN GINSBERG,
ROBERT CREELEY

From "A Commemorative Evening for Louis Zukofsky"

Celia Zukofsky: Louis didn't always associate with presumably the greats. He had a great many close and intimate friends and people who were not poets. But if he felt that there was an integrity and if he felt he liked them as human beings, there was a great friendship which he kept up all his life.

Allen Ginsberg: Robert Creeley was one of . . .

Celia Zukofsky: Oh, Robert Creeley was one of his dearest friends. I mean, Robert Creeley has a very private niche in Louis' spiritual world. If Louis had to pick the friends that were dearest and closest to him, it would be Ezra Pound, Robert Creeley, and William Carlos Williams for a while.

Robert Creeley: But I never knew that.

Allen Ginsberg: What were the first texts of Robert's that Louis liked?

Celia Zukofsky: *The Whip.*

Allen Ginsberg: That was the first text, then?

Celia Zukofsky: Yes, and then the book of short stories: *The Gold Diggers.* I should add that Creeley's displacing Williams was not necessarily because of whose poetry is better—it was a

Transcript of a PEN commemorative evening, April 18, 1979, at the PEN American Center, published in *American Poetry Review* 9, no. 1 (Jan./Feb. 1980): 26. Reprinted by permission. Permission to quote Celia Zukofsky material given by Paul Zukofsky. No one may use this material without obtaining the express permission of Paul Zukofsky, who now owns the copyrights.

question of rapport. He thought that he had a much greater metaphysical rapport with Robert Creeley than he did with Williams. Bill would frequently argue with Louis. They didn't see eye to eye, oh, about what books to read, what books not to read and so on.

Louis, in addition to being a literary man, was very learned in many branches of philosophy. Now, I don't just throw this off the top of my head, but he knew his Aristotle very well; his Spinoza—well, that was his Bible; St. Thomas Aquinas; Wittgenstein. Louis didn't just glance at books. He read philosophy as other people eat bread.

In Creeley, he felt that there was this rapport, this philosophical and metaphysical closeness. And when I say Creeley, I mean Creeley's work. He did not feel that rapport was always present in Eliot's work or even Williams' work. He felt that in Pound's work. He felt that in a good deal of Marianne Moore's work, but in a different sense. He always thought of Marianne Moore as one of the best American poets.

This is not to say that he did not esteem many other young people's work. He liked Robert Duncan's work very much. The one thing that bothered Louis very much about Duncan and Olson was the question of myth. Louis could not get that involved in mythology as Duncan is, and that always troubled Louis. He tried to understand it, but it was something that he could not really apply himself to as he would just so naturally take to Creeley's work or to Pound's work or even to some of Cummings' work, which he liked. . . .

SHERMAN PAUL

Gripping, Pushing, Moving

I

I suspect that Robert Creeley was always a letter writer and that he began to write voluminously—became a man of letters—simply because sometime toward the end of 1949 or the beginning of 1950 his dismay with the situation in poetry provoked him to publish, with his friend Jacob Leed, a little magazine. I hear myself saying, "Yet another little magazine!" and I say it now because the failure to launch the *Lititz Review*, which was only, finally, a mechanical failure, the result of a faulty press, remains instructive. These letters—the first two volumes of this projected multi-volume correspondence cover the brief period April 21 to September 21, 1950—are Creeley's show in the absence of many of Charles Olson's letters; and Creeley's concern with the magazine, especially as the correspondence itself clarifies the issues and proposes the work it should push, is very much part of the story. If nothing else, the letters, along with those to Leed, Pound, William Carlos Williams, Cid Corman, and Vincent Ferrini published or available elsewhere, provide an essential (heroic) chapter in the history of little magazines and American literature because, as it turned out, the failure of the *Lititz Review* was made good in *Origin,* begun by Corman in 1951, and the *Black Mountain Review,* begun by Creeley in 1954. The writers whose work Creeley had so arduously solicited became the nucleus of Corman's magazine (the first two issues featured Olson and Creeley), and Corman's achievement, somewhat distorted by the one-sided correspondence of Olson's *Let-*

Review of *Charles Olson and Robert Creeley: The Complete Correspondence,* vols. 1–2, from *Parnassus* 9, no. 2 (Fall/Winter 1981): 269–76. Reprinted by permission.

ters for Origin, is not diminished by recognizing how much in the matter of setting things in motion was Creeley's work. The new movement in American letters was to a large extent encouraged by letters—when, it should be noted, first-class postage was three cents.

The architect Daniel Burnham used to admonish his colleagues to "make no little plans," where Louis Sullivan asked them to "remember the seed-germ." Reading these letters reminds us that little magazines are seed-germs; that two people, one pretty much alone on a farm in Littleton, New Hampshire, the other about as solitary and unnoticed in Washington, D.C., may do greater things than they know by writing letters ("let language be our tie!" Olson exclaims early on), by thus confronting their isolation and transferring, and compounding, their energies. Of most importance then—and now—was the crystallization of ideas fostered by this correspondence; it formed two distinguished careers; and it gave rise to a new poetics, a new charter, to use Grant Webster's term. (" . . . isn't time," Pound wrote Creeley, "for Creel's generation to revolt against the dead hand, dating from Dial or before / backwash of aestheticism . . . ?") The letters themselves are sometimes drafts of what was subsequently published ("Projective Verse" and "The Gate and the Center") and are valuable because they deepen our understanding of projective writing, whether in verse or prose. They exemplify the very theory discussed in them, one of the best forms for projective expression, which Creeley acknowledged by publishing Olson's *Mayan Letters*—and Corman, too, by making letters a distinctive feature of *Origin*. The letters, then, are not merely documents; they bring us immediately into the current of life. Sometimes they are so stunning, of such force of mind and heart, that one feels compelled to say, as Creeley did on first recognizing Olson's work, "Too much! too much!" (a phrase, picked up from jazz musicians by Creeley, that Olson, his senior by sixteen years, asked him to gloss). Or compelled to cite Williams's reply to Creeley: "I am really startled at what you see and how clearly you see it. It's stimulating to me to realize your clarity of purpose . . . your drive."

To adapt Williams: no little magazines (of any worth) without ideas. And no little magazines without generalship. Discussing Creeley's force with my colleague Donald Marshall, he remarked that Plato was wrong about poets, that they, not philosopher-kings, should rule—which may not be wide-of-the-mark of Olson's belief in the sovereign power of the poet as pedagogue, a role he himself filled when he gave up a political career. Creeley's letters—these and the others, all notable for their various styles, each respectively taking the measure of the recipient—belie whatever impression of reticence, hesitancy, or stumbling his poems give, though these, one comes to realize, are hard ("conglomerates" is his word), evidence of the *grip* he so often demands in the letters, of having things directly in, and under, *hand.* The Creeley of the letters is forward, fearless, and commanding, so much so that both Pound and Williams, to whom he turned for help, took the trouble to keep up a correspondence with a young man of twenty-three.

Olson's letters are modeled on Pound's, though they soon become as open, as free formally and visually provocative, as those in *Letters for Origin* and *Mayan Letters.* Creeley's letters to Olson are composed of sentences broken into small breath phrases by heavy, unusual punctuation (colon and slash), marked by abbreviations and syntactical inversion. Their effect is of rapid fire, a brisk shorthand, even though they must be read word by word, as carefully as poems, alertly. And they are often poems, as in the following indebted to Charlie Parker: "Tell yez / wd, to get out, to get clear: to renew / this life. Give much to be anywhere / . . . chewing the fat / slide & slip. Going dead." They fulfill his demand for sound; they go by ear. There is the frequent aside, "like they say" (still a signature), and often a final turn, undercutting his aggressiveness and extremity of feeling with the knife of self-awareness. They are urgent, so it may not be far-fetched to recall the example of General Grant, whose prose-dispatch was prompted by the battlefield. (And didn't it require generalship to outflank Pound's campaign to use the magazine to his ends?) It is understandable, then, that in dedicating *The Maximus Poems*—begun at this time in a *letter* to Ferrini—Olson thought of Creeley as "the Figure of Outward," an "opposite to a / personality which so completely does (did) / stay at home." He was the person who enabled him by correspondence ("why *was* the pt. then to write Creeley / daily?") to have the " 'World.' "

That Pound and Williams needed Creeley as much as he needed them tells us a great deal about the situation in poetry in 1950. Creeley recalls that at Harvard his teacher, F. O. Matthiessen, didn't include Pound in the course on contemporary poetry, nor Hart Crane—avoidances whose importance he indicates when he remarks, in an unfavorable context, that "in 2000 years, maybe all such: will be grouped under general heading / Ez Pound."* The guiding poets of the time were Stevens and Auden, the former much respected by him though said to have "fallen to the questionable fact of a device" ("Stevens aint got the push, any more. It is a method / holds him up. NOT a content"), the latter dismissed for "a socially based use of irony [that] became the uselessly exact rigor of repetitive verse patterns. . . ." Creeley felt, as Williams insisted, that "the measure itself / had been lost," and that too many young writers of his generation had failed to school themselves in the *art* of poetry in the work of Pound and Williams—failed, as Olson has Yeats say in Pound's defense, to take up and carry on "the advances we made for you." When he wrote to Corman in December 1949, in what must be one of the first salvos of the advance, he complained of *Poetry* on two scores: its kind of lyricism ("I can't see very much that they've published in the last 4 or 5 years, new, that is, that's been worth the effort") and its failure to maintain its initial force ("And we don't need the tradition so much as we do the kind of force & straightness that brought it into being"). Creeley and Olson consider many little magazines in the course of the correspondence—they are busy submitting manuscripts to some of them and know the timidity and dilatoriness of editors, the lack of force and straightness; and they have been rejected, perhaps the most remarkable instance being the refusal by the *Kenyon Review* of a Creeley story, accepted and paid for but then returned when John Crowe Ransom concurred in R. P. Warren's opinion that it lacked "plot." It should not surprise anyone who knows this time that Creeley and Leed planned to devote an early issue of the *Lititz Review* to education, that is, to the University; that they took issue with it, knew that as much

---

*He comments extensively on Crane in the letters.

as the little magazines, the academy contributed to the tightness and settled state of things. By this time the New Critics dominated the schools and even the New York Intellectuals were turning to them, and to magazines like the *Kenyon Review,* for support. Corman wisely refused the institutional backing of Brandeis when he undertook *Origin,* and Creeley and Olson also stood outside the circle of such support. The obsessive words of their correspondence are *push* (noun and verb) and *move.* The mounting anger of these letters is caused by stasis, the impasse and impotence of thwarted hope and energy; the humor is caused by the fact, noted in "Le Fou" and probably recognized only by them, that "they are waving" (the others, standing still) and "we are moving."

The poetics that they work out in the letters—Olson from the vantage of poetry and Creeley from that of prose—is also one of push and movement, eminently projective. Its gist appears in Creeley's early comment that the head should determine form as "an extension of its own center," not do "menial / enclosed / work. . . ." Or phrased another way, "the compression & push of poetry: toward a single 'action' of comprehension. . . ." By restoring the "subjective," he would join art and life, make writing "personal," the work of what he calls the "Single Intelligence," that center from which one pushes his own content. It is "the usable content of a man," his "coherence"; and it is pushed/moved so that "what was of me, in, is it: out." (Turn the inside out, Williams said.) So form is the extension of content: in the very language, the literal activity, of the poem, we have the particular history (his-story, Olson would later pun) of a man who knows directly, and firmly grips, what he is writing about, delivers it straight, exactly. When given this notion by Creeley, Olson adduced Whitman.

Creeley adduces Lawrence, the prose writer whom, with Stendhal and Dostoyevski, he admires most, and, with some reservations, Crane, the poet, who, he believes, "push[es] way out," farther than Pound, Williams, and Stevens. To use one of Creeley's more recent formulations, Crane is an example of life tracking life. In the letters there is a statement addressing the heart of this undertaking: "Too much / those things. I mean: of the heart, that which can be tracked. . . ." Crane, he says, tracks the heart by feel, or as Olson says in another context, "he goeth by / langwitch." Charlie Parker, an exemplar for Creeley of the going by ear—the sound—both prose and poetry now require, is another who "live[s] by feel"; he "pushed out too far." Lawrence, too, goes "by the head & heart." Heart? Yes, taking one's feelings straight, as Creeley wished to advise Ferrini to do; permitting "a direct reaction," which has been blocked in recent poetry ("there are countries where men can cry"). This is why he frequently cites Williams' "Why do I write today" (from "The Apology") and why for him the value of the new poetics is that it doesn't "stifle feel/grip: by preconceptions . . . ONLY as the coming out: makes it."

Of the many implications of this poetics perhaps the most radical at the time and the most necessary for Olson and Creeley were the following: that content is the evidence of originality ("A man, each man, is NEW. If his method, his form IS the logic of his content: he cannot be but: NEW / 'original'"); that "conjecture," an active, searching attention, is requisite; and that memory must become a condition of the present ("You can't go 'back'—you got to pull 'to'"), a problem that Creeley was confronting in his stories and Olson would soon confront in working out the historiographical difficulties of *The Maximus Poems*. Creeley may be said to summarize the case, when, exasperated by reading anthologies of poetry, he says, "I don't want the remembering. I want the straight thing. The straight open breath of it, the freshness, the love, exact & living." Olson says it in a letter to Ferrini: "when I also speak of PV [Projective Verse] as propellant, I think of the man as his own muzzle—and charge." And as he remarked to Creeley at the outset, when he announced the battle: "a man . . . / has to come up with his own lang., syntax and song both, but also each poem under hand has its own language. . . ."

II

Of course, it is not necessary to join the battle or to use the letters as a textbook of poetics in order to enjoy them and welcome their publication. Their importance is assured: this is unquestionably one of the great correspondences of the twentieth century. So it is assuring to have the letters in the care of a capable editor and courageous publisher. George Butterick respects the text and doesn't tamper with it. His notes, as always, are ample and invariably helpful: resourceful. His Introduction, brief yet summary, is surely modest in the light of the many volumes of correspondence still to come. The illustrations he has selected for each volume are excellent, and the indexes of persons named in the letters and of works by Olson and Creeley referred to there are very convenient. The format of the volumes is the usual handsome one that identifies the Black Sparrow Press. Like many of the volumes John Martin has published, these confirm the value of his enterprise, his push, the way he keeps (good) things moving.

Like all great letters the appeal of these lies in their unguarded expression and revelation of human quality. They have *size,* as Olson said of the Sumerian kings, when, in "The Gate and the Center," he addressed the issue of education; they exhibit extensible energy and offer us the "IMAGE of possibilities implicit in the energy," that is, to cite his own statement of purpose at the end of *The Maximus Poems,* give us "an image / of man, 'The nobleness, and the arete.'" This installment also has the excitement of beginnings, of being on hand to witness what Olson called "Corinth." He said of the happy accident of Melville discovering Shakespeare that "Melville and Shakespeare had made a Corinth and out of the burning came *Moby-Dick,* bronze." This speaks for an intellectual event, where the Corinth of Olson and Creeley is that and also a personal event, the beginning of a lifelong friendship, more enduring than that of Hawthorne and Melville, but of that kind.

I read these letters as much as anything for such tokens of necessary generosity as Olson's almost immediate encouragement ("above all things resist, to be sick at heart: we are forward, and it is such gratification, that you are ready to go with me // love, / Olson") and his immediate remittance of the money Creeley needed to procure library privileges at Dartmouth College; and on Creeley's part for such admissions as "Because / much talk from the others: but from yrself: the facts of the poems / the prose of P / & the verse. The letters. That wd be enough, any one of them" and "Jesus / O / I ask nothing, absolutely, nothing from you but that you stay within reach: letters—let[s] build this thing." So much is moving inside, within them, and so little is moving outside that they have often to grapple each other close (Olson: "this / correspondence, you and me"; Creeley, echoing Lear?: "Let's you and I, by God, write for each other!"). And inescapable throughout the letters, almost from the start, is the groundtone of Creeley's desire to see Olson, whom, in fact, he didn't meet until March 1954, when he came to Black Mountain College—a disappointment as great as the failure of his magazine.

There is, inevitably, much here of biographical interest and much to satisfy the hunger, whetted by the distance of time, for literary gossip. Olson describes his curious working day from 1 to 9 P.M., determined, he explains, by his wife's "crazy" shift, and their apartment near the railroad tracks ("this small two room jewel in brick, with garden"). He notes, in speaking of particularists and generalizers, that T. S. Eliot has misused "my, *my* madonna, buona viaggi"—this before he had begun *The Maximus Poems* and Creeley could pick up the reference. Compared with Creeley, he's reticent, or maybe it's that what personally concerns him most in the letters is his relationship with Pound. He had broken with Pound two years earlier but mentions it only when Pound writes Creeley of Olson's defection: "Believe Olson FUNDAMENTALLY (not superficially) wrong, tendency which will sterilize anything it touches. i.e., AGAINST nature's increase, etc." Creeley found this kind of literary politics disturbing, and petty. It posed a serious question of loyalty for him, as it had for Olson, who said that "the big struggle, after the decision to leave politics . . . , was to leave Ez." Creeley admitted his struggle, and that he had been "holding to you, as against him. . . ." He knew what he owed Pound, recognized his power, his "ways and means," but almost immediately held with Olson, a decision of considerable consequence for his magazine and one that brought forward as its presiding elder the gentler, less officious Williams.

For his part, Creeley writes vividly of his life on the farm at Littleton and of the years preceding it, the time at Cape Cod, at Harvard, in India and Burma during the war. He explains his awkwardness in cities, how he went under in Boston ("cd not hold myself / or work"); his singleness ("I cant see that one writes / or does anything / to be among others: but only to be: himself"); his fierceness ("Christ: get there if you can and see the land you once were proud to own, etc., or: shit. Keep clear & go with & by yrself. Who is there / that can make that difference. I am ready, dammit, I am ready: to leave anywhere, anything: at any time"), and his egoism ("My egoism is very great. I believe in all sincerity that what I say is important"). So constituted what could he do but make his push with a magazine or, later, with the Divers Press? His dilemma: "how to take on what I think are valid/actual: responsibilities, without sacrificing the aloneness." He writes of his love of cars, his good relations with his mother, family history, the need for roots. His several accounts of jazz, especially of the "Bird," are notable (to "Le Fou," he appends, "Thank you—Charles Parker. Et tu— Thelonius Bach"). More than Olson he tells of his intellectual and social life, his reading, for example, of Lawrence ("Lawrence is worth 50,000 Pounds in any market") and Dahlberg ("Sick, sick bk/man"), the visits of Slater Brown, a valuable, generous friend and mentor, and of Mitchell Goodman and Denise Levertov, the latter, it seems, spoiling for him a much-used book, Rilke's *Letters to a Young Poet.*

But enough. There are riches here, and much advice to put with Rilke's. Olson dated postmodern, in these letters anyway, with Hiroshima. I hear postmortem in the word, but also postpartem. And I think of "La Préface," where Olson might just as well be speaking of Creeley as of Cagli when he says, "We are the new born" and this means that there is "no parenthesis." These letters are an opening, and bring us into the open. Creeley wrote in "Hart Crane," the poem that initiates his work, that for Crane letters proved insufficient. The measure of these letters is that they proved sufficient and enabled Olson and Creeley to make "the push // beyond. . . ."

MICHAEL RUMAKER

From "Robert Creeley at Black Mountain"

My first introduction to Robert Creeley was through Charles Olson reading Creeley's early poems and stories in his writing classes at Black Mountain College. Mostly they were read to us students in manuscript since little of his work was as yet published, the new work arriving regularly along with the almost daily letters from Mallorca, where Creeley was then living with his wife, Ann, and children, in the voluminous correspondence exchanged between Creeley and Olson. Neither had as yet met in the flesh. . . .

Creeley, having gotten out the first issue of *Black Mountain Review* on the island of Mallorca, was expected to arrive at the college to start teaching early in March, 1954. Excitement and anticipation generated by Charles became, as usual, contagious in the rest of us and had certainly built up in me. I was not only curious but eager to meet this writer whose poems and stories we'd been reading and discussing for many months now and whose presence, at least on paper, had played such an important part in my early student days.

Tom Field and I, both of us early risers, were up after dawn that morning in Meadows Inn, where we shared, each with our separate rooms, the whole first floor, along with Terence Burns, another student who only slept there, preferring to spend most of his time working at the farm with Doyle, the farm manager. Terence usually left before dawn and the first thing Tom did when he got up was to shut the door to Terence's littered bed-

From *boundary 2* 6, no. 3; 7, no. 1 (Spring/Fall 1978): 137–70. Reprinted by permission.

room, where the long-unchanged sheets on the bed had become the shade of a good strong brew of coffee, to "keep out the barn smell" from the rest of the house. Burns, a very good collagist and aspiring poet from Providence, a widely read and acutely perceptive reader with a quirky, eccentric intelligence, agreed evidently, along with D. H. Lawrence, that too much cleanliness "impoverishes the blood."

Fixing breakfast together in our communal kitchen, Tom pumping up the Coleman gas stove he'd installed after the college dining hall closed, checking to see if the block of ice in the old wooden ice box would make it through the day—no worry now since Tom was the newly proud owner, because of GI mustering out pay, if I remember right, of a gray, chrome-shiny 1950 Buick in good condition that sat parked out on the grass in front of Meadows Inn. We could make runs into town now whenever we needed supplies and, equally important, beer trips to Ma Peak's down the road, or even ride into Asheville for an occasional movie.

As we puttered about, we wondered, since he was due that morning, if Creeley had arrived, knowing that if he had, we probably wouldn't be meeting him till later in the day since we understood that Charles and he, after their enormous correspondence over the years, and meeting now for the first time, would undoubtedly spend the first hours together. At least we knew, from past experience, that Charles, in his excitement at finally having his "pen pal" (Tom's irreverent phrase) here at last, would determinedly see to that. . . .

I spotted Charles and a younger man in a dark blue beret, an eyepatch over one eye and what looked like rough, loose-fitting workclothes, sitting side by side on the park bench in Charles's front yard. The stranger of course had to be Creeley who, it turned out, had just arrived.

The two sat very close, almost of necessity, since Charles's girth and height was in itself enough to fill the bench. They didn't see me approach at first and I watched Charles talking earnest and close in Robert's ear, his huge body swung half around in relaxed and easy confidentiality. Robert, sitting stiff, listening with bowed head, stared down at the ground. My body tensed with anticipation, seeing for the first time the person whom I'd only known so far on typed and printed pages.

I planned only to nod and go on my way, mostly out of my own innate shyness but also respecting, as Charles had impressed on us, like a strong, tacit vibration (also conveyed to newcomers, verbally, by more seasoned students) his adamant insistence on his privacy in and around his own house. But Charles caught sight of me as I passed and lifting his long arm from around Creeley's shoulder waved to me and called out, with a radiant smile on his face, "Michael, come on over here and meet Robert Creeley."

There was something large and ungainly in Robert's hands dangling at his thighs, thick-wristed as they poked out from the dark sleeves of his jacket. He snapped halfway up from the bench as I crossed over the yard, the first glimpse of him was of some awkward, sturdy peasant, like a Basque, his face pale and tense, his movements jerky, agitated. I wrote this off as fatigue (Creeley, I found out after, had driven through the night in his battered old pick-up truck nonstop from New York to North Carolina), but it turned out that Robert was pretty much like this all the time.

As I approached, he sprang up from the bench as if poked from behind with an electric prod and plunged in my direction one of those large, work-roughened but very white hands. . . .

I liked him immediately because I discovered in that last instant he was as awkward and as easily embarrassed and uncomfortable as myself.

All that was exchanged then were some trivial pleasantries, and Charles, beaming, telling Robert, as if by way of "assurance," that I would be in his writing class, like Creeley had something to look forward to, which made me gawky and a bit panicky, fully aware of my own defects as student-apprentice.

My immediate sympathy with Creeley was enlarged by seeing in that one dark eye staring out at me—the one beneath the patch began watering rapidly and he dabbed at it in quick self-conscious swipes with a wrinkled dirty handkerchief—an attractive vulnerability, a desperate desire to be liked. In his eye was a mute appeal of the painfully shy (magnified by his low, barely audible words) to overlook his clumsiness and shortcomings, to look beyond them.

Those first moments of meeting him were also like being dropped into the presence of a fierce, impatient bird, strapped down, restricted, in a too tight ribcage of flesh, an entrapment of spirit so visible I could instantly identify with it, the only difference being that mine was more "controlled" and being gay and out of necessity for survival being the better actor, more concealed. What stood before me was a person who seemed totally undefended and who, consciously and without apology, revealed to all his inner exposure and need. As we mouthed the customary inanities of greeting, Creeley's body and face spoke, in gestures and tics of awkward sign language, of someone quite another: here was a kind of man I'd never encountered before in the rawness and abrasiveness of his physical presence. Olson's own presence was mitigated in the large openness of his generosity and charm and, an accomplished player himself, in the swagger of his own unquestioned rightness. Creeley appeared like a man shrunken and gnawed by tremendous doubts and uncertainties, if not the same, at least on an equal pitch of intensity to my own.

Although I didn't know it then, or have words for it, it was my first glimpse of someone who stood revealed without subterfuge, in every gesture (and, later I was to find, in his words, in his classroom), in complete and unadorned honesty.

Olson convinced Creeley not to waste any time getting down to work, and so that same evening Creeley held his first writing class in the big classroom on the lower level near the front of the Studies Building with about a half dozen students in attendance: Tom Field, painter and writer; Karen Karnes, the resident potter; Cynthia Homire, with long glossy black hair, barefoot early spring to late summer, in worn faded Levi's jacket and jeans, looking like Mother Courage herself, a part she actually played in Huss's production of Brecht's play; Laurie Forest, short cropped carrot hair, who loved Emily Dickinson and wanted to write but because of Charles's negative attitude on Dickinson took up potting instead, and who had a fine stash of wine in her apartment above us in Meadows Inn; Don Cooper, a music student from Philadelphia studying with Wolpe; Jerry Van de Wiele, painter and writer, ex-regimental aritst in U.S. Marine Corps, of all things; perhaps one or two others, perhaps even Terence Burns was there, taking time off from the farm.

I've told pretty much what that first class was like to Martin Duberman, who quoted it in his book on Black Mountain. That part of the interview, as written by him, is as follows:

The first class was the worst. It met in the large conference room of the Studies Building, which had a huge table that took up most of the space. Six students bunched up at one end, and at the other sat Creeley, forlorn, alone, staring sideways at the wall, mopping at his eye with a handkerchief (Creeley had lost the eye in an accident and usually covered it with a patch; but since the patch made him self-conscious, he'd left it off for the first class; only to have the eye—as always, when he got emotionally upset—run buckets). Creeley talked in a nonstop monotone so low and gravelly, that no one could understand what he was saying. After ten minutes or so, Karen Karnes asked him if he could speak up; he lifted his voice for a few minutes, but it soon sank back into a monotone. . . .[1]

When Creeley, casting a desperate eye, perhaps a desperately frightened eye that someone actually might have, asked if anybody had brought any writing, I piped up, apprehensive but wanting to be of "help," and said I did and read some excerpts from my Day ledger journal. I was surprised when Creeley responded favorably to two of the entries: one about a middle-aged drunk I saw one night getting out of a taxi in Greenwich Village, a blonde on each arm, hollering tipsily, "Toujours l'amour!" over and over; and another about a woman, alone and late at night, staring out the upper windows of an office building downtown. It was a generous response considering the slightness of the material and its observations, and it warmed me to an encouraging start with Creeley.

Robert gradually improved, losing his shyness as he got to know us, becoming more and more an effective instructor as his own confidence increased. Moving the class to the smaller Reading Room on the upper level of the Studies Building, just inside the lobby, helped too, creating a space more amenable to

Creeley's intimate and personal style. Also, given the snug size of the room, there were no more complaints about not being able to hear him, and Creeley seemed more comfortable, more relaxed, with the students gathered closely around.

Creeley's classes never met for more than two hours, often less, again, matching his style, contrasted with the endurance tests of Olson's marathon meets (or even Hilda Morley's, who gave three- and four-hour-long classes in metaphysical poetry). In Creeley's class we read and discussed at length William Carlos Williams's earlier poems as points of departure towards our own possibilities in American speech, as well as the poetry of Hart Crane and the jazz of Charlie Parker and Bud Powell. Now and again a student would read a poem or piece of prose they'd written (Creeley had no requirement, like Olson, that a student had to bring writing to class or else not be admitted), and we'd spend a little time talking about it, Creeley careful not to impose any absolutes or dogmas, respectful to leave space for openings. But mostly it was Creeley talking, and Creeley talking, on his best days, was plenty good enough, and I for one was an avid listener, respectful of the incisiveness of his intelligence, its live-liness, and the interpretation and range of his reading. He was more than just a fresh voice sounding within the Seven Sisters: he seemed to have his sights on and be in touch with every aspect of what was new and vital going on then.

After a few classes, Creeley began to say the two of us ought to get together to talk about my writing, not that I had anything much to show. He was impressed by the number of hours I spent in my study writing, in longhand, still not having a type-writer, never having had enough money to actually buy one. It was all pretty mechanical stuff, the short stories I was trying to write, awfully weak and spiritless, stenographic in detail. . . .

Creeley, who preferred to work, like Olson, late at night, jazz blaring on his phonograph, and then only in erratic fits and starts, finding a consistency of rhythmic work difficult (it was around this time he wrote "A Wicker Basket," starring Liz, the ancient college cat with one pink and one green eye, a poem on several levels on how Creeley was and was not "making it"), would say to me, "I see you writing all day. That's good. I envy you. Keep at it," which, I guess, was about the only and best thing he could say. "*Write, write, write,*" Olson used to say, and that was the main part of it then, a sort of grinding, plodding hope. . . .

After putting me off for a long time (I guess he'd gotten the drift pretty quick by this time that with what I was writing there wasn't too much to talk about), Creeley said we'd get together one particular afternoon in his apartment in the back of the Studies Building. I encountered Robert at the time of the meeting hanging up his laundry, which I took at first to be old cleaning rags, on a droopy clothesline slung under the open back area of the Studies, directly beneath his apartment. I was coming up from the library, taking the short-cut through the tall weeds and marsh grass (cut on rare occasions by student work crews with machetes and bolo knives). . . .

Creeley was skittery and jumpy—perhaps he'd just had *his* first encounter with the automatic washer, which certainly would've accounted for it—but it was really something a great deal more than that. His eye snapped from side to side, like it wanted to get around me, his body moved in quick sideways arm and shoulder jabs, like he wanted to escape, but couldn't, held trapped as he was, possibly, by his sense of obligation and responsibility, not only on this occasion of his talk with me but of his overall difficulties: his teaching classes for the first time, his adjusting to the place and getting down to a consistent rhythm in his writing, and I guess, what it really was, concern and loneliness for his wife with whom he'd been having troubles he hoped to patch up, and missing his children, too; not to mention the work to be done with the Spanish printer on publishing and editing future issues of the *Review*. At this point his heart and mind seemed more in Mallorca than at Black Mountain, himself a thousand miles away and more.

It started to rain, one of those sudden afternoon mountain rainstorms, tropical in its intensity and abundance of downpour. (Mary Fitton Fiore once showed me a rainfall map of the USA which revealed that the immediate Black Mountain area had more inches of rain per year than any other in the region, Black Mountain being a tiny black dot on the map, designating heavy rain, surrounded by a vast area of white, meaning relatively average or below average rainfall.) Water from the storm started blowing in under the exposed lower level and Creeley led the way up into the belly of the building on the open rickety wooden steps ("temporary" like some other features of the Studies when it was built back in the forties, and still so to that day) and down the narrow hallway lined with the shut doors of studies in the all but empty building to his apartment at the rear. When he opened the door he stood dead in his tracks, seeing sheets of rain blowing in through the large pushout windows he'd left open and around the piece of cardboard over the broken pane in one. He rushed to the window ledge, simultaneously yanking the windows closed and snatching up small pieces of paper lined up on the ledge. They turned out to be checks, new $2.50 per year subscriptions to the first four issues of the *Review*, most precious checks, given the necessarily slim financing for the project which was instigated by Olson in hopes of attracting monetary attention and students to the school.

It was an inauspicious time for our first one-on-one talk, to say the least. Having looked forward to it for some time now, I felt disappointed, and strained. Creeley was darting about the room, flapping the rain-splotched subscription checks in the air, trying to dry them as best he could, moving them to a safer place. He kept saying, "They'll be all right, I think," as if to reassure himself, glancing at me in agitated helplessness for some firmer reassurance. "They'll dry here, don't you think? I think they'll be okay, don't you?" He looked so pathetically vulnerable, like a boy caught slipshod at his chores, I only nodded agreement and made the best soothing noises I could as I helped him spread the checks on a dry surface away from the windows.

So our "talk," or rather Creeley's talk, chopped out in bits and pieces as he scurried about, didn't amount to very much, any more than some well-intentioned platitudes of encouragement. "Vary the length of your sentences," he told me, consistency and monotony of syntax being one of my many problems. "You'll be okay," and he gave a little nervous smile meant to comfort, the best he could manage under the circumstances. . . .

That was probably Creeley's last attempt at the tutorial process. As usual, much more was gained in casual talks over coffee with him in the kitchen in Meadows Inn or, more likely, over beers down the road at Ma Peak's tavern.

After that two months of teaching in March and April, Creeley left Black Mountain and returned to Mallorca to continue publishing the *Review* and also to attend to his seriously ailing marriage. . . .

When Creeley returned to Black Mountain from Mallorca in June 1955 the situation at the college had deteriorated and grown even more bleak financially and in morale than on his first trip. The scene at Black Mountain matched his own personal crisis regarding an impending break with his wife.

To say that he was in an extremely agitated state would be putting it mildly. He had been unsuccessful in mending his marriage and this failure became an obsession with him, dominating his talk as he poured into any and every ear, in compulsive necessity, the most intimate details of the breakup. He would look at you, his eye glaring and watering, a bit mad, but coaxing the sympathy out of you, as he shook his head in disgust, his brow wrinkling in bewilderment. "Can you imagine a woman saying *that* to her husband?" and he would pause to shake his head again before launching into another passionate monologue about how wronged he'd been.

In an atmosphere where sanity was often pushed to its limits, including my own later excesses, Creeley appeared at times in the weeks ahead to be not quite sane. Olson told me how Creeley had come to him one afternoon, drunk and high on pot, crying "crocodile tears" and complaining, "If this is the way the world is, I don't want it—If this is the way it is, you can have it." And Olson, who had been a paragon of patience and tolerance and support, was getting pretty fed up by this time with Creeley's boozing and pot-smoking, letting his attention to his classes go slack, bellyaching constantly about the bustup of his marriage; Charles, all but abstemious in those days, a few beers now and again, afraid of it I think, and with good reason, having seen him high on occasion; Charles, the private person, silent on his own impending breakup with Connie, sat down, after he'd gotten rid of Creeley, and wrote, out of anger and affirmation, the first draft, in what sounded to be a white-heat of energy, of "A Newly Discovered 'Homeric' Hymn."

Ahab's obsession with the white whale was as nothing compared with Creeley's obsession with the woman he felt had betrayed him and whom he was about to lose. It got so that people started ducking him when they saw him coming, not wanting to endure listening to yet another hour or so harangue of accusation and self-pity. Tom Field, who was docile and understanding up to a point, finally exploded to me once after a particularly long and earbending one-way talk from Creeley on his marital woes, Tom ringing in a change on one of Robert's own poems, suggesting the blindness obsessions are, exclaiming, "The night has a thousand eyes and *thou* but *one!*" Yet it was said not without sympathetic humor despite his chagrin.

Naturally, Creeley's teaching suffered, not to mention his students' suffering, since he often had to be dragged out of Ma Peak's bodily by one of them, usually Cynthia Homire, to get him back to the college in time to teach his evening class in the Reading Room.

And Creeley, even without the beer in him, wouldn't have been much good to give his best attentions and abilities to teaching (which were, when he left the first time, gaining steadily and which I hope I've made clear were considerable), possessed as he was by his marital demons. One night—I think it was Cynthia who once again got him out of Peak's this time—when he seemed to have had a few more than usual, sitting in his chair under the windows in the Reading Room, stiffly, acidly drunk, his "teaching" consisted of going around the class, student by student, with a quietly vicious and menacing appraisal of each one of our shortcomings as human beings and hopeless lack of abilities as writers. . . .

Creeley, no longer able to stand the isolation of his drafty apartment off in the all but deserted Studies Building, spent most of his time in Dan Rice's quarters in the rear first-floor apartment in Black Dwarf, where Hilda Morley and Stefen Wolpe lived, sharing the front apartment. There, Robert and Dan would hole up, drinking and talking—knowing Dan to be a good listener, I can imagine who did most of the talking— nobody laying eyes on them sometimes for days on end. Creeley had said about Dan in the afterword to the 1955 Jargon edition of *All That Is Lovely in Men,* "I have an immense hunger for such space as he knows. . . ." They shared two main things in common: jazz (Dan had done stints as trumpeter in the Stan Kenton and Woody Herman bands) and a love for the same woman, Cynthia.

Dan, an extraordinarily forceful and sensitive painter, whose status at that time at the college, neither student nor instructor, was more like hanging around because there was no other more likely place to go (he'd first arrived as a student in the late forties); yet his presence exerted a quiet, invisible force: it helped maintain a stoic, unspoken attitude, especially among the men. . . .

I was sitting on the front steps of Meadows Inn one evening after supper. Earlier, Tom had taken his Buick and driven down to Ma Peak's with Creeley, Dan Rice, and Jorge Fick. I don't know if I'd been invited to go along or not, or if I had, if I'd refused (refused maybe for lack of the buck or so for a couple of bottles of Ballantine Ale—ale got you high faster in the altitude—scarcity of money a constant fact each of us lived with daily).

I know for certain I was moony and lonely, feeling dissatisfied with myself, and wanted only to be alone that night, remember a feeling of relief that I was. . . .

I don't know how long I mooned along . . . as I sat clutching my knees on the dusty wooden front steps of Meadows Inn, but when I heard the motor of Tom's Buick as it echoed to a roar against the hills as the car wound up the twisting dirt road in the distance, complete darkness had fallen. I guess I'd been sitting there for several hours.

That snapped me out of my self-indulgent revery: Tom was returning, with Robert and Dan and Jorge in tow, and if they all decided to end the night in the kitchen of Meadows Inn, that meant endless exhilarated talk at increased volume from Ma Peak's beer into the small hours of the morning, additionally fueled by the six-bottle cartons they'd be sure to bring back with them.

Reluctant to move, unwilling to leave my sad delicious mood quite so abruptly, I sat where I was, determined to savor my solitude right down to the last few moments.

The car's engine grew louder, amplified as the sound of it pitched back and forth among the close hills. Presently, to the left, over the stream and through the trees now black with night, I saw its headlights slashing and cutting through the gaps in the branches and brush as it sped up the road, clouds of dust kicked up in its headlights.

Tom was driving faster than usual (and he was a pretty fast

driver), so I expected he must have gotten a snootful at Peak's. I could hear voices over the distance coming through the open car windows, hollering, but what they were shouting I couldn't make out. They sounded like they were arguing.

The car braked abruptly at Black Dwarf, the house up on the other side of the road where Jorge had an apartment upstairs above Dan's, so Tom must have stopped to drop Jorge off, and probably Dan and Robert, too. There was more shouting and hollering and slamming and unslamming of car doors, then I heard the car start up with a sudden lurch and watched its headlights through the trees as it swerved away from Black Dwarf and barreled into the dirt lane which turned down towards Meadows Inn by Olson's house.

The Buick gathered speed as it came fully into view now in the open grassy area, its headlights, blurred in swirls of dust, glaring directly into my eyes and lighting up the front of Meadows Inn. Someone inside the car, either Robert or Dan, was shouting, "Tom! Tom!" and then Jorge was saying in a loud voice, "Aw, Tom, come *on*" (so he, too, was still in the car). All the doors except the driver's were swinging open and shut as if the occupants were trying to jump out (perhaps the three of them had tried to back at Black Dwarf) as it came on in a loose zigzag, a fat low mushroom shape of chrome and gray metal, moving fast over the wide field and heading directly for the steps on which I sat.

Another voice shouting, sharper now, aware, "Whatta ya doing, man?! Hey, *Tom!*"

I sat there paralyzed, the way a wild animal must feel, frozen in the middle of a road at night, its eyes hypnotized by the beams of an onrushing auto. I kept thinking, "Sure he's going to stop. He's just drunk and kidding, give them all a scare. Sure he's going to stop."

But Tom didn't stop, and he must have had the gas pedal shoved to the floor, the car was moving at such a fast clip. Although veering eratically left and right, he kept it steered pretty directly for the front of the building, so large a target no matter how he went he couldn't have missed some part of it. I realized now in the hairsbreadth of an instant he was so close he couldn't stop even if he wanted to.

"*Tom!*" The car was so near I could see through the windshield and make out arms scrabbling over Tom's shoulders, trying to get at the wheel, and Tom's voice above the loud racing roar of the motor shouting, "If this is what you want, you're getting it! If this is what you want!"

With the car no more than a few feet from the steps and heading directly at the spot I was sitting in, at the last possible moment I clicked out of my hypnotic trance and suddenly leapt up, shoved open one of the french doors and bounded into what I decided in a split second would be the relative safety of the lobby, unsure as I'd been just which way the car was going to hit on the outside, deciding there might be more safety behind the thick and heavy stones of the fireplace where I now stood, a little way out from the front of the wide mouth of the hearth, facing away from it, stiff with apprehension.

All this happened only an instant before the front end of the Buick crashed into the fieldstone chimney directly beside the steps with a sickening punch of metal tangling against stone, a crunching impact that shook the entire house from the cellar up. The building shuddered around me, was still.

I stood a moment immobilized in the middle of the lobby floor, then slowly turned around. The crash had been so forceful I was surprised the chimney was still standing, even the front of the house. Staring out through the glass panes (curiously unbroken) of the french doors with the taut gauzy curtains Tom had put up, I watched the steam and smoke swirling up in the fractured beams of the headlights of the car which were, equally curious in my dazed mind, still on.

As often happens in such moments of shock, I became suddenly very calm. I hurried out the door to see Jorge wandering around in little circles on the grass at the rear of the car. I heard some moaning from the backseat, and in the driver's seat, his face illuminated by the still-lit greenish blue gleam of the dashboard, sat Tom, slumped forward, his glazed eyes staring out the windshield, his face red and glistening, muttering to himself, "I told them to stop—I told them I'd do it—I told them—"

I was amazed that any of them were still alive, let alone conscious. In the glow of the broken headlights that still lit up the rough stones of the chimney and the weathered green shingles in a stark eerie light, Jorge's pallid face was whiter than usual as he stumbled about in his heavy black boots, clasping and unclasping his hands to his head, stopping now and again to bend slightly at the knees and peer through the open rear door of the car. When I ran up Creeley was hunched near the floor in the rear seat, trying clumsily to pull out Dan who sat flung back, his head thrown against the far corner of the backseat, eyes closed, his mouth, pulled down at the corners, slightly open. Then I ran around behind the car and to the driver's side and leaning in the window asked Tom if he was all right. He said he wasn't sure, his knees were caught under the dashboard. His eyes were dull, unseeing. I managed to pry the door open and looking down at Tom and not seeing any blood, felt reassured, relieved at least they were all breathing, surprised, from the violence of the crash, not to see any blood at all.

As I jerked my head to the backseat, Creeley was still fumbling awkwardly around Dan, who seemed unconscious, his head twitching from side to side, his face ashen and deathlike.

Turning to Tom, I asked him, "Did you break anything?" He said he didn't think so, just his legs were stuck. I said I'd help him get out and after maneuvering his body and carefully easing his legs out from under the dash, he was able to move. I took his arm and gradually helped him out of the wreck but his one leg buckled under him, painfully. He couldn't stand on it and leaned on me heavily.

By this time Laurie and Naomi had come down from their upstairs apartment and were standing staring wide-eyed, uncomprehending at the scene. Several others began to appear: Olson and Wes Huss, Joe Fiore. I think Mary and Connie, too, but they might have arrived later.

There was so much confusion at this point I'm not certain of all that occurred, except that up till that time I was still keeping a pretty steady calm, helping as best I could, mechanically mostly. We got Tom and Robert into the lobby, Jorge being able to walk himself, and Dan was carried in and laid on a couch that was pulled up in front of the fireplace. Creeley sat there beside him.

Strange how, after over twenty years, a few details remain vivid in the aftermath of the accident: the bed Dan lay on, with

Creeley next to him, with its pink and rose coverlet with white and yellow stripes, in need of a washing, that Tom had picked up somewhere when we first moved in and had thrown over the old sour mattress on box springs to make a "daybed" out of it to help smarten up the lobby.

As I leaned over to see how Dan was, Creeley suddenly seized my hand and pulled me down on the bed to sit close beside him, squeezing my hand in a tight grip, a strength that surprised me after what he'd just gone through. Staring directly, intently, into my eyes, his own eye riveted on me in insistence, as if fearful my attention would leave him, he began to talk in a harsh quick voice, not about Dan, not about Tom or Jorge, not even about the accident, but about his wife and himself, in a nonstoppable rush of words, his hands squeezing mine tighter and tighter.

I felt uncomfortable, and annoyed, too, still stunned myself from the aftereffects of the wreck. Why was Creeley babbling on about this, now, all over again, what we'd all been hearing for months on end? I wanted to punch him. Instead, I tried to look away, to the side or down at the floor but his voice always pulled me back. Listen, listen, listen! was the demanding tone of it. Tears began to run down his cheeks and wouldn't stop running, like his words, which ran faster and faster, and for the first time Creeley didn't reach for a handkerchief to sop at them as he did in other times of agitation, but let them run freely.

I grew even more uneasy, like a fraudulent priest hearing the confession of an utterly desperate man. What perplexed me even more was that this man, whose writing and perceptions I respected so highly, that I had struggled to comprehend, with whom I felt (although he was only six years older than myself) very much in the position of novice writer and student in the face of all his own steady and solid accomplishments, who stood head and shoulders above my own bare achievements, whose uniqueness and whose personal life, in spite of its "unconvention," was in the main "acceptable," who could speak aloud and at length of it, and most certainly did, of its happinesses and unhappinesses, contrasted to my own buried dreads and forcibly stopped-up heart and silenced mouth, heard, in the low rasping torrent of words that came from a throat sounding as if it was choking with rage and fear and hurt, his asking me for forgiveness. And interspersed in his rapid talk now were phrases of "You're a lovely man, Mike," and "Tom is a lovely man," and beneath it all, in the tone of all he was saying, I could only hear, Forgive me, forgive me.

Forgive him for what I didn't know—that, as later came out, his, along with Dan and Jorge, digging at Tom was the main cause of the car wreck? Not knowing, all I did was sit and listen, not having any words, not having the space to speak them even if I did; or the ability to grant it, whatever absolution he so desperately needed, for whatever unspeakable crimes of the heart.

The brunt need of that low, fast-talking voice in its gravelly naked openness was like a tormented child baring itself in a breathless stumble of words. It had such an impulsion of necessity behind it, the need to speak and speak, as if words themselves could fill a particularly harrowing void made more numbingly empty in the aftermath of the suddenness and shock of the "accident," the jolt of bewildering recognition that, in its raw feeling, had nothing to do with words but only for the comforting resonance of their pure sound, the sound of the self like a falsely brave and stuttering noise in a fearful vacuum.

I kept silent. I listened. It was the only kindness I could do for him. . . .

Mary and I went down to visit Tom and Dan in the Veterans Hospital in Swannanoa, just off the narrow county road leading up to the college, a huge sprawling place that looked like a military camp, or a factory, with its large heating and generating plant with its tall smokestacks. I had passed it innumerable times, drunk and sober, hiking or riding back and forth between the college and Ma Peak's, but this was the first time I was ever inside; I guess for Mary, too.

Tom it turned out had broken a leg, and Creeley came out of it with a severely wrenched shoulder but didn't require hospitalization. Dan, the unluckiest, had his back badly dislocated and would be in the hospital for a longer period of time, and in a back brace even longer after that. . . .

As I look back now, what happened couldn't have been otherwise, this horrendous culmination of so many small and growing disasters of that summer. So many underlying and hidden malevolences seem to have been set loose in each of us in those last dying months of Black Mountain, as if the spirits inhabiting the space of the land itself had also finally turned against us and wanted us out of there, to rid the place of a certain destructive sickness which would only grow worse with our continued presence, the seeds of which were in, or touched on, everyone of us who had somehow survived and remained clinging in blind hope and stubborn belief right down to the desperate end.

Perhaps after so many negativities of experience, we no longer loved the place enough, secretly harbored hatred for it in our hearts, and the wild and green spirits of the mountainous forests picked up on those unvoiced emanations of hatred and turned their own malevolencies against us to preserve the spirit of forested spaces that, literally, we were helping to destroy, forced to lease out large tracts of the hilly woodland to timber cutters for meagerly extended survival.

Perhaps, too, and the most likely, it was that the hour had finally come, unaware to us, that the varied and multiple shapes and ideas and perceptions spawned at Black Mountain over its last years were ready to be scattered out into the world, after a long-protracted and overdue birth.

I can't leave it at this, since the uglinesses and violences, even the sillinesses of that time were in no way equal to or ever overshadowed the accomplishments in the work done at Black Mountain in those last years, in the ideas and enthusiasms and camaraderie that were exchanged on a daily basis. In trying to sum up (impossible task!) what it was like knowing Creeley and what Creeley's writing has meant to me, the impact of him in my own life, I'll try to say it this way, realizing there isn't any end to the saying of it:

His is a scrupulous and highly exact examination of conscious processes. His own clearances, then as now, are in areas of excruciating wakefulness. If his demons are "conscious" ones, they are, paradoxically, no less real and terrifying than those lurking in the dark under-roots of the unconscious. Yet much of his writing has the quality of dreams, in definitions of consciousness so newly realized they have a nether-worldly aura, so foreign are they, seen from the prospect of his unique and stripped-down acute angle of vision.

In the darkness of bedrooms, in the darkness of his own mind and heart, trapped in a head of the night that can't sleep, a head insomniac through the day, grinding in flinty obstinacy to strike a few precise sounds of conscious meaning in the opaque density of incomprehension that surrounds us all our waking and sleeping hours:

> My mind to me a mangle is

To press and press, on, to squeeze from the skin of one's own reality refractions of it that might possibly conflagrate—and in Creeley's writing often do—a larger illumination.

From the narrow base of his concerns, tight in its strictures, in its methods, whole formerly darkened and inaccessible areas erupt in veined light across the eyes, they are so physical and penetrating. Having read Creeley, who is, like all who are given the gift of a loan of the secrets and who challenge and claim a particular space as their own, none of us will ever see the same again.

What is sometimes taken away is given back double-strength in another place—with Creeley, half-sighted has been more than enough to focus and deliver the power of vision behind it. Through it, we have all been given additional sight.

NOTE

1. Martin Duberman, *Black Mountain: An Exploration in Community* (New York: E. P. Dutton, 1972), 393–94.

GILBERT SORRENTINO

From "Black Mountaineering"

It is difficult to remember the isolation a writer such as myself
felt in the fifties. The sense, the absolute insistence upon the fact,
that one had no peers that were of use or interest seemed de-
pressingly clear. There were magazines, of course: they made
the young writer even more depressed. Not only was there no
hope of being represented in their pages, but that writer whose
learning had come from the tradition of Williams and Pound
knew that his work, scattered and inchoate, had no relation to
the narrowly conceived policies of these respected journals.
There were attempts to provide showcases for the "new writ-
ers"—I think of *Discovery* and *New World Writing*—but it turned
out that these publications were edited by men who accepted the
given of that time and were simply looking for more of the
same, albeit by different names. Then there were the "experi-
mental" little magazines that would publish anything—any-
thing at all. Meanwhile, one worked in a kind of numb solitude,
unpublished and unread, and, more to the point, without access
to those works that could have acted as direction and buttress to
one's own false starts and scribblings. How fantastic it was,
then, to see the *Black Mountain Review:* a journal that not only
presented the work of men who shared one's concerns, but that
established a ground on which the American writer could stand.
It was, or so it seemed, against the grain. Now, of course, we
see that it was in the grain, and much of the work that was
treated with such exaggerated respect between 1945 and 1960
has revealed itself to be aberrant, nontraditional, and essentially
frivolous in its concerns. I mean to say that the viability and

From *Poetry* 116, no. 2 (May, 1970): 110–12, © 1970 by Gilbert Sorrentino.
Reprinted by permission of the author and the Editor of *Poetry*.

energy of that work done by Pound, Williams, Zukofsky, Oppen, H. D., Dahlberg, et al., *surfaced* in the *Black Mountain Review* in the verse and prose of a generation of writers that had been "officially" looked for by the entire literary establishment. Of course, when they showed up, nobody in that establishment knew they had arrived. It wasn't many years ago that Olson was called "an aging beatnik." Duncan is still referred to as an "experimental" poet, and so on and on. But the recognition of that ground was instantaneous to those who, like myself, had thought of their own conceptions of the poem as freakish. There it was, this magazine, clearly new, clearly arrogant, with a first issue that contained Olson's brilliant essay on Robert Duncan, "Against Wisdom As Such," and an attack on Theodore Roethke, thought of by many people as a major American poet.

A ground to walk on, a force, an encouragement for all young writers who felt themselves to be disenfranchised. So that it was a gathering place for all of them, whether they were published in it or not. It was indeed a subversive magazine, partly because its thrust into letters was positive, that is, the sense, the entire tone of the magazine posited the value of its own concerns; it was not a journal that devoted itself to a derogation of that work against which it was set, rather, it gave you Olson, it gave you Duncan, it gave you Burroughs, it gave you Rumaker and Selby. There was the example before you of its beliefs. It proved, along with *Origin,* which was neither as catholic nor as intelligent, the proposition that with the end of the war the dominance of an effete, academic, and European-oriented literature was also ended.

It is beautiful to me that the magazine has been so justified, that is, that those writers who appeared in its pages should show, now, as teachers of the young. That so many of them have been proved masters is obvious; what is more important is that those who have disappeared, or failed, left this residue, contributed a poem, a review, whatever, still valuable in trying to understand exactly where and how the unaffiliated made a stand. This is, of course, a tribute to the intelligence of the editor, Robert Creeley, a man who somehow got this fantastic engine going, and who edited each issue into a complete statement of *the fact.* As Creeley has said elsewhere, the writers of that time needed the dignity of their own statement—and this magazine provided it. The dignity of *their* own statement, not the dignity of *one's* own statement in some hostile context, that is, Duncan in, let's say, the *Hudson Review* of that time. Creeley clumped together the most disparate literary intelligences of the time, clear in the knowledge that they formed a true configuration of the new letters. . . .

CID CORMAN

A Requisite Commitment

Sixteen short poems in a handsome accurate format, handset and handbound, constitute this second collection of poems by a young New England poet living temporarily with his family in Mallorca.

Here is the title poem:

> Giving oneself to the dentist or doctor who is a good one,
> to take the complete
> possession of mind, there is no
>
> giving. The mind
> beside the act of any dispossession is
>
> lecherous. There is no more giving in
> when there is no more sin.

Yes: any such concentrated speech makes it, a poem. Where is the rule that will accommodate this act? Shall we angle for a generality that the sun may quickly dry? *This* is the kind of act of Robert Creeley. And that it is *his,* that particular e-motion of speech, which is true to his uses, gives it identity, shape.

But it is not only a private party, this; also the play of it lets us in (and the title of it invites). There is a danger and a requisite commitment to the sea in which this harried diver lives. His act, which never shirks the danger or the commitment, aims constantly at exposing through the large illogic of poetry, that perfection of speech, his inner tensions as they may cohere with ours.

Review of *The Kind of Act Of* from *Poetry* 83, no. 6 (Mar., 1954): 340–42, © 1954 by Cid Corman. Reprinted by permission of the author and the Editor of *Poetry*.

The poem should, it seems, grammatically open with the preposition "In." Three good poetic reasons exist for not doing so: (1) "Giving" is thus given prime emphasis, becomes immediately present as "theme," (2) its grammatical function is insufficient also for its running against "giving in" later in the poem, and (3) it is unnecessary. The poem, then, opens (or closes, if you will) into three complete sentences, set forth as if they followed one after the other with ineluctability; but what we are actually witnessing, seeing, and hearing the precise evidences of, is the poet's mind and vitals struggling to grasp the seeming passivity of "dispossession." True, but where does the struggle come in?

It enters *in the form*. The opening line sets the stage. It is lengthy (dramatically tightening into what follows), it needs qualification; the poet has some as yet undefined qualms. The next line breaks with a strong emphasis to underline the complete surrender of the act. This is left hanging in the main clause in the third line, *moving* us (as later too) to the next stanza and the paradoxical, somewhat unexpected, "giving" recurring. The poet has two items to build from now, as introduced: "giving" and "mind." He isolates them here, in the center of the poem, and the poem teeters these two elements, holds them in tension—which is not simply mathematics.

The line, breaking here, in a sense gives the pause wherein the poet feels his progress, a progress which is neither all mind nor all body, but both, poetry. He grasps, with some pain of discovery (he seems to realize *at the same instant we do*), that the mind cannot be a clean instrument, that though sharp, by its very nature, a dirt clings to it, a guilt. The word "lecherous" is clearly emotional in tone.

And then the poet in the last sentence realizes the struggle openly and fully, though with great succinctness. He defines the struggle by the almost aphoristic utterance and slyly takes us into what is not "aphorism" or "mere statement," but to his own depth, to a genuinely painful appreciation and understanding of our irreconcilable guilts.

An exaggerated reading? Not at all. Much more is here. This brief analysis tells something of the area made precise here and now, but to say "precise," as so many tend to understand it sadly, is not to say "scientifically" or "coldly." There is no coldness here; there is some terror; there is considerable edge of agony. There is a courage in the very act of it, finally. The very act of this poem is evidence of a courage. This brief and not wholly adequate analysis has been offered, not as a proof of one reader's perception of the poem, but to draw the reader's intelligence to the fact that Robert Creeley's poetry, which has so much to teach those of us who care for what can be done in poetry and what it does, is so likely to suffer the most casual silence and the most facile of rejections.

ROBERT BEUM

From "Five Poets"

If You makes one suspect that Creeley's ultimate poetics will be more eclectic than that of Williams, who has given him his direction: the poems show an increasing exploration of rhyme. The final stanza of "For Ann" (the whole poem, for that matter), the last poem in the book, should be enough to convince the most hidebound verslibrist that rhyme can be adapted to even a short-lined free verse unobtrusively, with musical effect, and to great advantage in securing conceptual unity:

> I loved you as well
> even as you might tell,
> giving evidence
> as to how much was penitence.

Otherwise, these eight poems are further demonstration that Creeley is the most successful of the many who have achieved an idiom close to that of Williams, yet distinct from it, suitable for individual needs and insights. Creeley's temperament is lonelier than Williams's and more introspective, less ebullient, less susceptible to vivid visual imagery, more compelled to a recognition of what is ironic and painful in subtle impingements of feeling and situation. Architectonically, Creeley continues to alternate between a classic transparency and the now much-mined exciting opacity of free association. "Air: 'Cat Bird Singing'" . . . is the only unsuccessful poem in the group. It is destroyed by a certain disjointedness and by the imperfectly motivated shouting of:

Review of *If You* from *Poetry* 92, no. 6 (Sept., 1958): 387–88, © 1958 by The Modern Poetry Association. Reprinted by permission of the Editor of *Poetry*.

> The trees, goddamn them,
> are huge eyes. They
>
> watch, certainly, what
> else should they do?

and in general the piece seems to follow what is worst, rather than best, in Pound and Williams.

LOUIS ZUKOFSKY

"What I Come To Do Is Partial"

As he says in his preface, Robert Creeley's honest metaphysical intention is: "—there is no use in counting. Nor more, say, to live than what there is, to live. I want the poem as close to this fact as I can bring it; or it, me." It is like Spinoza's definition of honesty—"I call that honest which men who live under the guidance of reason praise and which is not opposed to the making of friendship." With some disposition like that in mind Creeley can happily say: "I write poems because it pleases me, very much—I think that is true."

That one guiding and reasonable fact "Nor more to live than what there is", whatever way he "stumbles into" particular examples, should assure Creeley that these cannot be "hopeful and pompous." Considering the one fact moves all of his poems, it is understandable that Creeley—if he writes for anyone—may seem "now" to "know less of these poems" than the possible reader he imagines, who also knows it and sees the poems made by it:

> & the head could not
> go further
> without those friends

* * *

> I mean, graces come slowly

* * *

Review of *The Whip* from *Poetry* 92, no. 2 (May, 1958): 110–12. Reprinted by permission of the Editor of *Poetry*. Permission to quote Louis Zukofsky material given by Paul Zukofsky. No one may use this material without obtaining the express permission of Paul Zukofsky, who now owns the copyrights.

perpetuity
            (which is not reluctant, or if it is,
it is no longer important.

                    *   *   *

friendship, the wandering and inexhaustible wish to
be of use, somehow
to be helpful

when it isn't simple

                    *   *   *

            behind her there were
flowers, and behind them
nothing

                    *   *   *

            there
is the rock in evidence . . .

            What I come to do
            is partial

                    *   *   *

Where fire is, they are quieter
and sit comforted . . .
            If they speak
I have myself, and love them.

                    *   *   *

The poem . . . addressed to
emptiness—this is the courage

Necessary.

                    *   *   *

            If quietly and like another time
There is the passage of an unexpected thing:

to look at it is more
than it was.

* * *

But how account for love even if you look for it?
I trusted it.

* * *

A COUNTERPOINT

Let me be my own fool
of my own making, the sum of it

is equivocal.
One says of the drunken farmer:

leave him lay off it. And this is
the explanation.

* * *

Which one sings, if he sings it,
with care.

* * *

No man shall be an idiot for purely exterior reasons.

The poems are to be praised for not counting up to the "con-
ceit" of rhetoric, which a generation or so ago misnamed "meta-
physical", whose thought presumed more hope than the voice
of a limited body.

The Work of Robert Creeley

We think of the modern tradition as being indivisible, like water, but actually there are seven or eight strong traditions within the modern tradition, and a poet may have the strength and courage to participate in one or more of those traditions. It is obvious to everyone that Robert Creeley has some courage.

The work of Robert Creeley includes, I think, not only his poems, but also his work for the Black Mountain group; this group, to which he has devoted so much time, is perhaps for the first time in America, nearly a "school" in the French sense. Their work has made the *Black Mountain Review,* of which Mr. Creeley is the editor, an honest and intelligent review, and in some ways the most interesting magazine in America. The group includes Charles Olson, an American from New England, in Lowell's generation, who among other things wrote the book on Melville which Grove Press has published; Irving Layton, a Canadian in the same generation; Robert Duncan, now increasingly admired, also in the generation of the forties; and others, both older, such as Louis Zukofsky, the old radical, who is still writing on, and younger, such as Denise Levertov.

The poems of these poets have appeared regularly in the *Black Mountain Review,* in Cid Corman's *Origin,* certain California quarterlies, and of the more national magazines, only in *Poetry,* which has made an effort to represent them. The book publisher for this group has been, for the most part, Jonathan Williams, a young man in Highlands, North Carolina, who supports the press on his own income, has the books printed in various countries of the world, and has printed since he started in 1951 about thirty-five books. That is a lot of work. He published in 1953

From *Fifties,* no. 2 (1959): 10–21, copyright © 1959 by Robert Bly.

Creeley's *The Immoral Proposition* and in 1955 *All That Is Lovely in Men*, both now out of print, and in 1957 *The Whip;* and he also publishes the *Black Mountain Review*, which is now up to #8. Mr. Creeley has also published four other books elsewhere: *Le Fou*, Golden Goose Press in 1952, *The Kind of Act Of*, Divers Press in 1953, *The Gold Diggers* (short stories), Divers Press, 1954, and *If You*, Porpoise Bookshop, San Francisco, in 1956. The most available book of Mr. Creeley's is *The Whip*, a small book of selected poems, from which the poems quoted in this review are taken. . . . As Mr. Williams mentions somewhere, magazines such as the *Kenyon Review*, the *Partisan Review*, the *Nation*, the *New Republic*, and the *Saturday Review* have yet to review one of Mr. Williams's thirty-five books, but they are reviewed frequently in *Poetry* and occasionally in the *New York Times*.

The books of poems by men in this group occasionally have introductions by William Carlos Williams, whom they admire both for his long and independent creative life, and his rugged "local" quality. I know none of these men, but I gather they also respect Pound, not only for his daring of mind, and freedom from the old Georgian cant, but also for his continual hardheaded insistence that all is not well in America, this best of all possible worlds.

These poets are somehow politically more mature than the usual poet in, for instance, *Poetry,* and understand that some form of oppression today, even in America, is as common as beauty, for those who have senses which can grasp it. And they are all ornery men. If total oppression came, a poet like Robert Hillyer would probably become Poet Laureate, and these men, not formidable so much as ornery, would probably be shot instantly to keep them out of trouble. And that is some sort of compliment.

It must be said for William Carlos Williams that he has a kind of vitality which inspires a considerable amount of thought in younger men; in other words, he has disciples, and that certainly cannot be said for such men as Eliot or Jeffers or Tate, or even such a fine poet as Marianne Moore. We remember that the sources of the recent activity in San Francisco, namely Allen Ginsberg and Jack Kerouac, both profess also a strange relationship to William Carlos Williams, who in this case acts as a sort of windowpane, behind which they see Whitman, who is temperamentally much more unapproachable. With this common devotion to William Carlos Williams, we should not be surprised to see these men appearing in Robert Creeley's magazine. In fact, Ginsberg's best poem, "America," was first published there, and later, other San Francisco people have appeared in the *Black Mountain Review,* including Gary Snyder, and the good short-story writer, Michael Rumaker. Mr. Rexroth was also, several years ago, connected with the magazine.

In other words, this is an amorphous group, having in common a respect of William Carlos Williams and Ezra Pound, an interest in independent thought, a dislike of hacks and innocents, and what is perhaps not so healthy, a sort of American isolationism.

There is an anecdote about Yeats and Sandburg. Yeats was making one of his lecture and reading tours of America, about 1912, and he came to Chicago, I suppose in some connection with Harriet Monroe. After reading many poems on Irish themes, and perhaps, telling a few anecdotes of literary life in London, it seems Mr. Sandburg stood up and asked in an angry voice why, if Yeats was an Irishman, he did not live and write in his own country instead of in a foreign one? Mr. Yeats replied that Paris was the center of the world of poetry, but unfortunately he could not speak French; so he lived as close to Paris as a man could who could not speak French. Sandburg is then supposed to have gone into a rage, saying in effect, that all that about Paris being the poetic center was hokum, that Chicago could just as well be the center, and that they would make it so, etc., etc. America was as good as France, better because less exhausted, it had native inspiration, etc., lacked all that corruption, etc. Now after forty years, how has the story ended? Yeats is considered the greatest poet of the century in the English language, and Sandburg is in Arkansas with his goats and his guitar. These stories are not stories so much as myths, that happen over and over again.

The danger, it seems to me, of Mr. Creeley's group, and the San Francisco group, is that they will go the way of Sandburg.

In fact, there is a strange resemblance between the Chicago group of the 1910s and the San Francisco group of the 1950s. In forty years, the city has shifted 1,500 miles farther west, but there is still the moving attempt to raise up a culture in an isolated city by any means possible; in both movements there is the thought that poetry can only be written by the uncorrupted and innocent; an emphasis on street poetry and prostitutes; and an emphasis on the strictly "Amurrican," as Pound would say. One senses that the majority of the San Francisco group, with the exception of Mr. Rexroth, is all too ready to describe French poetry as "Rimbaud and all that"; we remember that Charles Olson, in Mr. Creeley's group, is an authority not on some foreign poet, but on the American, Melville; and that all the doctrines of the man they perhaps respect the most, Williams, emphasize the Americanism of material, words, meters, and attitude as subjects for poetry.

These thoughts about isolationism from the newer poetry of Europe are never too distant as we consider Robert Creeley's poems themselves. Robert Creeley has a lovely poem to William Carlos Williams, in which he is thinking perhaps of the troubles in Williams's life:

> The pleasure of the wit sustains
> a vague aroma
>
> The fox-glove (unseen) the
> wild flower
>
> To the hands come
> many things. In time of trouble
>
> a wild exultation.

What is the weakness in this poem? Obviously it is lack of images, just as the same thing is the weakness of Williams's poetry itself. The language suffers a kind of drought from lack of images. Yet the use of images is particularly the tradition of modern poetry which comes to us from abroad. Perhaps we can see the incompatibility of abstract words and images better in another poem. Mr. Creeley opens:

> By Saturday I said you would be better on Sunday.
> The insistence was a part of a reconciliation.

It is strange to see this. It seems to me that the greatest tradition of all modern poetry, and of the avant-garde for a century, has been the heavy use of images. Poems are imagined in which everything is said by image, and nothing by direct statement at all. The poem *is* the images, images touching all the senses, uniting the world beneath and the world above, as in Lorca's:

> Black horses pass
> And dark people
> Over the deep roads
> Of the guitar.

These wild images we first notice in French poetry of the nineteenth century, in Baudelaire for instance. There is a great blossoming in Mallarmé and Rimbaud, and in this century, it is made into a whole way of thought by the poets in the Spanish language. In French, also, images continue to be the strength of modern poetry, both in the Surrealists and in such poets as Eluard and Char. But in this poetry, or in America itself, this tradition does not exist.

There are other great traditions in modern poetry; a second great direction is that of going deeply into oneself, and returning like an explorer, perhaps saddened forever, but with strange kinds of knowledge—the tradition, for instance, of Rilke and Trakl. Yet, to anyone who knows this work it is apparent that the poetry of which we are speaking does not share this tradition—the connection with the world is never broken.

A third great movement of modern poetry, and an invention horrifying to the bourgeois, is the simple description of life in modern cities, life after the Industrial Revolution, life exactly as it is, of which the first poems were written by Baudelaire, as, for instance, in his "Dusk Before Dawn":

Houses, here and there, commence to give off smoke.
Women of happiness, with eyelids the color of ashes,
Mouths fallen open, sleep the sleep of beasts.
And women without a cent, dragging their thin and cold
      breasts,
Blow on their coals, and blow on their hands.
It was the time of night, when, among cold and pinching of
      pennies,
The pains increase of the women in labour;
Like a sob that is cut by a jet of blood
The cry of a cock far off slashed the smoky air,
A sea of fog bathed the monumental buildings. . . .

Like a face in tears which the gusts try to dry
The air is full of the whispering sounds of things that at last
      escape,
And man is sick of writing, and woman of making love.

Eliot in 1915 wrote:

They are rattling breakfast plates in basement kitchens,
And along the trampled edges of the street
I am aware of the damp souls of housemaids
Sprouting despondently at area gates.

To those who know Mr. Creeley's work, it is obvious that there is nothing of this sort here either: the poems like those of Pound, after he left London, exist in some indeterminate place which is never described. Some of Eliot's descriptions of cities, though written forty years ago, are still the best in the English language; in German, there are poems by Rilke and Gottfried Benn, but none in America at all.

A fourth of the great traditions of modern poetry is a kind of daring in self-revelation—one thinks immediately of La Forgue's wild descriptions of himself as a clown, an orphan, a weather-cock, a worshipper of the moon, a terrified admirer of women, a hunting horn, an eternal failure. This daring seems to start with Gautier. Baudelaire is nourished by it, and it occupies nearly the entire work of Corbière. But in the poetry of which we are speaking the poet clings to his own personality too tightly, as if he might lose it, and nothing can be achieved here. It comes as a start then to realize that this poetry, though presented in this country as avant-garde, does not share at all in four of the greatest traditions of modern literature or avant-garde poetry. This is true both of the San Francisco group and the Black Mountain group, as well as of Mr. Creeley's poetry itself.

Well, what is modern about it then? For it is obvious that Creeley's poems are modern, just as it is obvious, for instance, that William Meredith's poems are not. Let us compare a stanza of Mr. Meredith's with one of Mr. Creeley's. Mr. Meredith opens a poem:

> What will I ask, if one free wish comes down
> Along with all these prodigalities
> That we pick up like dollars in a dream,
> And what I urge you ask, is not that we
> Grow single in our passion without gap,
> Losing with loneliness dear differences;
> Not lust, to burn a lifetime resinously,
> Although that surely were a miracle. . . .
>
> (from "A Boon," by William Meredith, in
> *New Poets of England and America*)

Robert Creeley writes of his children:

> Where fire is, they are quieter
> and sit, comforted. They were born
> by their mother in hopelessness.
>
> But in them I had been, at first,
> tongue. If they speak,
> I have myself, and love them.

The first thing one asks, when one finishes the Meredith stanza, is, what kind of a man is it, that, speaking to his own wife or girl, would ever say:

> Grow single in our passion without gap,
> Losing with loneliness dear differences;

It is impossible. No one would speak like that. In Elizabethan times, and in another country, they actually spoke like that but that was three hundred years ago. Mr. Meredith writes of his emotions as if he were living in Elizabethan times, and the whole thing comes through to us, as it cannot help but do, with an air of phoniness.

When Mr. Creeley, speaking of the strange sense of self-possession one's own children give to a parent, says:

> If they speak,
> I have myself, and love them

it strikes us that people today speak with that voice. In syntax, in diction, in every way, tone, attitude toward love, these two poems about love are in total contrast. The greatest difference perhaps is in the words: in Mr. Creeley's poem, the words are honest and convincing—a quality which Mr. Creeley learned from William Carlos Williams, or perhaps, learned by himself, I don't know. One of the greatest of modern traditions is the use of our own words, of modern words. Somehow we are very reluctant to do this. We find it hard to admit the world has changed as much as it has, and we want to hedge our bets, so to speak, and use words the immortals used. Mr. Creeley has not done this. His poems exist in the modern vocabulary, or not at all, and his poems have been from the start sharp and without the apology of rhyme. As a result, he is very much at home in this language, and at times so much at home, that he plays, and decides to go farther out into slang:

> As I sd to my
> friend, because I am
> always talking,—John, I
>
> sd, which was not his
> name, the darkness sur-
> rounds us, what
>
> can we do against
> it, or else, shall we &
> why not, buy a goddamn big car,

                drive, he sd, for
                christ's sake, look
                out where yr going.

I think this is a fine poem, and that it makes most other poems in slang look silly. It succeeds in exactly the points where they fail, namely in a kind of sensitivity and resonance. In the use of this kind of language, which in one sense is the only language we have, almost all American poets are behind Mr. Creeley. This is one part of modern poetry in which his work does share.

The relationship between men and women as subject matter for poetry is another great modern tradition. It is hard for us to realize that through the nineteenth century of Wordsworth, Keats, Shelley, Tennyson, Hopkins, Bridges, etc., this poetry virtually dropped out of existence. The poems were not about the relationship between men and women, but Grecian urns, Chapman's Homer, Intellectual Beauty, the Lake Country, King Arthur's court, autumn, etc., and if women are discussed, it is in a dreamy "poetic" way. Suddenly real women have returned, at first in Baudelaire, and then strongly in La Forgue, in his case almost his entire subject matter, and in Eliot, in Eluard, in the magnificent poems of Neruda. In America this tradition has been represented by Eliot in his youth, and through his entire life by William Carlos Williams.

One of the most interesting qualities of Robert Creeley's work, as it is of Louis Simpson's, is the presence of women.

As he says in "The Warning":

                For love—I would
                split open your head and put
                a candle in
                behind the eyes.

Let us choose a poem in which the two traditions present in Robert Creeley coincide—the use of modern words and the presence of women. We find in him a man who will use modern words in a poem at any risk, even the risk of bad taste or being temporarily the tough guy, and a man who is evidently kind and gentle, and who loves and respects women:

Nothing for a dirty man
but soap in his bathtub, a

greasy hand, lover's
nuts

perhaps. Or else

something like sand
with which to scour him

for all
that is lovely in women.

In "The Carnival," writing perhaps of love, he says:

Whereas the man who hits
the gong dis-
proves it, in all its
simplicity—

Even so the attempt
makes for triumph, in
another man.

Likewise in love I
am not foolish or in-
competent. My method is not a

tenderness, but hope
defined.

A last invention of modern poetry I will mention here is poetry about the increasingly invisible, but increasingly apparent, oppression in all countries. García Lorca wrote some of the first of this poetry, and was shot by Franco. This element of his poetry is as important I think as the folk element, for which he is so much praised. When Lorca writes of the Spanish State Police:

Their horses are black.
The hoofs of their horses are black.

And:

With a patent leather soul,
They come riding down the road,
Hunched over and living at night,
Wherever they go, they cause
Silences made of black rubber,
And fears of fine sand.
They go by, if they wish to,
And in their heads they hold
A vague astronomy
Of heavenly pistols.

When Lorca writes so, he is writing a poetry of which, either in images or subject matter, we know very little in this country. This tradition does not exist in William Carlos Williams, nor, except in a sort of cloudy way, in Pound, and not at all in Mr. Eliot, who, in any event, is so much on the side of authority that he is obliged to forgive much of what they do. Lorca is quite a different man. The events in his *Gypsy Ballads* are a symbol of the increasing defeats of the poor in their battle with the rich. It is interesting to see this sense of oppression suddenly appear in Mr. Creeley's work, with a touch of bitter humor. He has a poem called "After Lorca," which I will quote entire:

The church is a business, and the rich
are the business men.
                    When they pull on the bells, the
poor come piling in and when a poor man dies, he has a
        wooden
cross, and they rush through the ceremony.

But when a rich man dies, they
drag out the Sacrament
and a golden Cross, and go *doucement, doucement*
to the cemetery.

And the poor love it
and think it's crazy.

This is a good poem too. We notice again the tremendous power
of contemporary words, when someone who understands them
uses them. In this poem, once more, the language often becomes
slang, as in the last word, upon which the whole poem depends.
If the poem is sometimes weak, as it is, it is not because of the
contemporary words, but because the poem is not contempo-
rary enough; the language is treated in too flat, or English, a
way—unlike Lorca, himself, whose wild attitude and wild, deep
treatment of the language make a strange unity.

This must be the end of a short tour through Mr. Creeley's
work. His poems give the sense of a man who has considerable
integrity and is difficult and stubborn. Though the resemblances
to old men such as Williams and Pound are too clear to be
mistaken, nevertheless there is a distinct originality, for when
we read his poems, we are led toward quite different thoughts;
the reverberations in our mind, so to speak, are different, and
certainly richer, than those from the rather barren work of such
earlier men as Larsson or Lowenfels. Still we feel a shock to
realize that this poetry, which is thought of in this country as
avant-garde, and perhaps is the most avant-garde we have, is
really not avant-garde at all. The poems seem quite isolated
from the great richness and daring of Spanish poetry, or French
poetry, and somewhat also from their delicate sensibility and
joy, as well as their savagery. Mr. Creeley has great sensitivity
to the American language, and great honesty, but it seems at the
service of a too narrow and barren tradition. These poems, and
those of the entire Black Mountain and San Francisco groups,
are based almost entirely, it seems to me, on the American tradi-
tion. The American tradition is not rich enough; it is short,
Puritanical, and has only one or two first-rate poets in it, and the
faults of the lesser poets are always the same—a kind of barren-
ness and abstraction. I think Mr. Creeley should try to deepen
his own imagination, perhaps by learning a new poetry in an-
other language, certainly by searching for more richness of lan-
guage and image. Mr. Creeley is still very young, and his

poems, even so far, are a contribution to American literature, but I think his work also shows that sheer honesty and the American literary tradition alone are not enough to make a rich avant-garde.

HUGH KENNER

From "More Than Pretty Music"

. . . Robert Creeley's *A Form of Women* . . . is a good specimen
[of Jonathan Williams's Jargon Books, "some of the most hand-
some, least pretentious volumes of verse since the heyday of the
Cuala Press: Unlike the work of the Parisian little presses of the
twenties, they do not stink of the luxury trade," Kenner says
earlier in the review]. It isn't the best Creeley, which is still to be
found in *The Whip* (1957). The poet has virtually abandoned his
often miraculous control of spoken American for dreamlike
spells articulated in loose quatrains of which he seems not yet
quite to have discovered the secret. Now and then the feat
wholly comes off:

> If you wander far enough
> you will come to it
> and when you get there
> they will give you a place to sit
>
> for yourself only, in a nice chair,
> and all your friends will be there
> with smiles on their faces
> and they will likewise all have places.

This poem, like many of Mr. Creeley's, turns on its title, which
is "Oh No." For all its enigmatic and transitorial quality, *A
Form of Women* is very likely one of the books for which every-
one will be combing secondhand lists in ten years. Its author is
one of the very few contemporaries with whom it is essential to
keep one's acquaintance current.

Review of *A Form of Women* from *National Review*, Nov. 19, 1960, 320. Re-
printed by permission.

KENNETH REXROTH

From "Bearded Barbarians or Real Bards?"

. . . Second only to Denise Levertov is Robert Creeley. Superficially his poems look like the cameos of Mallarmé—such still lifes as "Autre Eventail" or "Petit Air," or the intense little epigrams of William Carlos Williams—the plums in the icebox, the wheelbarrow glazed by the rain or the cat stepping over the [jamcloset]. On close inspection Creeley's poems turn out to be anything but Imagist. They are all erotic poems, but what gives them their terrific impact is neither love nor lust. Each is an excruciating spasm of guilt. In the last couple of years Creeley seems to have become more at ease in the world and less haunted by his relations with others, and his poetry is, however slowly, gaining in humanity and breadth. It is distinguished by a remarkable sensitivity to the inflections of speech.

From the *New York Times Book Review*, Feb. 12, 1961, 44. Used by permission of Bradford Morrow for the Kenneth Rexroth Trust. Copyright © 1961 by Kenneth Rexroth.

PART TWO *The 1960s: Into a Present, a Presence*

ROBERT DUNCAN

After *For Love*

And there to discourse of love . . .

"*E quivi ragionar sempre d'amore,*" the line goes in Dante's sixth
sonnet. To which Robert Creeley in an early poem, not included
in the canon of the book *For Love,* refers directly, taking his title
from Dante's first line—"*Guido, vorrei che tu e Lapo ed io,*" which
he translates in the opening of the poem:

> Guido,
> I would that you, me & Lapo
> > (So a song sung:
> > *sempre d'amore . . .*)

There is the common usage of "me" in the nominative series,
evidence of Creeley's care or ear for the natural eloquence of the
vernacular, a primary in his aesthetic which he shares with
Dante. "Instinctive feeling," so Jespersen in his *Modern English
Grammar on Historical Principles* tells us, seizes upon the similarity
or rime of the nominatives *we, ye, he, she,* so that *me* and *thee*
follow where the influence of sound governs: "likeness in form
has in part led to likeness in function." So, "Guido" leads to
"me" to form a phonic link and reinforces the vernacular ten-
dency. For the poet form and function are always at play as one,
and Creeley can delight to catch in a jargon the peculiar syncopa-
tion of feeling as a song. So, in the poem "The Man," he will
invert a syntax too in order to sing:

From *boundary 2* 6, no. 3; 7, no. 1 (Spring/Fall 1978): 233–39. This review of *For
Love* first appeared in *New Mexico Quarterly* 32, nos. 3–4 (Autumn–Winter
1962–63): 119–24. Some changes have been made by the author. Reprinted by
permission.

He toes is broken
all he foot go
rotten
now. He look

I don't have to establish the excellence of Creeley's art in poetry here. Others over the past decade have given clear testimony. "The subtlest feeling for measure that I encounter anywhere except in the verses of Ezra Pound," William Carlos Williams writes. Donald Hall more carefully remarks, "colloquial speech with accuracy and a fine sense of proportion."

Williams's superlative does not clarify. Not only Pound, but Williams himself in *The Wedge* (1944) and *The Clouds* (1948) gives the young Creeley his challenge of what form and measure in poetry must be and defines, more certainly than Pound, the particular mode or convention of the common-speech song with a persisting convention of two-, three-, or four-line stanzas, highly articulated to provide close interplay and variation, which Creeley is to specialize in and to develop toward his own poetic voice. Yet in the opening passage of the poem "For Love," as late as 1960, Creeley's voice is close indeed to its modal base in Williams's music:

Yesterday I wanted to
speak of it, that sense above
the others to me
important because all

that I know derives
from what it teaches me.
Today, what is it that
is finally so helpless

His articulation of the line here follows Williams in its phrasing, counter to the facilities of statement, a structure ready to register minute shifts in confidence, emotionally telling in its hesitations. The juncture between "to" and "speak," defined by the line, expresses in the raised pitch of the terminal "to" and in the increased stress of the word "speak" the exact contour of a searching consciousness, an exacting conscience in the course of the poem, that will not take "to speak" for granted in its ready formation but must find its exact way. So, Creeley speaking at once of instances of love and instances of form (poems) in his preface to the book *For Love* has his sense "the misdirected intention come right . . . wherewith a man also contrives a world (of his own mind)." Williams is, in this, Creeley's master—not his superior, but his teacher. Given the invention or development of the articulated line (appearing in Williams's work as early as 1916 in the poem "March"), a variety of lyric and dramatic forms have been derived. Louis Zukofsky, Charles Olson, Denise Levertov, Paul Blackburn, Larry Eigner, Cid Corman, and myself, as well as Creeley, have all taken over directly from Williams the operative juncture, the phrasing of a composition in which the crisis of the form is everywhere immediate. "It is the LINE," so Olson relays the dogma in his essay "Projective Verse" of 1950: "that's the baby that gets, as the poem is getting made, the attention, the control, that it is right here, in the line, that the shaping takes place, each moment of the going." It is the fact that no pattern can be taken for granted as a given procedure* but that every measure means decision, immediately carries the crux of the form, that demands the subtle feeling for measure, the accuracy and fine sense of proportion characteristic of Creeley's art.

Given the decade 1950–1960 defined by the book *For Love* and the specific form of the speech song with its highly articulated line and its set stanzas, Creeley has no superior but he has peers. Williams in this period no longer writes in stanzas but develops a three-phase line in *The Desert Music* and in *Journey to Love* that can be compared to Creeley's more traditional three-line stanzas. Zukofsky in *Some Time* and in *Barely and Widely* or Olson in certain poems like "O'Ryan" and in the "Variations Done for Gerald van de Wiele" have surely equaled Creeley's achievement in *For Love*.

Then there are poems of Creeley's—"The Warning," "The

---

*Creeley's adherence to the set convention of the stanza should modify this disallowance of the given procedure.

Hero," "The Flower," "The Hill," "The Cracks," "The Rose"—that take their place in my mind with poems of Denise Levertov's—"The Absence," "With Eyes at the Back of Our Heads," "The Goddess," or "The Park"—where moving images of a psychological process appear. We have to do in our appreciation of Creeley's art not with a lonely excellence or an idiosyncratic style but with the flowering of a mode, a community of feeling in poetry. Just as Dante's art has company in Guido Cavalcanti's and Lapo Gianni's (in *De Vulgare Eloquentia* Dante relates his art also to that of Cino of Pistoja), so Creeley's art belongs to a movement in poetry redefining the ground of feeling.

It was not only in order to trace Creeley's style that I referred to his concern with Dante's sonnet addressing Guido. I had in mind also Creeley's continued association of the poet with the Tuscan tradition and, further, his ever-returning subjects, the hero and love, with the cult of Amor, and back of that with a line of poet love-heros.

"The Spirit of Romance" Pound called the tradition, tracing it from *The Golden Ass* of Apuleius and from the *Pervigilium Veneris* of the second century A.D. through to Dante and Guido. One of the key reiterations of the tradition in our time is Pound's rendering of Cavalcanti's great "Donna Mi Prega" in "Canto XXXVI":

> A Lady asks me
> I speak in season
> She seeks reason for an affect, wild often
> That is so proud he hath Love for a name

which Creeley echoes in the poem "Lady Bird":

> A Lady asks me
> and I would tell
>
> what it is
> she has found the burden of.

The "Lady" then of the poem "Air: 'Cat Bird Singing,'" even of the rueful "Ballad of the Despairing Husband," and certainly of later poems—"The Door," "Kore," "Lady in Black," "The Cracks," "The Gift," or "The Wife"—is a power in women that Dante once knew in his Beatrice, and that, before Dante, troubadours of Provence addressed in their love songs and petitions. "The lover stands ever in unintermittent imagination of his lady (co-amantis)," Pound quotes from a chivalric code of the Courts of Love. For the poets of the Provençal movement that made the matter of Love paramount as once the matter of war had been, romantic love was adulterous love, the Lady was not to be the Wife. Dante, who was married, as a poet has no wife but adores a lady, virginal in his mind, though she was actually the wife of Simone de' Bardi. And Rossetti, who revives the tradition in English poetry in the nineteenth century, adores the woman he is married to as a lady, not as a wife. But at the turn of the century, Hardy addresses the woman as both lady and wife in one, and D. H. Lawrence continues. The pathos and strength of Williams's later work, the personal immediacy and the communal voice, springs from his concern with these powers a woman can come to have in a man's feelings. For Creeley too, the Lady is both archetypical and specific.

Thus, the wife's part in marriage in the poem "Wait for Me" is also to *give a man his . . . manliness,* a function of the Lady, and in the later poem "The Wife" Creeley tells us:

> I know two women
> and the one
> is tangible substance,
> flesh and bone.
>
> The other in my mind
> occurs.
> She keeps her strict
> proportion there.

"*La gloriosa donna della mia mente*"—the glorious lady of my mind—Dante calls Beatrice in *La Vita Nuova.* But for Creeley what is held in the mind is what is realized in the act, and a poetry arises in the constant working of tangible substance and idea at tension.

It is the perplexity of a life, as in the poem "The Whip,"

where the husband lies by his sleeping wife, unable to sleep himself because there is this *other* on his mind. In the scene we see two levels of the poem itself illustrated:

> . . . above us on
> the roof, there was another woman I
>
> also loved, had
> addressed myself to in
>
> a fit she
> returned. That
>
> encompasses it. . . .

As in the terms of the language, the vulgar and the noble are involved, and Creeley resolves an eloquent vulgate of his own, a vernacular elegance. It is a synthesis of a moral demand and an aesthetic demand, her "strict proportion," where song must take command over what had otherwise been a moral or aesthetic mandate. The song itself, the vent of the poem, is "for Love" and is given over to "her tired / mind's keeping," to Her who is this woman, wife and lady, and who is also beyond her the Lady—the Muse or Divine Being of the poem "The Door":

> I will never get there.
> Oh Lady, remember me
> who in Your service grows older
> not wiser, no more than before.

The common speech, the immediate expression, the contemporary style, the poetic tradition, take on new resonance in each other. Graves's book *The White Goddess* and Jung's theories of the Anima and feminine archetypes play their part here, perhaps. But Creeley, unlike Graves or Jung, insists there is no system: "one stumbles (to get to wherever) at least some way will exist." The faith of this poetry is not dogmatic but pragmatic, in a world where lessons are not learned, though we may derive our selves from them.

The serious reader may relate the reference to Campion in the poem "Air: 'Cat Bird Singing'" to Creeley's awareness of what the song has been in itself as a tradition and to his recall of Pound's dedication of the "Donna Mi Prega" translation (in the book *Make It New*): "To Thomas Campion his ghost, and to the ghost of Henry Lawes, as prayer for the revival of music." He may find the ghost of Dante haunting the poem "Heroes" when Creeley recalls Virgil:

> That was the Cumaean Sibyl speaking.
> This is Robert Creeley, and Virgil
> is dead now two thousand years, yet Hercules
> and the *Aeneid,* yet all that industrious wis-
>
> dom lives in the way the mountains
> and the desert are waiting
> for the heroes, and death also
> can still propose the old labors.

He may note Creeley's returning the image to the great thematic constants of Romance—the dark forest, the wind, the candle "lit of its own free will," the lady, the traveler the poet is, the company strangely come upon

> in a dream, in shapes
> of all this: faces and hands,
> and things to say, too.

It is in the quest not of some *Divine Comedy* that Creeley follows the lead of Dante but in the quest of the primaries back of the tradition, of depths of self that are also depths of Time, as in the poem "A Form of Women":

> My face is my own, I thought.
> But you have seen it
> turn into a thousand years.
> I watched you cry.

So that the old orders of feeling are brought into his own new orders, so that the immediate moment opens upon other worlds.

He turns to the world of story as he turns to the world of dream or of daily life, to find a door leading to a self he is that is not his, to a revelation that is beyond him and must be given: its secret is in a woman's keeping. As in the poem "The Rose":

> And all about a rosy
> mark discloses
> her nature
> to him, vague and unsure.
>
> There roses, here roses,
> flowers, a pose of
> nature, her
> nature has disclosed to him. . . .
>
> on them there is a mark
> of her nature, her flowers,
> and his room, his nature,
> to come home to.

"For the revival of music," but it is also "for Love": "Form is never more than the extension of content." As in the spoken song, what we would say finds itself only in the emerging melody, the rime, the moving numbers. Feeling, unborn were it not for the art of the poet, coming to life in a magic then. "Mighty magic is a mother," Creeley says in the poem "The Door": "in her there is another issue." In his craft he may have peers; but here, in the music itself, in the magic, he is unique; we are mistaken to compare. This art can go to the heart of things, the melody of this voice is, most rare, in love with song—

> Into the company of love
> it all returns.

CID CORMAN

"For Love" Of

Past that, past the image:
a voice! . . .

To start's not always at the beginning, but nevertheless a beginning. Nothing absolute, yet nothing not absolutely what it is, if a word can be kept to its shape, caressing, as it were, its contours, taming it, keeping it just so. No, not so, not ever quite that neat. Yet to start, as he does, Creeley, with Hart Crane, the very image of the gorgeous adrift, the lost confectioner's son

> . . . stuttering, by the edge
> of the street, one foot still
> on the sidewalk, and the other
> in the gutter . . .

From the start, then, hope was pinned to the word. Pico.

> The letters have proved insufficient.
> The mind cannot hang to them as it could
> to the words.

The poems in *For Love* are selected and placed in, so far as I can determine, fairly chronological order, if chronos is ever logical. There are omissions, some of which I miss, but there is a life in Creeley no blurb professes, that was (and is) intricate with his work and part of my sense of that work, unconsciously at least (assuming that the conscious is all-conscious, etc.), must draw upon that, a personal relation. But let that fall as it may.

Creeley's effort, if followed with the care he continually advocates and deserves, is remarkably open. He bespeaks relations

Review of *For Love* from *KULCHUR* 2, no. 8 (Winter 1962): 49–64, reprinted in *At Their Word* (Santa Barbara, Calif.: 1978), copyright © 1978 by Cid Corman.

to others, without any attempt to conceal them—with Williams and Crane and Pound, Olson, Zukofsky, or Campion.

> It's all in
> the sound. A song.
> Seldom a song. It should
>
> be a song—made of
> particulars . . .
> . . . something
> immediate, open . . .

The Williams "Poem" frankly takes its closing "centrifugal, centripetal" from Whitman and in turn brings us to Creeley's "Song":

> I had wanted a quiet testament
> and I had wanted, among other things,
> a song. . . .
>
> (A grace
> Simply. Very very quiet. . . .
>
> A song.
> Which one sings, if he sings it,
> with care.

Which, in its turn, comes more recently to Denise Levertov's "Music":

> . . . a
> singing
> sung if it is sung
> quietly

It would be a sad error, if any reader should imagine me interested merely in noting influences as against what does concern me: the continuity with divergences along a given still vital line. For no poet who is "with it" can afford to have missed a line of promise. And Creeley has sprung, no more full-blown than the mythical Rimbaud, from a past and leads clearly to a future, meaning he is precisely here with us now.

And, indeed, to touch the present in such a way, as he so often does, that it keeps vibrating, keeps presence, despite "What one knows . . . not simple." Or perhaps that questioning presented, that keeps throwing the listener back upon himself, rocking him back on his heels, jolts. As in "The Crow." But I run ahead of myself. For I want to trace a development within the man's work (1950–1960), as it now stands, moves, addresses me, within covers, within its own order, letting contingencies occur, relations, as they must, as they do.

Creeley's poems have as an element, or aspect, to be more accurate, in their development a push toward tighter formal means, a stricter discipline, without leaning over backwards but rather, out of whatever past, pulling weight forward, toward more intimate structure. Merely to riffle the pages of this book "in order" is to "see" it. Signs of it come at once, but it strikes one *in* its formality most quietly and forcefully first in a poem like "The Innocence." To point up, however, what he has accomplished, it may serve to set before it a passage from a writer with whom he has a certain affinity but who tends to work different formal means, Samuel Beckett. This is from near the beginning of *Molloy* (which Creeley reviewed at about the time his poem was written):

> . . . They turned towards the sea, which, far in the east, beyond the fields, loomed high in the waning sky, and exchanged a few words. Then each went on his way. Each went on his way, A back towards the town, C on by-ways he seemed hardly to know, or not at all, for he went with uncertain step and often stopped to look about him, like someone trying to fix landmarks in his mind, for one day perhaps he may have to retrace his steps, you never know. The treacherous hills where fearfully he ventured were no doubt only known to him from afar, seen perhaps from his bedroom window or from the summit of a monument which, one

black day, having nothing in particular to do and turning to height for solace, he had paid his few coppers to climb, slower and slower, up the winding stones. From there he must have seen it all, the plain, the sea, and then these self-same hills, that some call mountains, indigo in places in the evening light, their serried ranges crowding to the skyline, cloven with hidden valleys that the eye divines from sudden shifts of colour and then from other signs for which there are no words, nor even thoughts. But all are not divined, even from that height, and often where only one escarpment is discerned, and one crest, in reality there were two, two escarpments, two crests, riven by a valley. But now he knows these hills, that is to say he knows them better, and if ever again he sees them from afar it will be I think with other eyes, and not only that but the within, all that inner space one never sees, the brain and heart and other caverns where thought and feeling dance their sabbath, all that too quite differently disposed. He looks old and it is a sorry sight to see him solitary after so many years, so many days and nights unthinkingly given to that rumour rising at birth and even earlier, What shall I do? What shall I do? now low, a murmur, now precise as the headwaiter's And to follow? and often rising to a scream. And in the end, or almost, to be abroad alone, by unknown ways, in the gathering night, with a stick. It was a stout stick, he used it to thrust himself onward, or as a defence, when the time came, against dogs and marauders. Yes, night was gathering, but the man was innocent, greatly innocent, he had nothing to fear, though he went in fear, he had nothing to fear, there was nothing they could do to him, or very little. But he can't have known it. I wouldn't know myself, if I thought about it. Yes, he saw himself threatened, his body threatened, his reason threatened, and perhaps he was, perhaps they were, in spite of his innocence. What business has innocence here? . . .

THE INNOCENCE

Looking to the sea, it is a line
of unbroken mountains.

It is the sky.
It is the ground. There
we live, on it.

It is a mist
now tangent to another
quiet. Here the leaves
come, there
is the rock in evidence

or evidence.
What I come to do
is partial, partially kept.

Here we have the horizon as distance, as what is there to be seen, objective, what one sees, more firmly, via distance, to be grasped, realized: a past a future present, but how things grow vaguer growing closer, impinge, and one leans outward to grasp at something, anything, solid, to hold onto. To add one's own make, a little, to what is there. The placement, the weave, of "there" and "here" is beautifully pointed and carried. And the increasing uncertainty, as against the fixed "line" first (immediately) established, finds a quiet pathos at the close. A poem trying to find ground: "The rites are care . . . trace of / line made by someone."

But Creeley, Olson's "figure of outward" (Olson's prow-head?), is the seeker of inwardness, grace, the searching "single intelligence" he early accepted as his limit and to which all his prefaces earnestly attest. One of his most telling "early" pieces is "The Crow":

The crow in the cage in the dining-room
hates me, because I will not feed him.

And I have left nothing behind in leaving
because I killed him.

And because I hit him over the head with a stick
there is nothing I laugh at.

> Sickness is the hatred of a repentance
> knowing there is nothing he wants.

The poem, which has all of Creeley's potent concentrated presence, builds in a series of rationalizations to insinuate and then bluntly (but intricately) state an overwhelming guilt, self-hatred. The poem, as elsewhere for this poet, becomes an act concurrent with itself of self-immolation, a release "*in* tension." Some of the rhythmic invention reminds me of Paul Blackburn's work in *Proensa* contemporary with it. But Creeley consistently brings other men's accents into his own. And often perfects them, gives them a truer pitch. As here. As in the muffled rhyme of "wants" (presaged in the "at" that picks up the "hit") that sticks at the end in one's craw.

A young friend, shown the poem, said, But why does he say "there is nothing I laugh at?" After all, who *expects* him to laugh at anything at that point? Ah, but that's just it: after such an event one wants to laugh it off somehow, to "get out of it." But there is no exit. The poet keeps having to come back to the nothing he has left behind him.

This is evidently not Stevens's "Snow Man," no "supreme fiction," and yet it is one of the mortal twists of the mind, of something that eats in us, that takes a stick to us, that threatens us, as our own device. Creeley reaches us where body and mind break most painfully, whereas Stevens makes a code of the imagination, is "out of the skin," a "necessary angel." Angel Creeley is not.

There is something, to be sure, of the clipped Puritan accent, a faintly religious undertone, say, in "The Immoral Proposition," in

> . . . The unsure
>
> egoist is not
> good for himself.

that Marianne Moore quite naturally apprehends as possible to her own poetic inventory. So that there is a curious, almost perverse, neatness of finish at times that makes doubt teeter more. But the curiousness itself stops us, I feel, and makes us "go back" to see how we got there, how the poet ever got us into this mess, whether

> . . . My method is not a

> tenderness, but hope
> defined.

or

> . . . There is no more giving in
> when there is no more sin.

"The Crow" finds further declension elsewhere, as in "The Operation," where the poet describes his relationship to his very sick wife in terms that make of it a sickness too and justly says at the end

> Cruel, cruel to describe
> what there is no reason to describe.

And one is tempted to ask, Why, then, *do* you describe it? Unless it be to *be* cruel, to flay yourself in public.

The turn is to couplets, tercets, quatrains, small tight stanzas, spilling over carefully, truly. But no amount of formality calls us away from the inner event. On the contrary, the form more and more evokes it. The struggle. For self-possession. And hopefully, also, surrender. The pity is that the terms remain those of "contention," though Creeley himself has written me often enough of his opposition to "oppositions" (dualities). The stage is Creeley, the words entering, Creeley's, villain and hero and sometimes tired man, Robert Creeley and Virgil's Aeneas, "proposing the old labors."

Yeats's famous statement comes to mind here, to get into what, in particular, the poet's work is:

We make out of the quarrel with others, rhetoric, but of the quarrel with ourselves, poetry . . . we sing amid our uncertainty; and, smitten even in the presence of the most high beauty by the knowledge of our solitude, our rhythm shudders . . .*

This is a statement that has resonances at least as far back in poetry as Sappho, but in its more modern convolutions it reaches us through Baudelaire and the breakdown of religion into "faith," "myth," "symbol," "belief" on into self-torment, self-questioning, self-doubt and the relief, short-lived and desperate of every kind of drug, hallucination, kick, until the one question "What is real?" (meaning nothing is) comes to dominate modern "thought," as we face the manifestations of science-fiction and the now always less fictional possibility of nuclear wipeout. Death becomes the hopeful death of mankind more contagiously, as Lawrence had already felt.

But I'm carrying the thing too far. The line that Creeley develops thematically relates to Baudelaire, Rimbaud, Mallarmé, and has analogies in Roethke and Lowell and the other "sick" poets of our time. But not one of these has so abandoned the "world" outside as Creeley has. Roethke always has his father's hothouse and marshy childhood to fall back into, Lowell always his father to beat, his family's incestuous inbreeding and "history." Both are "case histories" as poets: their poems are essentially psychoanalytical.

There are touches of this in Creeley too when he begins to pick his mother apart. But his numerous dream poems are not finicky clinical, but imaginative self-appraisals: the arc remains one of exploration, the inner trying to find "out." The only contemporary I can think of at this moment whose labors parallel Creeley's closely is Cesare Pavese, whose journals are painfully lacking in "things." It is strictly a world of no one else.

So it is notable that Creeley, who has lived in many places: Mallorca, Provence, New Hampshire, Guatemala, New Mexico, has never evoked geography or place. His poems are always located precisely and *only* within himself. I can think of no one, in fact, who has more stubbornly carried on his duel with the

---

*From "Per Amica Silentia Lunae," in *Mythologies.*—ED.

"single intelligence." He is, in a sense, the logical offspring of a poet like Baudelaire and so, predictable. But it takes a certain courage, nerve, if you like, and innocence, perhaps compulsiveness (whatever that means), to have maintained so difficult a way and to have done so with such high result.

But encomiums aside, and they are of no use unless you, you who read me, who hear poetry, can feel how finely Creeley has brought himself forth, and with what intensity.

Dr. Williams has written:

When a man makes a poem, makes it, mind you, he takes words as he finds them interrelated about him and composes them—without distortion which would mar their exact significances—into an intense expression of his perceptions and ardors that they may constitute a revelation in the speech that he uses. It isn't what he says that counts as a work of art, it's what he makes, with such intensity of perception that it lives with an intrinsic movement of its own to verify its authenticity . . .*

As in his own "To Elsie" with its sharply phrased thrust-at-us conclusion:

No one
to witness
and adjust, no one to drive the car.

Creeley's own original desire to write in Basic English, and he very nearly does even now, would hardly find exception in Williams's quoted lines, but the good doctor exploits an openness of concern, perhaps inevitable *as* a doctor, a certain outgoingness, that one can never honestly hope for Creeley, but only a slow coming to relation with himself and maybe a few others and with us, in his life, in his poems.

But to get back and on to how language can and does work

---

*"Author's Introduction" to *The Wedge* in *The Collected Later Poems* (New York: New Directions, 1963).—ED.

and again how more often it just don't, here is Louis MacNeice's recent "The Wiper" to set beside "I Know a Man":

THE WIPER

Through purblind night the wiper
Reaps a swathe of water
On the screen: we shudder on
    And hardly hold the road,
All we can see a segment
Of blackly shining asphalt
With the wiper moving across it
    Clearing, blurring, clearing.

But what to say of the road?
The monotony of its hardly
Visible camber, the mystery
    Of its far invisible margins,
Will these be always with us,
The night being broken only
By lights that pass or meet us
    From others in moving boxes?

Boxes of glass and water,
Upholstered, equipped with dials
Professing to tell the distance
    We have gone, the speed we are going,
But never a gauge or needle
To tell us where we are going
Or when day will come, supposing
    This road exists in daytime.

For now we cannot remember
Where we were when it was not
Night, when it was not raining,
    Before this car moved forward
And the wiper backward and forward
Lighting so little before us
Of a road that, crouching forward,
    We watch move always towards us,

Which through the tiny segment
Cleared and blurred by the wiper
Is sucked in under our wheels
  To be spewed behind us and lost
While we, dazzled by darkness,
Haul the black future towards us
Peeling the skin from our hands;
  And yet we hold the road.

I KNOW A MAN

As I sd to my
friend, because I am
always talking,—John, I

sd, which was not his
name, the darkness sur-
rounds us, what

can we do against
it, or else, shall we &
why not, buy a goddamn big car,

drive, he sd, for
christ's sake, look
out where yr going.

Not to say too much. For I think one would have to be deaf
dumb and blind to miss the wallop of Creeley's poem *and* not to
feel the subtle handling of it, the way words and feelings are
"scored" freshly. But it should be noted that MacNeice's poem
becomes, laid cheek by jowl with Creeley's here, mightily fac-
titious. MacNeice's management is nice and refined and stan-
dard. But the Creeley poem suddenly calls the MacNeice poem
into question and answers it! It is a trait of Creeley's best work,
as here, that it makes us hold judgment in abeyance, makes it
seem superfluous, irrelevant. The event is so immediate and
true. The speed, in this poem certainly, that the abbreviated
notation implies, seems wholly consistent with what is going
on. Part of the dissolution. Where MacNeice labors, filling,

Creeley, even within the growing complexity and difficulty of the situation, where we are, sings. How simple! And how movingly concentratedly profound! How that broken "surrounds" envelops us, the self-criticism and the obsessiveness of ". . . because I am / always talking . . .", the loneliness and projection of "which was not his / name," the excitement in the penultimate stanza and the sharp painful braking of the last, the urgency of it, the feeling of near disaster, throwing us back upon the futile wish of "a goddamn big car." Every syllable pulls its weight and no punch pulled. There isn't "time," least of all to embroider.

As later in "Anima Hominis" Yeats adds:

> . . . I think that we who are poets and artists, not being permitted to shoot beyond the tangible, must go from desire to weariness and so to desire again, and live but for the moment when vision comes to our weariness like terrible lightning, in the humility of the brutes. . . .*

Perhaps even truer if the Yeatsian flamboyance is cut and found again, more illuminated, in Dante's:

> . . . For in every action what is principally intended by the doer, whether he acts of natural necessity or voluntarily, is the clarification of his own image. Thus is it that every doer, to the extent of his doing, delights in it, for everything that is desires its own being; and since in doing the doer's being is somehow amplified, delight necessarily follows. . . . Nothing, therefore, acts unless it may thereby manifest whatever it is. . . .

To watch Creeley's mutations of what is to hand, or ear, is to see, to hear, how the inward draws to itself every possible (usually subverted) relation, stratagem, to make fun of it, almost, as in

---

*"Per Amica Silentia Lunae," in *Mythologies*.—Ed.

> *. . . give a man his*
> I said to her,
>
> *manliness: provide*
> what you want I
>
> *creature comfort*
> want only
>
> *for him and herself:*
> more so. You
>
> *preserve essential*
> think marriage is
>
> *hypocrisies—*
> everything?
>
> *in short, make a*
> Oh well,
>
> *home for herself.*
> I said.

And here's the model, Williams's

THE TESTAMENT OF PERPETUAL CHANGE

Mortal Prudence, handmaid of divine Providence
    Walgreen carries Culture to the West:
hath inscrutable reckoning with Fate and Fortune:
    At Cortez, Colorado the Indian prices
We sail a changeful sea through halcyon days and storm,
    a bottle of cheap perfume, furtively—
and when the ship laboreth, our stedfast purpose,
    but doesn't buy, while under my hotel window
trembles like as a compass in a binnacle.

a Radiance Rose spreads its shell—thin
Our stability is but balance, and wisdom lies
      petals above the non-irrigated garden
in masterful administration of the unforeseen
      among the unprotected desert foliage.

'Twas late in my long journey when I had clomb to where
      Having returned from Mesa Verde, the ruins
the path was narrowing and the company few
      of the Cliff Dwellers' palaces still in possession of my
      mind

The switch to the highly-charged personal, the relations almost invariably "screwed-up" between a husband and wife, between Creeley and his woman, is characteristic. Yet I doubt if any poet has ever more doggedly explored the ramifications of what goes on between two human beings, presumably adult, who live under one roof, who sleep in or use one bed, or what does *not*. And the scrupulous examination he constantly subjects love to. No longer "romantic" or not in any usual sense.

THE BUSINESS

To be in love is like going out-
side to see what kind of day

it is. Do not
mistake me. If you love

her how prove she
loves also, except that it

occurs, a remote chance on
which you stake

yourself? But barter for
the Indian was a means of sustenance.

There are records.

I think it is Valéry who emphasizes his delight in poetry consists in its "transitions," how thought in it "turns." In Creeley what we would tend to call, if it were not inevitably jargon, the "intuitive" predominates. More than "thought" turns here: the movement worms its way forward through a logic of feeling rather than that specifically of thought, though it has seemed crucial to me that thought itself be recognized as feeling, and that feeling itself is a way of thinking, by no means "primitive." (Indeed, formal thought often has struck me as being as naive as it is constipated by its adherence to set structures.) Anyhow, it is, when it works in Creeley, a source of astonishment and deep delight, to move with him, to feel the implication of risk (though the question seems to dawn only when "yourself" is put on the line) in love's open exchange and how risk *is,* clearly, what there is that sustains. The opening lines have Creeley's already remarked cryptic utterance, simple, so simple as to be startling, and revealed wholly as the poem gradually reveals it. To know, that is, where one is, by giving oneself to it, going out into, to see.

Creeley's wit, I might say in passing, is never quite light-hearted. It is not irrelevant that he called his early small collection of "light verse" a "Snarling Garland." A wryness persists, a taking oneself to task, an effort, difficult surely, to begin to laugh at oneself. Salutary, at any rate.

The tightness works its way out into an ever cleaner sense of economy, of form:

LA NOCHE

In the court-
yard at midnight, at

midnight. The moon is
locked in itself, to

a man a
familiar thing.

Which bears an odd resemblance to a haiku by Kikaku:

                    locked & bolted
                    the castle-gate
                    winter moon

   In the whimsicality of "Juggler's Thought" there is an under-
riding pathos, of lost Eden. And with the second section, 1956–
58, come some of the unhappiest love poems of our time. As in
the final stanzas of "A Form of Women":

            My face is my own, I thought.
            But you have seen it
            turn into a thousand years.
            I watched you cry.

            I could not touch you.
            I wanted very much to
            touch you
            but could not.
                [notice the break between "to" and "touch"]

            If it is dark
            when this is given to you,
            have care for its content
            when the moon shines.

            My face is my own.
            My hands are my own.
            My mouth is my own
            but I am not.

            Moon, moon,
            when you leave me alone
            all the darkness is
            an utter blackness,

            a pit of fear,
            a stench,
            hands unreasonable
            never to touch.

But I love you.
Do you love me.
What to say
when you see me.

In such poems it is amazing to see a man hold on, grip structure
for salvation, making the rope while climbing it, for that is what
one feels. Or even as Stevens put it, proven here, "the poem is
the cry of its occasion."

Beyond the poems that mock romance:

She walks in beauty like a lake
and eats her steak
with fork and knife
and proves a proper wife.

or

Out of the table endlessly rocking,
sea-shells, and firm,
I saw a face appear
which called me dear.

where the frank doggerel is used to bitter effect, the crisis is
openly vented:

A MARRIAGE

The first retainer
he gave to her
was a golden
wedding ring.

The second—late at night
he woke up,
leaned over on an elbow,
and kissed her.

> The third and the last—
> he died with
> and gave up loving
> and lived with her.

(Which might be compared to Elizabeth Jennings's bland study of her parents.) It could hardly be more clinched, and final. Gradually, however, he works his way out of that pit. And it may be said that in all this too private a despair is being displayed. And so it would be, and in many other instances is, if the poet were incapable of finding the center of the experience, of saying it true, so that we know the pain only for what we feel, as the poet gives it to us, is lost, is a love.

Out of this despair comes more and more quietly again a singing. A belief. A strand. As at the end of "The Door":

> I will go to the garden.
> I will be a romantic. I will sell
> myself in hell,
> in heaven also I will be.
>
> In my mind I see the door,
> I see the sunlight before me across the floor
> beckon to me, as the Lady's skirt
> moves small beyond it.

At least there is a teasing saving presence of hope, grace, something. What follows is lustration. Rhyme in water. Lucid dream.

> God is no bone of whitened contention.
> God is not air, nor hair, is not
> a conclusive concluding
> to remote yearnings. He moves
>
> only as I move, you also move to
> the awakening, across long rows, of beds,
> stumble breathlessly, on leg pins and crutch,
> moving at all as all men, because you must.

Which suddenly sounds as though Stevens were addressing us.

In "The Rain," with its recollected music of Duncan's "O let me die, but if you love me, let me die," the final two stanzas yearn for outwardness:

> Love, if you love me,
> lie next to me.
> Be for me, like rain,
> the getting out
>
> of the tiredness, the fatuousness, the semi-
> lust of intentional indifference.
> Be wet
> with a decent happiness.

It is both Creeley's strength and weakness that when he speaks we feel him personally present, an authentic personality, as against, say, Duncan of "The Albigenses" I quoted, where the poet speaks in the role of "poet." Creeley is up against it, wherever he is, we feel, and out of it emerges a voice, but transmuting harshness to intensity, toward music, into poetry. The shapes of that poetry, the heart of his effort, seem to contradict his avant-gardistic position, for they demonstrate a strict relation to the tradition of the lyrical quatrain. Of the final thirty-eight poems in this collection; that is, his most recent work, only three are *not* in quatrains. Rhyme is always an immediate possibility, yet never anything but another sounding of edges, an adjunct to the total "ring" of the poem. A pulling in together of the music meaning engenders in language, felt meaning, meaning feeling for meaning. Or the poem dedicated to Louis Zukofsky,

THE HOUSE

> Mud put
> upon mud,
> lifted
> to make room,

house
a cave,
and
colder night.

To sleep
in, live in,
to come in
from heat,

all form derived
from kind,
built
with that in mind.

So much of this effort is one that brings poetry back to each of us as each. Not that the literary doesn't crop up, or lacks validity anyhow, but that every poem is an occasion that one man comes to, came to, finding for us, while finding himself, words for our occasion.

From here the act is, more even than Olson realizes in his "figure of outward," the primary one so easily lost sight of, so much again more difficult, the "major aim" of the poet as Zukofsky so beautifully puts it:

> . . . not to show himself but that order
> that of itself can speak to all men.

Not that a man doesn't stand more and more revealed as his art discovers him in it, to others' eyes, but that personal private revelation must become each beholder's, listener's, partaker's, realization.

So that I don't finally urge you to go out and buy Creeley. Why should I buy or sell anyone or anything? But I would urge those of you who have not partaken, to do so, and those of you who have, to attend.

JOHN WILLIAM CORRINGTON

Creeley's *For Love*

In complete candor, I believe *For Love* is clear and present evidence that Robert Creeley is one of the most exorbitantly overrated poets practicing today. Not that Creeley's work is valueless: with the tiny confines he has chosen to work, Creeley frequently does very well indeed. As a kind of latter-day Metaphysical, Creeley can lay claim to being the twentieth century's equivalent of Thomas Traherne. But his admirers—and they seem to be legion—will not have it so: Hugh Kenner says with a lavishness scarcely to be comprehended, that Creeley is "one of the very few contemporaries with whom it is essential to keep current." I take such a remark to indicate that Kenner judges Creeley a shaper and a major figure in modern writing. This he is not.

It may seem disingenuous to argue the value of writers presently at work, but once such valuations as Kenner's are made—and made so frequently as to become received text among certain audiences—it becomes essential to make observations of a sort that may serve to balance excessive praise. To leave the job undone serves only to color falsely the entire spectrum of literary values. If Creeley is a "major" poet, then I suspect it may be necessary to reshuffle the whole complex matrix of critical attitudes and stipulations that have more or less obtained for the past several hundred years.

Major poets have had few things in common, but richness of language and width of vision and expression are common between Shakespeare and Eliot, Dante and Dylan Thomas. Taking

From *Northwest Review* 6, no. 3 (Summer 1963): 106–10. Corrington's review originally appeared with another review by David Bromige under the title "Creeley's *For Love:* Two Responses." Reprinted by permission.

the question of language first, it seems to me Creeley manages to disqualify himself from contention almost at once:

> What I took in my hand
> grew in weight. You must
> understand it
> was not obscene.
>
> Night comes. We sleep.
> Then if you know what
> say it.
> Don't pretend.
>
> Guises are
> what enemies wear. You
> and I live
> in a prayer.
>
> Helpless. Helpless.
> should I speak.
> Would you.
> What do you think of me.
>
> No woman ever was,
> was wiser
> than you. None is
> more true.
>
> But fate, love, fate
> scares me. What
> I took in my hand
> grows in weight.

At this point I do not wish to take up Creeley's meaning, or even the mode of thought his lines suggest. I am interested particularly in the language that he chooses as his vehicle. Creeley has said, "I care what the poem says, only as a poem. . . ." He has further urged the redemptive power of language. Whether these ideas are viable or not is of no importance here: the question is whether Creeley's language, his use of words, produces anything of much value *qua* language. I think not. In the poem quoted above, and in dozens of other poems, I discover little or nothing that could be termed poetry—little or nothing different from the sort of writing one finds in a newspaper or perhaps the pages of *Fortune* magazine. Putting aside Creeley's content (and this is done at his own suggestion, one must remember), one is faced with a kind of barren analytical prose, a kind of gnomic sparseness in which one finds no pleasure, no glory, no outrage or benevolence—in which, briefly, emotion and evocative feeling are rendered as sterile as in a page of Kant's *Critique*. In terms of language alone, Creeley's work is as bereft of imagination as a set of orders tacked to a regimental bulletin board. If, as Creeley has said, he depends upon words for his redemption, then the working out of that redemption will likely have the character of a legal abstract rather than a psalm.

Beyond this careful poverty of image and figure in Creeley's language, there is a clipped, tight-lipped rhythm in all but the earliest poems (and, to my taste, the first poem in the volume, "Hart Crane," is the most satisfying). It is a kind of oracular briefness of line and phrase that frequently causes a reader to turn the page, unable to believe that the poem has jolted to its conclusion.

The other characteristic of Creeley's work which seems to me clearly second-rate is its ideational content. The majority of his poems would classify, I think, as extended epigrams: short, terse bits of insight in which idea and turn of phrase join to produce an effect perfectly described as *tour de force*. Now there is nothing wrong with epigrams. Jonson and Donne wrote a number of them, and as "entertainments" (Graham Greene's word to distinguish his light fiction from his serious work) they frequently succeed brilliantly. But neither Jonson nor Donne considered these clever brevities the foundation of his reputation. Donne writes,

Your mistris, that you follow whores, still taxeth you:
'Tis strange that she should thus confesse it, though it be true.

and sophomores guffaw. In the tradition of "throw-away" humor, the lines are indeed clever. They are seen, appreciated, and put aside. Reading Carew's epitaph on Mary Villers,

> Though a stranger to this place,
> Bewayle in theirs, thine owne hard case:
> For thou perhaps at thy returne
> Mayest find thy Darling in an Urne.

one smiles at the bizarre propriety of the lines. In both poems, there is a neat felicity that engages despite the essential inconsequence of the ideas which generated them.

Then there is Creeley:

> Mind's heart, it must
> be that some
> truth lies locked
> in you.
>
> Or else, lies, all
> lies, and no man
> true enough to know
> the difference.

Confronted with lines like these, one hardly cares enough to ask precisely what the "mind's heart" is, where it resides, or what function we should expect of it. One wonders whether the poem is a translation from the Chinese, or Creeley's attempt at an Anglo-Saxon riddle. Again:

> Moon
> and clouds, will
> we drift
>
> higher
> than that we
> look at,

<pre>
        moon's and
        mind's
        eye.
</pre>

If this is an English approximation of haiku, it should be remembered that, since the quantitative system of Japanese verse has no application in our language, what we have—as an *English* poem—is a blurred and pointless epigram. Again, one is no more moved to scratch beneath the cliché of "mind's / eye" than of "Mind's heart."

There is, finally then, a banality of thought, a transcendant invitation to boredom in Creeley's work that constantly undermines whatever purpose he sets about. He has a way of failing even when he succeeds:

<pre>
        My lady
        fair with
        soft
        arms, what

        can I say to
        you—words, words
        as if all
        worlds were there.
</pre>

Here Creeley's theme is that of a hundred popular songs ("I Can't Begin to Tell You," etc.), and is little better handled than in many of them: it is, after all, a massive platitude that language must give way to a more pointed tool in the presence of love, and while Creeley's clever and subtly placed cliché (My lady / fair) and irrelevancy (with / soft / arms) illuminate his thesis, they (and the opaque referent of the demonstrative "there") do nothing to make that thesis more than yawn-provoking.

I have no wish to stamp the whole of Creeley's work as valueless; I simply find that his reputation and the work upon which that reputation is based have little in common. If Creeley, in fact as well as in widely circulated fancy, is to become a major poet, he has an enormous amount of work ahead of him. *For Love* is hardly a beginning.

ROBERT PETERS

From "Robert Creeley's *For Love* Revisited"

Thomas Hardy

Part 3 of *For Love* reveals affinities of tone, diction, and manner with Thomas Hardy's poetry. Creeley has absorbed the older poet well. My feeling is that if the truth were known Hardy would prove one of the most influential of all turn-of-the-century poets on later poets. But critics generally remain myopic. In Creeley's "Song" the agents, like Hardy's, are elemental forces, sparely realized. Rivers, land, sea, wind, trees . . . these are the agents against which the weather of the poet's feelings prevail. The simple quatrain stanzas provide an illusion of concreteness, and are forms loved by Hardy; the elemental force of wind finding trees to move is curiously specific. Whether the setting is Dorset or New Mexico doesn't matter. The sudden personal, philosophical turn is also reminiscent of Hardy, as are the hesitancies behind the questions and the direct simple rhymes:

> And me, why me
> on any day might be
> favored with kind prosperity
> or sunk in wretched misery.

The simplicity of the form: dimeter, trimeter, followed by two tetrameters; the simple rhymes—two plain monosyllables set against two polysyllabic rhymes; the use of old-fashioned phrases—"kind prosperity," "wretched misery." And what

From *The Great American Poetry Bake-Off* (Metuchen, N.J.: Scarecrow Press, 1979), 34–35. Reprinted by permission.

could be simpler than the response to the question "why me?" An apothegm: "be natural, while alive." And once dead we "go another / course, I hope." Creeley's tentativeness reflects a similar stance frequent with Hardy.

"Kore" similarly deals with simple, elemental acts. The first stanza risks the sort of inversion Hardy liked to include as part of his poetic carpentry; it was as if he wished to maintain some mark of the crude, of the adze, on his work. Here is Creeley:

> As I was walking
> I came upon
> chance walking
> the same road upon.

Even the most casual reader of Hardy is aware of chance as a prime mover. In "Kore" chance produces a vision in a light green wood of a lady led by goat men, moving to a flute. "The Rain," as in Hardy's poems about rain, is the occasion for self-reflection and an uneasiness about that self, implicitly religious, implicitly romantic. Love, like rain, enables the poet to escape fatuousness, fatigue, indifference. The problem is to soften the ego's edge—finding one's self at last "wet / with a decent happiness." For both Hardy and Creeley time is essentially one. The present is for questioning one's purpose and destiny. Past and future, as parts of the present, yield some comfort in the fact that they are cut from the same die. The questionings never end. Hardy's "Ah no, the years, oh," the refrain of "During Wind and Rain," his finest lyric, finds echo in the concluding stanza of Creeley's "The Plan":

> the way, the way
> it was yesterday, will
> be also today
> and tomorrow.

Hardy called himself a meliorist, which means that things are bad but that in a mysterious way they are getting better. Creeley puts the idea thus in "The Immoral Proposition," on behalf of the "unsure egoist" who knows that "God knows // nothing is competent nothing is / all there is." One's salvation and strength, it seems, reside in one's ego. Says Creeley, the healthy egoist must be sure; the "unsure // egoist is not / good for himself." *For Love* is an impressive revealing of one hesitant poet's effort to vivify and starch up his ego. Perhaps because Creeley's ego fails as often as it advances these poems remain human and poignant, despite the passing of over twenty years.

ROBERT CREELEY

Versions

after Hardy

Why would she come to him,
come to him,
in such disguise

to look again at him—
look again—
with vacant eyes—

and why the pain still,
the pain—
still useless to them—

as if to begin again—
again begin—
what had never been?

•

Why be
persistently
hurtful—
no truth
to tell
or wish to?
Why?

•

The weather's still grey
and the clouds gather
where they once walked
out together,

greeted the world with
a faint happiness,
watched it die
in the same place.

CHARLES OLSON

Introduction to Robert Creeley

I take it there is huge gain to square away at narrative now, not
as fiction but as RE-ENACTMENT. Taking it this way I see
two possibilities:

    1. What I call DOCUMENT simply to emphasize that the
events alone do the work, that the narrator stays OUT, func-
tions as pressure not as interpreting person, illuminates not by
argument or "creativity" but by master of force (as space is
shaper, confining maintaining inside tensions of objects), the art,
to make his meanings clear by how he juxtaposes, correlates,
and causes to interact whatever events and persons he chooses to
set in motion. In other words his ego or person is NOT of the
story whatsoever. He is, if he makes it, light from outside, the
thing itself doing the casting of what shadows;

    2. The exact opposite, the NARRATOR IN, the total IN to
the above total OUT, total speculation as against the half man-
agement, half interpretation, the narrator taking on himself the
job of making clear by way of his own person that life *is* preoc-
cupation with itself, taking up the push of his own single intel-
ligence to make it, to be—by his conjectures—so powerful in-
side the story that he makes the story swing on him, his eye the
eye of nature INSIDE (as is the same eye, outside) a light-
maker.

    Both *1* and *2*, both methodologies drive for the same end, so
to reenact experience that a story has what an object or person
has: energy and instant. Here is their gain, over the fictive—not

---

From *Human Universe and Other Essays*, edited by Donald Allen (New York:
Grove Press, 1967), 127–28. This essay first appeared in *New Directions XIII*
(1951), 92–93, along with several short stories by Robert Creeley. Copyright ©
1951, 1965, 1967 by Charles Olson. Reprinted by permission of the Estate of
Charles Olson.

to spill out these bloods, but to keep original force in at the same time that that force is given illumination.

There is another reason why I am sure that the choice now is one or the other of these two attacks on the problem. They are the only way that narrative can take up that aspect of verse which is its multitude. For variations—"motion"—lies out there in the meat of reality, not in the small paper of egos or lyric soullessnesses. Events have outreached narrators, have overmatched them, because narrators have either succumbed to them or, as silly white to that ridiculous black, have taken themselves to be more interesting. They are not. Poets could have told them. For "things" are what writers get inside their work, or the work, poem or story, perishes. Things are the way force is exchanged. On things communication rests. And the writer, though he is the control (or art is nothing) is, still, no more than—but just as much as—another "thing," and as such, is in, inside or out.

What it is, is two geometries, now, for the storyteller: either he lets things in and manages them so well that they get curved back by his pressure outside and make a self-existent sphere (the law is gravitation) or he takes on himself the other law (they are recognized now to be identical) and, as center, as core to the magnetic field, he causes the things to pull in to make their shape.

I take it that these stories are of the second way, of the writer putting himself all the way in—taking that risk, putting his head on that block, and by so doing giving you your risk, your commitment by the seriousness of his—constituting himself the going reality and, by the depth and sureness of his speculating, making it pay, making you-me believe, that we are here in the presence of a man putting his hands directly and responsibly to experience which is also our own. It is his presence that matters, for it rids us of artifice as such (as the whole of the story), instead only uses it to keep the going going, to make the reach of what is happening clear. For his presence is the energy. And the instant? That, too, is he, given such methodology. For his urgency, his confrontation is "time," which is, when he makes it, ours, the now. He is time, he is now, the force.

Which is multitude. It is human phenomenology which is reinherited, allowed in, once plot is kissed out. For the moment you get a man back in, among things, the full motion and play comes back (not parts extricated for show or representation) but the total bearing, each moment of the going—as it is, for any of us, each moment, anywhere. "Mr. Blue," for example.

LINDA W. WAGNER

Review of *The Gold Diggers*

Robert Creeley's recent collection of short stories has been praised and damned—for essentially the same reasons: "form-lessness" and an intense concern with language. Actually, the two characteristics are inseparable, for Creeley is trying in most of these stories to re-create one *real* moment in life. Because a moment may not have "rising action" or chronology, the story may not have a standard form. But also, because there is just this one time and place of focus, this single incident through which to show character, word choice must be exact. The most precise writing may not always be the most graceful. As in the following description, for example, the qualification which slows the sentence is often its most important part:

> At noon the glasses and sandwiches sat on the table, and they before them, and they both ate without haste, or eagerness, but more as occasion, usual, for which there was custom. Still, looking at them, together, it was to catch some of the reason for them being together. There seemed to be a reason. She was short and he was tall and both were somewhat dark with brown hair, eyes, rather oval, long faces, and then their bodies, having some sense of strength in them, and one thought that they would look better without the clothes than with them.

This early paragraph from "The Lovers" reflects in style the characteristic indecision of the protagonist. He dreams, he thinks, he detests the commonness of his wife—yet he partakes

From *Studies in Short Fiction* 3, no. 4 (Summer 1966): 465–66. Reprinted by permission.

of it because that is his situation. His wife has her cats; he has only her. Accordingly, the tone of awkwardness and constraint in the prose parallels their relationship, and also his character, torn as he is between his desire and his reality. Creeley concludes another story, "Three Fate Tales," with this comment: "a reality, before it becomes our own, is often tricky and can be easily mistaken." So he suggests here in the lines about *custom* and *reason*.

As I describe them here, Creeley's stories sound as if they are very much in the mainstream of modern writing. Yet these stories are different from those of Gold, Updike, O'Connor, Cheever. For one thing, they are extremely short. A character appears for a brief scene, sometimes in dialogue, again in isolation. The emphasis is frequently on man in himself, to himself, rather than on man as social being. Creeley's stories also interrelate. The tone is consistent: the protagonists think alike and usually behave alike, in the midst of relatively hostile (or perhaps indifferent) surroundings. Yet there is no repetition. Each story presents different people and achieves a somewhat different theme, despite the single impression of the collection as a whole.

The primary reason for these differences lies in Creeley's purpose for writing stories. As he explains in the preface, "Had I lived some years ago, I think I would have been a moralist, *i.e.,* one who lays down, so to speak, rules of behavior with no small amount of self-satisfaction." Since the writer can no longer perform that function, he has left only "the tale, and all that can be made of it." The word *tale* is essential here, I think; and in Creeley's concept of tale as an art form devoted to realities may lie the difference between his stories and those of other modern writers. It may also be the reason that several sets of primary themes dominate the stories.

Man in Creeley's world is nearly always alone, frighteningly alone. The stark figure of the gold digger waiting eagerly for his companion, a man whom he dislikes greatly, symbolizes the condition of all but a few of Creeley's protagonists. Whether misunderstood or geographically isolated, man is separate. The poet of "The Book" searches for a woman to sing the songs he carries with him. Peter, the husband in "The Dress," longs for companionship, as he takes his wife into his underground hollow: "through a small opening in the floor, pulled her down, into where *he* lived." But he saw on her face only dismay, followed by laughter, and then, again, dismay.

Many of Creeley's protagonists are family men, but even this relationship does not insure love. "The Grace" is a poignant account of the husband-wife relationship broken into by the cries of their young son. Each time, the woman goes to him, at the cost of alienation from her husband. Yet finally, the man himself goes, his anger turning to pity for the boy's need.

Frequently in Creeley's work, even the smallest children reflect the morality that surrounds them. The three children of "The Boat" sail over their father as he swims before them in much the same way as his wife openly encourages her lover. Amos, the widow's only child in "A Death," is also cruel at times, as are her in-laws and their children. The prevalent attitude toward life is that of brother-in-law James, who "wanted not quite to see." The attitude Creeley champions, wistfully, is that of the widow who thinks, "One saves all one's life, against the one instant it is all real, and all enough." But to her family, the widow is "foreign," a corruption.

Man's position, then, will be lonely so long as his aims are different from those of his culture. Like the gold diggers of the title story, modern man may also be isolated because of his purpose in life. As Creeley has expressed that difficult aim in his novel *The Island,* in his poems, and in many of these stories, men need "one action, definite, to place them all in that place where time shall have no dominion."

J. P. FREEMAN

Review of *The Gold Diggers*

Robert Creeley is better known for his poetry, which has been appearing in collections since 1950, than for his prose, a novel and the stories collected in *The Gold Diggers*. . . . There are clear parallels between his poetry and his prose, but it may be that the stories deserve more attention than they have had in comparison with the poems.

To read *The Gold Diggers* is to experience an assault. One is conscious at first less of a collection of narratives—indeed most of them hardly fit that description anyway—than of an invitation to see the world in a peculiar, and, it seems at first, perverse way. The activity of reading becomes an argument between this quite justified suspicion and any accommodations that one can make. The writer takes no part in this debate: his position is settled. Hence the extreme reactions his work in prose and poetry has aroused; one either subscribes to the "monkish cult" of Creeley, or, with Karl Miller, dismisses it as just that. There seems to me another possibility—not to call it a "middle" between the equally nullifying effects of simple acceptance and rejection—which is to find this book's qualities, precisely because of one's resistance, a continuing and disturbing challenge. If that is what makes writing "significant," then Creeley's work is significant.

Yet his world, or that of his characters, is both rich and claustrophobic. The people are like sea anemones waving sensitively in the currents of their thoughts, emotions, and physical rhythms. They can be decisively affected by small things because the wider context of time and space is shadowy, and only what is before them is real. When, as is often the case, nothing

From *The Cambridge Quarterly* (U.K.) 2, no. 4 (Autumn 1967): 414–20.

much is happening, the stasis is correspondingly total and tangible. This structuring of experience is perhaps only possible for people outside any larger current of society and its corresponding large-scale and long-term involvements; it is the life of people for whom these social rhythms no longer modify their own and those of their small group. One is considering life lived, as it were, inside oneself; the whole work is a study of singleness. Even the studies of the relations between men and women—most of these tales have something to do with that theme—show the life of these relationships as insistently something worked out within each individual, for whom the other is very markedly "out there," and indirect, however forceful, in significance. Escape from the self and from self-consciousness, and its attendant nervous tension, is rare. The distinctive style in which the stories are written is nervous, involved, full of qualification and careful dislocation or readjustment of familiar usages: not Joycean verbal pyrotechnics but insistent reminders of the thought process, the medium of its communication, and the presence of the writer, contributing to the same continual self-consciousness. It is pursued with such single-mindedness as to make one sense a perverse cultivation of a subnormal, subvital contraction of personal horizons, a coming to terms with life on a lower level.

It is this coming to terms, however, this exploration of the self-consistency of a life which is totally delivered to the timeless moment and permits it to redefine the whole of experience at every turn, which is the essence of what Creeley offers, and the reviewer who senses something new and important in it, if he is not to accept it unreservedly as the gospel of the true life, must try to indicate the strengths attained by its deliberate limitation. Some of them are perhaps implicit in what has been said already. Total exposure to the moment allows that moment to be lived with a purity and sensitivity which offers its own kind of integrity: and it is this consistency which Creeley traces as the form underlying the sometimes incoherent appearance that his characters' lives would present if described or seen in less inward terms. To find this consistency is to restore to their experience the meaningfulness that it appears to lack; it is to express their dignity. But what is involved is at least part of all our lives, the underlying pattern of inward experience which emerges to never wholly adequate expression, and which we falsify as well as transcend by dealing with larger, less personal concerns. It is perhaps also a larger part of more people's lives in a context of social disintegration than in any other, so that Creeley is also reporting on a largely unexplored modern situation of weakening social ties; but the emphasis is on the extent to which this is a common experience and not merely that of a few. Leroi Jones has written: "The 'people' in Creeley's stories are perhaps more intense than the 'average American,' certainly more tortured; but their difference is one that Creeley has proposed aesthetically. They are people better revealed, but they are not different people, as the characters in a Rechy or a Selby story are." That "aesthetically" shades into "morally" perhaps in the way I suggested earlier that to restore the formal coherence of a life was to restore our sense of its dignity. Certainly Creeley does make explicit moral claims, and most of the stories have a definite moral substructure. I take the story called "A Death" to be a test case not only because it seems to me the best—others are good in quite different ways—but because the moral issue is the key one in Creeley's work that gives us the implied orientation of the rest. It describes a scene on a beach—where is left unspecified—involving a widow who has come from New Zealand, which appears to be a long way, with her spoilt, inconvenient six-year-old son Amos, to visit her brother James—the only other named person—and his conventional and complacent wife. All these people, with James's children, arrive in a vague pervasive sense of latent tension and hostility, on the beach. Amos throws a stone at one of the other children, and his mother, though nothing has been said, offers some defiant defensive remarks about him. As these drop into the silence she takes Amos down to the water to swim.

Looking at Amos, she now wondered what she would change, if she could. His eyes were blue, almost shut in the intensity of their color. Perhaps he would be a great man in spite of them. His hair had bleached almost white, and under it the darker tawny color came through. But his arms were very thin and stick-like, and his chest corded with little muscles. He was like a goat, an obscenely precocious goat, who had no use for people.

Taking off their clothes, she put them in a pile, and then put a stone on top of it. Amos giggled. She had forgotten the bathing suits, and they were in the basket, high up on the hill with the others. Even so she slipped into the water quietly, and calling softly to Amos, drew him in after her.

Above them, James fumbled in his embarrassment. His wife smiled again, and watching him, thought only of his remarkable innocence. It was pleasant that it should be so. He was very unmarked, and untouched by so many things. His sister might well be a photograph, she thought, which he wished to be proper and in focus. Otherwise she was a nuisance, as, for example, she paddled away down there, with the boy, and seemed almost completely foreign. James coughed, he wanted not quite to see. The bodies went under the water, to leave their heads free, then they too ducked under.

Still watching him, his wife said, what do you think of it, James. As she had said, three days earlier, to a young man on the beach with them, do you see how he treats me?

But what was so simple about it. Make me happy, she said. Don't please think of her. James was very much in the middle and began to know it. He knew love was not multiple, or could not be here divided. He said, be patient with her. He let it all rest on kindness.

The water around them changed all that, on their bodies, very much on their bodies. Amos jumped up, shrieking, and she loved him more than she admitted. Look, she said. The small fish darted out, past their white feet, and then back again to the darker places. But Amos had seen them. It was lovely.

Then she left him, swimming out and free of it. The water was buoyant, so that she hardly swam but floated, lifted out on the wash of the waves as they fell back. Beneath her the colors changed from the green to blue, and then to a darker blue, and then black. She dove and felt the tips of her fingers touch bottom, and on her hands the weeds were very light and brushed them gently.

Far away she thought that the house was now gone. Her husband loved no one anymore. At last they were also free of him. He sat in the yard in a chair which he had made. There was no car. The street was long, and at the end there was a tram-stop. People spoke English but he answered them, *no se*. He was a Greek with rings in his ears, and his hands were folded in his lap.

So one could change it as he might. She held to that, and here the water helped her, taking her as she was. One saves all one's life, against the one instant it is all real, and all enough. Why, she said, tell me now otherwise! Tell me nothing.

If it is obscene, she said. Her husband's mother was obscene. Of her own husband she had known nothing, she had not even known his body. And when at last he grew sick, to die, she took off his clothes for the first time, and saw the body for the first time, dying.

Gulls flapped off the rocks behind her. Amos slapped at the water with a stick he had found. The quiet grew over all of them.

A struggle begins between James's wife's hostility to his sister and his own pacific desire for compromise and tolerance, a struggle which James eventually loses by siding with his wife in prudence and calculation, though without her satisfaction. He is abject even beside her, but there is a bigger contrast with his sister, on whom most of the emphasis rests, and which concerns the moral issue which I suggested was in a way the crucial one. It is she who lives with an intensity and openness which seems truly alive, despite her awkwardnesses and failures. In the pleasure and freedom of the swim to which she gives herself up, the past and future fall into place in a spontaneous vision in which her own values are established at least for herself, against the atmosphere on the beach and the correctness of her sister-in-law. It is because Creeley has the kind of concern he does that he can capture so completely the vivid sensuous pleasure she takes in the swim and the total change it brings about in her world. Another character and another author would not manage the purity of that experience and without that the tale is nothing. It is only in relation to that living moment that her thoughts about the past and her husband, whose death supplies the title, and the future of her son arrange themselves.

But because a fishing boat passes near enough for the sailor to see her swimming naked in the water, James and his wife are scandalised and consider they will not be able to use the beach again. This seems to James a sufficiently decisive event to make him side wholly with his wife. Thus when the sister returns to them it is more thoroughly than before to the tension and hostility from which she had been liberated in the swim. The showdown is near. Her superiority and triumph are the way she transcends these constrictions and brushes them aside.

> Such a lovely swim, she said. The water was so lovely, and refreshing. And the boat, the wife asked. But did she really say it. Her own children were safe behind her and never again would she really let them go. Amos giggled, he pulled at his mother's skirt, raising it, and James saw the tight thigh, and the brown, close flesh. Did you see the boat, his wife said. She knew it was her brother's wife. She knew her own husband was dead. She saw the faces all in front of her, and if she cried out at them, she was still in love with everything.

That final flourish, which may look sentimental, is, I think, justified in the context of the whole story; it seems to be earned by the fullness with which her exhilaration has been conveyed and to be literally true. The contrast between her own involvement and the people before her is clear, and in that her moral superiority consists. She is a sympathetic figure to an extent that few of the other Creeley people, usually more imprisoned by tension and scruple, seem to be: but all the stories have a kind of seriousness and intensity that correspond to that treated in this story and which account for some of the quality one senses, whatever one's reservations, in the whole book. It is from this intensity that his cautious and idiosyncratic style gets its justification, and when it loses touch with its source it comes close to preciosity and self-parody. But the form is certainly essential to the effect: Creeley has a poet's developed sense of the possibilities of words and uses rhythm and suggestion in a way which makes these stories things, constructions, as closely worked as poetry, to imitate the kind of conditions he describes. He can make what he has to tell us meaningful because of his concern for form, and it is only in this form that the originality and force can survive. In chapter 6 of his novel *The Island* he reworks what appears to be substantially the same material as he uses in "A Death," giving a more circumstantial account of the characters' lives, their occupations, appearance and past histories—the kind of information which occurs in the short story only as it occurs in the minds of the characters; more than the other stories, "A Death" does manage to focus a sense of a whole life span without betraying the closeness of its attention to the moment. In the novel some of the details are different but the relationships and the incident of the boat are the same. The woman is Australian, her husband had been an English wool-buyer, she has read Lawrence all through, we know more of her mannerisms. The pathos of her situation is more explicit: her brother has paid for her trip but is not likely to pay for another; it is her last freedom. Her unattractiveness is emphasised more. The novel's central figure, John, sympathises with her overtly. Yet in the end this account is not a powerful and original piece of writing as the story is. Whatever Creeley has to say, it can only be said in his way, and that when he is at his best. Indeed it is a question of demonstrating rather than saying, demonstrating a kind of purity that is limiting but capable of intensity and power. His work is often polemical enough in intention to count as a manifesto for that purity as a way of living; a kind of almost religious concentration on the essence of personal experience. It is an example of a kind of excellence, and perhaps important enough to be one of those various landmarks by which we take our bearings.

LINDA W. WAGNER

The Poet as Novelist: Creeley's Novel

As well as being a good first novel, Robert Creeley's *The Island* is an interesting illustration of the close relationship which exists between poetry and prose. Creeley is but one of many contemporary writers who move easily between the two mediums. Thomas Hardy might be taken as the great example by modern poets; and in our own time novels have been written by such poets as Robert Graves, Conrad Aiken, E. E. Cummings, William Carlos Williams, Allen Tate, Robert Penn Warren, and others. Even T. S. Eliot has apparently published short stories: see Gwenn R. Boardman's article in the Summer 1961 *Modern Fiction Studies*. The list of "younger" poets who are also writing prose fiction is almost interminable: Charles Olson, Howard Nemerov, Delmore Schwartz, Stanley Kunitz, Robert Duncan, Karl Shapiro, Robert Lowell, Kenneth Rexroth, Denise Lever-tov—all show their command of verbal skill by writing well in both poetry and prose.

Now Robert Creeley has published his first novel. That he should turn to long prose fiction is not surprising in the light of his past work with criticism and short stories. Not only has he written much prose, but he also has used prose techniques to a great extent within his poetry.

Granted, a great deal of contemporary poetry relies at least nominally on prose techniques—much of it avoids restraining rhyme patterns and the obvious artifice of allusions and some figures of speech; it uses "normal" syntax and colloquial vocab-

Review of *The Island* from *Critique* 7, no. 1 (Spring 1964): 119–22. Reprinted with permission of the author and the Helen Dwight Reid Educational Foundation, 4000 Albemarle St., N.W., Washington, D.C. 20016. Copyright © 1964.

ulary. This may be true because the modern-day poet finds himself facing a distrustful audience. As Dr. Williams once warned, people have been alienated from poetry through ignorance about it; anything that sounds like traditional poetry is suspect. Therefore, according to Dr. Williams, poets of today must use the vocabulary and rhythm of common speech if they are to communicate. Since Creeley too aims for a wide audience ("How much I should like to please!"), he bases his expression on contemporary idioms:

> Let me say (in anger) that since the day we were married
> we have never had a towel
> where anyone could find it . . .
>
> > ("The Crisis," *For Love,* 19)

> The one damn time (7th inning)
> standing up to get a hot dog someone spills
> mustard all over me.
>
> > ("The Ball Game," *For Love,* 25)

Creeley's language here reflects speech patterns with noticeable accuracy. The long sentences, at times ungrammatical, characterize both his poetry and prose. Short sentences and phrases punctuated as sentences are used frequently for contrast and restatement. Creeley's line division is also meaningful in that it indicates phrasal units; in reading his work, the poet pauses after each line, regardless of length. These excerpts from *The Island* show the same pattern, basically long sentences interspersed with short:

He watched his grandfather pare the apple, the strip coming off in one continuous band, and then the spoon the old man used to eat it, making straight, clean scoops. Teach me that. (68)

If people could be taken apart successfully, inside there would be a complexity of jutting hooks, and places for such hooks to fit into, and what people consider as relationships would be the fact of a complement of such hooks and places, fitting together, until some external shake or jarring pulled them apart. (164)

In addition to this basic idiomatic vocabulary, contemporary poetry and prose have also been united through similar techniques. Both have moved steadily toward the classic principles of poetry. Poetry itself has become more suggestive than it was during some recent periods; and for the past forty years the short story and novel have aimed toward a concern with *being* rather than narrative, an interest in time as a state of flux rather than a rigid division of hours, a concentration of detail, and an emphasis on suggestive and consequently widely meaningful experience. As a result, prose works have generally grown shorter and more intense in effect, again paralleling poetry.

All of the above generalizations are true of *The Island*. Although the novel could be considered the account of a marriage, its emphasis falls on the character of the poet-protagonist John in his search for identity, "place," realization. The concern is like Creeley's presentation of it—a timeless one. The actual plot structure requires several months; the reader, however, experiences relevant happenings from John's entire lifetime—as well as some probable future events. Creeley achieves this inclusion through standard devices like flashback interwoven with the recreation of John's consciousness. Although told in omniscient third, the entire novel is John's account. Creeley uses no quotation marks, no arbitrary means of separating objective material from his protagonist's introspection: all the man sees, hears, and experiences becomes a part of him. Both past and immediate are depicted as present, the thread of John's thought binding all into one tense. Creeley's technique here is reminiscent of that used within his poems where the protagonist is consistently recognizable—although appearing sometimes as "he," sometimes as "I," and again as "John"—and exists nearly always in a continuous present.

So far as achieving the suggestivity which enables the novel to "mean" universally, Creeley works through a structure of repeated motifs which have less than symbolic significance but more than representational. The distinction here is that the themes of the beach, conception, debt, and place have no consistent referents; they often denote a feeling John experiences—his bewilderment over debt, for example—but their significance can change with context. The beach in its isolation is commonly a source of pleasure but in some passages it is the site of sacrifice and again a cruel torment. Through his use of this ambiguity in the repetition of motifs, Creeley re-creates the very real complexity of a perceptive mind.

He also uses heightened description to add to the import of scenes which could easily be considered "simple." When the drunken Artie comes to John and Joan in the early morning, Creeley describes the breakfast scene in this manner:

> Joan brought in their breakfast of eggs and a little bacon, and some of yesterday's bread, coffee. They sat in a union of small necessities. . . . (12)

Although the compact details are realistic, they also have thematic importance. It is the ostensibly "small necessities" with which *The Island* deals—chief among them being man's need for valid human relationships.

Recognizing the impossibility of a pat solution to this constant problem is the culmination of John's experience within the novel. *Place* provides no assurance, although for much of the book it appears to. Neither does mutual interest: John and Joan, though united through love for their children and each other, through like ambitions, through sex, and through years of memories, find little help in one another; John's artist friends become sources of nothing but concern. John finally concludes that "all that was, was in," yet at the end of *The Island* he has realized that even self-reliance is too simple an answer. In his preface to the novel Creeley had expressed what he felt was the only solution: "I have found that time . . . carries one on, away from this or any other island. The people, too, are gone."

This central theme is a continuation of one of Creeley's primary poetic motifs. As he wrote in "The Immoral Proposition," "If you never do anything for anyone else / you are spared the tragedy of human relation- / ships." However, with his characteristic awareness of human complexity, Creeley con-

cluded this poem, "The unsure / egoist is not / good for him-
self." In "Love Comes Quietly," the poet asks,

> What did I know
> thinking myself
> able to go
> alone all the way.

He concludes here* that "Into the company of love / it all
returns."

Like many of his poems, *The Island* also creates the tension of
the writer's personal anguish. Because John is an intensely sen-
sitive man, his life is filled with the despair which observation
brings. His restless nights contrast vividly with Joan's snores; his
concern over what money may do to their friendship, with Ar-
tie's casual borrowing; his sadness over the "shifting vagueness"
of relationships, with Joan's "love" for Rene. Throughout the
novel John bears the weight of his awareness, his only release—a
temporary one—in art.

It is a literary adage that all segments of a good writer's work
should be of a piece, should have distinguishing marks. Yet for a
single work to be so capable of identification does not insure
quality. *The Island* is not a good novel primarily because it is the
logical outgrowth of Creeley's poems and short stories. It *is* a
good novel because in it Creeley depicts personalities with ac-
curacy and life, presents a fluent narrative which deals with basic
human problems, and achieves both the former through his
skillful and deliberate employment of words.

---

*The lines that follow are not from "Love Comes Quietly" but from the title
poem of *For Love*.—ED.

FREDERIC WILL

To Take Place and to "Take Heart"

René Char says that "the act, even repeated, is virgin" (*l'acte est vierge, même répété*), and no production in language could bear him out better than some of the poems in this collection. I will concentrate on those particular poems, which, if they open out, will show something about the whole of this book.

Several of these poems ("Waiting," "The Fire," "Walking," "One Way," "Some Place,") seem to me in this sense to lie at the center of *Words*. Each of them is dealt out, through careful arrangement of line-lengths and frequent punctuations, into a shape which trembles with breathed hesitations and processes itself difficultly toward a conclusion. What each poem is working toward has chiefly to do with this quality of coming into being.

It would be misleading to say that these poems are not about anything. They tell no stories, but they are stories; intimate—often epistemologically so—workings out, through words, of states of awareness, attention, and intention. This kind of being a story is one thing that the dealing out, which these poems are, naturally becomes. But there is more to say, about the stories these poems are. They all both are, and are about, the surprise, quality, and finality of coming into being, of occupying the unique point at which the poem has just arrested itself. "The Fire," "Walking," and "One Way" are this coming into being as it takes place in worded eventualities which the poet has made of a girl's eyes, a walker's direction, and a domestic scene's particular, otherwise meaningless, thereness. "Waiting" is the most perfect of these poems, because it is a story, of the kind

Review of *Words* from *Poetry* 111, no. 4 (Jan., 1968): 256–58, copyright © 1968 by The Modern Poetry Association. Reprinted by permission of the author and the Editor of *Poetry*.

sketched above, about the risk involved in trusting oneself forward through language from one phrase to the next. That risk, which is "all there is," is the unique condition of the poem in question. It is the act which, forever repeated by us in our forever incomplete effort to be human, is forever repeated and forever new.

The perfection of "Waiting" is what I mean by an opening which says something about this whole book. Through such an opening we can see the system of progressing yet always static words which each poem in *Words* is. This poetry is peculiarly about itself, and as such, when we look to it for its relationships, seems peculiarly without them; without links to its maker, or to the field of phenomena which we call the "world." The great importance of Creeley's book rests on this philosophically original situation. Of *Words* one would want to say first, and in a sense which is quite fresh, that it is an event in the history of language.

In a special and cathartic sense this book, which has happened to language, marks a new moment in twentieth-century American poetry. How can we place it? It is a far less subjective poetry than Creeley wrote in *For Love,* or than Olson or Duncan have favored. Compared to *Words,* the expressionism of the Beats seems dated. *Words* is cool. But not by any giving in to the other. There is here no complicity with things or society, as is importantly the case, say, in Snyder or Bly. *Words* lies in the center, is a given, in language. It is not something iconically given, not poetry static because it is frozen as wit or conceit, but the processually given, a special kind of futureless taking place. This is what is so heartening about the book. I can think of only one other, on the American lyric scene in recent decades, which gives such strength: Oppen's *This in Which*.

JOHN THOMPSON

From "An Alphabet of Poets"

In contrast to what I have said about Berryman's poems, very
rarely in Creeley's appear a place, a time, an event, or—and
about this there should be a quarrel from his school of poets—a
human voice. This is strange in a poet who so often invokes
William Carlos Williams, whose motto was, "No ideas but in
things." Creeley's motto might be, "No things, thus no ideas."
Such things as are present in these poems are usually generic:
"the seasons, the sun's light, the moon, the oceans, the growing
of things. . . ." Creeley is particularly fond of the gerund, as in
"the growing of things," a way of generalizing action so that
what takes place has no particular time. He likes to compound
tenses, so that time is confused or denied. "She moves, she had
moved. . . . The bodies fall, have fallen. . . . Then the place *is* /
was not ever enough. . . . Then it all goes, saying, here they
were, and are. . . ." He likes confusions of identity. "There is
nothing I am, nothing not. . . . This and that, that one, this and
that . . . Who am I. . . ." "If all women are mothers, what are
men. . . . I wanted the man you took me to be. . . . Again, let
each be this or that, they, together. . . . The man who says hello
to me is another man, another comes then. . . . You there, me
here or is it me *there,* you *here*—there or there, or here—and
here."

It should be clear what the technique of the poems is. In the
word of the oldest member of this school of poets, Charles
Olson—but not as he seems to have meant the word—this is
"projective" verse. The words are so general, the situation so
vague, the personages so ectoplasmic, the action, if any, so small

Review of *Words* from *New York Review of Books,* Aug. 1, 1968, 35. Reprinted by
permission.

and obscure, that the reader is invited to fill this vacuum by himself in "projection." The reader projects into these nearly empty forms not some memory of a feeling like that presented in the poet's specific occasion, as in Berryman's poems, but whatever he wants to put there. This is quite different from what I called earlier a search for analogues.

It would appear that many people enjoy doing this. Perhaps at its most intense it gives them a vague and pleasant feeling of being one with the universe, Freud's "Oceanic" feeling, derived from unconscious desires to return to the protected environment of the womb, where, of course, one truly was united with the surrounding elements. A stanza of Creeley's invokes this vision with suitable generality. It is the last stanza of a poem called "The Rhythm," about the eternal cycle of life and death.

> The rhythm which projects
> from itself continuity
> bending all to its force
> from window to door,
> from ceiling to floor,
> light at the opening,
> dark at the closing.

This is an example of one of Empson's subtypes of ambiguity, a passage that sounds expository and explanatory but which owing to the extreme vagueness of the subject and the resolute inscrutability of the verbs, remains impossible to follow. Empson's example was the famous passage from "Tintern Abbey," where Wordsworth tells us of the "presence," the "something," "a motion and a spirit," that is "far more deeply interfused," "dwells everywhere," that "impels" all things and "rolls through" all things. Creeley's "rhythm" only "projects" and "bends," but it is the same kind of thing. It invites readers of like mind to join in this experience if they care to. And why should they not? We each of us have different requirements, require different verbal constructions, different strategies of definition and thought and connection of thought, before we are able to be convinced. Those who have what might be called high thresholds have no occasion to be indignant because others can satisfy themselves more readily. Particularly there is no cause for disparagement when those who are finding quiet enjoyment in filling these voids also know what they are doing. Creeley has a poem about this. It is called "Joy."

> I could look at
> an empty hole for hours
> thinking it will
> get something in it,
>
> will collect
> things. There is
> an infinite emptiness
> placed there.

I quote it all, not only because it might be a motto for him, but because it gives an example of something I have not commented on, the arrangement of his words into lines. You will have seen that this arrangement has nothing to do with ordinary meter—syllables, stresses, and all that—nor does it have to do, directly, with the structural phrases of English. Briefly, I would guess that its intention and its accomplishment are consonant with the other qualities of the verse, in this way. Take the clause "thinking it will get something in it." We can suppose that when the line ends thus, "thinking it will"—we pause. (I have not heard Creeley himself read this poem.) In ordinary matter-of-fact speech we would not pause there; we might even slide subject and compound very rapidly together; "it'll get something." When we pause between the two parts of the verb, we create an expectation that what follows will be of some unusual importance, whether we are deliberately withholding for suspense, or just trying to think of what to say next. There is, of course, no way to guess, in verse like this, as there would be in old-fashioned meters, whether we should say, "Thinking it will . . . GET something in it," or should say, "Thinking it will . . . get SOMEthing in it." It makes a difference, but probably not very much.

Anyway, the breaks in these lines do invite the reader or the listener to believe that what he is getting is somehow important.

That, I believe, is their purpose and function. Now, many people seem to have few enough occasions to feel they are in the presence of important incidents of language. If they can lend to these words their yearning for significance, if they are able to believe they are filling this emptiness (their own emptiness or the poem's), with instincts of value, then who would wish to deny them this harmless pleasure?

Indeed, I would say in praise of Creeley's poems that they do not invite vicious feelings of any kind, he seems to offer little opportunity for arousing or projecting aggressive sentiments or sentiments of scorn, expressions of personal superiority, greed, or any kind of socially disfunctional sentiment. Rather he appears benevolently to give opportunities to his readers or listeners for the invocation of the polymorphous, the inarticulate, the wistful, for "feelings" about nothing in particular, felt by nobody in particular, and quite charmingly without consequence.

This mood has always had an appeal for certain kinds of gentle adolescents; some years ago, for instance, it was satisfied by the nebulous religious effusions of Kahlil Gibran. There will always be people whose satisfactions in literature are reserved from the harsh world in a dreamy bubble of the "poetical." A fragile refuge, doubtless; but if there is any harm in it, it is only that the location of the more tender sentiments in this vacuum may leave them, under the pressures of life, unavailable for real things. But if we started to ask poets to be responsible for the well-being of their client's sentiments, there would be no place to stop, short of Plato's edicts. To define tastes and not to dispute them, that is our proper task. I do wish, a little, that I could induce Robert Creeley's readers to consider what they are doing when they respond to his words; but that they respond to any words at all deserves our appreciation.

ARTHUR FORD

Words

To repeat: "It is the way a poem speaks, not the matter, that proves its effects."[1] A platitude certainly in postmodern aesthetics. How else does a Braque or a Franz Kline painting speak to us but through the form it takes, the "way"? The planes, the textures, the colors, these and not the matter speak to us. The way a poem then speaks, the statement it makes, is through its form. By Creeley's own insistence, this speaking succeeds through what Olson points out is basic to poetry: the syllable and the line. Syntax and sound are established by manipulating the syllable, and the poem is given physical substantiality through the line, a line determined literally by the breathing of the poet. Furthermore, for Creeley the poem is given even more substantial form by the inclusion of specific American speech patterns, patterns that Creeley insists do exist and that he identifies most strongly with William Carlos Williams's "local."

I Rhythmic Precision

What . . . we . . . see in Creeley's 1967 collection, *Words,* is a basic concern with rhythmic precision, with matching the rhythms of each poem to the impulses of that poem and thus in effect causing the rhythmic pattern to become the vehicle through which the poem speaks. In *Pieces* Creeley literally caused the rhythm to carry the statement; in *Words* the rhythm most often works concurrently with a discernible image. An examination of several poems written in the early 1960s will illustrate both the organic matching of rhythm, image, and statement, and the range and variety of rhythmic possibilities.

From *Robert Creeley* (Boston: G. K. Hall, 1978), 58–72, 144–45. Copyright 1978 and reprinted with the permission of the author and Twayne Publishers, a division of G. K. Hall & Co., Boston.

The sun's
sky in
form of
blue sky
that

water will
never make
even
in
reflection.

Sing, song,
mind's form
feeling
if
mistaken,

shaken,
broken water's
forms, love's
error
in water.[2]

The first two stanzas constitute a syntactically easy sentence: a reflection of the sky in water is inferior to a direct perception of that sky; however, the sentence itself is slightly elliptical—the sun's sky in (the) form of (a) blue sky—and even incomplete; and the short lines produce a broken, jagged effect. The second half of the poem extends this perception of a physical phenomenon to its human parallel, the incapacity of a person's feelings, love perhaps, to respond sufficiently to the cause of that feeling; and, once again, the form is broken, now even more elliptical, more insistently fragmented. The perception revealed can best be understood by comparing the poem to a high-speed photograph of gently agitated water with each facet of a wave, diamondlike, reflecting only a portion of the sky. The parallel to the inadequacy of human feelings then becomes clear—and hangs there suspended in time. Rhythmically, each brief line, even each syllable, underscores the fragmentary quality of the reflection and the perception, especially when each line is heavily punctuated by Creeley's reading. But the handling of syllables is subtler than that. In stanza 1 "Sun's / sky" and "blue sky" reflect each other rhythmically except for the juncture in the former. No such parallel occurs in the second stanza, which asserts water's inadequacy in reflection. The shift to human feeling is made in the first line of stanza 3, "Sing, song," a shift from one realm to another, the form echoing the earlier sound parallels ("Sun's / sky" and "blue sky") and anticipating the next line, "mind's form." But then these parallel double accentual units disappear in the insistence of single accents: "mistáken," "sháken," "bróken," reflecting the fragmentary quality of these human feelings before the final easing into "love's / error / in water." This is not to insist that such choices were conscious on the part of the poet; rather, the choices were likely made in the act of creation.

Another poem that matches form and content, "Quick-Step," suggests rhythmically the easy grace of the dance.

> More gaily, dance
> with such ladies make
> a circumstance of dancing.
>
> Let them lead
> around and around, all
> awkwardness apart.
>
> There is
> an easy grace gained
> from falling forward
>
> in time, in
> simple time to
> all their graces.

(41)

Here the lines are lengthened primarily by using more unaccented syllables and by using devices such as assonance ("all /

awkwardness apart"), alliteration ("grace gained," "falling forward,"), and internal rhyme ("circumstance of dancing"), that aid the smooth movement of the line. These are traditional poetic devices, of course, and they promote a correspondence between the poem's form and the concept of the dance, the fluid shifts in the tempo of the quick dance reflected, for instance, in the hesitation at the end of stanza 3 ("from falling forward") and the effortless recovery at the beginning of stanza 4 ("in time, in / simple time"). Furthermore, the poem is not a poem about dancing or even about the movements of a particular dance, but rather the poem itself, the sounds, the rhythms, is a dance.

A third poem, "Song," produces still another rhythmic variation:

> The grit
> of things,
> a measure
> resistant—
>
> times walk-
> ing, talk-
> ing, telling
> lies and
>
> all the other
> places, no
> one ever
> quite the same.

(28)

Here the lines are once again short, and, once again, the poem is "about" the rhythm it produces. The precision of the poem does not come from the image—"The grit / of things" is as specific as the poem's image becomes. Rather it results from the precise rhythmic rendering of the idea of grit, namely a grinding hesitancy resulting from the introduction of a foreign substance, as sand, into machinery. In terms of the poem's rhythm this would be "a measure / resistant—"; in terms of human contact it would be "telling / lies." The hesitant rhythm is introduced then in stanza 2 between these two corresponding ideas, the counterrhythm resulting from the simple division of words: "Walk- / ing, talk- / ing." The voice must pause unnaturally at those line breaks, whereas before and after, the lines proceed smoothly with syntactically acceptable breaks (although more so in the first stanza than in the third). The temptation when reading a poem such as this is to search beyond it for application. Does the poem suggest the counterproductivity of lying? Is it supporting rhythmically subtle poetry as opposed to the mindless regularity of popular verse? Again, the poem is not about a "measure / resistant," it is a measure resistant. As a Klee abstract is a complete object in itself, so is a Creeley poem. Reverberations occur, but in reverse of the normally understood pattern. Picture a movie of an exploding house—shown in reverse. Rather than the poem expanding out to many applications, it brings other applications into itself. The "point" of "Song" is what it is doing on the page and what it does when it hits the ear—and mind—of the listener; and that is presented here with precision.

II The Physical Object

The pressure for precision found in Creeley's careful placement of syllables and lines results quite understandably from a poet's instinct and from a craftsman's concern for his materials; however, in Creeley's poetry this rhythmic precision is only one part of the larger concern with rendering the precise moment of a poem's coming to creation. Thomas Duddy is correct when he says, in his review of *Words,* "What Creeley is left with, and it is a unique poetic attention, is a limitless particularity of experience in which each moment acts out the fragmentation of time. So that the moment which the poem is *about* is indistinguishable from the moment *of* the poem."[3] . . . [In *Pieces*] Creeley attempts to capture that moment by insisting on the sufficiency of words: they are objects in themselves as sounds, as presences on the page, and they need not represent some other thing. Earlier, in *Words,* Creeley's attention focused on a similar attempt to prove the sufficiency of objects, of things. For some time he had

been repeating Williams's dictum, "No Ideas but in Things";
now he insisted, "There is nothing / but what thinking makes /
it less tangible," ending that poem, "I Keep to Myself Such
Measure . . . ," with "I hold in both hands such weight / it is
my only description" (52). Although *Words* may be read in dif-
ferent ways, it can be seen in large part as an attempt to discover
and reveal the physical presence and substantiality of the object
in the poem, its *dinglichtkeit,* by locating it precisely and by
scraping off abstract associations. The movement from this con-
cern for the physical substantiality of the object in *Words* to the
physical substantiality of the word in *Pieces* then becomes ob-
vious and can be seen in many poems from this volume.

The link between physical object and physical language ap-
pears overtly in the poem called "The Language." Love is by
common usage the most abstract of all words. How to make it
real? How to change "I love you," that most overused of all
expressions, into something alive? These are questions of human
relationships and of linguistics.

> Locate *I*
> *love you* some-
> where in
>
> teeth and
> eyes, bite
> it but
>
> take care not
> to hurt, you
> want so
>
> much so
> little. Words
> say everything,
>
> *I*
> *love you*
> again,

then what
is emptiness
for. To

fill, fill.
I heard words
and words full

of holes
aching. Speech
is a mouth.

(37)

As is true of Creeley's best poetry, this poem appears as simple statement but stretches out gently to touch related themes and images, creating a hovering on the page rather than a conclusion. "Speech / is a mouth" of course emphasizes that love is made real through its presence and through its physical utterance rather than through the concept of it; actually speaking the words is a literal act and thus more real than the thought. But again (and this became even more the issue in *Pieces*) the attempt is never successful. In fact it cannot be successfully concluded because then the poem would be a static result rather than a dynamic process. The first half of the poem particularly insists on pushing and probing. . . . Creeley stops at the end of each line when reading; . . . notice the effect of the juncture between "bite / it," "want so / much so / little" before the temporary ease of "Words / say everything" with the juncture at the normal break between subject and verb. A comparable pattern is found in the second half of the poem, beginning with "I / love you" and ending with "Speech / is a mouth," syntactically and thematically recalling the earlier "Words / say everything" but intensifying that statement by switching from the abstract to the concrete. As is love, words are holes aching to be filled, a recurrent image in Creeley's poetry with its linguistic as well as its sexual associations. "The Language" then insists on the physical substantiality of literal objects (love becomes holes to be filled) and the physical substantiality of language itself (words become holes to be filled).

In poem after poem, Creeley reaches out for the substantial in the poem. In "A Place" he remembers a scene: "The wetness of that street, the light, / the way the clouds were heavy" and then laments, "I do not feel / what it was I was feeling." Somehow he needs to go back to that experience and not simply describe it. Finally, he must "open // whatever door it was, find the weather / is out there, grey, the rain then and / now falling from the sky to the wet ground" (85). This is real, the weight of the wetness, achieved or at least approximated through a synesthetic mixture of touch, pressure, sight, and sound. In "Some Afternoon," a "world elsewhere" is rejected in favor of a world here where "the tangible faces / smile, breaking / into tangible pieces" (60). In a short poem, "Pieces," the pain of one person hurting another is made real by three final words, each occupying its own line: "meat / sliced / walking" (104). And finally, in a brief poem with the innocuous title "Hello," Creeley makes vivid the shock of human contact far beyond the average experience of that contact. The poem begins:

> With a quick
> jump he caught
> the edge of
>
> her eye and
> it tore, down,
> ripping.

(40)

These and countless other examples from *Words* illustrate Creeley's reaching out for the real in the physical, a desire that he shares with many poets of this century. Creeley differs, however, in the degree of his insistence and in the frustration at what he feels is the failure of his attempt. In fact, he often uses that frustration in his poetry. His poem, "A Method," can be seen most clearly within the context of this frustration:

> Patterns
> of sounds, endless
> discretions, whole
> pauses of nouns,

                    clusters. This
                    and that, that
                    one, this
                    and that. Looking,

                    seeing, some
                    thing, being
                    some. A piece

                    of cake upon,
                    a face, a fact, that
                    description like
                    as if then.

                                              (100)

Sound arrangements become cake on a face become fact. "A
Method" suggests also the poem "For W.C.W.," which in-
cludes the lines, "There, you say, and / there, and there, / and
and becomes / / just so" (27), as well as these lines from his poem
"Enough": "You / there, me // here" (126). And even more
insistently, in "The City" he says, "Again, let / each be this or /
that, they, together," then "vegetable, / flower, a crazy orange
/ sun, a windy / dirt" (91). Finally, Creeley has included in
Words several poems that baffle by their sheer minimal quality. A
poem such as "The Box" seems to do nothing until it is seen as
an attempt to nail the thing to the wall:

                    Three sides,
                    four
                    windows. Four

                    doors, three
                    hands.

                                              (116)

Out of sheer frustration, the poet seems to be pointing his finger
and saying, "There, that's it. Nothing more, nothing less. Just
that." A precision of focus such as that and a brazenness that can
come only from frustration may have resulted in "A Piece," a

poem easily ridiculed and easily misunderstood—the total
poem is

> One and
> one, two
> three.

(115)

—but a poem that can also be seen as the logical, perhaps inev-
itable extension of Creeley's doomed attempt to place the phys-
ical object on the page.

III   The Substantial Self

All of which leads to a corollary theme in *Words*. As Creeley
attempted to substantiate physical objects, so he attempted to
substantiate the self, not by looking within but by placing the
self somehow outside the consciousness expressing it. In many
poems in this volume Creeley refers to the self as something
with a physical, independent existence, an existence just as ob-
jectively real as a tree or a house. The poet, dreamlike, is in the
position of watching himself in action, as seen in these lines from
"The Dream":

> In the dream
> I see
> two faces turned,
>
> one of which
> I assume mine, one
> of which I assume.

(53)

The experience described in this poem and others is quite com-
mon. We have all at one time or another, waking or dreaming,
seen ourselves as though we were an outsider or observer; how-
ever, within the thesis being developed in this chapter, the re-
cording of this phenomenon by Creeley can be seen as another
extension of his doomed attempt to fix the physical object (in

this case the self) on the page. If a tree or a house has a physical presence that can be at least in part captured, why not the self? And how else to do it than to capture a moment in time—a concern that became much more prominent in *Pieces*. The poem "The Measure" begins with a realization of the self's predicament in time:

> I cannot
> move backward
> or forward.
> I am caught
>
> in the time
> as measure.

(45)

While in "Walking":

> In my head I am
> walking but I am not
> in my head.

(36)

In still other poems the split between the consciousness producing the poem and the self is made even more overt, as in an early part of the poem "A Sight":

> . . . *He/I*
> were walking. Then
> the place *is/was*
> not ever enough.

(101)

or even more strikingly in the outwardly autobiographical poem, "I," which begins with the title and continues " 'is the grandson of Thomas L. Creeley,' " thereby making of the first person pronoun a third person noun as though "I" were the name of Thomas L. Creeley's grandson. This device produces a curiously disjointed impression of the self, especially since he keeps the first person possessive elsewhere in the poem.

167

I, is late

But I saw a picture of him once, T.L.
in a chair in Belmont, or it was his invalid
and patient wife they told me sat there, he
was standing, long and steady faced,
a burden to him she was, and the son. The
other child had died

They waited, so my father
who also died when I is four gave all
to something like
the word "adjoined," "extended"
so I feels

I sees the time as long and wavering
grass in all about the lot in all that
cemetery again the old man owned a part of
so they couldn't dig him up.

                                                    (33–34)

In this poem the third person "I" creates a greater sense of objectivity, a viewing the thing out there, separate, hence in a better position to be analyzed. In another poem, however, the "I" is split into an outside–inside relationship, creating complex connections between the two "I's" and thus allowing Creeley to say something with greater precision than if he had stayed with the single "I." The poem titled "The Pattern," begins:

As soon as
I speak, I
speaks. It

wants to
be free but
impassive lies

in the direction
of its

words.

Creeley here separates the self into the man ("I speak") and the poet ("I speaks"), allowing the man to comment on the poet as a third person object ("It / wants to / be free"). He is obviously describing the role of the poet, which is as a third party agent to the creative process. The poem arrives through its own insistence upon the poet who "lies [in two senses of the word] in the direction / of its / words." This passive function is presented dramatically by splitting the poet's self in two and having one observe the other.

IV   Love and Loneliness

And finally, to feelings, or more specifically love, a major subject of the poems in *Words,* as in all of Creeley's writing. How to make a vague, elusive emotion precise and tangible? In "The Language" the words "I love you" became real, but what about the feelings behind those words? Here we come back again to rhythmic precision. In a poem titled "Song," Creeley asks a difficult question with an even more difficult answer, an answer—or at least its difficulty—suggested by the *way* the question is asked:

> What do you
> want, love. To be
> loved. What,
>
> what wanted,
> love.

(79)

Once more the heavy end stops provide the crucial play between normal syntax and the poet's insistent voice. The simple desire to be loved is impossible to know until the feeling becomes not abstract words but "a simple / recognition," and, finally, the feeling and recognition are stripped bare becoming "two things, / one and one." Hesitant insistence also marks a poem called

"Going," which begins, "There is nothing / to turn from, / or to, no // way other / than forward." The line breaks correspond to syntactical junctures except, crucially, between "no" and "way" (a break between stanzas also occurs here), the result being a phrase broken in two and hanging suspended for the moment. The poem ends with a similar pattern, but softer this time as a degree of reconciliation is achieved: "Let me / leave here a / mark, a / way through / her mind" (90). These soft hesitancies are used most effectively in a poem Creeley wrote to his wife, Bobbie, which demonstrates how subtly he modulates his voice through rhythmic precision:

> What can occur
> invests the weather, also,
> but the trees, again,
> are in bloom.
>
> The day will not
> be less than that. I
> am writing to you,
> wishing to be rid of
>
> these confusions. You
> have so largely
> let me continue, not
> as indulgence but
>
> then to say I
> have said, and will,
> anything is so
> hard, at this moment.
>
> In my mind, as
> ever, you occur. Your
> face is such
> delight, I can
>
> see the lines there
> as the finest

mark of ourselves.
Your skin at moments

is translucent. I
want to make love
to you, now. The world
is the trees, you,

I cannot change it,
the weather
occurs, the mind
is not its only witness.

(97–98)

Briefly, this poem speaks of loneliness and of love overcoming that loneliness. The woman becomes real "in my mind" as the trees bloom, as "the weather / occurs." But the poem is much more than this. Somehow Creeley manages to capture that precise configuration of reaching out, touching and not touching—physical separation diminished by love but not completely destroyed by it. Both love and loneliness remain, and in precise ratio to each other, a ratio achieved by mixing easy syntax with occasional slightly less normal line breaks. The first five lines, for instance, follow normal syntactical grouping. Line 6, however, ends with the first word of a new sentence, "I" sitting there alone, a pause, and then the release into the next line. Stanza 4 comments on the difficulty of the moment's loneliness in awkward rhythms and slightly disjointed syntax, followed by the simple statement of the next stanza, the image returning "In my mind, as / ever."

V   The Critical Reception

This is the artist's complete control over his material, consciously and instinctively. In fact, such poetry approaches at least what Creeley apparently intended in this volume, to make the *way* of the poem and not the matter the point to be demonstrated. In 1960 Creeley had written, "I mean then *words*—as opposed to content. I care what the poem says, only as a poem—

I am no longer interested in the exterior attitude to which the poem may well point, as signpost. . . ."[4] A simple concept certainly, a concept obviously used by painters such as the abstract expressionists (Franz Kline had said, "Painting is paint," and Creeley approved), by contemporary minimal sculptors, and by composers, in fact almost always by composers; but a concept causing much controversy in Creeley criticism. Many of the reservations in the reviews of *Words* might be traced to a misunderstanding of this concept. John Thompson, for instance, writing in the *New York Review of Books,* refers to these poems as abstract and general, appealing to "soft, naive, dreamy readers";[5] while Ronald Hayman, reviewing the English publication of *Poems 1950–1965,* which contained the first two-thirds of *Words,* called these poems insubstantial and mannered.[6] At least two reviewers left no mistake about their dislike for *Words.* Peter Davison, writing in the *Atlantic Monthly,* said:

> His earlier poems, though limited in range, displayed subtlety of sound and intricacy of feeling. In *Words* his range has narrowed to the vanishing point, and his energy has subsided almost into catatonia. These poems are so exiguous, so limited in emotion, language, and movement as to be hardly perceptible. . . . Creeley's new work announces the victory of the inarticulate. A battle against glibness has been won, but at a terrible price: almost all the organs of language have been removed. These poems vary neither in tone, in form, in imagery, nor in intention. . . . Creeley's poetry has reached a dead end of self-limitation. . . ."[7]

And John Perreault in the *New York Times Book Review* lamented the direction of Creeley's verse:

> In what appears to be his search for greater purity, clarity and efficiency of language, he has almost completely eliminated the freshness of viewpoint that occasionally enlivened his earlier efforts. The same subjects remain: personalized versions of love, pain, sex and death, but whittled down to "breath units" of often breathless banality. Sometimes, it must be admitted, the thinness of vision and the absence of imagina-

tion is effectively disguised by what can only be described as esthetic control. . . .[8]

Most reviewers, however, saw what Creeley was attempting to do, even if they did not always approve of the attempt. Louis Simpson said in *Harper's Magazine* that in *Words* "everything is style; there is no subject but the poem talking to itself. Such visible objects as were present in his early poems are missing here. These are syllables, breathing pauses, whispers."[9] True, but one senses here a note of regret. No regret is suggested, however, in reviews such as G. S. Fraser's brief, complimentary note in *Partisan Review*,[10] or in Donald Junkins's review in which he called *Words* "an extraordinarily fine book," observing that "the setting is . . . the mind itself, and the poems are conceptual, nonimagistic, anti-romantic."[11] And still other reviews both praised the book and noted Creeley's accomplishment. Thomas A. Duddy observed that "Creeley's poems act out the hesitancy of their own coming to be and serve as reminders of the silence they are situated in."[12] This view of a Creeley poem as process in action, or energy construct as Olson said, is echoed in one other highly favorable review in *Poetry*, always receptive to Creeley. Frederic Will sees *Words* as a group of poems hovering on the point of just having been made: "They all both are, and are about, the surprise, quality, and finality of coming into being, of occupying the unique point at which the poem has just arrested itself," concluding that this volume "marks a new moment in twentieth-century American poetry."[13]

High praise, but even more important, valid observation of the poems in *Words*. Creeley has moved to a greater precision of rhythm than in his earlier poems and has exhibited a greater faith in the *way* of the poem to prove its effect. Matter is still here but is pared more to the minimal, anticipating the poems of *Pieces* and beyond. Creeley himself saw where he had been and where he was going in 1965: "Still, it was never what they [poems] said *about* things that interested me. I wanted a poem itself to exist and that could never be possible as long as some subject significantly elsewhere was involved. There had to be an independence derived from the very fact that words are things too."[14] Words as things became a major theme in Creeley's later poems; here those words are used to attempt the impossible: to fix the object, the self, even love, wriggling to the page.

NOTES

1. "The New World," in *A Quick Graph: Collected Notes and Essays* (San Francisco: Four Seasons Foundation, 1970), 207.

2. *Words*, 22. Further page references will be given in the text.

3. Thomas A. Duddy, "On Robert Creeley," *Stony Brook* 3/4 (1969): 385.

4. "A Note," in *A Quick Graph*, 32.

5. John Thompson, "An Alphabet of Poets," *New York Review of Books* 11 (Aug. 1, 1968): 35. [Reprinted in this collection.]

6. Ronald Hayman, "From Hart Crane to Gary Snyder," *Encounter* 37 (Feb., 1969): 77.

7. Peter Davison "New Poetry: The Generation of the Twenties," *Atlantic Monthly*, Feb., 1968, 141.

8. John Perreault, "Holding Back and Letting Go," *New York Times Book Review*, Nov. 19, 1967, 97.

9. Louis Simpson, *Harper's Magazine*, Aug., 1967, 90.

10. G. S. Fraser, "A Pride of Poets," *Partisan Review* 35 (Summer 1968): 474–75.

11. Donald Junkins, *Massachusetts Review* 9 (Summer 1968): 598, 601.

12. Duddy, "On Robert Creeley," 387.

13. Frederic Will, "To Take Place and to 'Take Heart,'" *Poetry* 111 (Jan., 1968): 257. [Reprinted in this collection.]

14. "Poems Are a Complex," in *A Quick Graph*, 54.

IRVIN EHRENPREIS

A World of Sensible Particulars

Robert Creeley's new collection, *The Charm,* is mainly made up of works the author failed to reprint in earlier volumes, and might properly be read not on its own but as a supplement to *Poems 1950–1965* (published in England four years ago). Yet this miscellaneous sample does suggest Creeley's appeal and his range. The blocks to one's enjoyment of the poetry are big enough; they are not immovable. In too many poems Creeley seems to defy the reader with the question, "Who is speaking?" or "What am I thinking about?" He has been known to ask listeners whether or not he is audible and then to tell those too far back to hear well that he would spoil the effect of the lines if he raised his voice.

The truth is that his technique limits him to a fairly small number of subjects; if one keeps those in mind, one can usually sift out the meaning. Anyhow, Creeley could only produce his bright but ambivalent illuminations behind the screen of his impudent vagueness. Often the subject is a curious detail of somebody's sexual habits. In "Two Times" he compares the inexperienced lover's shock on being handled by a woman with the experienced lover's ease:

I

It takes so long to look down,
the first time thinking it
would then and there either
shoot up or else drop off.

Review of *The Charm* from *Times Literary Supplement,* Aug. 7, 1970, 871. Reprinted by permission.

> One hand on
> the trigger one
> hand on the hand.

The blurred reference of "it" is a mark of Creeley's style. He is fond of nouns like "thing," pronouns without clear antecedents, demonstratives that seem to point nowhere. The effect (when it succeeds) is to make the reader an accomplice of the poet: we are presumably both on such good terms that the reference will be clear.

The complexities of the relation between men and women are a favourite subject, especially as shown in marriage. Human nature depends on loyalties that last. Yet close, deep-rooted ties snarl one another and make people frantic. Creeley plays with the oscillation between mutual need and mutual rejection, marriage as grace and marriage as yoke. Here is "For an Anniversary":

> Where you dream of water
> I have held a handful of sand.
>
> My manners are unprepossessing.
> I stand here awkward, and a long time.
>
> I am mainly an idiot.
> You are almost beautiful.
>
> We will both be miserable
> but no one is damned

The arbitrary changes in tense suggest Creeley's preoccupation with time, his insistence that whatever was meaningful in the past becomes part of the present. The variety of verb forms in the poem—not only tenses but persons, numbers, voices—suggests the variety of experiences contained by the marriage. In this effort to make syntax expressive, one meets a normal element of Creeley's style.

The act of composition itself often becomes part of the poem if not the central subject. In "The Late Comer" Creeley rewrites the poem as he goes along, and comments at the end, "(better)." In "Chasing the Bird" he suggests that each time the poet tries to convey his experience of "night," the task grows harder:

> The sun sets unevenly and the people
> go to bed.
>
> The night has a thousand eyes.
> The clouds are low, overhead.
>
> Every night it is a little bit
> more difficult, a little
>
> harder. My mind
> to me a mangle is.

When Creeley shifts without warning from the theme of nightfall to the theme of writing about nightfall, he acts in character. The reader must simply identify himself with the poet to the point of "acting" with him, and seeing what "it" refers to. The passive reader will miss out. In the expressiveness of the rhythm (if one stops for what Creeley calls "terminal juncture" at the end of each line), in the change from the mildness of the first half of the poem to the harsh movement of the second, one can hear the most subtle of Creeley's accomplishments. Fuller demonstrations of this rhythmic power appear in "The Rhythm" and "The Woman" in *Poems 1950–1965*.

Finally, there is the examination of selfhood or consciousness, implicit in all Creeley's work—for the creative imagination is only a purified form of the human sensibility—but primary in a number of poems. The relation between perception and recognition, experience and memory, the difference between the self as agent and the self as witness, the "I" who *am* and the "I" who *is*—these themes provide centres for Creeley's verse, essays, and fiction. On the poet's uncorrupted mind the world of sensible particulars imposes its fresh objects; these the poet grasps, giving them meaning as he embeds them in his associations; and

thus he joins several different times with the place of the imme-
diate experience. In "Not Again," a poem about self-con-
sciousness, Creeley enacts the sudden appearance of the "I" as
witness before the "I" as agent:

> It was a breeze and a seashell
> brought in Venus—
> but I can be here
> without going anywhere.
>
> So goodbye
> until we meet again,
> and when you come, walk right in.
> It's I.

The comic slyness that suffuses this poem and many more
alternates or mingles itself with a despair that rises as easily. So
long as a man upholds the integrity of his soul while reaching
out to those who love and resist him (especially his wife and
children), he is bound to feel regularly defeated. Yet he must
keep renewing the effort. These conflicts find an audible outlet
in deliberate and often mischievous bathos.

Disappointment with people verges on disappointment with
self—the failure of the imagination to work well against routine
monotony and anxiety. Fears of death, of losing creative power,
may be embodied in despair or transcended in the ironic pathos
of a poem like "Hélas"—here are the opening lines:

> Hélas! Or Christus fails.
> The day is the indefinite. The shapes of light
> have surrounded the senses,
> but will not take them to hand (as would an axe-edge
> take to its stone . . .)

Creeley's style, tentative and recapitulatory, slows down the
surges of feeling without explaining them away. It sounds like
his hesitant, low-pitched voice. The movement between poet
and world becomes the quietest possible drama but draws in
every resource of language. When his lines break off or dwindle

into ellipses, they evoke the poet's rueful admission that no words are right for some reflections, or else his confidence that the sympathetic reader needs no further hint. When the voices speaking in a poem change with hardly a sign, Creeley implies that all the voices—despair, humour, confidence, and lyric passion—emerge ultimately from the single poet who represents the human spirit.

KENNETH COX

Address and Posture in the Early Poetry of Robert Creeley

A number of Robert Creeley's poems, certainly most of the best, are in form addresses to another being. They differ from the absolute subjective outcry addressed to no one in particular or the universe in general (lyric) and from statement attributed as if objective to various persons addressing one another (drama). In the category to which these poems belong the writer speaks in his own person to someone else. Among the verse forms used in English the sonnet became for a long time practically identified with it.

It is of the nature of the address that the being spoken to should remain mute. The poems are obliged to perform their act or exercise without benefit of participation and without the aid of answer or cue: for any such aid they can only look to the practice of self-examination. In this one-sidedness they partake of the nature of an act of homage or worship, an oblation to a divinity, a gift to a friend, a love token. There may be response supposed, but none which really influences the act. Nevertheless the act has an object and a direction from which it must not part. In this it differs from genres of pure self-regard—meditation, monologue, self-portrait.

There is an early poem of Creeley's about postmen who burnt the mails, so disrupting a system of multiple bilateral communication. It leads to the reflexion that their conduct was not of great importance because the absolute statement, made without

This essay originally appeared as "Address and Posture in the Poetry of Robert Creeley" in the *Cambridge Quarterly* (U.K.) 4, no. 3 (Summer 1969): 237–43. Reprinted in *boundary 2* 6, no. 3; 7, no. 1 (Spring/Fall 1978): 241–46. Reprinted by permission.

recipient in mind, is the ideal to aspire to: "The poem supreme, addressed to / emptiness—this is the courage // necessary" ("The Dishonest Mailmen" [*For Love,* 29]). But the aspiration includes a feeling that, for the writer of this poem, such a mode of utterance is difficult or unnatural. There are among the other poems examples of utterance released from the attraction of an addressee, some of them labelled *songs,* but they are as it were absent-minded addresses. Other apparent exceptions are addresses at one remove: observations on the difficulty of formulating the address, reports of what was said on an occasion in the past.

If this analysis is anywhere near correct it is reasonable to ask what a third party, the reader of the book, can expect to get from poems addressed by the author to a second party. At first sight the reader would appear to be in the position of an eavesdropper or wiretapper. All he could expect to get from a reading of the poems would on this view come from an analogy of substance between what he has overheard and his own relation to another (fourth) party. He might also pick up hints on how to make good addresses of this kind.

Something like these do indeed seem to be the basic uses of Creeley's poems, but they do not entirely exhaust the functions his poems perform. In making addresses his poetry also discusses the making of them and at high points attains a general validity. It would of course be impossible for the poems to have meaning if they could not appeal to some similar experience. And even if the appeal should be mistaken, the analogy false, the meaning would not for this reason be any the less real although the social usefulness of the poem would be lessened

Many of Creeley's poems may perhaps be regarded as paradigms which attempt to provide the verbal elements of the thing required to be said. An attempt which succeeds would then serve a purpose similar to that of the prototypes of physical measurement, the bronze yard still kept in the House of Commons or the wavelength of orange light from pure krypton 86 which replaces a bar as the international standard of the metre. Occasions when recourse to the standard is needed will be very few, but a standard needs to be kept lest deviations multiply and produce error.

The introduction of the notion of standard is not intended to imply that the statements made in the poems are invested with authority or even deserve much attention. In their preoccupation with the infinitely small as also in their discreet adventurousness, the poems have more in common with pure mathematics than with law: they may be considered studies in the reformulation of expression whose experimental formulae have possible but unpredictable applications. If they avoid received usage it is because this omits meaning bolder or finer than its terms admit. At best they reject accepted values by continual never-satisfied negation, at worst they deny the possibility of satisfaction, wallowing in their own shortfalls.

Here or hereabouts may be heard an objector uttering the word *precious*. It is absent from the present description for three reasons. First, as the ambivalent senses of the word themselves indicate, it is by no means clear how the trivial and the morbid differ from the ingenious and exquisite, or where one passes into the other; and until this is sorted out the word can hardly count for much. Secondly, when the differences are apparent to taste, *precious* is true of a great deal of American art—if the quality originated in the conscience of seventeenth-century New England, it is extended and established by the superrefinements of twentieth-century technology—and the question arises whether the word does not express a cultural prejudice. Thirdly, and most important of all for any attempt to assay the work of a living writer, Creeley's is *prima facie* morally in earnest and technically of interest. In their constant concern for what is just right his poems administer a standing rebuke to brash feeling and conventional phrase.

The poems apply their own corrections, each phrase or step evading a slide into what is merely expected of it. They prefer to stop short rather than go wrong. They catch themselves out, detaining a phrase before it is completed or diverting it as it falls. The extreme shortness of the lines assists the action: with each new line a slight hiatus or breathing, not so strong as a stress, sustains the attempt a little longer, turns it in a different direction, prolongs the hesitation and, still deferring a conclusion, brings it a little nearer to the thing intended to be said. All but a few keywords are emptied of their mass. They float "like a /

clear, fine / ash sifts, / like dust // from nowhere" ("Words" [*Words*, 92]) till an experimental landing can be made. Any statement eventually attained stands with so much the greater strength.

The tentativeness of the definition seems to provide an assurance that the thing to be said, even if not yet formulated, has at least not (yet) suffered distortion. Silence still leaves open the possibility of getting it said right, whereas saying it wrong would close the possibility: in spite of self-corrections what has been said cannot be unsaid. Creeley uses this fact of time in the statement which contradicts itself ("I / do not want what // I want" ["The Dream" (*Words*, 54)]) to leave the idea in its faintest possible trace or cut its life to the minimum. For even if the statement was right when it was made it may have ceased to be right with the saying of it. The temporary validity of the statement expresses awareness of the discontinuity of consciousness.

Another method Creeley uses to lighten a word and limit its acceptation is that of the rhyme word introduced not to pattern sound but to provide a near alternative to the sense. Throughout his vocabulary *walking* is practically a doublet for *talking:* "and keep on talking / and keep on walking" ("The Joke" [*For Love*, 116]), "Where do they walk now? / Do they talk now" ("The Rose" [*For Love*, 148]), "In my head I am / walking" ("Walking" [*Words*, 36]). Words of very similar sound may have very different meanings but in course of time, if the meanings are within range, they attract and contaminate each other, producing equations capable of solution. The technique as used in poetry may be said temporarily to speed up the process of linguistic change. The doublet *walk/talk,* for example, approaches the single meaning *move legs or tongue.* Motion of body and speech being then equated, metaphors carried across from one to the other, such as *stumbling* speech or *mincing* gait, become literal. In Creeley's usage the forward movement of walking is also the creative formulation of the word: "He pushes behind the words" ("Waiting" [*Words*, 24]), "Let me stumble into / not the confession" ("For Love" [*For Love*, 160]). And the syllable *for* of course dedicates the movement.

Other examples of equating rhymes are: "God is not air, nor hair" ("The Awakening" [*For Love*, 107]), "mistaken, //

shaken" ("Water" [*Words*, 22]), "I cannot relieve it / nor leave it" ("The Mountains in the Desert" [*Words*, 23]). Or one and the same word-sound is used in two senses: "right (write)" (*Words*, 72), "mark / time" (*Words*, 90).

The total effect of the devices described may be compared with that of the optical illusions of baroque architecture, the ambiguous puzzles illustrated in books on Gestalt psychology or the bewildering dazzle of op art. In all such examples a number of individually scarcely perceptible deviations are contrived to convey a preliminary confusion, suggest possibilities of resolution and postpone a decision on which aspect is to be represented as the real. The poems thus voluntarily accept the risk of being seen to miss the mark. When examination of conscience precedes the composition of a poem, then the poem is its fruit and conclusion. But when, as often in Creeley's, the examination itself constitutes the composition and is conducted in the presence of an invigilator, then the risk of visible failure is the price of success. The odd situation may arise where the failure of a poem is itself the subject of the poem. On these occasions the reader may apprehend with alarm that what he is witnessing, performed in the interest of poetic truth but at the instance of some self-defeating movement of the mind, is the immolation of a poetic faculty.

The question may then be asked whether the purpose of such puritan scrupulosity is to exhibit the attainment of a conclusion subtler than ever before or to evade conclusion by demonstrating the impossibility of it. Part of the hesitation in approaching the simple conclusion is due not so much to the difficulty of the operation as to horror of self-exposure. In a solo performance without supporting cast external help is needed to give courage.

Apart from the spiritual help that comes from the being addressed, help of another kind is available from the past. Poems cannot be nothing but statements addressed by the writer to a listener and overheard by a reader. At least at moments of critical revision the writer must know that he is going to be overheard: in addressing his listener he will to some extent bear his reader in mind. Grammatically his approach may be defined as first person speaking to second (mute) with awareness of unknown third. The awareness of the third person may have been smaller when sonnets were circulated in manuscript and may sink to zero in the case of a completely private communication but even then the writer cannot help making use of a language already marked by the successes and the failures of his predecessors. An unknown reader carrying memory of the language stands at a pole opposite to that of the person addressed by the writer. The words chosen by the writer consequently vibrate at the point of intersection of two lines of force, one produced by the example of the past and bearing on the reader, the other due to the obligations of the present and directed to the person addressed.

The writer's response to the tensions thus set up causes what may be called his posture. By this is meant simply the position of his mind, the word *attitude* being avoided because of its ideological implication and the word *pose* to prevent insult. If *posture* has attracted some of the insinuation of *pose* the word *stance* may be substituted, but nothing deliberate or athletic is intended. Placed amid its tensions the mind cannot but adopt a position towards them just as the body must be in some posture.

The colloquial ease of Creeley's poems camouflages the artifice by which he maintains and changes posture. At times a literary origin is not disguised. Some of the poems even proceed from quotation or allusion and then modify the posture under influence of the address: "She walks in beauty like a lake" ("The Bed" [*For Love,* 66]). To appeal exclusively to the reader's acquaintance with language and literature, abandoning the object of the poem, would be to commit treason and play to the gallery. To attend solely to the person addressed would be to end in uninteresting repetition and in blank statement. Creeley's poems dart and hover between these two extremes. There can be no resting place, no answer to the problem. At best one can try to understand it and observe proportion.

A crucial and conspicuous illustration of the problem lies in Creeley's use of the word *lady.* It is not customary now for a man speaking English to address the woman he loves as *lady,* yet the word appears often in the poems, at least till about 1960. It relates the postures of Creeley's poetry to the late medieval tradition which in England fizzled out with the Cavalier lyricists. The modesty, subtlety, and cunning of his diction also suggest a debt to medieval poetry, and the best of his poems, like "For Love," express and examine the nature of the most intimate of addresses in a mode which descends, if deviously, from the "Donna Mi Prega."

The poetry of this school, though addressed to the woman loved, is not a manoeuvre in courtship. It does not give vent to the emotion of the moment, describe the excitement of the pursuit or the anxiety of the approach, wheedle or rail or flatter. In seeking rather to define the male experience of loving the poem allows itself familiarity and adopts a persistent exploratory movement which, imitating the act, becomes itself an act of love. Equating the organs of speech and sex, it puts value on penetrative ease, fluency, fluidity. Only the male speaks: he accepts responsibility for the emotion, exposes himself, leaves marks, makes mistakes, corrects himself but in the end "cannot / be more than the man / who watches" ("The Name" [*For Love*, 145]). The physical object of love scarcely appears. The consciousness of the object of love comes in Robert Creeley's poems like the irruption of a god in Homer or a change of weather in a modern novel: in the word he insistently uses it *occurs* ("The Awakening" [*For Love*, 107], "The Wife" [*For Love*, 154], "To Bobbie" [*Words*, 98]). The occurrence of the consciousness of the object of love clinches the self-examination and the exercise. The creation of the reality of imaginative love then justifies and ends the poem, having manifested that "the mind / is not its only witness" ("To Bobbie").

RICHARD HOWARD

Robert Creeley: "I Begin Where I Can, and End When I See the Whole Thing Returning."

We may—and if we are poets we must, or risk bearing nothing else—learn to bear the indignities of success, as we have borne those of failure, in order to get on with the task:

> The poem supreme, addressed to
> emptiness—this is the courage
>
> necessary. This is something
> quite different.

The charge is a particularly American lesson (think of the "success" of Gertrude Stein, the "failure" of Melville)—one which requires, at least, a particular diligence of its American students, who are likely to find themselves hoisted up, with wisps of obloquy and neglect still clinging to the anfractuosities of a temperament not yet entirely sanded down by public relations, onto an eminence or, say, a plateau of publicity which surrounds their every utterance with—with platitude, precisely. We Americans are, or are made, leaders on a grand scale before we have left off skirmishing in the gang wars of our poetry, and it must be a strong as well as a good character which can resist all the platforms made available when a desk-top is the only relevant surface. To stick to one's last, as an American poet of achieved success, then, is to abide as well by one's first, is to

From *Alone With America: Essays on the Art of Poetry in the United States Since 1950.* Copyright © 1980 Richard Howard. Reprinted with the permission of Atheneum Publishers, Inc.

> . . . take oneself
> as measure,
>
> making the world
> tacit description
> of what's taken
> from it

—to pursue one's initial impulse undeterred—and undiluted—
by the imitations of oneself which one is urged to bestow upon a
world thirsty for reasonable facsimiles, making "a pardonable
wonder / of one's blunders."

Diligent, strong and good are surely the epithets which attach
to Robert Creeley's aspiring character ("my method is not a /
tenderness, but hope / defined"), for this poet shows, in his *poetry*
at least, none of the distractions pressed upon him by the tenden-
tious praise of *both* Leslie Fiedler and Hugh Kenner (poetry, what
alliances are made in thy name!), by the *imprimatur* of William
Carlos Williams and the impertinence of John Simon ("there are
two things to be said about Creeley's poems: they are short; they
are not short enough"), and most distracting of all, by the clam-
orous mimicry of his juniors:

> The sound of waves killed speech
> but there were gestures—
>
> of my own . . .

Steering what he always accounts for as a highly tentative course
("I make a form of assumptions . . . or better, a jerking leap /
toward impulse"), the contributor to *Wild Dog, Quagga* and *Fuck
You: A Magazine of the Arts* acknowledges in return the "contri-
bution" of the Guggenheim and Rockefeller Foundations to a
career which, at just past forty and however uncertain of the
Muse's patronage—

> But the lady—
> she, disdain-
> ful, all
> in white for

                              this occasion—cries
                              out petulantly, is
                              that all, is
                              that all

—has conferred upon him the status of a *chef d'école*. The school, though, is one of knocks and pratfalls, an academy of tumbling in which the "grace gained / from falling forward" specifically suggests Frost's account of his own poetics:

> I have the habit of leaving my toys where people would be pretty sure to fall forward over them in the dark. Forward, you understand, *and* in the dark.

Indeed, it is astonishing that a poetry which questions so eagerly the very possibility of poetry, even as it queries the constitutive notion of the poet ("the mind's / vague structure, vague to me / because it is my own"), should have become so popular, or at least so influential; but we must remember that the scandal of the negative, the destructive energies of an enterprise of cancellation always light up the sky with an infernal glow. Frost's Myth of Daemonic Incoherence makes peace, Creeley says, with what is easy: there is every excuse for Creeley's war against poetry (for out of it, out of the experience of an impossible end, an intolerable return, comes what poetry is possible to him:

                              and there
                              it was, a little

                              faint thing
                              hardly felt, a
                              kind of small
                              nothing

—a poetry of the *given,* whose emphasis is on the feel of specific sites and moments as if they were totally detachable from the rest of life, not to be repeated, discriminated, or even named; the expression in literary form of certain enormous repudiations) but no excuse, unless they would share his *gran rifiuto,* for those who imitate him, even for those who "like" him.

Immensely out in the open now ("in private you are you," Creeley quotes Gertrude Stein aptly, "and in public you are in public and everybody knows that"), exploiting his forebears ("a quiet testament / a song / which one sings, if he sings it / with care"), explaining his followers ("the lines / talking, taking, always the beat from / the breath"), Creeley yet continues to explore his own function—or his failure to function—as a *poet* with a splendid unconcern for external relations, preferring to harbor his most freakish and obvious faults quite as if they were his most original and valuable impulses (and perhaps they are— in any case they are indistinguishable from his virtues in the ultimate effect of his work: thus Creeley quotes Valéry's definition of *lyric* as that mode of poetry in which the content and the form are realized simultaneously—neither one can precede the other as a possibility). So consistent, indeed, with themselves, so characteristic and even queer are Creeley's poems, all collected now in two volumes published—on a field argent, a very narrow rivulet of print between ample meadows of margin—in 1962 (*For Love*) and 1967 (*Words*), that they loom, or unravel, as much more like themselves than they are like any other poems, even poems by William Carlos Williams and Charles Olson. That is an extreme quality, the same quality which makes Gertrude Stein say that American literature is quite alone because in its choosing it has to be without any connection with that from which it is choosing; and in order to account for such extremity I shall have to ignore what is perhaps a certain drift in the course of the poems toward mediation ("now, as I begin to relax," Creeley says, incredibly, "as I grow . . . more at ease in my world, the line can become, as you say, more lyrical, *less afraid of concluding*"). After all, Creeley has chosen to remain alive in the world, which means there are occasions when he has recognized the necessity of relating or concluding or repeating an experience—"it is necessary," he says, "to suppose a continuity, though none comes readily to hand." Indeed, if there is in any conventional sense—remembering that a convention makes easy what would otherwise remain difficult—a *development* in the art of Robert Creeley, it is a development toward not away from extremity, toward the limit of experience which makes it possible to know what the experience is by learning

what it is not, and away from the center where things are neigh-
bored, accommodated, solaced by propinquity. What we get in
Creeley, what he *wants* to get, or is compelled by his nature to
give, is a "hammering at the final edge of contact" (his phrase,
from a 1954 note on Williams). He is what Melville calls an
isolato, not acknowledging the common continent of men, but
rather the island of ego, the atoll of solipsism which life itself, as
he says in the preface to his novel *The Island* (1963), forces us to
leave:

> This island, in which the world will be at last a place circum-
> scribed by visible horizons, is, finally, not real, however tan-
> gible it once seemed to me. I have found that time, even if it
> will not offer much more than a place to die in, nonetheless
> carries one on, away from this or any other island.

But in a novel, surely, the supposed continuity is more necessary
than in poems—that is why Creeley writes poems, not because
of some ulterior inclination of literary temperament:* poems are
the one chance he has of focusing upon experience without a
shift of view or voice ("I grew up on a farm. It gave me that
sense of speech as a laconic, compressed way of saying some-
thing to someone. To say as little as possible as often as possi-
ble"), without, in every sense of the word, *relating.* No connec-
tion and above all, no return. This notion of return (of
recurrence and therefore of recollection, as Stevens has said that
the poet is "he that of repetition is most master") is crucial to
any art of verse, as the word *verse* itself indicates—Creeley
writes not anti-poems, as has been said, but anti-verses. "The
issue is the poem, a single event," Creeley insists, and by issue
he means outcome, the specific and reified recognition of the
momentary experience: "a poem is some *thing,* a structure pos-
sessed of its own organization in turn derived from the circum-

---

*"I feel poems and prose equally are given me to write; I do not feel *I* create
them, I have no patience or sympathy with writing which dictates its concerns as
a *subject* proposed by 'choice.' 'Choice' for me is more accurately recognition. I
want to live in the world—not 'use' it. . . ."

stances of its making." A poetry without recurrence, then, is a poetry without verse; a poetry without return or ending—

> things continue, but my sense is that I have, at best simply taken place with that fact. I see no progress in time or any other such situation. . . . What I think to say is of no help to me—

is a poetry without rhyme or reason (*ratio*); for rhyme and reason do go together, since the aim of both is to bring things to an end in order that they may begin again; a poetry, as Yeats called it, of precision but no rhythms—there is not a single sentence anybody will ever murmur to himself. And that is just what Creeley is after, or rather, he is not *after* something but seeking to be *present* with it: a poetry that cannot be murmured, remembered, but rather encountered, confronted; as his mentor Charles Olson puts it:

> What really matters: that a thing, any thing, impinges on us by a more important fact, its self-existence, without reference to any other thing, in short, the very character of it which calls our attention to it, which wants us to know more about it, its particularity. . . .

Experience, then, is for him a matter of separation, the substitution of incoherence for subject matter (hence the titles of Creeley's two books, which are concerned with precisely the subjects most often thought to involve connection, *love* and *language*, and which for Creeley afford a kind of ecstasy of isolation, each instance of the use of his body and of the use of words as discrete, singular, insistently unique:

> now screaming
> it cannot be
> the same)

—and the poem a strategy to avoid pattern (Creeley on Swinburne: "a tedium of accumulation and patterned manner"), to dissolve continuity and what used to be called the *keeping* of imagery; what is sought is the *losing,* an imagery out-of-keeping, an imagery kept out:

> an egg of obdurate kind. The only possible reason of its existence is that it has, in itself, the fact of reality and the pressure. There in short is its form—no matter how random and broken that will seem.

This question of the broken form, of something made to be—or to appear—fragmentary, partial, incomplete is of great importance to Creeley's work; "the poems come from a context that was difficult to live in, and so I wanted the line used to register that kind of problem . . . now the truncated line, or the short, seemingly broken line . . . comes from the somewhat broken emotions involved." It is as though the contours of regular form must blur, dim, and deceive us until we lose contact. Only the broken surface reveals the truth:

> tear impression
> from impression
> making a fabric
>
> of pain.

And the lines of cleavage will be irregular, the lunatic fringe of existence where we "live / on the edge, / looking." *Only disconnect,* Creeley urges; if I forget what *was,* I may be able to exist *now:*

> . . . in the memory I fear
> the distortion. I do not feel
> what it was I was feeling. I am im-
> patient to begin again, open
>
> whatever door it was, find the weather
> is out there, grey, the rain then and
> now falling from the sky to the wet ground.

It is the first time in the history of poetry that a man has written a poetry of forgetting:

> There are ways beyond
> what I have here to work with
> what my head cannot push to any kind
>
> of conclusion

—a poetry without any of the axiological signs and spells which serve to hold it in the mind; without images or rather with an imagery pulverized beyond the recognition of shared contours, an imagery hugged to the self, "played" close to the chest:

> The
>
> mind makes
> its own
>
> forms, looks
> into its terror
>
> so
> selfishly
>
> alone. Such
> a fact so simply
>
> managed there is
> no need for any
>
> one else.

—a poetry without rhyme, or rather with a sonority parodied beyond belief, a music jeering at conventional accords:

> . . . rhyme, of course, is to me a balance not only of sounds, but a balance which implies agreement: that's why, I suppose,

I stay away from rhymes . . . except for this kind of ironic throwback on what is being said.

—a poetry without any constants in its rhythmic behavior (for when the rhythm is variable, there is no *rhythmic* point in the run-on line: Creeley's enjambments are not a departure from something, but a coming *to* something, a dislocation "until the mind itself is broken, breaks back, *forcing the world to declare itself*"), though its rhythmic behavior is always the same in its very inconstancy, a kind of insistent unpredictability ("the slip-shod, half-felt, heart's uneasiness in particular forms") which affords the single self its final locus, an ultimate accommodation of what Shelley said was "conscious, inseparable, one":

> I wanted
> one place to be
> where I was
> always. . . .
>
> Oh when regrets stop
> and the silence comes
> back to be
> a place still for us,
>
> our bodies will tell
> their own story, past
> all error,
> come back to us.

There are clusters here, a sense of energies focused in "the virtues of an amulet / and quick surprise," but no way of telling that the set-up on the page must be one way rather than another, no way of discovering not only that the poem might not have been, but also that it could have been no other way than it is, the two discoveries *together* making what Valéry calls the Beautiful. Hence Creeley's method, a treatment rather than a technique, of destroying expectation, of *forgetting* in order to avoid ending, which would mean having to reopen the healed, scabbed-over trauma—instead, everything is kept raw and ruined here, giving or enforcing the impression both of debris:

> some echoes,
> little pieces,
> falling, a dust

and of contusion, the incurable wound:

> My nature
> is a quagmire of unresolved
> confessions . . .

> We change, not multiplied but dispersed,
> sneaked out of childhood,
> the ritual of dismemberment.

Yet though there can be no doubt about the dismemberment, preferred to any remembering, it is precisely the ritual which is in question, for Creeley's poetry is in opposition to all ceremony, all politeness, which is inevitably a long poem since it is full of recurrences. Here there is but "a drunken derision / of composition's accident" and a mockery of the mnemonic devices we employ to keep experience *in mind:*

> The mind
> fast as it goes, loses

> pace, puts in place of it
> like rocks simple markers,
> for a way only to
> hopefully come back to

> where it cannot. All
> forgets. My mind sinks.
> I hold in both hands such weight
> it is my only description.

We hang a jingling padlock on the mind, Pope said, and Creeley would release us from the bondage of that chime, not concerned like his moderate mentor Dr. Williams with the ideas in things (after all, when you say *no ideas but in things* you still assert the possibility of ideas), but with

> the grit
> of things,
> a measure
> resistant . . .
>
>   no
> one ever
> quite the same.

When the mind is unlocked, released from any servitude of repetition, when no experience is "quite the same," then we get a poetry without ending and without climax (for climax is what happens when things meet in a form and have an ending), a poetry without recurrence and without memory: a poetry of confession—"I write what I don't know"—of centripetal illumination, of paralyzed auto-fascination. Wordsworth's famous criticism of Goethe—that his poetry was not memorable enough—applies more aptly still to Creeley's fragments of a great confession, save that—and it is literally the *saving grace*—Creeley *wants* no poem remembered, wants each poem to enrich himself and us by what it reveals of his poverty, for in the entrancement of isolated experience the first obstacle to action is the absence of obstacles, of a resisting *norm* from which to vary:

> . . . the interminable
> subject all but
> lost to my mind . . .

The masters of linguistics tell us that there is no reason for the sentence, in its unconditioned state, to end—ever. There is every reason to suppose that we all, unwittingly, spend our lives within one and the same sentence, a single locution which is coterminous with our own bodies. This is what Robert Creeley means when he says that "words are common, and language knows more than one man can speak of"; it is his power (and, as well, his pathos) to have added his voice—sour, stumbling, secretive—to that enormous and obsessive murmur which sometimes rises from literature and which is perhaps its justification, the utterance of our becoming. "There is no more to live," Creeley says darkly in his preface to *For Love,* "than what there is, to live. I want the poem as close to this fact as I can bring it." He has brought his poems so close to that "no more" of his, to that irreducible absorption in what is *there,* that he speaks, or we hear him speak, out of an absolute gist of solitude—honorable certainly and enriching to us, as I have said, though I think too that it must be the greatest impoverishment to live in a world without recurrence, a world where nothing can happen more than once:

> One is
> too lonely, one wants
> to stop there, at the edge of
>
> conception.

Robert Creeley and the Pleasures of System

> *Experience (in a manner usual enough) created by a system—The*
> *spatial relations made by a house, for example, the distribution of*
> *movement in an arrangement of streets, etc. . . . . Mind experience, or*
> *however to isolate it if that's possible, taken as the possibility of*
> *system.*
>
> —A Day Book

Charles Olson, Robert Duncan, Allen Ginsberg—these are some of the poets Robert Creeley has associated himself with during the past thirty years, and they are dwarfing company for a poet like Creeley. These three figures, like Whitman before them, are seldom at a loss for an encompassing proposition. They are poets with systems who, one feels, given time and opportunity, could confidently find a place for anyone or anything in their writing. But Creeley? "Well, I've always been embarrassed for a so-called larger view. I've been given to write about that which has the most intimate presence for me, and I've always felt very, very edgy those few times when I have tried to gain a larger view. I've never felt right. I am given as a man to work with what is most intimate to me—these senses of relationship among people. I think, for myself at least, the world is most evident and most intense in those relationships" (*Contexts of Poetry,* 97). That embarrassment "for a so-called larger view" has periodically returned to Creeley, sometimes in the form of a desire to escape his own precedents and specializations—"Short intensive poems. Short intensive stories" (164).[1] Between 1967 and 1969 he resolved to try the high road of his three friends: *Pieces* is Creeley's first attempt to make chronological time serve the inclusive ends of a system of belief (192). More than twenty

---

From *boundary 2* 6, no. 3; 7, no. 1 (Spring/Fall 1978); 365–79. Reprinted by permission.

years of short poems, some of them wonderful, led to that deliberate shift away from his poetic past.

Most of the poems I return to eagerly come from these first twenty years, but they bear a curious relation to this matter of a "larger view." Many of the best of these poems reinforce—sometimes by teasing—the assumption that human experience is intelligibly ordered within definable spheres, and the more ambitious assumption that the world at large is intelligibly ordered. This is to say that Creeley has always, in an important though unusual sense, been a systematic poet. He presumes that people conduct their affairs in orderly fashion, and that the poet's task is to reveal the order behind human behavior as a delicately articulated but binding system of understanding. In this regard, Creeley is an empirical poet: whereas Olson, Duncan, and Ginsberg *constructed* systems in order both to write poetry and to answer questions about history, Creeley *discovers* systematic behavior in the people he observes or imagines.[2]

It is easy for Creeley to assume that personal experience is intelligibly ordered; convention quietly weaves the lines of personal relationship into a dense, fine fabric. But the relationships between classes and institutions, these Creeley approaches obliquely—at times, through another poet's vision. Here is "After Lorca," which first appeared in 1952:

> The church is a business, and the rich
> are the business men.
> When they pull on the bells, the
> poor come piling in and when a poor man dies, he has a
> wooden
> cross, and they rush through the ceremony.
>
> But when a rich man dies, they
> drag out the Sacrament
> and a golden Cross, and go *doucement, doucement*
> to the cemetery.
>
> And the poor love it
> and think its crazy.
>
> (*For Love,* 27)

The intelligibility of social relationships is posited as directly by the manner of the first two lines as by any proposition the poem advances: before *Pieces* Creeley's poems characteristically open with an assertion; the definitive copula is still his staple predicate. His manner, like Olson's and like Dorn's, is discursive; this is appropriate for poets who proceed on the assumption that life is explainable by general laws. The first two strophes nicely elaborate the sort of class analysis common in political verse and oratory, but Creeley's poem really lies in the concluding lines. That the church and businessmen systematically enforce the prerogatives of class structure on the community's worship could surprise no one. That these prerogatives arouse bemusement rather than resentment among the poor is more startling. The poor understand the class system perfectly, and they delight in its misplaced discriminations. To see clearly a system's symmetries disarms that system's oppressive significance; systems analysis and good humor supplant politics.

Political questions do not engage Creeley. The social relationships he deftly analyzes fall within the province of manners. "The Lover," published in 1953–1954, takes it for granted that rules routinely govern social behavior:

> What should the young
> man say, because he is buying
> Modess? Should he
>
> blush or not. Or
> turn coyly, his head, to
> one side, as if in
>
> the exactitude of his emotion he
> were not offended? Were
> proud? Of what? To buy
>
> a thing like that.
>
> (*For Love,* 41)

Routine is no more interesting than the dull hum of an electric clock, but at the edges of convention, where a system is ill-known (as here) or under strain (as in "Hello" [*Words,* 40]), its delicate workings slip into place as astonishingly as in high art. Through these angular lines, Creeley uncertainly pursues the young man's options. Postured "exactitude" would be one possibility, but the analysis produces a more systematic conclusion—signaled chiefly by a period where one more question mark might have inverted the sense of the poem: to buy Modess is, for the generic young man, a rite of passage, one of those points at which the social system escalates its terms.

Creeley is especially interested in rites of passage; they are junctures within a social system which momentarily seem to be hiatuses rather than turning points: the young man gropes for the determinacy of a systematic imperative, for what he *should* do. Creeley's best poem about these apparent hiatuses is "The Business" (1955):

> To be in love is like going out-
> side to see what kind of day
>
> it is. Do not
> mistake me. If you love
>
> her how prove she
> loves also, except that it
>
> occurs, a remote chance on
> which you stake
>
> yourself? But barter for
> the Indian was a means of sustenance.
>
> There are records.
>
> (*For Love,* 44)

Creeley is testing the apparatus of intellectual analysis on the theme of love. He begins with the syntax of a universal proposition: apparently, he is about to define the nature of love when the poet's tool ("like") comes to the aid of the sanguine analyst.

But it is awkward aid: the simile attempts to illustrate a state by referring to an action, and the analyst resolves to try again (lines 3–4). This time he draws out the apparatus not of definition but of validation ("how prove she / loves also"). Yet the syntax of validation is no more complete than that of definition; in place of an "unless you" clause completing the conditional syntax comes a clause which dissolves the possibilities of validation: "except that it occurs. . . ." The point behind Creeley's dissolution of syntactic structures seems to be the obvious one that love is beyond the eager, assured reach of discursive understanding; in James Merrill's phrase, love "is everyone's blind spot."[3] Love is apparently where systems end: change is another word for lawlessness, or indeterminacy. And yet this surrender to contingency ("going out- / side to see what kind of day / / it is") is only a disguised and rudimentary form of systematic behavior: barter. Creeley suggests that although, in the absence of general laws, the requital of love seems only "a remote chance," the power of barter is such that requital "occurs." Love offered is taken; love taken, returned. That archaic circle of exchange shows that love seems chancy chiefly because it involves a part of the social system which we naively think we have surpassed.

Manners, the system of acceptable social behavior, are not easily surpassed and can only briefly be interrupted. Human nature is a delicate thing and cannot take its experience raw. There is a fine poem on just this subject, "Something," written in 1963:

> I approach with such
> a careful tremor, always
> I feel the finally foolish
>
> question of how it is,
> then, supposed to be felt,
> and by whom. I remember
>
> once in a rented room on
> 27th street, the woman I loved
> then, literally, after we

had made love on the large
bed sitting across from
a basin with two faucets, she

had to pee but was nervous,
embarrassed I suppose I
would watch her who had but

a moment ago been completely
open to me, naked, on
the same bed. Squatting, her

head reflected in the mirror,
the hair dark there, the
full of her face, the shoulders,

sat spread-legged, turned on
one faucet and shyly pissed. What
love might learn from such a sight.

(*Words*, 35)

Creeley nicely frames this anecdote with invitations to interpretation; the title, "Something," shows how little he is willing to say about "What / love might learn from such a sight." Among the notions covered by that one word, "Something," is the awareness of how time measures and places even intimate experiences. "A moment ago" she had been completely open to him; but he cannot complain, for she is that woman he "loved / then." She had carefully placed their intimacy in the immediate past; Creeley forcefully assigns his love of her to the now distant past. Love might learn that people need and cherish the relieving distance that comes with even small increments of time. In the opening sentence of the poem, Creeley expresses the onerous burden of intimacy, for intimacy sets one in the interstices of the system of manners, scrambling, like the young man in "The Lover," to deduce proprieties. In this awkward moment, when the sink must serve as a toilet, she needs the screening sound of water running, just as the poet, in order to capture her delicacy, needs that euphemism "to pee." And in her shy distance she is as engagingly beautiful as ever: "the hair dark there, the / full of her face, the shoulders. . . ." What love might learn is the care people take with themselves and require of each other.

But why is Creeley so taken by systematic behavior? Why is a poet who is unwilling to formulate "a so-called larger view" so consistently engaged by the *idea* of a larger view? One might answer with the claim that the explain-all is a national resource. The following passage shows Creeley tapping this resource in the customary way:

> It is all a rhythm,
> from the shutting
> door, to the window
> opening,
>
> the seasons, the sun's
> light, the moon,
> the oceans, the
> growing of things,
>
> the mind in men
> personal, recurring
> in them again,
> thinking the end
>
> is not the end, the
> time returning,
> themselves dead but
> someone else coming.
>
> (*Words*, 19)

These lines from "The Rhythm," written in 1961, open *Words;* after the first stanza they show Creeley following Whitman and Emerson in tracing the concentric circles of cosmic cycles. But this poem has too much of the generalized credo about it to be characteristic of Creeley at his best. He seldom declares his faith in such centralizing systems; he prefers to uncover systematic order in commonly overlooked corners of experience. This short poem, "Midnight," was written in 1959:

When the rain stops
and the cat drops
out of the tree
to walk

away, when the rain stops,
when the others come home, when
the phone stops,
the drip of water, the

potential of a caller
any Sunday afternoon.

(*For Love,* 111)

Creeley's sense of system is vaguer than Whitman's or Emerson's—less cosmic, more ordinary, more amiable. His images suggest the completion of a number of small processes and activities—the rain, the cat taking shelter in a tree, the expedition of "the others," the phone ringing. These completions reinstate stability—"the drip of water." Yet for Creeley, stability, in the inclusive system of simply observable phenomena, is a context for novelty: "the / potential of a caller / any Sunday afternoon." For as surely as the repetitive, insistently rhymed "when" clauses, after momentarily devolving on the cat's four-line exit, create the expectation of a resolving predicate (which never comes), so the steady drip of water in a quiet house full of its occupants leaves one awaiting disturbance—as though people, weather, and plumbing obeyed a set of laws as abstract and predictable as those of English syntax. Abstractness seems to be exactly Creeley's point. The particular significations of a system are seldom his focus; relations are more binding than referential significance. Specific signification sometimes seems a source of oppression in Creeley's poetry.

Although it is hard to say why Creeley is lured by the idea of a system—hard, that is, to ascribe one cause to his systematic imagination—one can easily locate the first systematic moment in his poetry. And this early poem, "Return," which opens his collection of early poems, suggests that Creeley's systematic bent once expressed a response to the political climate of the midforties:

> Quiet as is proper for such places;
> The street, subdued, half-snow, half-rain,
> Endless, but ending in the darkened doors.
> Inside, they who will be there always,
> Quiet as is proper for such people—
> Enough for now to be here, and
> To know my door is one of these.
>
> (*The Charm,* 3)

Creeley's poems generally seem timeless in a simple sense: when they refer to a context, it is often so personal as to be beyond reach. "Return," however, is an exception. It was written in the winter of 1945–46, when Creeley came back to Harvard after driving an ambulance in the Burma-India front. Thematically, it belongs with poems like Lowell's "Exile's Return" and Wilbur's "Mined Fields"—poems about how to return after the war. Creeley's strategy for return: to discover in domestic Cambridge a systematic order clean of the taint of ideological combat. The people of Cambridge are silently, permanently governed by laws whose simple propriety is reassuring. Creeley will not push the subject too far: the genesis of that domestic order, the relation between domestic and other, larger and smaller, systems of order, the claims and obligations of domestic order—he will not broach these matters.

> Enough for now to be here, and
> To know my door is one of these.

Why that satisfaction? Such self-restraint here means staying on a plane of abstraction where questions of genesis and consequence are not allowed to arise. Creeley has explained that during these postwar years he felt distrustful of analysis:

> I wanted to get out of that awful assumption that thinking is the world. I was thinking how things have shifted, literally,

in my experience of the world from that time of the forties when mind was thought of as the primary agent of having place in the world. I think that came probably from that sense of getting out of the whole nightmare of the Depression by being able to think your way out. And isn't that characteristic of Roosevelt's administration that there enters into American government in political circumstance a sense of expertise— the ability to think your way out of dilemmas; that is, to deal with the national economy by thinking of a way out. I mean, even the Second World War was a mind game. You confront one agency—isn't Hitler, for example, thinking the world is one thing; and then there are those obviously involved thinking it another. (*Contexts of Poetry*, 166)

Like any number of his contemporaries, after the war Creeley wanted to locate his writing beyond ideology.[4] He avoids the iron reference of particular ideologies by turning to the system of manners with the abstract delicacy of an anthropologist's attention. After the spectacle of World War II, he wanted no part of the proud construction of systems of belief; his taste for systematic order would be satisfied by discovering the operation of systems of behavior which make no claim to historical meaning.[5]

Increasingly in the sixties, however, the systems which engaged Creeley were more constructed than discovered by the human mind. On occasion this sense of the mind as a spidery weaver of systems led to anxiety, as in "I Keep to Myself Such Measures," because mental systems, in their abstractness, can deprive one of the world (*Words*, 52). More typically, though, the notion that systems are constructed leads the poetry to playfulness and humility. The play is clear in "Numbers": Creeley meditates on the psychological valences of an arbitrary construct, the decimal system (*Pieces*, 21). He is interested in the way feelings have accrued around a purely formal set of conventions; the feelings have nothing to do with the signification permitted by the system, only with its structure. His humility in this regard is clear in this first section of a meditation on death:

> We'll die
> soon enough,
> and be dead—
>
> whence the whole
> system
> will fade from my head—
>
> "but why the
> tort-
> ure . . ." as if
>
> another circumstance
> were forever
> at hand.
>
> (A Day Book, 70)

Mortality, the loss of consciousness, is referred to austerely as a "circumstance"—as neutral and uneventful as the light around us. Yet mortality lies behind the system Creeley likes to imagine; the mind, under the pressure of its own dissolution, constructs a system as an elaborate way of giving ground before the inevitable:

> We resolve to think of ourselves,
> insofar as one of us can so speak
>
> of the other, as involved with
> a necessary system, of age and its
>
> factors.
>
> (A Day Book, 102)

The "necessary system" is not just biological: by the power of collective resolution people invent other dimensions for the system. Mortality is the mother of necessity, and what are known as manners are finally the "factors" of age. All delicacy follows from the fact of impending death. *A Day Book,* written between

1968 and 1971, expresses a deeper perception of systematic behavior than the earlier volumes did; in this recent book, Creeley elaborates an elegiac perspective on human conventions.

Creeley's sense of style is consistent with his interest in systematic order. I have observed that his manner is characteristically discursive; his poems commonly begin with a definition or a proposition and then proceed to qualify and illustrate that proposition. (In addition to "The Business," quoted above, some distinguished examples of this type of poem are: "The Immoral Proposition" [*For Love,* 31], "Air: 'The Love of a Woman'" [*For Love,* 142], and "On Vacation" [*A Day Book,* 112].) This is not to say that his poems are exactly verse-essays, but rather that, like Williams, Creeley intends his poems to display "all the complexity of a way of thinking" (*Contexts of Poetry,* 16). Creeley's many attempts to disclaim a discursive motive (*A Quick Graph,* 54, 57, 72, 207; *Contexts of Poetry,* 91, 127) or to assign that motive to the distant past (*The Charm,* xi) should not go ignored—especially since, in verse, he has wittily undone the discursive ambition:

> Do you know what
> the truth is,
> what's rightly
> or wrongly said,
>
> what is wiseness,
> or rightness, what
> wrong, or well-
> done if it is,
>
> or is not, done.
> I thought.
> I thought and
> thought and thought.
>
> In a place
> I was sitting,
> and there
> it was, a little

```
                    faint thing
                    hardly felt, a
                    kind of small
                    nothing.
                                              (Words, 87)
```

Those last five lines show how small his esteem of the Big
Questions addressed by poets with systems, poets such as
Olson, Duncan, and Ginsberg. Yet, as I have shown, Creeley
often tries to relate his poems to a general system. "Had I lived
some years ago, I think I would have been a moralist, i.e., one
who lays down, so to speak, rules of behavior with no small
amount of self-satisfaction" (A Quick Graph, 3).

On the level of style, one can speak of Creeley as a systemic
poet with less qualification. In 1951 he wrote "Le Fou," a gentle
parody of the Olson manner:

```
       who plots, then, the lines
       talking, taking, always the beat from
       the breath
                   (moving slowly at first
       the breath
                   which is slow—

       I mean, graces come slowly,
       it is that way.

       So slowly (they are waving
       We are moving
                       away from        (the trees
                           the usual        (go by
       which is slower than this, is
                           (we are moving!
       goodbye
                                              (For Love, 17)
```

The style here is grammatical in that it advances by reference to
antecedent phrases and clauses. Both Olson and Creeley make
their poems move with constant reference to the rules governing

English usage; their styles are systemic in the sense that by underlining the grammatical grid behind the clauses and by favoring the small systemic, nonspecific words—such as prepositions, conjunctions, and pronouns—these poets declare at nearly every turn that poems are generated as much by the systemic properties of language as by individual temperaments. This poem opens with a subordinate clause so that its first words refer back to a preceding term (the title, "Le Fou," or the dedication, "for Charles") which can preside over this syntax. The many pauses punctuating the poem mark off the boundaries of grammatical units, phrases and clauses—the terms of the system of utterance. There are a number of ways in which the poem is made to seem a web of internal relationships: each of the nine pronouns in these fifteen lines dispatches attention to the rear, as though words were generated by antecedent words or statements. And they are: in the second line, "taking" clearly issues from a phonological resemblance to the preceding word, "talking"; likewise, the tenth line—"we are moving"—is born out of the syntactic analogue ending the ninth line—"they are waving." Still more obviously, out of one word in the fourth line, "slowly," come at least the following five lines; that single word keeps bobbing up, apparently compelling the poet to the brink of inarticulateness: "I mean, graces come slowly, / it is that way." Yet, of course, this is not fully Creeley's style; it is, as the title suggests, more an acute but playful parody of Olson's.

Creeley knows, though, that his own style too leans on the systemic symmetries of language. In 1957 he placed this poem, "A Song," on the page facing "Le Fou" in *The Whip:*

> I had wanted a quiet testament
> and I had wanted, among other things,
> a song.
> > That was to be
> of a like monotony.
> > > (A grace
>
> Simply. Very very quiet.
> > > A murmur of some lost
> thrush, though I have never seen one.

Which was you then. Sitting
and so, at peace, so very much now this same quiet.

A song.

And of you the sign now, surely, of a gross
perpetuity
          (which is not reluctant, or if it is,
it is no longer important.

A song.

Which one sings, if he sings it,
with care.

(For Love, 18)

Like Olson, Creeley uses simple repetition ("I had wanted . . . /
and I had wanted") and subordinate clauses branching out of
pronouns ("Which was you then"; "which is not reluctant";
"Which one sings") to keep the poem going. But his tone is so
different from Olson's that the comparison will not hold for
long. This poem seems at several points (lines 9–10, 12–13, 17–
18) about to conclude or expire when it draws another shallow
breath; its small fitful movements are part of Creeley's design.
For the poem should seem to have been written almost inadver-
tently: his reluctance to write the "quiet testament" for his first
wife is overcome or forgotten ("it is no longer important") in
the course of talking about the poem he once wanted to write.
This fiction about the poem's genesis depends upon a literary
convention which Olson never invoked: that of sincerity—the
convention to end conventions—which Creeley understands,
after Pound's Confucius, as "*Man standing by his word*" (*Contexts
of Poetry,* 188). That steadfastness, Creeley claims, may gain "a
political term of responsibility" (*Contexts of Poetry,* 83). In a time
when political immoralities are conducted by means of linguistic
contortion, the sincere use of language may imply a political
challenge to step free of the predictable deceptions of ideology
(83–84).
    Creeley's use of the literary convention of sincerity is tricky,

213

though. His claims to sincerity are convincing enough to allow him outrageous liberties: here, not just the artlessness of simple repetition, but also the use of three "very"s—two of them back-to-back—in the course of nineteen lines. But the first words indicate a counter-pressure: "I had wanted. . . ." The past perfect tense stands for a characteristic distance. Though regularly claiming sincerity, Creeley customarily tries to indicate some measure of alienation from his own avowals. Those throwaway clauses—"among other things"; "though I have never seen one"; "or if it is, / it is no longer important"—cool down the tone, as though the poem commanded no more than the surface of Creeley's attention. He often looks back on his creations with a measure of disgust: "the sign now, surely, of a gross / perpetuity." Similarly, his diction is seldom so homogeneous that it might, in some context, be spoken of as "natural." The polysyllables, "testament," "monotony," "perpetuity," glare out of the page as though they might, amongst so many "low" words, require footnotes to the dictionary. Speech, for Creeley, is an idea more than a method.

His method is, rather, to set at odds a personal subject matter and an abstract, generalized manner of treatment: that tension represents Creeley's attempt at impersonality. (For an example of this method, see "In an Act of Pity" [*The Charm,* 43].) This abstract manner is the stylistic expression of Creeley's systematic imagination; it offers the discipline of distance from the emotions behind the poem. "The Operation," written in 1953, shows Creeley's suspicion of this technique of tension:

> By Saturday I said you would be better on Sunday.
> The insistence was a part of a reconciliation.
>
> Your eyes bulged, the grey
> light hung on you, you were hideous.
>
> My involvement is just an old
> habitual relationship.
>
> Cruel, cruel to describe
> what there is no reason to describe.
>
> (*For Love,* 34)

The occasion of the poem is apparently Creeley's seeing his first wife immediately after surgery (this moment is narrated in *The Island*). Creeley submits the anxiety of the occasion to the defusing cool of his impersonal diction: "The insistence was a part of a reconciliation." That, evidently, is Creeley's mannered way of saying that his desire to patch up differences with his wife made him express the hope for her recovery. He himself cannot swallow the antiseptic impersonality of this contrived manner. In the last two lines, he reproaches himself for the abstract meanness of the poem, and especially of the preceding couplet. Sincerity, then, recovers control of the poem in time to dash it to a close: self-exposure is filtered through the screen of an impersonal style. Creeley acknowledges, in these final lines, that this abstract style deals with other people no more civilly than a predator does. Yet he never dismisses the impersonal manner completely, for

> In the narcotic and act
> of omniscience
>
> a gain, of the formal,
> is possible.
>
> *(The Charm, 56)*

That gain will always lure Creeley, whose poetry hovers near the brink of inarticulateness; without the sometimes histrionic "act" of omniscience, some of his poems would not achieve form of any kind.

Creeley's poetry, then, is intimate and disembodied at the same time, like a late-night phone call. He moves back and forth between the convention of sincerity and the discipline of systematic abstraction. His work can be underestimated if either term of this relationship between sincerity and systematic abstractness is taken as the last word. In recent years, Creeley has tended to move away from his discursive mode; the didactic form which has come to interest him, beginning with *Pieces* (1969), is the epigram. He has written some short poems which seem, in isolation, naively sincere; but fairness to Creeley demands that they not be taken in isolation. Behind even so slight a poem as "One Day"—

One day after another—
perfect.
They all fit.

(*Thirty Things*, 67)

—lie more than twenty years of pressing the pieces of experience for systematic meaning. Creeley is a minimalist only in the sense that he needs little to work with. The ends of his art are as far-reaching as those of his friends Olson, Duncan, and Ginsberg. Like them, he has his own way—abstract, unspecific, yet empirical—of responding to political history, and he too, sometimes just by his style, urges understanding of a "larger view"; he allows for no isolated detail.

It
all drops into
place.

(*Words*, 38)

NOTES

1. See also *Contexts of Poetry*, edited by Donald Allen (Bolinas, Calif.: Four Seasons Foundation, 1973), 40, 74.

2. The distinction I am making between a *systematic poet* such as Creeley, and *poets with systems* such as Olson, Duncan and Ginsberg, resembles a distinction discussed by Ernst Cassirer between the Enlightenment *esprit systématique* and the seventeenth-century *esprit de système* (*The Philosophy of the Enlightenment*, trans. Fritz C. A. Koelln and James P. Pettegrove [Princeton: Princeton University Press, 1951], 8).

3. James Merrill, *Nights and Days* (New York: Atheneum, 1966), 46.

4. This desire later allowed Creeley remarkable optimism concerning the "counterculture" apoliticism of the late sixties; see *Contexts of Poetry*, 181–82.

5. For Creeley's remark to Robert Duncan that he is not interested in history, see *Contexts of Poetry*, 156.

GEORGE F. BUTTERICK

Robert Creeley and the Tradition

Praise a good education, or a man careful enough to obtain one. What struck me repeatedly while editing Robert Creeley's extensive correspondence with Charles Olson was how well grounded Creeley was in the inherited literary tradition, not only in his letters, with their constant references to Stendhal, Dostoyevski, Gide, Unamuno, etc., but also in his verse from the late 1940s and early 1950s. I was also reminded how useful he found the tradition at critical moments throughout his early career (that summarized by the collections *For Love* and *The Charm*) as he sought to develop his individual voice. What might be explored, then, are some of the uses Creeley made of the tradition—and not only the regularly acknowledged influence of Pound and Williams, Campion and Charlie Parker. Generally, what is the role of the tradition in his writings and in his efforts to achieve a satisfactory poetics? How does he participate in the inherited tradition and incorporate it, formally, into his poems? A series of close readings may make this clear. Specifically, it might be of interest to explore how several of Creeley's poems owe their success to a purposeful variation of traditional beginnings, and how even in his most personal lyrics he might introduce other men's words, mostly in an effort to find an alternative to the dominant and oppressive forms of the day. In this, he and Olson were partners in restlessness.

Creeley's earliest poems reveal the struggle toward form. Several will serve as examples, although the fact that the poet left them out of *For Love* indicates he was aware of their limita-

From *Sagetrieb* 1, no. 3 (Winter 1982): 119–34. Reprinted with permission of the author and the National Poetry Foundation, University of Maine, Orono, Maine.

tions. The syllogistic wisdom of a poem like "Sanine to Leda" (*The Charm,* 9), written in 1948, is in progression of content not very different from such later poems as "The Immoral Proposition," except in spacing. (First it must be made clear that the classical allusion of the title is misleading, an editor's error in the poem's original appearance in the Harvard *Wake*.[1] It is not an allusion to the queen of Sparta, in the fashion of Yeats, but introduces an address to the "Lida" [Lidia Petrovna] of Mikhail Artsybashev's novel, *Sanine*. Lida's brother Sanine is speaking— in tones far different from those that might be addressed to the ancient beauty, in potential competition with the great Swan himself.) Creeley's poem begins:

> Beyond this road the blackness bends
> in warmth. Two, then three or four,
> lovers with wisdom for themselves
> enough are sitting there in vague,
> unbending poses. They sit.
> The quiet grass holds roses. . . .

There is a jammed quality to the lines; "enough" of line 4 is misplaced, the principle obeyed seems to be mere visual symmetry. The lines cling somewhat desperately to the margin as if it was a subway pole. The metric is neither speech nor strict regularity, and as music it falls flat in spots like an old hotel ballroom's wooden floor. The poet has neither a grip over traditional forms, nor the desire to make them work; otherwise "roses" in line 8 and "poses" in line 10 (themselves wonderful eye rhymes with "loses" and "chooses" in the final line to come) would have been end rhymes in a more intricately rigid scheme. The poem does work, however—not as music overall, but in the rhyme at the end. "Look. / Each loses what he chooses" is no different from conclusions such as "Laughter releases rancor, the quality of mercy is not / strained" ("The Crisis"—and itself a clever use of a familiar allusion), "No man shall be an idiot for purely exterior reasons" ("The Rites"), "There is no more giving in / when there is no more sin" ("The Kind of Act Of"), "Sickness is the hatred of a repentance / knowing there is nothing he wants" ("The Crow"), or "The unsure / egoist is not / good for himself" ("The Immoral Proposition")—each poem titled by "The." The endings are assertions; the poems, no matter how lyric, are logical constructs. Poetry is definition.

Much of Creeley's earliest verse is poetry aching toward definition. Preoccupation with form continues in "Still Life Or," collected on p. 19 of *The Charm*. Originally written in November, 1949 (a copy sent to Leed, November 14, 1949), and like "Sanine to Leda" published in *Wake,* it was sent to Olson on June 1 the next year, in its same original, unrevised state—four regular stanzas of 5–4–6–5, mostly six-syllable lines each, visually tight and symmetrical. It was revised by Creeley, however, for *Le Fou,* his first collection, in accordance with his understanding of poetics as they had begun to emerge from the discussion with Olson underway.[2] The significant thing is that at this stage of Creeley's development, only the line arrangements are changed in the revision. Every one of the original words remains the same (except for the substitution of an ampersand for the word "and" in line 9), indicating that in this early experiment in projectivism, at least, the form was rearranged *post facto.* The new version represents perhaps an effort to gain back the original, heard rhythms of the lines, but at the same time, strictly speaking, such a revision violates the basic tenet and purity of projective verse, that the issuance be direct, that the poet "can go by no track other than the one the poem under hand declares, for itself,"[3] that there be no intervention by craft or reason. Creeley has not yet begun to rhythmically *think* with his poems.

Creeley again shows his impatience with inherited form in a two-part poem from late 1949 titled "Notes on Poetry," directly influenced by his reading of Wallace Stevens. The second part, a variation on Stevens's "Anecdote of the Jar," is of interest for reasons similar to "Still Life Or." The section appears, revised, as the initial part of "Divisions" in Vincent Ferrini's *Four Winds* in the summer of 1952 (*The Charm,* 33). Like the previous "Still Life," the lines of the original version are patterned in stiff, indeed self-conscious, symmetry:

> Order. Order. The bottle contains
> more than water. It is surrounded.
> In this case the form is imposed.

As if the air did not hold me in,
and not let me burst, from what-
have-you, or inveterate goodwill!

To make it difficult, to make a
sense of limit, to call a stop to
meandering, one could wander here

in intricacies, unbelted, somewhat
sloppy. But the questions are,
is it all there or on some one

evening will I come again here,
most desperate and all questions,
to find the water all leaked out.[4]

In the revised, "opened" version, the stanzas remain the same, a
few words are omitted, but mostly the lines are rearranged to
follow the rise and fall of speech:

Order. Order. The bottle contains
more than water. In this case the form
is imposed.

As if the air did not hold me in
and not let me burst from what-have-you or inveterate
goodwill!

To make it difficult, to make a sense
of limit, to call a stop to meandering—
one could wander here . . .

A careful comparison of the two versions (not fully possible
here) will reveal what was gained by the revision, and, perhaps,
some of the characteristics of projective or open verse as under-
stood by Creeley at this time, along with its differences from the
formalistic "closed" verse leading up to it. For example, "form"
(line 2 of the revised version), being the actual subject of the
poem, is emphasized, suspended for our attentions to seize. In

the next stanza, there is a similar pause at the end of the second line—for a sneer—as "goodwill!" is spit out. In the third stanza, the same rhythm: "sense" is suspended; the line is broken where the word would have been italicized—i.e., stressed—in speech. The lines in this version advance by phrasing (in the musical sense as well), they are not bound in a bundle, like fasces (the fascism of form, one might say heavily). This is, thus, a preliminary stage before Creeley entrusts himself to the newly emerging projectivism and the rhythms of indigenous speech.

"Hart Crane" and "Le Fou," written in June and July of 1950 respectively, while he was deep in correspondence with Olson, are readily recognized as Creeley's breakthrough poems. "Hart Crane," properly selected to lead off *For Love* (15–16), was originally in five parts and, more surprisingly, titled "Otto Rank & Others" (though still dedicated to Crane's old friend, and later Creeley's, Slater Brown).[5] The final version is a weaving of thinking-out-loud (pushing with the head) and remembered comments by Brown about Crane in a discontinuous narrative, a conversation between Creeley, Brown, and the reader, alternately. Its original ending was less effective, more hurried:

> *And so it was I entered the broken world*
> Hart Crane Hart

—which becomes more deftly choreographed in the final version:

> Hart Crane.
> *Hart*

(without final punctuation, so that the name—and possibly its homonym "heart"—reverberates on and on). All of Crane's verse and presence is summoned into that penultimate (in the original version), italicized line—taken from Crane's "The Broken Tower"—in preparation for the end when Creeley's poem lifts from its ground in a self-sustained, all-encompassing mixture of cry and statement of fact: "*Hart.*" A single word, a simple awe. "Le Fou," in its turn, with its subject of "breath" and movement (a train or car—metaphoric of poem—taking off), is a direct embodiment or poetic equivalent of "Projective Verse," at least the first part of that essay (not necessarily the second, where Olson calls for a new heroism). "A Song" (*For Love,* 18) follows in November, and Creeley is well on his way. In most general terms, his tradition is the familiar enough one, the measure of speech. He writes forcefully to Olson, May 19, 1952: "Well, I came up from the bottom, rock of sorts, and fell, now, I am *not* going to toss out the one thing I got from it: speech. No man is going to get me to let that go. I heard everything, as a kid, and felt, then, shy & unfamiliar—often started by any words too hard, or couldn't find those flip answers my friends could, etc. In fact, my friends: one was in prison the last time I heard, another working in some garage in Acton, the rest I don't know. But speech, I heard the craziest, shouted, or whatever—the deepest, most permanent contempt for any 'written' word any man ever wrote."

What is of interest henceforth is that Creeley, in this advanced drive, returns to the larger literary tradition for periodical reactivation and refreshment. He always was a very competent mimic, with a good ear for the old forms. See, for example, "Song: 'Rough Winds Doe Shake . . .'" (*Olson & Creeley* 1:75–76) beginning with an echo of Shakespeare but blasting beyond, or the more sustained "Doggerel for O" (*Olson & Creeley* 1:131–34). Part of the impulse is the natural exuberance any poet finds in language, in any form he can get it. Creeley sent Leed a "Ballad of the Goodly Fader," signed "John Drippings" with an address of "Ham-On-Rye / Echolalia, Ill." and itself a parody of a parody, opening:

> Yez IS ole, fader William,
> the yng man sd,
> & yr balls hang down to yr knee.
> Can yez possibly tell
> how you can do well
> with yng ladies, if yez cant PEE?

He also sent Leed a very skilled imitation in fifteen octosyllabic quatrains called "To Robert, That He Maketh Much," beginning:

When to his lady oft he slips
and with much musick gaily trips,
methinks, he's moved by none but whips:
or, so it seems, from sorrow. . . .

and ending:

So to make much of, to enjoy
all that is fine, our wits employ
and let it be all joy, all joy,
which all from us shall borrow.[6]

Schoolboy ventriloquism, no doubt, but the point is he prac-
ticed it, took pleasure in it, was capable of it (Frank O'Hara in
his early poems similarly). He embraced a rhythmical and musi-
cal tradition, not just a semiotic one.

This deliberate, allusive playfulness is different from some of
Creeley's earlier incorporations of other men's lines into his
own. Borrowings are seen most notably in "Hart Crane," al-
ready pointed out, or in "Love" (*The Charm,* 27), written in
June, 1951, where a line from William Carlos Williams's own
"Love Song"—"*The stain of love is upon the world!*"—is included
with such self-consciousness that Creeley finds himself using the
occasion to force an end upon his poem, saying—after present-
ing the line in italics—"Which I have not written." As a result,
"Love" becomes a statement of admission. He is not able to be
so conclusive; the subject is as complex as ever; he is still learn-
ing how to write about it from an immediate master. There is
also "Hélas" (*The Charm,* 20), which directly absorbs a passage
from Olson's "La Torre" (in lines 4–5) as well as a passage from
Williams's "The Wind Increases" (lines 13 ff.), as Creeley seeks
out a language of his own.

Documentation continues with "From Pico & the Women: A
Life" (*The Charm,* 14–15)—reduced from an original five-part
poem titled "Pico & The Women: A Life" (thus the "From" in
the final title)—which opens with a passage from Pico della
Mirandola as it appears in Pater, unidentified in the poem other
than by italics: "*Love God, we rather may, than / either know Him,
or by speech / utter him . . .*" (see *Olson & Creeley* 1:41 and 4:70).

It is an example of how another's language is useful to explore not only for meaning, but, more importantly in the present instance, can provide the rhythmic start of the poet's own word-flow. It is classic "variation on a theme": language begetting language. Directly relevant is what Creeley tells Olson, April 8, 1953: "I have felt that if, say, in any poem I can manage the rhythms of one line, and feel their necessity, actually, then I have made the way altogether for all the lines subsequent." This is exactly what happens in the case of "From Pico" as well as, as will be seen subsequently, "The Bed" and "Just Friends." The same realization holds true many years later, when Creeley writes in "Notes Apropos 'Free Verse'" from 1966 (*A Quick Graph,* 58–59): "For my own part I feel a rhythmic possibility, an inherent periodicity in the weights and durations of words, to occur in the first few words, or first lines, or lines, of what it is I am writing." When the initial words are someone else's rhythm, Creeley, any poet, is off and running, at liberty to respect or rebuff the borrowed measure as the need arises and content demands.

More rarely does Creeley invoke the tradition like Pound or Olson, to support an argument or illustrate his method, although "Air: 'Catbird Singing'" (*For Love,* 69) does just that. It is a summation of poetics as much as a personal lyric. That the poem is in a tradition of such "airs" is made clear by the introduction of a line from Campion—"follow thy fair sunne unhappie shadow"—which serves to illustrate the melody (defined in another letter to Olson, April 3, 1953, as "sound in progress"). It thus stands as Creeley's defense of the brief lyric form, which had become by that point in his career his chief mode and which he was unduly self-conscious about, just as Campion defended his "short and well seasoned" airs against those who "will admit no music but that which is long, intricate, bated with fugue, chained with syncopation, and where the nature of every word is precisely expressed in the note—like the old exploded action in comedies, when if they did pronounce *memini,* they would point to the hinder part of their heads; if *video,* put their finger in their eye." Reading either writer's "airs" today will assure a reader no defense was ever needed.

Creeley understood why someone like Lawrence might reject

traditional lyricism, but for himself, with more ironic sharpness and a greater speed in the poetic line than Lawrence, as well as greater historical distance from Romantic attitudes (Pound, Eliot, Williams, Stevens, and other masters of modernism having intervened), he could feel free to use the traditional lyric as he saw fit. Also, in a growing disillusionment with marriage and romantic love, the lyric would have to be confronted for even more personal reasons. In musing on poetry in a letter to Olson, March 29, 1952, and specifically on the traditional English ballads, Creeley writes: "I don't recall any mention or much emphasis on, the English lyric (pre-Elizabethan) or that form" in Lawrence's writings, continuing, "My own thought, that the lyric, there, was too much the cover of a ground he was himself attacking . . . I.e., the sexual, the blood finally, is what he wanted to extend to." Lawrence, he finds, is "the most forward, here; of all those I know, the only to go onto this ground, clearly, as against, for one, Melville's PIERRE, and that failure. Lawrence was *on* it, the sexual, was standing exactly on that ground. Hence," Creeley concludes, "my own mentor, finally the only one I can have." He would, however, take the lyric on tighter turns than Lawrence was capable of, made possible by the spontaneities of speech and American jazz.

In that same letter to Olson, Creeley reports being struck while reading Pound's introduction to the *Analects* of Confucius by the statement, "It is an error to seek aphorisms and bright sayings in sentences which should be considered rather as definitions of words." He comments: "Not that it's new, but the recall, to that emphasis, was very damn helpful. As of poetry, to constitute definition. It is a damn exciting biz. Or is to me, that by these uses, one can define the word itself, exact." This may help to account for the many Creeley poems beginning with the article "the." The title is a focusing device; the poem is its definition. It is not, broadly, *a* (for *any*) wicker basket, it is "*The* Wicker Basket," particular to Creeley and already charged with a drama that the poem will make manifest. The article immediately and conveniently concretizes the abstract: "The Crisis," "The Riddle," "The Rites," "The Rhyme," "The Innocence"—almost half the 133 poems in *For Love* are so titled.

In his quest to define by poetry, juxtaposition of relatively abstract statements without subjective intervention becomes Creeley's principal technique. His important January 7, 1953, letter to Olson discussing the poem "The Kind of Act of" (*For Love*, 28), suggests the title is to be read as running on into the first line: "The kind of act of / Giving oneself to the dentist or doctor. . . ." The poem, then, is a definition of a particular kind of act, the twin desires of the mind to both give of itself and to possess:

> to take the complete
> possession of mind, there is no
>
> giving. The mind
> beside the act of any dispossession is
>
> lecherous. There is no more giving in
> when there is no more sin.

All turns on the paradox of "taking" and "giving," and specifically on the repeated "giving," with the addition of "in" (line 6) adding a new connotation to the word's previous plain appearance. Creeley's comments to Olson in the letter make clear he is very aware of the flat "statement" aspect of the poem and the fact that it seeks its success through juxtaposition or what he calls "conjecture," possibly with the word's root meaning of "throw together" more actively intended than the usual meanings "inference" or "guess." It is a useful understanding, in that sense (and, oddly, a less than common term in critical discussions of this basic compositional technique—more familiar as collage, stream of consciousness, association of ideas, etc.), because of its connotations of speculation, imaginative exploration, and even the vague hint of "conjure." "Conjecture" is Creeley's favorite theoretical word at this time, his parallel to Olson's "projective." He is aware there is no necessary logical relation between or among his poem's lines, that they represent an assertion, a leap beyond inference. (Assertion itself thus may be a significant aspect of the act of definition.) Maintaining the proper balance between inference and assertion creates the most desirable balance of tension in these early poems. As Creeley says, "I wanted the *fastest* juxtaposition possible, and the *least* explanatory manner."[7]

Several more examples of Creeley's use of the tradition might be examined. Also in *For Love* is the ballad "The Three Ladies" (61), which begins with an echo of the old English (or Scots) ballad, "The Three Ravens," that Creeley may very well have come upon in *The Viking Book of Poetry of the English-Speaking World,* edited by Richard Aldington (New York, 1941), where, p. 39, it begins: "There were three ravens sat on a tree, / They were as black as they might be."[8] Creeley starts his ballad with heavy rhyming—

> I dreamt. I saw three ladies in a tree,
> and the one that I saw most clearly
> showed her favors unto me,
> and I saw up her leg above the knee!

—although the rhyme disperses as the poem progresses. The initial line is masterfully broken up by the period—a brilliant sense of rhythm, since the elision occurs anyway in the reader's mind. A spirit of independence over the form is gained. Creeley's rhyme, despite its forceful beginning, is inconsistent; or rather, he feels no need to maintain the heavy consistency of end rhyme that characterizes the first stanza. Instead, he rhymes where sound is accessible—enough for a sophisticated modern ear, which may hear regular rhyme as too great a thump, too monotonously obvious. Rather, the rhyme scheme fluctuates, occurring wherever the poet wants to strike a harmony and refresh the ear, end or mid line. There are rhymes within a line such as "dead in his head" (line 15), but also near rhymes of "complacent, expectant," and, in the penultimate stanza especially, the perfect crowd of rhyme—"night! Light shows . . . nobody knows," etc.—a carnival of sound. As the dream extends, sound and meter tumble in splendid disarray, to be brought up newly regrouped by the concluding couplet, *"Oh one, two, three! Oh one, two three! / Three old ladies sat in a tree."* The count resumes; the refrain rounds out the poem (a traditional enough device for Creeley—cf. "Chanson" and "If You"), although incrementally, with change: the ladies are now

227

"old." It is an italicized, choric, awakened voice: along with reality, anti-Romanticism triumphs.

"The Three Ladies" is only five quatrains (plus concluding couplet) long. More sustained—though it too is interrupted by a fresh voice and final irony—is the popular "Ballad of the Despairing Husband" (*For Love*, 76–77), a parody of courtly tradition, for the most part. Generically, it has everything Helen Adam might approve of: hearty octosyllabic iambics, rollicking content, all the pointed exaggeration of a sirvente, although Creeley, in some comments, quickly reminds us the last lines can also be "whiningly sincere." In responding to Cynthia Edelberg's questions, he cites the basic autobiographical element to the poem, indicating that in addition to it being in the spirit of Paul Blackburn's Provençal translations, he had actually hoped that his wife—from whom he was separated and to whom the poem was addressed—would appreciate the petition of the ballad, especially its last stanzas: "I hoped that she still had some virtues of a sense of humor. At that point, hopefully, [the poem] turns into fun. And the last lines of the poem are obviously whiningly sincere."[9] In any case, the beat is infectious, the way that sounds of a polka at a party light up faces. Rhythmically, it is the most primal kind of poetry, prior to all our introversions.

But it is the more sober and deliberate adjustment of tradition that marks Creeley's accomplishment: not simple irony or parody, but a dexterous mastery of all effects, as the occasions arise. It is speed that enhances his early work, range (to the point of obliquity) and flexibility of craft—even to the extent that craft gives way in the face of honesty or other urgencies (as in "The Three Ladies"). Most of all, it is the acceptance of discovery, even if that should scare the poem off its tracks or, in his later writings, obsessively reduce the poem to its most minimal relations and language itself to an exploration of its own congruities.

"Chasing the Bird" (*The Charm*, 59), written in June, 1953, is an example of how Creeley makes use of the traditional to twist a poem closed. The title is that of a Charlie Parker tune, in which by implication the rest of the band (Miles Davis on trumpet, Bud Powell on piano, Tommy Potter on bass, and Max Roach on drums, in the most popular recording) scampers to keep up with the high-flying Parker, whose solos draw the group on.

(Though, of course, it could simply be the record that Creeley has on in the background—or in mind—at the time.)[10] The tune is not a frivolous piece, nor is it one of Parker's most light-hearted; it is a very competent and deliberate excursion, a tight display of controlled virtuosity. The descriptions with which the poem opens are themselves flatly competent:

> The sun sets unevenly and the people
> go to bed.
>
> The night has a thousand eyes.
> The clouds are low, overhead.

There is nothing ironic about the images, nor are they imbued with any aura other than what they state, although "The night has a thousand eyes" tends toward romanticism, perhaps testing those limits, perhaps even intentionally misleading, since the poem continues:

> Every night it is a little bit
> more difficult, a little
>
> harder. My mind
> to me a mangle is.

In retrospect, the "eyes" become—if pushed that far—para-noiac, insomniac. The seriousness of the poem's intent is seen in the gentle but deliberate rhyming of "bed" and "overhead," followed by a rejection of all rhyme (in keeping with the poem's sense of a mind disordered, at sixes and sevens). The rhyme (given weight by the preceding comma in line 4) threatens a certain inevitability, a trap of regularity, like the pattern of lives invoked. The people who go to bed with the sun are as stolid and predictable as the subject-predicate order of the first four statements (lines 1–7) and, almost, that of the fifth (begun in line 7)—until the surprising and comic inversion of the last line subverts all prior orderliness. The outcome is not fully prepared for, either rhythmically or in terms of meaning—as was Parker's wont as well. Thus, again, the title.

229

The repetition that follows the descriptions of the opening four lines—"a little bit / more difficult, a little / harder" (including the assonance of *i*'s)—is part of the progressive negativism of the poem. At the same time it prepares for the concluding statement that summarizes and subjectively encloses the presented world. The poem ends as its title began, with an allusion. The final sentence is split, purposely, over two lines, to save the surprise: "My mind / to me a mangle is." (Creeley, of course, intends "mangle" in the somewhat neologistic sense of "mess" or "botch," nominalizing the familiar verb, rather than the sole dictionary definition of the noun, a machine for pressing cloth.) The alliteration, even the word order, is comic, perhaps seriocomic, as are the perfectly regular iambs. But just as important, the ending is actually an echo—and reversal—of Sir Edward Dyer's late sixteenth-century "My Mind to Me a Kingdom Is," beginning:

> My mind to me a kingdom is;
>> Such present joys therein I find,
> That it excels all other bliss
>> That earth affords or grows by kind:
> Though much I want which most would have
> Yet still my mind forbids to crave.

It probably caught Creeley's eye as he leafed through Aldington's large and convenient anthology, which he had with him in Europe at the time, enabling him to have a useful survey of the tradition at hand.

"Chasing the Bird" is a confessional poem, in which revelation is withheld until the end, with its head-shaking display of self-knowledge. The final statement is not so much a comment on previous observations or an attempt to draw truth from description (the opening lines) as it is a release or sigh of admission, with the dark but evident wit (including the sophisticated literary echo of Dyer) and self-mocking syntax to save it from wallowing. The conscious reference of the title and the ending, together with the dignified progression of opening statements, indicate the poem is more controlled and self-critical than self-pitying. The concluding statement in which "mangle" is substituted for "kingdom" may be less an allusion to Dyer and his world of self-confidence—which Creeley may have found ultimately smug—than it is a parody of such sentiment. A new tradition of wry defiance (embodied by Charlie Parker) is superimposed on the old Elizabethan optimism. The anguish and relativism of existentialism has been substituted for the autocracy of faith.

It was a difficult time in Creeley's personal life; old attitudes toward love and traditional lyricism appear shaken. Both "The Bed" and "Just Friends," published side by side in *For Love* though written almost three years apart, are poems of utter bitterness and disillusion. "Just Friends" (*For Love,* 67) from the summer of 1956[11]—with its possible irony and any reference to a particular personal relationship notwithstanding—is probably named after the popular song of that title, which Charlie Parker had recorded (with strings) for producer-impresario Norman Granz. The poem, like the song, is a mood piece. It begins structurally the same as "The Bed," as will be seen, with a distorted classic line: "Out of the table endlessly rocking. . . ." The Whitman echo kicks the poem off, mocking the familiar classic, mocking, indeed, the vulnerability of Whitman's own title (the way Parker may have derided the strings with his solos). "Just Friends" does not profess the sweep and profundity, the full orchestra, of Whitman's poem of passage and initiation. Instead, it invokes such a poem of large mood to belittle not so much that earlier poem but rather its own mood and the speaker's own predicament.

The image the poem ends with is, at its most maudlin, one of bleary self-pity: "Everything is water / if you look long enough." It is possibly a weighty ontological or cosmological statement, although not meant to be a reiteration of Thales, for whom water was the substance of which everything is made and consists. The "wisdom" of such a statement is potential at best, and self-serving no matter how accurate, though it may be as profound as it is clever. It seeks to do several things: it certainly is heavy enough to close the poem firmly, i.e., the reader has enough to think about. It is conceivably, metaphysically true, and thus faces the perennial question of appearance versus reality, which can never be exhausted and can be ignored only at peril. It is meant to be provocative in all its simplicity. Upon each successive reading, meaning ripples—from the negative, to the symbolic, to the trivial, to the merely clever, to the cynical, to the Job-ish, to disillusionment or disappointment, to the literally, physiologically true. The basic question is, is the statement metaphoric or not? Very much like the surface of water itself, it reflects whatever light the reader brings or cares to bring to it, in whatever mood.

"The Bed" (although it appears before "Just Friends" on p. 66 of *For Love*) was written April 24, 1959 (Novik, 88). It is launched with a parody of another classic—Byron's famous exaltation of woman's perfection, "She walks in Beauty, like the night . . ." (whose concluding lines may have particularly rankled Creeley—"A mind at peace with all below, / A heart whose love is innocent!"). Such an opening simultaneously rouses attention and satirizes the Romantic vision of woman. (And if any reader has forgotten that it is "the night" not "a lake" that Byron's raven-tressed beauty is compared to, Creeley's next rhyme of "knife" with "wife" might be the aural encouragement, a nudge toward remembrance.) In this case it is Byron, just as previously it had been Whitman, but it could have been any familiar or too-familiar line deconstructed to set the mood and provide the rhythm, like the words from Pico della Mirandola in "From Pico." Such a practice automatically gets the words flowing at a pace, a usable measure, at the same time as the parodic twist quickens the wit. A most convenient device.

Meanwhile, Byron's octosyllabic line is broken after the initial parody into a basically four-syllable line (though there is also one line of six syllables and one long pentametric line, the most intricate and evasive in the poem, that teeters before allowing the final ending). The strict rhyming of the opening *aabb* quatrain immediately gives way to a delightfully unpredictable but completely appropriate play of rhyme, very much as the opening statement of the bop tune gives way to the improvisation of the various solos. Creeley will space and time his rhymes as Parker did his riffs and phrases. It is the same procedure that he had followed in "The Three Ladies," the breaking up of the too heavily patterned rhyme scheme to allow room for a more authentic voice. Rhyme thus placed in no way slows the poem, and even, in this instance, helps resolve the ambiguities of the final stanza.

The thrust of the final stanza depends on to whom the "decry" is addressed. Is "oh god" (line 9) an actual invocation (like Creeley writes in "For the New Year," "Oh God, send me an omen . . ."), or exclamation of despair or dismay, or is the speaker addressing himself, ironically? And is not "common finery" itself nearly oxymoronic? To "put the need / before the bed" sounds apothegmatic, nevertheless ambiguous. What does it mean? Cultivate desire before one has the means to satisfy it? Or is it an encouragement to seek satisfaction directly? Is it a petition, one placed before she-who-awaits in the metonymic bed? And how does the rhyme help resolve ambiguity? Does the final "indeed" make "the need" two lines earlier forever more essential than even beds and like quotidian utensils of domestic love? Or is it the bed that is essential "indeed," in deed? At least we know that the Byronic, the falsely Romantic attitude has been undercut. The "lie" lies in the marriage, evidently. But is to "make true" a "lie" to rectify a betrayal or resolve a tension (such as a relationship), to practice hypocrisy or to expose such? With the rhyme, there is at least a musical resolution even though intellectual speculation may reel on.

In these early poems of Creeley, such echoes are refrains, touchstones which serve both to remind the reader how different and removed this new poetry is from its past and yet how conscious and in touch, in a self-determining, controlled way, it remains. Most important is the sense that the tradition can be returned to at will. One is neither bound to it slavishly nor so foolish as to seek to shun it altogether, which is a squandering of another order. Two beliefs, themselves a tradition, prevail. Creeley writes Olson, June 21, 1950 (*Olson & Creeley* 1:118): "A man, each man, is NEW. If his method, his form, IS the logic of his content: he cannot be but: NEW/'original.'" And some years later, in a letter to Olson from December 4, 1954: "I know that however much I read and come to love any man's practice, no matter what dates, my own forms must come from my own rhythms, and my own ear." It is a practice that never allows diffidence, as he moves from it, from the tradition, and on into the hazard of the poem.

NOTES

1. Noted by Creeley in a letter to his old Harvard friend, Jacob R. Leed, Nov. 13, 1948 (now in the Literary Archives, University of Connecticut Library).

2. Revisions made by Nov. 30, 1951, when a copy was typed out for Olson in a letter of that date (among Creeley's papers at Washington University Library, St. Louis).

3. Charles Olson, "Projective Verse," in *Human Universe and Other Essays,* edited by Donald Allen (New York: Grove Press, 1967), 52.

4. TS sent Leed ca. Dec., 1949, in Literary Archives, University of Connecticut Library. This and other unpublished writings by Creeley throughout this essay are published by permission of the author, with all rights reserved.

5. The psychologist Otto Rank, whose *Art and Artist* Creeley had bought, he tells Leed in a letter, June 21, 1948, "to find out something more about the psychologist personality." The chief value he seems to have discovered in Rank was a "rejection of Freud's idea of the artist as a thwarted neurotic whose basis of creativity depends on the sexual." This might explain the early title of the poem on Crane, whose life was so haunted by the sexual, especially a Crane made vivid and personal to Creeley through Brown's stories. A TS of the poem was sent Leed (in Literary Archives, University of Connecticut Library).

6. TSS sent Leed in Literary Archives, University of Connecticut Library. There was also a more serious "Epithalamion" (down to the traditional "Hymen, Hymenae" refrain) from 1948. Its opening is of special interest: "I have no form to go by / but that which I can remember. . . ."

7. Letter to Olson, Jan. 7, 1953 (Washington University Library). Creeley writes Olson again concerning the larger issues of poetics and specifically of "conjecture" and "assertion" in relation to projective verse or "composition by field" on Apr. 8, 1953: "To think of the poem as a 'field' means, beyond everything else, that one thinks of the poem as a place proper to the act of conjecture—and to effect conjecture in form, can only come to—total assertion."

8. Creeley reports having the volume at hand some years earlier in a letter to Olson from Aix-en-Provence, Nov. 19, 1951 (Washington University Library).

9. "Talking on Your Notes," in Cynthia Dubin Edelberg, *Robert Creeley's Poetry: A Critical Introduction* (Albuquerque: University of New Mexico Press, 1978), 167.

10. See *Contexts of Poetry,* edited by Donald Allen (Bolinas, Calif.: Four Seasons Foundation, 1973), 31–32. However, since Creeley may not have had a record player in Majorca at the time—a source of occasional complaint in his letters to Olson—most likely the title is an allusion, in evocation of the wry dexterity of Parker, with traces of Creeley's homesickness for the American scene.

11. Mary Novik, *Robert Creeley: An Inventory, 1945–1970* (Kent, Ohio: Kent State University Press, 1973), 89.

REED WHITTEMORE

Review of *Pieces*

Let it be chronicled that in the Terrible Sixties scores of poets banded together and went about the country telling people off. The people needed telling off, of course, and seemed to like hearing of their deficiencies of language and feeling; but the evangelicism of the poets confused them some (after all, the poets kept preaching that poetry itself was not preaching). Still, a little confusion about poetry was hardly new, and some of the poets were marvelously forceful. At least *they* weren't confused.

Among the most respected of the crusading poets was Robert Creeley, who looked the perfect noncrusader. He was shy, reticent, uncontaminated by any sort of platform exhibitionism. His poems were strange and ended suddenly; they said quiet things about immediacy and love; sometimes they were funny and tricky; always they were low-keyed and antirhetorical. Creeley didn't seem a preacher-teacher type at all, except that there he was preaching and teaching.

Now the sixties are ending. One more Creeley book has sneaked in under the wire, and I must report that it shows us Creeley preaching and teaching shamelessly. Even the pose of antipreach is abandoned; I keep being reminded of the famous poem by MacLeish I have never liked, where he laboriously distinguishes between meaning and being, and sticks poetry with the latter. Creeley is not so pretentious, but he is on the same kick. He keeps giving us classroom demonstrations of how poetry works. Some of the demonstrations are comical and gamey, some are serious commitments; but all or nearly all have the demonstration manner about them. The teacher in Creeley has gotten the better of the poet, so that even as he preaches

From *New Republic,* Oct. 11, 1969, 25–26. Reprinted by permission.

immediacy and directness he sounds faintly abstract and be-mused, a man drawing illustrations of life on a blackboard.

One of the chief demonstrations has to do with the notion of a poem as a unity, a one. Creeley is bored to pieces with poets and critics who insistently treat a poem as an inviolable aesthetic and intellectual whole; therefore, he has named his book *Pieces* and has pieced it together so that all the conventional white space around the beautiful unities called poems is missing. Where a piece begins or ends is obscure. Good idea. The book is meant to seem less like a formal book of poems than notes from a poet's journal. Unfortunately the idea is undermined by the constant pedagogy. The pedagogy makes the informality seem a teacher's device rather than an attempt on the part of the poet to tell us his private thoughts. The notebook seems a hoked-up notebook, a notebook for classroom use to show that poems are put together like notebooks.

There are other demonstrations. Creeley is against metaphor and simile. He is against the war, the government, politicians. He is against details, plots, knowledge. All these annoyances provide him with opportunity for small lectures.

Then there are numbers, which he seems to like (perhaps he would like to teach math?), and they provide him with the long-est unified sequence in the book—a series of reflections about the numbers one to nine and then zero. Zero is apostrophized thus:

> What
> by being not
> is—is not
> by being.

The classroom or demonstration flavor of it all finally threw me off completely. Even what I agreed with I didn't like. The-oretically I sympathized, for example, with his efforts at infor-mality and piecemealness, if only because I have been exhausted by poets mapping out the shapes of their poems at readings ("Now I begin the second part of my seventh section, in which . . ."). Yet, theory aside, I found the fragmentation of *Pieces* oppressive. Instead of the sense of informality and imme-diacy that the pedagogue was beaming my way, I got a sense of emotional and experiential emptiness. I am much too old and confused to have clear notions of what a poem should be, but as a teacher-poet I feel the doubleness of my life keenly. And when a poem of my own emerges as *merely* a demonstration, an illustration, an instance of some fine aesthetic device, I feel bad; then I think I haven't written a poem but a lecture. Creeley made me feel this way constantly in *Pieces*. Luckily it was Creeley, not me, lecturing.

I blame Creeley's trouble on the company he has been keeping, the company of other poets and of the sixties. Before the sixties the company of other poets produced at worst an excessive aestheticism, an unnecessary preoccupation with literary matters. The Terrible Sixties added several measures of social indignation and missionary zeal that in this book Creeley seems to have swallowed completely.

This is too bad, some sort of error at the factory. The normal flow of Creeley's aesthetic energy remains in the other direction, to the rendering of private experience cleanly and without side. May the seventies restore us all.

LOUIS L. MARTZ

From "Recent Poetry: The End of an Era"

Robert Creeley's new book *Pieces* has a strange kinship with Lowell's [*Notebook*], since Creeley's mind too is playing out over the contemporary scene and attempting to find in his own consciousness a source of unity in the present world. Yet Creeley's interest in human beings is curiously different from that of Lowell. We hear of friends but we do not come to know them; we hear of places and yet we seldom see them; we hear of suffering and yet we do not grasp its reality. Everything in Creeley's book is seen through the lens of intellectual analysis, through a mind like a prism that refracts the world in segments. It is a universe rather like that inhabited by Camus's Stranger, that is to say, a world in which the individual consciousness provides whatever sense of reality is possible, while the outer forms of existence have only a dreamlike presence:

> Listless,
> the heat rises—
> the whole beach
>
> vacant,
> sluggish.
> The forms shift
>
> before we know,
> before we thought
> to know it.

Review of *Pieces* from *The Yale Review* 59, no. 2 (Dec., 1969): 256–61, copyright © 1969 by Yale University.

The mind
again, the manner
of mind in the

body, the
weather, the waves,
the sun grows lower

in the faded
sky.

This is one mode of apprehension; on the other hand there are
sharper moments:

Bird flicker, light
sharp, flat—the
green hills of the two
islands make a familiar
measure, momently seen.

And there are, amid these wandering forms and glimpses, cer-
tain poems that heave up formally out of the mist, as in the short
poem entitled "The Moon," one of the few poems in which a
sense both of human and of natural presence is sustained for
more than twenty lines:

she bent her head and looked
sharply up, to see it.
Through the night it must
have shone on, in that

fact of things—another
moon, another night—a
full moon in the winter's
space, a white loneliness.

I came awake to the blue
white light in the darkness,
and felt as if someone
were there, waiting, alone.

More often this groping for actuality in the mind represents a search that ends with a sense of some evasive presence, as in "The Finger." Here the finger turns out to be the mind reaching out from "that time [when] I was a stranger" toward the apprehension of woman as an abstraction of all the ancient mythological qualities named Aphrodite or Athena; not *a* woman, then, but rather the varied presence of woman-ness:

> She was young,
> she was old,
> she was small.
> She was tall with
>
> extraordinary grace. Her face
> was all distance, her eyes
> the depth of all one had thought of,
> again and again and again.
>
> To approach, to hold her,
> was not possible.

It is not possible because her loveliness exists only in theory; what he holds in the mind is, as he says in another poem, the "apparent forms" of being. The word "apparent" is in fact a key word in this volume, for it implies that whether the figure is "in or out of the mind" (as he says at the opening of "The Finger") "a conception overrides it." In this mental world of shifting, momentary, unstable, apparent forms, it is significant that the finest sequence in the book should be found in a group of ten poems entitled "Numbers," and dedicated to the painter, Robert Indiana, so famous for his skill in delineating numerical forms in spinning shapes and receding perspectives. In each of these poems, running from "One" through "Nine" and returning to "Zero," the physical image of the number becomes a point from which the mind's conceptions move into the apprehension of a rich, suggestive aura. Thus in the poem . . . "Two" we have a glimpse of the original act of Creation:

> When they were
> first made, all the

earth must have
been their reflected
bodies, for a moment—
a flood of seeming
bent for a moment back
to the water's glimmering—
how lovely they came.

That is, from the moment of Creation, human beings have lived within a mental locus:

This point of so-called
consciousness is forever
a word making up
this world of more
or less than it is.

Thus the sequence of numbers develops a process of creation that rests now and then in moments of full security, as with this excellent evocation of "Four":

This number for me
is comfort, a secure
fact of things. The

table stands on
all fours. The dog
walks comfortably,

and two by two
is not an army
but friends who love

one another. Four
is a square,
or peaceful circle,

celebrating return,
reunion,
love's triumph.

But as we come to "Nine" we find the poet saying: "There is no point of rest here"; this "triad of triads" leads to a question asking: what is resolved "in the shifting, fading containment?" And then, as we return to "Zero" the process of creation and recreation begins all over again, as the poet says:

> There is no trick to reality—
> a mind
> makes it, any
> mind.

This process of intellectualizing creates some fine poems here, such as the meditation on a bedpost, with its "extraordinary shape," "its conical cap and bulging middle," and its horizontals linking the manufactured and the human:

> I have not
> seen this elsewhere except
> as the cross bar of the collar
> bone, my own, or those of others.

These abstract, often geometrical images serve then to link a world together in the mind of the speaker and for brief moments the world coheres, although one has a sense that the words are receding even as they are pronounced:

> Late, the words, late
> the form of them, al-
>
> ready past what they were
> fit for, one and two and three.

Thus "all in the mind it comes and goes" with a significance that Creeley sums up when he says, of his own thinking: "Like old 'romantic' self-query, come of obvious unrest and frustration."

Read at a sitting, these pieces grow together, live together, after the manner that Creeley describes in one of his best poems:

> Grey mist forms
> out the window,

> leaves showing green,
> the dark trunks of trees—
>
> place beyond?
> The eye sees, the
> head apparently records
> the vision of these eyes.
>
> What have I seen,
> now see? There were
> times before
> I look now.

This is a strenuous volume, requiring the most intense effort on the part of the reader to actualize the abstractions through which this poetry works, in its search for "a locus of experience, not a presumption of expected value":

> Moving in the mind's
> patterns, recognized
> because there is where
> they happen.

It is impossible, I believe, to become more abstract without destroying the very presence of poetry. Yet Creeley manages to hold himself at the taut edge of poetic existence. It is a dangerous technique, impossible, I imagine, to imitate successfully, but a unique and worthy achievement in its own right.

DENISE LEVERTOV

Review of *Pieces*

Creeley's early poems were concerned with mental processes, the intellect if you will, evidences of the intelligence. Then they became concerned increasingly with feeling as distinct from intellection, but still feeling handled by the intellectual intelligence. "Kore," supremely beautiful, was an exception, and of course there were other exceptions, but that's my retrospective sense of the general tendency. "The Door" seemed to open up a new direction because, even aside from its autonomous strength, the deep authentic dream experience of it (all of his poems are authentic but not all go that deep) it was, more than any other poem of his up to that time, not an examination of what happens but an immersion in what happens—and this affected the form of the poem, so that though from stanza to stanza it was not atypical, its totality—in length, the *staying with it* rather than *whittling down*—was. The reflections upon the event are completely a part of the event; and at the same time "The Door" has a very clear narrative line. But for a while the kind of exploration adumbrated by this poem didn't seem to be pursued. Creeley went on writing mostly more *conclusive* poems: many of them are of a ravishing perfection, but sometimes it has seemed as if that perfection were a limitation, a sealing off when one wanted him to go on, to go further, not to be obsessed with refining what he had already done impeccably.

In *Pieces* something different happens—or *is happening,* for it is anything but a static work. Somebody glancing through it who did not know Creeley's earlier books might get an impression of sloppiness and ask, What's this guy think he's doing, publishing unfinished drafts? Someone who knew and dug his work, its elegance and concision and (most of the time) its clar-

From *Caterpillar*, no. 10 (Jan., 1970): 246–48. Reprinted by permission.

245

ity—dug it just for those attributes—might similarly think *Pieces* weak, self-indulgent, a falling off. But it's not. Its very sprawl and openness, its notebook quality, its absence of perfectionism, Creeley letting his hair down, is in fact a movement of energy in his work, to my ear: not a breaking down but a breaking open.

Titled poems (including "The Finger," a poem that does relate pretty closely to "The Door," and "Numbers," which goes deep into a long-present obsessive interest) alternate with untitled poems and fragments, and bits of prose; often it's hard to tell where one poem ends and another begins, even if you refer to the table of contents: and it doesn't matter, it's good, they are all related, it's a complete book, the way a notebook or diary has its own completeness and coherence, a relatedness of part to part that is not identical with the coherence of the deliberately arranged. One poem says,

> Such strangeness of mind I know
> I cannot find there more
> than what I know.
>
> I am tired of purposes,
> intent that leads itself
> back to its own belief. I want
>
> nothing more of such brilliance
> but what makes the shadows darker
> and that fire grow dimmer.

It is in keeping with the spirit of *Pieces* that there is no introduction. Creeley's prefatory notes in the past have seemed to me unnecessary, defensive. Here, in place of such a note, is an epigraph—these lines from Allen Ginsberg:

> yes, yes,
> that's what
> I wanted,
> I always wanted,
> I always wanted,
> to return

                    to the body
                where I was born.

I don't think (whatever Allen meant by it) that means a desire to
return to the womb; it's one's own body, the primal, the in-
stinctive and intuitive basics one started with, that is being spo-
ken of. His own body that he was born in, and that the mind,
the way we live, keeps wandering from. The freedom in *Pieces* is
also a kind of wandering, but back to sources—even literally (as
in the poem "I" in *Words*—"is the grandson of"):

                Falling-in windows—
                the greenhouse back of
                Curleys' house. The
                Curleys were so good
                to me, their mother
                held me on her lap.

A piece like "Mazatlan: Sea" begins with highly wrought,
finely written stanzas, and drifts off into scattered notes; peters
out, almost: but I can't see it as sloppy or arrogant to publish
such irresolutions, as it would be for someone without Creeley's
body of accomplishment behind him. Having that work in back
of it, a book like this is, on the contrary, an act of trust and
humility.

"Gists and piths"—Pound quotes the Japanese student defin-
ing poetry. Inadequate, like all definitions of the complex; but a
damn good try. Well, some poetry is stronger in one element
than in the other; in fact, "classic" could be equated with piths,
and "romantic" with gists. In that sense *Pieces* is a romantic
book, by a poet whose previous work has often been (im-
pressively) "classic." Because of its energy, candor, mystery,
and try-anything courage, I find it exciting. It moves me, not
only poem by poem (and there are some that don't say anything
to me, taken by themselves) but as an organic event. If Creeley
has seemed to be building himself, year by year, an elaborate
box, he has now revealed its door; the process is shown to have
resembled the way an Eskimo builds an igloo, from inside out,
the exit last.

RUSSELL BANKS

Notes on Creeley's *Pieces*

"My plan is / these little boxes / make sequences. . . ." And
they do. In turn, the sequences make a single sequence, the
sequence of an argument-form or syllogism—a gestalt that
slowly pulls free of the ground which is Creeley's life, revealing
not so much an image, however, as a structure—again, like an
argument-form. It appears gradually (rather than unfolding in a
linear role) and cumulatively, and by the end of the book it
stands free of the ground altogether—intact, integrated, and in
motion.

It's impossible to break the whole down into its component
parts and thereby give any sensible impression of the whole, but
if such were possible—to break the whole down into compo-
nent parts—and if the relations *sequentially* between the parts
could be shown, it might help to illuminate some of the less
apparent aspects of the whole poem. (*Pieces* is a book of indi-
vidual poems, yes, but it reads like a single, book-length poem,
e.g., sequentially.)

Generally, there seem to be seven or eight groups of seven or
eight individual "boxes." But the lines of demarcation between
groups are not clear, are more nearly *zones* than lines. The poem
moves the way an event moves in time.

The first group of poems is focused directly on the theme of the
unassailable unity of one—the assertion of particularity: "No
one / there. Everyone / here." But, starting with particularity of

From *Lillabulero,* no. 8 (Winter 1970): 88–91. Reprinted by permission.

the self, one moves naturally to the isolate specificity of the objective world, as in "The Family":

>Father
>and mother
>and sister
>and sister
>and sister.

>•

>Here we are.
>There are five
>ways to say this.

Yet, returning from there to here, the monad remains intact:

>If I were you
>and you were me
>I bet you'd
>do it too.

Gradually, and increasingly, as if drawn by a magnet, the poems concern themselves with the necessary duality of the monad: here/not-here; me/you: inside/outside; more/less. Until the connection with motion is made: "The car / moving / the hill / down. . . ." Or better yet, in the poem preceding that one: "a road, going by, / cars, a truck, animals, in crowds." And just before that poem:

>The way into the form,
>the way out of the room—

>The door, the hat,
>the chair, the fact.

With these three poems, one can see the shift from a concern with duality to motion. See also, for lengthy explorations of these themes, "The Finger" and "Gemini."

There follows then the group of poems that concerns itself with experiences asserting the unity of the present (motion, phenomenologically, being a present-tense experience). " 'Follow the Drinking Gourd . . .' " is for me the foremost expression of this experience—a truly beautiful and important poem, crucial to the thrust of the book and to an understanding of Creeley's vision, its breadth and literal precision.

From a concern with the unity of the present, the poet's "I" moves to an understanding, deeper than before, of motion, which leads him to a sense of continuum that is at the heart of an absurdist's vision of the world. Thus numbers, zero, and the Fool appear as images. As *images*. The book of poems now begins to resemble a poetic quest: an ontological chase in which the moral self is the prize. The search is a skeptic's search for a metaphysical safety that will match a Christian's, with right reason and moral integrity corresponding to faith—as means.

From a depth of anxiety, reached right after "Numbers" with "The Fool," and, between these two, the short poems about Nothingness ("When holes taste good / we'll put them in our bread" is not *cute* or funny in any way—except in the way that Beckett is funny: picture Chaplin munching doughnut holes), from this antic depth, the poems begin to glimpse an Other: "What she says she wants / she wants she says." The turn comes just after "The Fool," in the "bedpost" poem. Particularizing the Other through the sexual associations, this poem continues and uplifts the bogged-down quest by achieving the necessary transition from self to Other:

> . . . But the
> bar, horizontal, joining
>
> the two posts, I have not
> seen this elsewhere except
> as the cross bar of the collar
> bone, my own, or those of others.

What follows are "Names"—"Friends," "Citizen," "NYC," "Chicago," "America"—people and places named with words. Connecting. Getting into the world. Crossing bars.

The book, were it merely didactic, might've ended there. A reason it doesn't is that this group of poems also shows how the connection is locked into the present (Creeley is always *in* his poems, the way Pollock is in his paintings, Cage in his music):

> Late, the words, late
> the form of them, al-
>
> ready past what they were
> fit for, one and two and three.

Which leads him to considerations of times-past: mirror-images, echoes, histories, personal and otherwise. And slowly the poems turn away from a despair with the facticity of the past, its ambiguous claim on us, to an internalization of it, making for him a subjective Other:

> Nowhere one
> goes will
> one ever
> be away
>
> enough from
> wherever
> one was.

And: "Thinking of Olson—'we are / as we find out we are.'" Thinking of Olson in other ways, too—how Olson is *in* Maximus of Gloucester and not vice versa. Both poets agreeing, however, that "One wants *one*."

It's at this point, and no other, that the reference to Zukofsky appears, which is important: "Want to get the sense of 'I' into Zukofsky's 'eye'—a locus of experience, not a presumption of expected value." And see what follows (remembering that the struggle up to now has been to keep this 'I' intact without destroying the Other): "Here now— / begin!" So here, almost at the end of the book, he's finally got it all together, and the last poems are demonstrations of this. If . . . then. If all that has gone before in this poem is true (as it would be true for Wittgenstein, not Sartre), *then* I am in the world. I am in the world, with the unity of self established, in motion and in time, its past differentiated from, yet linked to, its future, the self, through words, "a locus of experience, not a presumption of expected value." All pulls together. One may freely ride back to the basic insight of "The Finger": "The choice is simply / *I will*—as mind is a finger, / pointing, as wonder / a place to be." But on this ride the difference is that now the choice has been made (an act possible for Creeley, the Puritan of "The Puritan Ethos"— "Happy the man who loves what / he has and worked for it also"—only because he's earned it). And thus the book/poem ends by turning in wonder, as prescribed, toward other people, confident, touching, connecting—a connection that, once made, gives Creeley *joy*. For him, a moral condition. As for most true Christians. Describing this joy, he says: "I felt, as though hearing / laughter, my own heart lighten."

To be consistent with itself (and a syllogism must be consistent with itself), the poem should end with a demonstration, rather than a claim, and it does.

PETER COOLEY

Review of *Pieces*

It's hard when you've consistently admired a poet to admit disappointment in what he does. But when you keep coming back to that feeling, it has to be confessed. Creeley is among the dozen most important poets writing in English today and *Pieces* is a real attempt to write his kind of long poem. On the whole it's not a success.

The book derives from nothing so much as *Paterson;* it even makes some specific references in that direction. As far back as *For Love,* of course, Williams was a major influence, not an undigested but an assimilated one. From Williams, Creeley learned the tendency to make the speaking voice a point of view which would try to identify with the thing perceived until it was both the creator of the thing and the thing itself.

> As the cat
> climbed over
> the top of
>
> the jamcloset
> first the right
> forefoot
>
> carefully
> then the hind . . .
>
> (Williams, from "Poem")

From *North American Review* 255, no. 2 (Summer 1970): 74–76. Reprinted by permission.

> Mud put
> upon mud.
> lifted
> to make room,
>
> house
> a cave,
> and
> colder night.
>
> (Creeley, from "The House")

This continued in *Words,* but there the place of things in the world rendered as an activity of perception (that root of Williams which Levertov has developed more than anyone) was less important than the speaker's voice cautiously talking to and about itself as if listening for its own echoes. Now it was evident that the subject of Creeley's talk could only be discovered in the process of discussing words' failures to hold on to experience—even as these words were its embodiers.

> The mind,
> fast as it goes, loses
>
> pace, puts in place of it
> like rocks simple markers,
> for a way only to
> hopefully come back to
>
> where it cannot. All
> forgets. My mind sinks.
> I hold in both hands such weight
> it is my only description.
>
> ("'I Keep to Myself Such Measures . . .'")

The individualized Creeley idiom took shape here: the self-conscious, stylized use of flat, monosyllabic words archly spaced on the page as if they were building blocks so that we can read connectives and prepositions with as much weight as if they were nominal:

254

With a quick
jump he caught
the edge of

her eye and
it tore, down,
ripping. She

shuddered,
with the unexpected
assault, but

to his vantage
he held by
what flesh was left.

                                        ("Hello")

This idiom was so perfected you could try "Creeley talk" out
on your friends. And why not? What's open to real parody
unless it's individual?

But in *Pieces* Creeley has taken off from the tradition of the
American epic which *Paterson* follows to write a more personal
poem which tries to objectify his own fragmentation. That old
American epic quest for relationship between self and other in
the midst of cultural and individual chaos is as old as *Leaves of
Grass* and as continuing as *The Maximus Poems, A 1-12* and
Snyder's *The Back Country*. Creeley gives up, however, the
framework of narrative, history, persona, or landscape for a
concentration on the self and its words over time, calling into
question the validity of expressing the self at all in words. This is
the book's major break with tradition, its innovation. What
loosely places *Pieces* in that American epic tradition, though, is
the definition of a self through language and the self-generating
motion of the speaker's words with their ringing insistence on
self-renewal and the consequent flat passages where self and lan-
guage are recharged.

In the search for that recharging, Creeley risks some genuine
open middles where the poem willingly floats for a while with-
out direction. Sometimes the result is exciting, sometimes it's

tedious. *Paterson* tried this, too, but it always had its self-confected mythology to fall back on. Creeley's chancier delimitation leaves him only himself and the words as they occur. And they do *occur;* some really seem diary entries without dates.

Pieces' speaker makes a shadowy journey across parts of geographic and thematic America; he tries to connect somewhat with others, but most of this concern is for fleshing and questioning his own vision of language and reality as it emerges in words. The form of an object or experience—Creeley's rendering of his relationship to it in an enacting language—is still one of his primary interests:

> No forms less
> than activity.
>
> All words—
> days—or
> eyes—
>
> or happening
> is an event only
> for the observer?

But in the midst of the voice's stumbling, it will come out with a whole, rounded-off poem in its own authentic idiom:

> Push yourself in on others
> hard enough, they beat you
> with sticks and whips—the birth
>
> of love. E.g., affection aroused,
> it moves to be close, touch, and
> feel the warm livingness of an-
>
> other, any other, sucked, stroked,
> the club itself possibly a symbol of
> the obvious. My mother had hair,

and when I grew older, so did
I, all over my face, which I wanted
to be there, and grew a beard henceforth.

("The Boy")

The concern with mediating the relationship between inner
and outer—in and across the self—is related to the spatial-tem-
poral problem of hereness-thereness and facts vs. abstractions:
these weave through the whole book. From the spare, enacting
language of the early poems, Creeley moves into sections in-
terlocking easily in image or theme (echoes, distance, move-
ment, and vision) and on to a range of discontinuities where the
connections seem overly private and the language extremely
self-conscious if not pretentious. Look at these three quotations,
from the beginning, middle and end respectively:

I cannot see you
there for what you
thought you were.

The faded memories
myself enclose
passing too.

. . . .

Your opaqueness, at moments,
would be the mirror. Your
face closed as a door—

that insists on nothing,
but not to be entered—
wanting simply to be left alone.

. . . .

Each moment constitutes reality,
or rather may constitute
reality, or may have *done*
so, or perhaps *will?*

Good? Hardly. Even in the first quotation the language of maxim is far removed from the gnomic originality of *For Love,* in lines such as "Be wet with a decent happiness" or "There is no more giving in / When there is no more sin."

In the sequence "Numbers" Creeley plunges into the numerology he uses as image-source throughout to do a full theme and variation on the ontological problems that elsewhere seem rather trumped-up. If the sequence is sometimes predictable, its relations of form and subject are always skillfully fused and fun to follow:

THREE

> They come now with
> one in the middle—
> either side thus
> another. Do they
>
> know who each other
> is or simply walk
> with this pivot between them.
> Here forms have possibility.

As in *Paterson,* Creeley drops prose passages into chinks between poems. Most of them are his own and represent more undistilled experience than what is in the "poetry" or are abstractly agonized reflections on the problems of being, of expression or relation to others:

> When and/or if, as,—however, you do
> "speak" to people, i.e., as condition of the
> circumstance (as Latin: "what's around")
> a/n "im(in)pression." "I'll" *crush* you to
> "death"—"flying home."

These passages vary the poem's texture but could have been used to represent a variety of "reality" against which the poems could play as "made" objects. If this seems like a rewriting of the book, it's at least a more organic approach to prose included with poetry than Creeley's merely mechanical distinction in *Pieces.*

Consistent with the poem's progressive deterioration in language is its loss of a social-political landscape present in the early pages ("Chicago," "NYC," "America," "Citizen," "The Puritan Ethos," "The Province," "Calendar"); there seems no functional reason for this disappearance; its sporadic reappearances are not very convincing:

> "It's rare that the city of Buffalo
> gets to shape its own destiny . . ."

> Take advantage of this,
> take advantage of what's downtown
> and link the two with a
> rapid transit system . . .

I wish, too, with the poem's hyperconscious and atomized language there were more moments of genuine self-mockery like this one: "Lift me / from such I / makes such declaration." Without them, many readers are going to find the voice overly earnest and turn off.

Perhaps I'm approaching *Pieces* with too many of those earlier, iconic Creeley poems already in my head; if so, I can blame Creeley for writing so individually and convincingly in *For Love* and *Words*. Whenever I read him I think of two other poets who may or may not have been "influences" but who each knew how to confront emptiness—as he does—in an individual way: Dickinson and Mallarmé. Both, like Creeley, often wrenched their poems into compressed lines that seem to bend as you read. And haunted, though in very different ways, by the *beyond* as lover-God or *l'azur,* which is finally unapproachable, both Dickinson and Mallarmé fall back into the domain of limited self which Creeley begins from. In his earlier poems Creeley has made the poem itself that act of reaching out beyond himself— even when he sounds onanistic. In *For Love* and *Words* Creeley wrote by listening to himself as he spoke; we were a part of that echo and in some sense he wrote emblematically for us in merely being himself. I grant him the right to share his fragments, but has he cleared a space for us among the ruins in *Pieces* where we can sit down and listen? So we can speak, too?

PART THREE   *The 1970s: A Life*
Tracking Itself

LATER POEMS

M. L. ROSENTHAL

Problems of Robert Creeley

Despite a tendency to regard as quintessential poetry any twist of phrase that happens into his mind, Robert Creeley has written some real poems—the lovely "Kore," for instance, and the self-fraught, intellectually engaging " 'I Keep to Myself Such Measures. . . .' " His new volume, *A Day Book,* adds a few more poems of interest among its many varied offerings. Like his 1969 volume, *Pieces,* it presents a mixture of rather diffuse and arbitrary notes with a number of short, lively poems and with several longer, serious ones that give the book its most decisive coloration.

A Day Book, though, is more than merely a new collection. It is, actually, a sequence. It could have become, I think, a rather marvelous sequence had the poet removed the dead matter, edited himself rigorously, and waited himself out. One thing he needed to wait for was an appropriate poetic line to carry the full surge of thought and feeling at peak moments along the way. But that problem aside, the reader who wants to ride with *A Day Book* from beginning to end has to step around a welter of hasty, awkward, ill-written passages and of dropped names— Alan and Allen and Louis and Charles and Stan and whomever else the book concerns.

The basic organizational plan, the jacket explains, is of "a record of experience." The implicit aim is to embody poetic process, the way we get from our daily empirical consciousness into a self-transcendent art. Almost half the book's approx-

Review of *A Day Book, Listen: A Play,* and *Contexts of Poetry: Interviews 1961–1971* from *Parnassus* 2, no. 1 (Fall/Winter 1973): 205–14, copyright © M. L. Rosenthal 1973.

imately 165 pages is made up of prose entries in a journal; the rest consists of poetic entries, often parallel or at least reciprocal to the prose. Since the book is unpaginated (an annoyance, given its size, whenever one wants to go back and find anything in it), and since no time divisions within its span of more than thirty months are specified, we have the impression of an almost undifferentiated drift of consciousness. Yet the sequence retains a fundamental, sometimes absorbing *promise*. Who can tell what will show up next in the float, partly confessional and partly atmospheric, of events, conversations, gossip, crumbs of literary or philosophical thought, introspective moments, aperçus, outbursts of erotic fantasy and memory, and moments of defeat by or triumph over depression that the drift carries along with it? If we take into consideration the poet's varied interests in jazz, drugs, varieties of sexual behavior, being on the move, and the confusions of love and family life, we have an ambience not unlike the television documentary *An American Family,* with modulations—would God that side were more consciously striven for!—toward Proustian recollection. When that Proustian effort does occur, as in the long poem "People," we see how moving the whole work might have been.

The link between the chaotic ambience of day-to-day life and the nature of poetic process is one clear motif of the book. There is a strong implication (or perhaps only a strong hope) that the real poem lies in the ambience, the casual drift of consciousness. At the same time, the overall organization—the prose entries followed by a partial recapitulation and heightening of the same material in poetry—would also suggest that Mr. Creeley wants to demonstrate an interaction between his raw materials and the results of aesthetic conversion, as Lowell does in *Life Studies.* Now there is nothing shocking or new in this kind of thing, but the problem is perhaps the most difficult and central one in both art and criticism, as Pound once pointed out very harshly to Williams: "Your interest is in the bloody loam but what I am interested in is the finished product." Everything depends, finally, on the quality of conception and execution. "Among School Children" and *The Man with the Blue Guitar* are certainly about the process and, at the same time, embodiments of it. So too, at least in good part, is *Paterson.* And so, in quite another way, are Lowell's excursions round and about his *Notebooks*. What counts is the pitch of language and realization, and the discovery of a dynamics that defines the poem's right curve of movement and helps strip bare the issues at its heart.

A Day Book does not get that far, yet it has its thread of progression and its emotional soundings. Its protagonist must deal with a depressed sense of loss, waste, and inadequacy, dramatized in the initial ambiguous indications of a personal crisis involving his wife's infidelity or at least his fear of it. There are countereffects—assertions of energy (often in memories or fantasies of sexual experience, especially fellatio, as a sweet relief that is more an almost infantile addiction than a delighted relationship) and confidence and a kind of joy. The depressive element remains, too heavy to be overcome though each of the two sections ends with a sufficiently "positive" emphasis; both the prose section and the verse section indicate a desire to continue in the real world despite the suicidal note at certain moments.

Looked at with complete sympathy, the sequence is an opening out in each section from the initially disturbed situation into the speaker's whole wide float of subjective associations, and then into an acceptance of despair without absolute surrender. In both sections the depression is traced to childhood sorrows and family tragedy. In the prose section the speaker asks: "Was my father, like they say, a deadbeat? . . . Now son makes deathly silence, in return, as though he were the tradition somehow of that deadening silence. . . . At least I won't live to see the end of it." And in the poetry love is seen as an anodyne (which indeed it often is) rather than a source of adult strength:

LOVE

Tracking through this
interminable sadness—

like somebody said,
change the record.

I hope that I have suggested how interesting the play of thought can be in *A Day Book*. With more power and depth, and with less clutter, it would be something to range alongside the truly accomplished American sequences rather than being a catchall with some finely interesting things in it. There are too many passages, too, done either in telegraphese or in a comma-spiked, anti-idiomatic style that befuddles one's memory of the English tongue. Some examples:

1. When Leslie comes he speaks, in his lecture, of the fact, to him, that prose has rejected the self image or the sorrows of Werther kind of fiction.

2. He wanted to fuck his wife all the time now. Yet having done so, would have his head fill with "things to do," almost lists of them, as if the relief of coming, like they say—and though understandable, it's an odd phrase finally to mean the emission of semen, but must mean something like, *it's me, I'm here?,* whereas "emission" would have the slightly military sense of, that which has been sent forth. . . .

3. There was a joke of girl at water fountain in factory who bending over to drink finds herself then caught by nipples of each breast by fingers which pinch, twisting them. The sharp, quick flood of wanting. She gasps. But couldn't it be equally, someone else's voice interrupts, it just hurts like hell? That's the joke probably, either way. And for years is sense of, if one does it, that way, the consequence is as stated.

4.
        I'm almost
        done, the hour
        echoes, what

        are those words
        I heard, was
        it *flower, stream,*

        Nashe's, as Allen's
        saying it, "Brightness
        falls from the air"?

                        (from "Echo")

It hardly seems necessary to spell out why the first three of these quotations are bad prose. Their cozy gawkiness (including Mr. Creeley's most obsessive mannerism: "like they say") evades an essential problem of style; to write intimately and informally and well is not just to muck about with language. Similarly, the fourth passage exploits our modern openness to the colloquial tone in poetry. Few effects are as satisfying as the assimilation of natural speech into a powerful and melodic poem—one could demonstrate from all the masters, past and present. But again, this does not mean there are not enormous qualitative differences possible, or that a loose and stumbling casualness automatically makes for good writing. I have just quoted the opening stanzas of Mr. Creeley's poem "Echo." The first two of these stanzas are relaxed and facile, but suggestive in their dreamy, halting, listening movement; and the poem will return to that tone in the unquoted portion after the third stanza. But that third stanza! I *think* Mr. Creeley is alluding to the way Allen Ginsberg recites Nashe's line, mutilated here, of course, by the way it is broken. But that is not as important as the sheer failure of the language and rhythm.

This problem of breakdown of diction and syntax is pervasive, though it is interesting that in the best Creeley poems—such as the short, witty, musical "Walking the Dog" or the long, beautifully serious "People"—the incidence of distracting mannerisms and limb-tangled syntax is sharply reduced. But not entirely. In "People," we find a passage like this one:

> If you twist one
> even insignificant part
> of your body
>
> to another, imagined
> situation of where it
> might be . . .

The intensity of the poem's concentration, however, enables us to discount such lapses, and even to attribute them to a desire to hold so much in the mind simultaneously: a remembered world of childhood fantasy, and the transmutations of that set of mem-

269

ories in patterns of adult awareness and longing. The abstractions do get out of hand, as does the language at times, yet these problems do not defeat the poem. "People," with one or two of the other longer efforts, is the main reason we can feel that *A Day Book* is concerned to make a sustained voyage of inward emotional discovery.

Before leaving *A Day Book,* I shall turn to just one more of the better poems in it to suggest a possibly important consideration. The poem is called "The Edge." Within the larger sequence, it is part of a brief series of poems and fragments on the theme of love: a movement of meditative tones that is calmly appealing. "The Edge" itself is a brief variation on a poem by William Carlos Williams, curiously unacknowledged considering how often Mr. Creeley speaks of the significance to him of Williams's work. I shall quote "The Edge" first, and then Williams's poem, "Love Song."

> Place it,
> make the space
>
> of it. Yellow,
> that was a time.
>
> He saw the stain of love
> was upon the world,
>
> a selvage, a faint
> afteredge of color fading
>
> at the edge of the world,
> the edge beyond that edge.

And:

> I lie here thinking of you:—
>
> the stain of love
> is upon the world!
> Yellow, yellow, yellow

it eats into the leaves,
smears with saffron
the horned branches that lean
heavily
against a smooth purple sky!
There is no light
only a honey-thick stain
that drips from leaf to leaf
and limb to limb
spoiling the colors
of the whole world—
you far off there under
the wine-red selvage of the west!

Williams's poem is rich and full-bodied. It isn't just that, as
Mr. Creeley has it, "He saw the stain of love / was upon the
world." Williams's "yellow, yellow, yellow" is an active image,
the projection of the lover's desire over the visible universe. In
"Love Song," that universe is tangibly out there. Its organic,
natural patterns are absorbed ("eaten," "stained," "spoiled")
into the driving emotion of the speaker until its limits are reached
in that wonderful image, "the wine-red selvage of the west,"
which receives and contains the poem's male force and suggests
female response and sexual fulfillment. The Creeley poem echoes
all this but makes it almost static and reduces the emotion to an
abstraction. Without Williams's phrasing—"yellow," "stain of
love," "upon the world," "selvage"—it would have neither
vigor nor concrete reference. It is a pulling back from Williams
and toward Louis Zukofsky, another of Mr. Creeley's chosen
ancestors but one more congenial to a less robust imagination
than Williams's, with a thinner melodic line and less possibility
for technical variation.

When I came upon "The Edge," I first thought to look into
Williams's 1948 play *A Dream of Love* to find "Love Song,"
which the play's poet-doctor hero reads to his wife in the bril-
liant opening scene. The scene underlines the fact that the poem
is directed by a real, grown-up man in the real, everyday world
to a real woman. Both characters are intelligent, sensitive, but
durable people baffled by the complexity of their relationship

and even of their identities. The dialogue certainly reveals a whole philosopher's-bookcase-full of problems, but without belying the earthy realities in which the characters are rooted. The original poem had been written more than a quarter-century earlier, and Williams repossessed it for the play.

The accident of going back to *A Dream of Love* first instead of to *The Collected Earlier Poems* led me to another, related realization. The scene between the hero and his wife that I have mentioned parallels the dialogue in Mr. Creeley's play *Listen,* which I had been reading just before *A Day Book.* The difference between the plays is like that between the two poems. *A Dream of Love,* whatever its weaknesses by the time it comes to its end, is physically very much alive. It strives to imply the copresence of many different selves in the literal, often absurd situations of its characters. *Listen,* with its two characters named "He" and "She" and its quotations from R. D. Laing and from Wittgenstein (e.g., "The I, the I is what is deeply mysterious" and "The I is not an object") is a gently, pleasingly abstract treatment of the same theme. It is somewhat academic and derivative, with traces of Eliot here and Williams there and Pirandello somewhere else, and with charmingly pedantic interruptions of the "action" while He gives instructions to the director which also instruct the reader in what he is to appreciate. There is also an appendix of "production notes" by Mrs. Bobbie Creeley to instruct us in how the lines should read. Her "monoprints" in this edition, incidentally, are imaginative examples of photomontage, and in a sense they illustrate the drift of the He-She conversation in the play. Because of their necessarily visual combination of literal human figures (the same man and woman in the same shot, but seen in different degrees of clarity and in different contexts) with a vague landscape and abstract forms around them, they lend a sensuous conviction and lyrical vibration mostly absent from the text.

Mr. Creeley's vague but assertive poetics may be examined at length in *Contexts of Poetry,* a collection of ten interviews with him by various people between 1961 and 1971. The interview as a way of getting at people's ideas and artistic practice is a not altogether satisfactory form, but it does bring out what the victim is likely to say when compelled to be relatively spontaneous in the face of his own self-consciousness. I found these interviews particularly useful for biographical information; the one with Lewis MacAdams, especially, throws light on the psychological background of the poet's interest in inarticulateness as a mode of expression, but the conversations with David Ossman and with John Sinclair and Robin Eichele are helpful in this way, too. The most *articulate* interview, on the other hand, is the well-prepared one with the very intelligent and purposeful Linda Wagner. Interesting points concerning rhyme and structure arise here, and Mr. Creeley points to Williams's observation that "a poet thinks with his poem" as a valuable touchstone of method. In this interview, too, he quarrels with Eliot's thoughts on the "objective correlative." He cites his own poem, "The Immoral Proposition," to show that an apparently abstract statement about feeling can convey its emotion through the weight and distribution of the words when it is spoken in the right way. He rather oversimplifies Eliot's thought; Eliot would doubtless agree with his general theoretical statement, though he might well disagree about the quality of "The Immoral Proposition." The important thing, though, is the way Miss Wagner gets Mr. Creeley to state his positions more clearly than he has in his essays.

On the whole, these interviews do bring out the range of the poet's concerns. There is plenty here to agree and to disagree with—the great point is that, as he says, "What is interesting . . . is that which one *does* say, over and over, without being really aware of it. For better or for worse, these insistences must be the measure of one's acts." I agree, and should like to speak to one of those measuring insistences—the notion that Whitman and Williams were neglected until quite recently. "The figure the New Critics and the universities to this day have conspired to ignore," we are told, "is Walt Whitman." So much scholarly work and criticism has been done on Whitman (Newton Arvin, F. O. Matthiessen, Gay W. Allen, and many others) and he has been well anthologized in so many scholarly anthologies, such as Harry Hayden Clark's *Major American Poets* (1936) and Matthiessen's superb *Oxford Book of American Verse* (1950), and taught in so many courses, that one does not know what to make of this assertion. As for Williams, Mr. Creeley is equally wrong in saying that "in 1945, I don't think [he] was even regarded as a minor poet." Just for starters, I suggest he look into Fred B. Millett's *Contemporary American Authors* (1943).

To get back to *A Day Book,* it's there, I think, that the lessons of Whitman and Williams have been, not neglected, but incompletely studied.

CYNTHIA DUBIN EDELBERG

"In London"

The poem of the mind in the
act of finding what will suffice.
*   —Wallace Stevens, "Of Modern Poetry"*

The Form

The first half of *A Day Book* (1972) is a prose record of Creeley's day-to-day experience. This section, based on family life, gives the volume its apt title. The second half is a sequence of poems inspired by travel and called "In London." As M. L. Rosenthal has pointed out in his critique, the two parts complement each other: "Almost half the book's approximately 165 pages is made up of prose entries in a journal; the rest consists of poetic entries, often parallel or at least reciprocal to the prose."[1] Creeley tends in his writing to explore his preoccupations at the time, regardless of which particular form the writing takes. For instance, his short stories collected in *The Gold Diggers* and his novel *The Island* are, in the main, thematic companion pieces to his poems in *For Love* and the first part of *Words. Listen,* a radio play, and *Presences, A Text for Marisol,* an autobiographical novella, deal with many of the same issues considered in *Pieces* and *A Day Book.* Despite Creeley's feeling that "distinctions between the forms are purely technical,"[2] that his work is "a continuing song, so that no division of its own existence can be thought of as being more or less than its sum,"[3] his poetry can stand free of the rest. The focus in this chapter is on the poetic sequence "In London" itself.

The epigraph for "In London"—"But what to do? and / what to do next?"—is taken from William Carlos Williams's *A*

From chapter 4 of *Robert Creeley's Poetry: A Critical Introduction* (Albuquerque: University of New Mexico Press, 1978), 136–57, 178–80. Reprinted by permission.

Voyage to Pagany. This quotation is appropriate for several reasons. Both works concern travelers who set out with serious intentions and high expectations. *A Voyage to Pagany* is a subjective account of the year-long European trip Williams made in 1924, a sabbatical from his medical practice in Rutherford he arranged partly in response to Pound's urging: "You'd better come across and broaden your mind."[4] When Dr. Evans, the protagonist, arrives in Pagany (Europe) he is not quite sure what he is looking for but he hopes he will discover values of elemental profundity: "Something may happen" to rearrange his life.

> He wondered what luck he would have on this trip. And always he kept saying: Perhaps this is the time. Something may happen and I shall not return.
>   But what to do? and what to do next?[5]

Similarly, the unnamed wanderer in "In London" attaches life-ordering significance to a series of trips through London, St. Martin's in the French West Indies, Belgium, and New England: "I wanted to find something / worthy of respect."[6] Like Dr. Evans, he hopes "to / get all the confusions at last / resolved"; and like Dr. Evans, he learns that his own interests and idiosyncrasies are more to the point than any of the places he visits. Both travelers return home with renewed interest and fresh energy, perhaps because nothing of remarkable importance happens to Dr. Evans to keep him in Pagany and, similarly, because Creeley's protagonist is unable to resolve the confusions. It is not that he is able to solve them at home; rather, it is that "all the confusions" seem to trouble him less in Bolinas than elsewhere.

Both Creeley and Williams subordinate descriptions of topography and manners to their emphasis on the narrator's personal impressions and responses. Dr. Evans's self-directed reflections taken together constitute the real subject of Williams's most lyrical novel. In his introduction to *A Voyage to Pagany*, Harry Levin says this novel "cannot be regarded as a travel book"; instead, he calls it "a spontaneous flow of autobiographical reality."[7] According to Levin, Williams relied heavily on the diary he kept in 1924 "to nudge his memory" which in turn helped him create the illusion of artless spontaneity.[8] Creeley, more daring, offers us his unrevised journal entries in their strict chronological sequence. "In London" is a compilation of loosely connected insights set down on the spot: some are related to particular cities and the associations they bring to the speaker's mind but most are self-contained observations of his own nature. These poems, then, are not unified by the poet-traveler's itinerary but by his distinct personality and by his recurrent preoccupation with death, love, and home.

Creeley's decision to present "a spontaneous flow of auto-biographical reality" is the logical consequence of his current attitude toward his poems. An appreciation of "In London" depends to an extent on an appreciation of Creeley's present aesthetic rationale. It is useful, therefore, to outline the changes in Creeley's thinking about the publication, composition, and organization of his poetry through the years with a view toward defining his recently formulated aesthetic reflected in "In London."

From the time Creeley entered the world of letters he was determined "to get his poems out where they ought to be" as quickly as possible.[9] Thus, he established the Divers Press on Mallorca in 1954 to print his own work and work by his friends. For the same reason, he sent individual poems to sympathetic editors in reply to their questions about his current work. He also welcomed the publication of a group of poems in a small pamphlet as soon as the opportunity occurred. To offset the limitations of his freewheeling publication policy, Creeley selected what he considered his finest poems written during a particular time span for the important Scribner's volume and arranged these poems to complement each other. For instance, he chose the best from among his earliest poems for part 1 of *For Love* (Scribner's, 1963), subtitled the section "1950–1955," and altered the chronology in several places to achieve a particular curve of feeling. The dozens of poems he wrote between 1950 and 1955 but rejected for the Scribner's volume could still be found in little magazines such as *Origin* and *Black Mountain Review* as well as in five hand-set chapbooks: *Le Fou* (1952), *The Kind of Act Of* (1953), *The Immoral Proposition* (1953), *A Snarling Garland of Xmas Verses* (1954), and *The Whip* (1957).

Creeley's first major statement about his changing attitude

toward publication came in July 1967, when he wrote a preface to *The Charm*, a collection of poems written during the fifties but omitted from *For Love*. In this preface, he explains that when he first began writing he was "very didactic and very involved with 'doing it right!'"[10] He therefore debated the merit of each one of his poems and dismissed those he felt were unacceptable.

> . . . whenever there was a chance to publish a small pamphlet or book, my temptation was to cut from it any poem that did not seem to me then and there to make adamant sense as a *poem*, and consequently I tended to ignore a kind of statement in poetry that accumulates its occasion as much by means of its awkwardnesses as by its overt successes.

Creeley goes on in this preface to explain how he came to realize that poetry "that accumulates its occasion . . . by means of its awkwardnesses" should be offered seriously to the general public. He refers to a conversation with Ginsberg during the 1963 Vancouver Poetry Conference that convinced him poetry should reflect "the fact that we are human beings and do live in the variability of that order," including the awkward. Thus Creeley justifies the publication of his early and uncollected poems.

Creeley's enthusiasm for his awkward early poems, first expressed in the 1967 preface ("Selfishly enough, I can often discover myself here in ways I can now enjoy having been—no matter they were 'good' or 'bad'") determined the final shape of "In London." The sequence is an all-inclusive record of his poetic activity from October, 1968, to June, 1971. It is not surprising that virtually all of these poems were printed earlier in one of a variety of magazines ranging in character from the ephemeral *Best & Co.* to the established *Partisan Review,* or in slim pamphlets devoted exclusively to his most recent work, *In London* (Bolinas, Calif.: Angel Hair Books, 1970) and *St. Martin's* (Los Angeles: Black Sparrow Press, 1971), to name two of them. What is new is that Creeley persuaded Scribner's to publish all of these two-hundred-odd presumably unrevised poems in the precise sequence in which they were written.

The preface to *The Charm* also makes it plain, however, that more was at stake than Creeley's decision not to offer Scribner's a selected volume. At the same time that he began to consider the merit of his awkward poems by different standards, he began to explore the possibility of spontaneous composition. He thanks Ginsberg, both in the 1967 preface and more explicitly in an interview taped several months later, for reassuring him that an alternative to his previous method of reworking, polishing, and judging his writing did exist, that is, "the possibility of *scribbling,* of writing for the immediacy of the pleasure and without having to pay attention to some final code of significance."[11] Creeley also acknowledges his debt to Robert Duncan, who convinced him that poetry of impulse has an integrity of its own because "there is a place for everything in the poem."[12] Duncan, Creeley says in his preface to *The Charm,* "always insisted, with high intelligence, I think, that poetry is not some ultimate preserve for the most rarified and articulate of human utterances, but has a place for *all* speech and *all* occasions thereof."

One of the first results of Creeley's spontaneous method was "A Piece," a poem written in 1966, which reads "One and / one, two, / three," and about which he says:

> When *Words* was published, I was interested to see that one of the poems most irritating to reviewers was "A Piece"— and yet I knew that for me it was central to all possibilities of statement.[13]

"A Piece" was not important because it became a model; there are comparatively few of its nature in *Words, Pieces,* or "In London." Rather, the poem "was central to all possibilities of statement" because it signaled to Creeley that he had gained a freedom in writing which allowed him to write for his own pleasure, "to forget that kind of signification that formal criticism insists on."[14] This newfound sense of freedom enabled him "to include a far more various kind of statement" in his poetry than his pre-1966 habit of writing almost exclusively "in a small focus, in a very intensive kind of address" made possible.[15]

By the time Creeley wrote *Pieces,* he was able to compose a diversity of poetic statements which ranged from the emotionally taut, his trademark, to the frankly trivial. As Denise Levertov has noted in her review of *Pieces,* he was moving away from what she calls "evidences of intelligence," carefully wrought early poems, many "of a ravishing perfection":

> In *Pieces* something different happens—or *is happening,* for it is anything but a static work. Somebody glancing through it who did not know Creeley's earlier books might get an impression of sloppiness and ask, "What's this guy think he's doing, publishing unfinished drafts?" Someone who knew and dug his work, its elegance and concision and (most of the time) its clarity—dug it just for those attributes—might similarly think *Pieces* weak, self-indulgent, a falling off. But it's not. Its very sprawl and openness, its notebook quality, its absence of perfectionism, Creeley letting his hair down, is in fact a movement of energy in his work, to my ear: not a breaking down but a breaking open.[16]

The "sprawl," the "openness," and the "notebook quality" Levertov discerns in *Pieces* are equally apparent in "In London." The chief formal difference between the two sequences has to do with the organization of material.

Though the structure of *Pieces* is substantially more flexible than the rigid thesis-antithesis pattern of his early poems collected in *For Love,* and more flexible than the loosely associational form of the long poems in *Words,* the romance convention shapes *Pieces* overall. With "In London," Creeley ventures into the "field" Olson defines in "Projective Verse": "From the moment he ventures into FIELD COMPOSITION—put himself in the open—he can go by no track other than the one the poem under hand declares, for itself."[17] "In London" moves seemingly in accord with the poet's unforeseeable impulses, not in accord with any a priori plan.

Despite the fact that Creeley has been associated with Olson and "Projective Verse," it seems that it was Ginsberg who was able to persuade him that the form of the whole should not be predetermined but should "follow the sequence of perception in the course of the writing, even if the route became as irrational, intuitive, and discontinuous as the shape of the mind itself."[18] Ginsberg, identified with a poetry of "undifferentiated consciousness," absorbed the idea from William Burroughs, who relied on the "cut-up" method to externalize, dramatically, what "is happening," and from Jack Kerouac, who wanted prose and poetry to record "an undisturbed flow from the mind." Kerouac's "The Essentials of Spontaneous Prose" and Olson's "Projective Verse" have so much in common that Kerouac could complain convincingly in his *Paris Review* interview: "I formulated the theory of breath as measure, in prose and verse, never mind what Olson, Charles Olson says. I formulated that theory in 1952 at the request of Burroughs and Ginsberg."[19] The question of who formulated the mid-twentieth-century American version of the theory of spontaneity is not the issue. The central point is that the unusually free notion of juxtaposition that orders the open literary structure of "In London" was probably influenced more by the Kerouac-Ginsberg-Burroughs nexus than by Olson. It may be that Creeley is acknowledging a debt to Burroughs[20] in the following passage from "In London":

> Small dreams of home.
> Small of home dreams.
> Dreams of small home.
> Home small dreams of.

But whether or not Creeley was thinking of Burroughs is not important. The importance here is bound up with the emphasis on spontaneity, the key word linking the theories of the Beat poets and of Olson.

Though Creeley has been called a projectivist poet since the publication of Olson's "Projective Verse" in 1950, "In London" is the first collection of poems that show he has completely assimilated ideas about a poetry of process, ideas associated with projectivism. Too much attention has been paid to Creeley's statement—quoted by Olson in his essay—that "form is never more than an extension of content," a definition of lyric poetry Creeley knowingly borrowed from Valéry.[21] Not enough attention has been paid to the fact that until "In London" Creeley did not allow the form of the whole "to go by no track other than the one the poem under hand declares, for itself." Creeley's actual contribution to "Projective Verse" concerned not the form of the poem but the form of the line. Portions of his letters to Olson in which he responded to Olson's insistence that the poetic voice must be true to the complexities of the human speaking voice—ranging in scope from idiomatic ease to anti-idiomatic stammering—became part of the seminal essay:

> And then those letters actually became incorporated finally in that essay on projective verse—in the first section, where he is talking about the significance of the syllable, the sense of breathing, the sense of where the intelligence is operating and the choice of the language where the whole physiology of man is at work in the poem.[22]

Even in his earliest published poems, Creeley was able to make the individual line register his "sense of breathing," though it was often with Olson's help.[23]

Between the time Creeley said "form is never more than an extension of content" and the time he made full use of the idea that content is revealed by form, more than twenty years had passed. In 1971, Creeley explained to Michael André why free form, the theory he spoke about during the late forties, became a workable mode for him at last. Contrary to his previous tendencies, he was able "to trust writing." If he were not completely comfortable with words "by the age of forty or forty-five," he reasoned, it was "obviously too late to learn."[24] Feelings such as these led Creeley to believe that the rhythm of life as it was actually lived, as he recorded it on impulse in his journal, would provide the organizing principle for the sequence. The un-polished, experiential sequence, "In London," reflects his decision to trust to the writing "to locate coherence in the most diverse and random of occasions."[25]

To help induce the effect of untampered-with immediacy the sequence attempts to convey, the pages are unnumbered, and many of the poems untitled. Creeley explains that "there was no need to draw a distinct formal line around each poem as though it were some box containing a formal statement."[26] The poems are separated by dots: "three dots indicate that that was the end of a day's accumulation, and the single dots most usually indi-cate division in the writing as it's happening, as I was sitting down to do it."[27] This conspicuously casual format—a visual testament to the spontaneity of the whole—thrusts the several motifs which naturally recur throughout this unrevised travel diary into the forefront.

The Content

In an attempt to mediate an argument between Creeley and Corman in 1951, Olson wrote to Corman:

> . . . That is, Creeley, is a subtle & beautiful man, worth more than all the rest of us you have published—and then some. Your magazine *Origin* shall be known in the history of writing because you there first published the stories and letters of this man. . . . You see, Cid, he is a grave and serious man, & his work of an order that causes him to demand back what he gives: utmost care & openness in discussion of. On top of that, he has, like any of us to whom the thing is already our life stretching down to our death, a sense of responsibility of the act of writing by anyone anywhere. . . .[28]

Though Olson felt Creeley's effectiveness as a writer derived in part from his sense of life's wholeness, from his mature understanding as a young man that "the thing is already our life stretching down to our death," Creeley seldom dealt with life as a total experience in his poetry, and he rarely mentioned death. With the exception of a silent elegy for his stepdaughter Leslie which begins "For you there ought / to be words as something / at least to say" (*Words*), and several passing references to his father's death, Creeley avoided the subject.

A central issue in "In London," however, is the inevitability of his own death. Milestone events, usually associated with middle age, such as the death of his close friend or the sudden realization that his daughter Kirsten is "a woman now / entirely," add to his concern with the fact that he is getting old. Minor events, some only related peripherally to aging, gain significance because he views them in the light of his preoccupation. For instance, a slight illness becomes a somber occasion for reflection: "The senses of one's / life beginning / to fade." That his "eye seems / to blur at close print" leads him to philosophize

283

sadly: "Pieces / fall away dis- / closing another place." "A sense of time passing surely" frames the whole.

His death, he fears, is almost at hand. Near the beginning of "In London," this all-pervasive theme is introduced in explicit terms and considered at length:

What is the
day of the
year we
sit in with
such fear.

WE'LL DIE
soon enough,
and be dead—

whence the whole
system
will fade from my head—

"but why the
tort-
ure . . ." as if

another circumstance
were forever
at hand.

•

Thinking of dying
à la Huxley on
acid so that
the beatific smile his
wife reported
was effect possibly
of the splendor of
all *possible* experience?

Or else, possibly,
the brain cells,
the whole organism,
exploding, im-
ploding, upon
itself, a galaxy
of light, energy,
forever more.

                •

Die. Dead,
come alive.

At first, the gasping poet, seemingly stunned, sounds virtually hysterical; Creeley achieves this breathy effect by breaking the opening lines on the frontal sound and then by beginning the next line with a frontal sound as well. As the speaker continues to reflect on "dying," his voice relaxes as he regains his composure. He might, he reasons, consider death an appreciated release from life. Instead of mitigating his apprehensiveness, however, the result of his speculation is to redirect his attention toward life itself. He wonders if his life should or could be different, more satisfying, a question Creeley continually asks himself in his poetry. Tortured by his desire to live "all *possible* experience" in the known world, he consoles himself here with the supposition that death is not an end but a continuance. Thus the poet achieves a measure of control over his fears; the series of poems ends on a note of optimistic resolve: "Die, Dead, / come alive." The poet has recovered his wit: his own mere words are capable of resurrecting the dead. Nonetheless, the serious issues he has raised in this passage about life and death remain unresolved by his cleverness.

What is wanted is a positive attitude toward death at the least or a sure sense of immortality at the most. The poet has neither. As an alternative to the idea that death is a meaningless finality, Creeley envisions a metaphysical state in which the living are at last gathered up into the eternal flux from which they came, a mystical circumstance analogous to the phenomenon of perpetual energy interchange in the galaxy. Of the several poems in this sequence that focus on the implications inherent in this transcendental possibility, the finest is called "Dying."

If, the poem proposes, he can believe that he as an individual is truly part of a "veritable multiplicity!" then he will be on the way toward finding the reassurance he is after. Creeley does not offer the concept of "oneness" as an accepted fact. Rather the poem, which turns on its first word, celebrates the hope:

DYING

If we are to exist,
a *we* of an imagination of
more than one, a

veritable multiplicity!
What a day
it is—what

one of many
days and many people,
who live here.

You may bring it
in now
to me. That,

one says, is
the multiplicity—
dying.

Creeley strikes the delicate balance between his longing for faith and his cynically wise understanding which argues against such faith. Hence, the poem comes to the verge of making a religion out of imagining a "veritable multiplicity!" but stops short of it just in time. With mock authority, the poet announces pompously that he is ready for death—"You may bring it / in now / to me"—thereby depending on irony to register the tenuousness of his philosophical position. By the end of the poem, he denies personal responsibility for the sophomoric idea by shifting the pronoun from "we" to "one says." Yet belief in a "veritable multiplicity!" would have been the basis of a magnificently fearless solution. For an instant in the poem, it seemed to exist: "What a day / it is—." What the poet would like to have is played off against what he knows he cannot accept; this emotional juggling accounts for the tension generated by "Dying."

When Creeley deals with the idea of a "veritable multiplicity!" as an established rationale, the result is unfortunate. In a long poem called "People," the eternal, collective life-force is personified as "myriad people" who "live // now in everything, as everything." As one of the myriad, he feels connection with the universe. He is not "isolated" but believes he has "continuous / place" in "visions of // order." These comforting notions related to the idea of "the myriad" were part of his childhood. As a child, he "knew where they were" and he assumed his sister "possibly . . . was one, / or had been one / before." Though Creeley says near the close of the poem "Some stories begin, *when I was young*— / this also," "People" itself is not a wistful, backward glance to a child's vision of immortality. Creeley neither develops his hope concerning the myriad as a fragile possibility about to vanish from his adult mind altogether, nor does he focus on his actual fear of death, which compels his present speculations. Instead, he presumes the reality of the myriad throughout the major portion of the poem as he does in this passage:

> I'll never die or else will
> be the myriad people all
> were always and must be—
>
> in a flower, in a
> hand, in some
> passing wind.

Though elsewhere in "In London" Creeley lovingly describes his felt affinity with the natural world within a recognizably human context, in this poem his delight in "a flower" or "some /

passing wind" is subordinated to his assumptions about pantheism. With utter seriousness, he speaks about "myriad people" who "live // now in everything, as everything" as a reasonable man would speak in the company of other reasonable men. However, the thought that there are "little people" who live in "a flower," "a stream of smoke," "under rocks," and even in "every insignificant part / of your body" so that if you "twist" your finger "you'll / feel the pain of all / such distortion" and the voices "will // flood your head with / terror" is surely not a serious notion.

"People" is burdened by a misplaced emphasis.[29] By dwelling at length on his ideas about the "little people," Creeley effactually sabotages the impact of even the finest passages in the poem; yet his fears about death, which, by implication, spawned these fantastic notions, lurk in the background of the poem and lend a shade of melancholy to the whole. The best poems in this sequence that present the recurrent fear-of-death motif are those in which the speaker's determination to control his apprehensiveness is set against his inability to do so completely.

In a poem titled "Moment," for instance, he thinks about what he should do with the time remaining to him. Though his meditation takes place in a graveyard, he strikes a casual posture by assuming a conversational tone and a utilitarian perspective. The only hint we get that he is troubled, that he is on the brink of losing his composure, is relegated to the naggingly provocative phrase "still preys":

MOMENT

Whether to *use* time, or to *kill* time, either
still preys on my mind.

One's come now to the graveyard,
where the bones of the dead are.

All roads *have* come
here, truly common—

except the body is moved,
still, to some other use.

Another effective way in which Creeley expresses his fears about death is first to indulge his feelings and then to castigate himself angrily for having done so. Despair followed by self-deprecating contempt is one of the characteristic emotional combinations in Creeley's poetry. In the closing stanzas of "Time," his self-pity predictably gives way to his disgust:

> . . . My time,

> one thinks,
> is drawing to
> some close. This

> feeling comes
> and goes. No
> measure ever serves

> enough, enough—
> so "finish it"
> gets done, alone.

Technically, the poet's struggle with his sadness is made evident through the articulation of the lines "some close. This" and "and goes. No" wherein the punctuation forces the reader's voice to dramatize the pull of continuing on despite the poet's impulses to the contrary. At last, the poet refuses to resign himself to his despair. His various self-urgings culminate in an angry, self-mocking outburst. He must, he demands of himself, adopt a more stoical attitude toward death despite his realization that "No / measure ever serves // enough."

Within the context of poetic association, his flat pronouncement about the inadequacy of every measure is colored by his previously expressed longing to live "all *possible* experience" before he dies despite his understanding that he will never attain such satisfaction. Again and again in this sequence, the restless poet wonders if he is taking from life all that it offers: "why / shouldn't there be // the possibility of many lives, / all lived // as one. I don't know" ("Smoke"). The curve of feeling in "Echo" is typical. The poem begins with a premonition "I'm almost / done," and goes on to convey his vague, amorphous discontent:

> Was I never here?
> The hour, the day
> I lived some
>
> sense of it?
> All wrong? . . .

He concludes with defiant resolution that borders on resignation: "*Here, here,* / the only form // I've known." Regardless of how the line "No / measure ever serves // enough" was intended or how it is interpreted, its impact derives from the poet's feeling that his time is running out. In similar fashion, the effect of many poems in this sequence is molded by this underlying omnipresent foreboding.

Perhaps Creeley's most specific statement apropos of his fear of death comes in "Somebody Died":

SOMEBODY DIED

What shall we know we don't know,
that we know we know we don't know.

•

The head walks
down the
street with
an umbrella.

•

People
were walking
by.

They will think of anything
next, the woman says.

Everything in this fragmented poem bears away from the fact that someone died. The effect is to rivet attention on it. The poem begins with a sample of giddy double-talk, moves on to a description of the present activity that aims self-consciously at precision ("*an* umbrella"), and, at the close, repeats an overheard snatch of conversation. By concentrating on the trivial and the irrelevant, the poem comments on the speaker's refusal to face the reality of death, a refusal perhaps cultivated in deference to his inability.

Creeley's preoccupation with death, which gives this sequence its distinctive character, lends a sense of urgency to his various attempts to formulate a suitable attitude so that he might die with a "beatific smile" as Huxley reportedly did. The idea that he will survive "*forever more*" because he has a place in the eternally alive "All" appeals to him; but his efforts to explore the implications inherent in this transcendental reassurance end dismally. A secular man by his own assessments as well as by familial predisposition—his grandmother, he says in "The Teachings," sought out a long lost son but decided never to speak to the "fool" again when he tried "to teach her / religion"—he pits his impulse "to love all / worlds" he lives in, "to / love everyone alive!" against his fears. For a while in the sequence it seems as if Creeley might explore the possibility that love is enough, that a "*voracious*" outpouring of affection would infuse life with meaning even in the face of death. At one point he calls himself the "poet of love" and at another he defines himself as the embodiment of "love" itself, "tracking through this / interminable sadness." His is a "slip-shod insistent sense of affection—," both eager and receptive:

> LOVE—
> let it
>
> Out,
> open up
>
> Very,
> very *voraciously*—
>
> Everywhere,
> everyone.

However, the nerve-wracking reality of his suffocating relationship with his second wife, Bobbie, argues in practical terms against his realization of this hope. The press of time aside, Bobbie is the villain of "In London." In literally every one of the many poems in which he refers to her, his impulse to love is checked, distorted, or blocked altogether. We do not get an account of the dynamics of their problematical relationship. Nor do we get a sense of Bobbie's own situation though we gather that her inner resources are severely limited. Such remarks as "GET IT anyway / you can but first of all / eat it" and "'I don't want / my tits / particularized,'" at any rate, show a lack of subtlety. In the main, Creeley gives us the speaker's response to his own frustrations. For him, for instance, her presence often conjures up thoughts of the minimal, the meager: "LOVE'S FAINT trace . . ." and "little bits" of love. He associates her with "the stain of love,"[30] thus laying bare his contempt for sex, a contempt perhaps designed to mask his insistent though unfulfilled need for love. Nonetheless, he refuses to confront the distressing reality of his marriage squarely; he refuses to end it. We are expected, presumably, to conclude that he has been victimized by her and to sympathize with his charitable attempts to reconcile their relationship:

> I DON'T HATE you lately,
> nor do I think to
> hate you
>
> lately. Nor then nor now—
> lately—no
> hate—for me,
>
> for you.

Despite the extent to which he has been disappointed in his marriage, he affirms the necessity of their relationship because he must define himself in terms of love. Even in the delicately ambivalent love song called "The Act of Love," which is his most generous expression in the sequence of his confused feelings for Bobbie, his careful tenderness seems to stem more from his painful, insistent longing to love "Everywhere, / everyone" than from his affection for this particular woman, with whom he always remains hesitant and on guard.

The poet's fear of loneliness accounts in part for his ongoing involvement with Bobbie. His uneasiness at the prospect of being left alone, often an implicit concern barely beneath the surface in many of his poems, is repeatedly an explicit issue, as just four of many similar passages make plain:

> In

> bed I yearn
> for softness, turning
> always to you. Don't,

> one wants to cry,
> desert me! Have I
> studied

> all such isolation
> just to
> be alone?

>> (from "An Illness")

> Why is it an empty house
> one moves through, shouting
> these names of people there?

>> (from "Rain [2]")

> . . .want

> you there,
> here, *be*
> *with me.*

>> (from "Smoke")

> what was the way
> which brought us here?
> To have come to it alone?

>> (from "Roads")

The poetic effect of these passages about loneliness is particularly shaped by the all-pervasive death motif. The poet imagines death to be the ultimate isolation. What he seems to fear most about death is that he will be alone; what he seems to want above all is the assurance that he will be included. If, "In London" proposes, the assumption about metaphysical "oneness" is beyond credibility, then at least its human counterpart—the feeling of camaraderie—is possible. Within Creeley's poetic world, a sense of belonging with valued friends becomes a substitute for the promise of eternity. Intense though fleeting moments of well-being with friends take on a religious aura. Of the several poems in the sequence that present spiritually suggestive idyllic scenes, the finest is "For Benny and Sabina":

FOR BENNY AND SABINA

So lovely, now, the day
quiets. What one hoped
for is realized. All

one's life has
come to this, all
is here. And it

continues taking place
for a long time.
The day recovers

itself, air feels
a wet, heavy quiet.
Grey, if one could see the sky.

I felt around myself
for something. I could
almost see you in wanting you there.

It's a hard life at times,
thoughtful, very careful
of all it seems to find.

Until anxiety intrudes, the hoped-for sense of serenity is realized: the peaceful, quiet afternoon and the pleasure of unquestioned friendship. Throughout "In London," treasured experiences such as this one are accorded the highest value because they reassure the skeptical poet, who at one point defines himself as a "wondering two-footed / notion of abeyance," that he has "a *place*" in the world ("Persons"). At ease with Mike and Joanne, he "finds / happiness // delicious . . ." ("Soup"). "For Betsy and Tom" portrays him as "happy, foolish," slightly drunk, and reveling in the self-abandon possible in the company of friends who share his love of peace: she is "charming in // the peace she so manifestly / carries with her." As these poems in "In London" attest, serenity has replaced analytical thinking—"I used to / think of the / reasons as if I // knew them" ("Song")—as the ultimate desideratum in Creeley's scale of priorities.

A cumulative effect is engendered by these isolated moments of uncompromised loveliness. Taken together, ephemeral instances of well-being create an illusion the poet would like to believe; that is, connection does in fact exist between the one and the many, between people and the world in which they live. The prized serene experience, rooted in credibly human situations with mystical overtones, reaches its epitome in a long poem near the close called " 'Bolinas and Me . . .' " in which the several motifs in the sequence are recapitulated and tentatively resolved. The poet and those he loves stand "in the open clearing" surrounded by a "circle of oaks." "The sun going west, a glowing // white yellow through the woods," makes this place seem a "holy place." It is in this "holy place" that the traveler-poet of "In London" comes as close as he will ever come to achieving a "beatific smile."

The poet's fear of death and loneliness, and his hope for love and serenity, come together to inform a single line that functions as a pleading refrain in this sequence: "I want to go home." "Home" refers both to the literal reality and to the metaphysical possibility; thus the statement is frequently appropriate. However, "I want to go home" is repeated so often in "In London" it comes dangerously close to sounding like a whine. Creeley relies heavily on the reader's willingness to respond to this line with complete sympathy, a ready willingness on the reader's part

Creeley initiates and shapes by creating a warm relationship between the speaker and reader from the start of the sequence.

In his *Paris Review* interview, Creeley says: "I feel when people read my poems most sympathetically, they are reading *with* me. So communication is mutual feeling with someone, not a didactic process of information."[31] The poet's deliberate attempt to establish and sustain "mutual feeling" with the reader is a motif *per se* in the sequence. The most obvious way in which Creeley tries to elicit and control the reader's accepting viewpoint is to address him openly and often. About one-quarter of the lines in "In London" are either direct or rhetorical questions as in this early passage:

> *Come fly with me*—like,
> *out of your mind* is
> no simile, no mere
> description—what "mere,"
> *mare, mère, mother*—
> "here then," is what you want.

> •

> Emily—simile.
> What are you
> staring at?

> •

> I wanted to find something
> worthy of respect—like
> my family, any one one knows.

> •

> What are you crossing all
> those out for. A silence lasting
> from then on . . .

Congenial and unpretentious—

I WAS NEVER SO upset
as when last I met

another idiot walking by
with much the same preoccupations as I.

—the poet plainly invites the reader's empathy and tries to maintain this rapport throughout "In London." Apart from creating sympathy for the speaker, the dynamics of the speaker-reader relationship generate energy in the sequence. This, and the fact that the speaker is usually involved in intense conversation either with himself or with seemingly dozens of friends, contributes to the feeling that a great deal is happening in these poems. Creeley would probably want the poetic achievement of "In London" to be measured in terms of how much energy the poem "explod[es], im- / plod[es], upon itself." When Jerome Mazzaro asked him what he looks for in reading other poets, Creeley answered: "Activity. Energy of thought."[32] From the standpoint of the complex of hopes and fears Creeley wrestles with in "In London," "Activity. Energy of thought" is a firm assertion of life though death is near.

The poems of "In London" follow the poet-traveler on his way "home." They show that he makes what he can of his condition with the means available to him. Unable to alter his essentially rational viewpoint, he considers the mixture as he finds it, the loneliness of it, the final tragedy of it, the peace of it. Once home in Bolinas he wonders about "all the confusions" still. But such activity has come to a quiet point, temporarily. The last paragraph of Creeley's recent essay "The Creative" would make a fitting conclusion to "In London," which ends with an essentially similar interplay of settled and unsettled feelings and ideas:

If I could just create the kind of world I'd really like to live in . . . I wouldn't be there. "I" is an experience of creation, which puts up with it no matter. There's a lot to get done. You've been born and that's the first and last ticket. Already he changes his mind, makes the necessary adjustments, picks up his suitcase and getting into his car, drives slowly home.

He lives with people whom he has the experience of loving. It's late. But they'll be there. He relaxes. He has an active mind.[33]

NOTES

1. M. L. Rosenthal, "Problems of Robert Creeley," *Parnassus* 2, no. 1 (Fall/Winter 1973): 205. [Excerpt reprinted in this collection.]

2. Aram Saroyan, "An Extension of Content," *Poetry* 104 (1964): 46.

3. Robert Creeley, *A Quick Graph: Collected Notes and Essays* (San Francisco: Four Seasons Foundation, 1970), 124. Creeley is describing Louis Zukofsky's attitude with which he feels an affinity.

4. William Carlos Williams, *A Voyage to Pagany*, introduction by Harry Levin (New York: New Directions, 1970), xi.

5. Williams, *A Voyage to Pagany*, 15.

6. Citations in the text of this chapter are to Robert Creeley, *A Day Book* (New York: Scribners, 1972), unnumbered.

7. Williams, *A Voyage to Pagany*, xvii, and xvi.

8. Ibid., xiv.

9. Creeley, *A Quick Graph*, 12.

10. Citations in this text of the 1967 preface are to Robert Creeley, *The Charm* (San Francisco: Four Seasons Foundation, 1969).

11. Creeley, *Contexts of Poetry: Interviews 1961–1971* (Bolinas, Calif.: Four Seasons Foundation, 1973), 42.

12. Ibid.. 192.

13. Ibid., 42.

14. Ibid., 193.

15. Ibid., 192.

16. Denise Levertov, "Review of *Pieces*," in *The Poet in the World* (New York: New Directions, 1973), 239–40. [Reprinted in this collection.]

17. Charles Olson, *Selected Writings* (New York: New Directions, 1966), 16.

18. John Tytell, *Naked Angels: The Lives and Literature of the Beat Generation* (New York: McGraw-Hill, 1976), 214.

19. As quoted by Tytell, *Naked Angels*, 199.

20. Ibid., 115. Burroughs learned the "cut-up" mosaic technique from Brion Gysin, who tape recorded a message that became a touchstone for him:

I come to free the words
The words are free to come
I come freely to the words
The free come to the words

The similarity between the passage associated with Burroughs and the "small dreams" passage in "In London" seems too close to be unintentional.

21. Creeley, *Contexts,* 26.

22. Ibid., 21.

23. Philip L. Gerber, ed., "From the Forest of Language: A Conversation with Robert Creeley," *Athanor* 4 (1973): 10. Gerber asked Creeley to describe "Creeley poetry." He answered:

In my own rather semi-conscious understanding of what it's like, my poetry tends to be often in the emotional situation of being "uptight." It's nervous. In fact, at times, when I read, people assume that I'm in a highly nervous state, because the poetry sounds of this order. But when I was still quite young, just beginning thus to write, Charles Olson pointed out to me one of my dilemmas. In trying to achieve an effective line, I was extending it—the result of my interest in Wallace Stevens and respect for him—in ways that my own energy couldn't sustain. I tended to speak in a short, intensive manner. My thought, the line of my thought, Olson generously said, was rather long; but the statement of my thought was characteristically short and intensive. Olson had never met me at this time. He was getting this completely from the characteristic letters and writing I was sending him."

24. Creeley, *Contexts,* 193.

25. Gerber, "From the Forest of Language," 12.

26. Creeley, *Contexts,* 7. Creeley suggests his indebtedness to Jackson Pollock and John Cage.

27. Ibid., 193. Creeley is speaking here about the poems in *Pieces.* The same is true about the poems of "In London."

28. Charles Olson, *Letters for Origin: 1950–1956,* edited by Albert Glover (London: Cape Goliard Press, 1969), 87.

29. "People," first published in a single-poem volume titled *1°2°3°4°5°6°7°8°9°0* (Berkeley: Shambala; San Francisco: Mundra, 1971), is dedicated to the artist Arthur Okamura. Okamura's eighteen delightful drawings of "little people" in the shapes of flowers, letters of the alphabet, and the like accompany the stanzas. Apart from being of interest in their own right, Okamura's designs remedy the misemphasis on the serious in "People" by illustrating the whimsical element inherent in the ideas the poem presents. "People," as it appears in "In Lon-

don," suffers without them. Incidentally, it would seem that the name of this handsome ninety-page volume would refer more appropriately to "Numbers" (*Pieces*), a poem Creeley wrote at the suggestion of Robert Indiana (*Contexts,* 201) and dedicated to him.

30. Creeley also used the phrase "the stain of love" in one of his earliest poems inspired by his unhappy first marriage. In both "The Edge" (1971) and "Love" ("Not enough.") (1951), Creeley makes much of the phrase he borrowed from Williams's "Love Song." Whereas in Williams's poem, the deliciously sensuous "honey thick stain" suffuses "the colors / of the whole world," bathing the world in love, in both of Creeley's poems "the stain of love" refers to sexuality as a blight, literally as "the stain."

31. As quoted by Jerome Mazzaro, "Robert Creeley, the Domestic Muse, and Post-Modernism," *Athanor* 4 (1973): 23.

32. Gerber, "From the Forest of Language," 14.

33. Robert Creeley, "The Creative," *Sparrow* 6 (1973), unnumbered.

ROBERT DUNCAN

A Reading of *Thirty Things*

for Michael Davidson and Michael Palmer

I

"When the ten thousand things have been seen in their unity"—
in my memory of the passage I had got the number of "things"
as 1,001, the number of tales in the cycle of *Arabian Nights,* and
built up an authoritative sounding reference to the number as
linking the Far East and the Arabian world of Scheherazade—
"we return to the beginning and remain where we have always
been" (Ts'en Shen).

After the daily calendar of *A Day Book* and given a deliberate
format in Robert Indiana's design for the cover, we might go on
in the new work to read "thirty" as the number of days in a
given month. And there is the feel of days going by in these
poems—even better, the feel of the calendar sheets tearing off
and blowing away as in the conventional motion picture lan-
guage. "A wind / blows steadily / as we sit" in an imaginary
film would turn the calendar pages and stand for the passage of
years. There is the feel of camera shots, a language of things seen
in a sequence of frames, in the sequence of poems that unreel the
book.

It is a book of Time passing. Creeley formed in jazz comes
into the kingdom of a people formed in rock. The time passing
from the Creeley song on through Ebbe Borregaard's postrock
song. "Echoes preponderantly / backwards." The poem "Sur-

From *boundary 2* 6, no. 3; 7, no. 1 (Spring/Fall 1978): 293–99. Reprinted by
permission.

geons" for the readers of Creeley will remind them of the poet's father, who died in Creeley's childhood; and in "Post Cards," the phrase

> Dad's mother's
> death

may have been taken up even as it was overheard in one of Creeley's daughter's conversations.

"Kitchen" addresses the passage of time directly:

> In the silence now
> of this high square room
> the clock's tick adjacent
> seems to mark old time.

And in "Photo," the woman

> . . . leaves
> a very vivid sense,
> after her,
> of having been there.

If "the ocean under / the road's edge" is Time, the road is the Life Way, and Time's erosion comes to mind. Here, especially, where the cliff edge at the Pacific is ever continually falling away, undermined, and the road must be reconstructed to go on.

"One day after another" would verify my initial sense of thirty days. Hath November April June and September. But come Xmas—that's December, with thirty and one. In the poem "Master of All," "Days have gone by / as I have been here"; and the matter of Time is there again, "abstract clock / literally so ticks"—so I write; but the word is "ticks." Things "click" into place.

II

The Ts'en Shen sentence appears as the epigraph to Maria Dermoût's life story *The Ten Thousand Things*. It is meant to be an old woman's book—she was sixty-seven in 1955 when the novel was finished—a novel about living in the after-fullness of one's time. Creeley's announcement of this "Master of all things / wisdom's fine ending / in the air begun with" belongs to such an after-fullness or poetry of afterthought. It is the "silence" of "in the silence now" in the poem "Kitchen" or the "still" of the poem "Still," where even as the theme of silence comes into "still the same day" and the title "Photo" may echo as a double exposure in the title, as the doubling arouses our suspicions, language in the still of the poem may be condensed into an intoxication of confused meanings.

The "alone" of the poem "Characteristically" refers to this silence around the event of the poem in which words are charged with meaning to the utmost possible degree. This is to read the "book" as a total field in which each word in its place charges the disposition of every other place. At last—lastingly alone—in one's "own" time—looking at it—thinking "where to end." In the fit, "feel it / in two places"—"places of fabulous intent" then, "mirrors," "echoes": the book proposes how it is to be read as it is written. It is, of course, that wisdom-as-such that Charles Olson so sharply spotted and rebuked among my own leanings.

I go back to read in the midst of this reading of Creeley's *Thirty Things*, Maria Dermoût's *The Ten Thousand Things* that Barbara Joseph first called to my attention. Not by the rime and contrast of the titles alone—the proposition of an abundance in the fullness of Maria Dermoût and of a scarcity, a Puritan scarcity, in the fullness of Creeley—am I led, but there is something else, for both write of living known in the lengthening shadows.

These things I have to declare at Death's customs—the ten thousand—thirty things.

It is not a matter of growing old in itself. The idea of growing old and coming upon death was years ago so lovely in my mind, the seductive line of a perspective that sharpened each "thing" in the course of life and drew it toward the remote proposition of a vanishing point and horizon, even as the idea of being a child was lovely, was "ghostly," each "thing" coming forward into life from a point—it was just this that was my "wisdom as such," this proposition of the Child consciousness throughout, that left me, in Olson's view of it, always "less [a child] or more [an old wise man] than I was"—this romance of living in perspectives of beginnings and endings has always been strong in my responses so that I have been ready indeed for the late afternoon stillness of these poems, as I was ready to love the late afternoon stillness of Maria Dermoût's little masterpiece. At fifty-five [fifty-eight now in 1977] am I any closer to "old" than Robert Creeley who in 1973 was but forty-seven? "Age," like "childhood," exists only as we create it. Oddly enough, how we "remember" it to be.

> Still the same
> day?
> Tomorrow.

Creeley has it.

In Maria Dermoût's realm we are reminded throughout of the ocean's being there: "On a stretch of beach under the plane trees, where the little waves of the surf flow out: three waves, one behind the other—behind the other—behind the other." It comes in from the first as the key to the mode of remembering itself, thinking like the sea; and as the lead motif then of the insistence of life itself: "where the surf came in from the ocean 'with its steadily repeating equally heavy beats' he had written." As Creeley in turn keeps reminding us of the ocean:

> wind on the ocean
>
> ("The Temper")

> and the sea
> opens below you,
> west
>
> ("As You Come")

> The road
> goes out to the channel
> of the water
>
> ("As We Sit")

Hear

the ocean under
the road's edge

("Place")

water, land's place
in it

("Master of All")

Natural enough, in a sequence of poems written in Bolinas, the ocean just off there where it is. Dying.

WHERE.

"Laughing" / "Who enters this / kingdom." These thirty things present a specific realm: laughing, we must enter. "As You Come" specifies (as in the *Mysteries of the Other World*— whether the Orphic tour or the map instructions of the Bardo state) the route. "As you come down / the road, it swings / slowly left and the sea / opens below you, / west." Read it as a student of a mystery searches a text where language has been "charged with meaning to the utmost possible degree" and speech grows oracular.

"Echoes preponderantly / backwards" may also then in the poem "Characteristically" be taking soundings of where it is, where the poem is at large, where the immediate poem finds itself to be in the line. The change—it is the change announced in the poetry itself—is from "the highway" to a byway in the art: "and drive up a country road."

then: "no nearer here / than there." In the poem "As We Sit," sightings are given again: "The road goes out to the channel / of the water." "Here . . . where there / is"—two worlds, more and more this emerges as the shamanistic mode in which the poet would trip out beyond "his own life," "what a small / place to be."

The poem "But" recites the rime of "where" in "there" again, and "[REPEAT]" signifies, a road sign pointing, a round.

The woman who "leaves / a very vivid sense . . . of having been there" in "Photo" may have been to the other world the poet begins to dwell upon the thought of. She may belong to the "ending," "in the air begun with." "There" is just beyond "here" everywhere now. We are not far from the poet of *The Four Quartets* and his "In my beginning is my end" thematic refrain. Where the field composition of Olson in *Maximus* was an onrushing moving picture projection, Creeley's field is a still life. This is still life. The "INSTANTER" here is an instant arrest.

It is true to this arrest of motion that the doubling of worlds and meanings in one nexus appears. There is no springing from here to there, but "there" is "here." Where in Olson we have to do with a dialectic, in Creeley we have to do with a developing exposure. We begin to see what is in the picture.

In the poem "Post Cards"—postcards that must go somewhere, have come from somewhere, arriving in the mail as they do— we find "Heaven must spell something." "Death," the poem message reads.

On the following page (the last of seven messages—the number of days in the week ending in Sunday—given a page of its own, becomes ambiguously a poem in itself, to make thirty and one, the number of days in the month that contains Xmas) I find "Up on the top the / space goes further than / the eye can see." Prepositions of place ring out in the sequence: "in," "down," "below," "before," "under" in one sequence; "out" (as in the vernacular of the day, *far out*), "up," "above" in another. I would read back ("echoes preponderantly backwards") to note the drive "up" a country road (this "kingdom," this "country," this "there," this "Heaven" spells what?) at the end, I think, a road that, in living, we were coming "down" ("as you come down / the road") returns "a long / stretch of sky / before us." If the expression "far out" sounds in the poem "No"— "No farther out / than in— / no nearer here / than there"—the meaning of "high" current in the drug culture certainly is there in "Xmas Poem: Bolinas": "Come Christmas / we'll get high / and go find it." And one cannot avoid the word "high" then in "the highway," which becomes "the high way"; yet throughout the proposition of going "over the hill," going beyond life of

> up here, calling
> over the hill

redefines the evident. I would read then "it" as "this kingdom," "Heaven" close to the sense of the Tao in Lao-Tze; here the road of life leads down to bring us "up," the sequence is haunted throughout by the sense of a trip to a spirit place. And the road instructions read "As you come down the road" back (as the sign in the poem "But" insists "[REPEAT]") to "up here . . . over the hill" "in the air begun with" that the Master of All knows, in order to see in the first line of the thirtieth poem, "Colors," "colors of stars" above; then below: "Cars / lights, wet streets." Again. "There," "here." "Feel it / in two places," the poem "Two" tells us.

III

"All you people." Who are "the people / formed in rock"? They are the following generation after Creeley who was formed in jazz, and their names appear in dedications of the poems: Ebbe (Borregaard) addressed in "For Ebbe," Joanne Kyger, addressed in the poem "Photo," and Tom Clark in "For Tom": three poets who define the Bolinas scene "here" for Creeley; and the filmmaker Stan Brakhage (as I read it a key to how much we are to read these poems as being of the order Creeley sees in Brakhage's own development of brief film things, *études,* or, as he calls them, poems, moving stills): these four are further demarked by Bobbie Creeley's (Bobbie Louise Hawkins's) use of their likenesses in her illustration of the volume. Then Bob Grenier and Ted Berrigan complete the identification of those poets who came after Creeley. The cast is discretely drawn: "stars," as Creeley reads it, of a firmament yet to come.

So, it may be that as more and more evidently Creeley finds himself moved upstairs into the firmament, "he has arrived; he is THERE," we say, down here where we are.

And (I would recall here that Creeley is a grandfather) one enti-
tled as in the poem "Hey" to address a new one coming along
the road to pass by—"Hey kid" who is entirely "flesh filled / to
bursting."

Then, the people who have gone before him: it is the address of
the poem "Surgeon"—it is in the full admission of death that we
admit fathers who were once babies coming into this world,
passing out of this world. "No farther out," he notes in the
poem "No," "than in"; then—"here"; "there." The "outside /
inside" of the poem "A."

   "Post Cards" 6: "Dad's mother's / death," and in "Home,"
family portraits again: "Patsy's / brother / Bill—," "Meg's /
mother—," and then, the "Father's // home" which may mean
"this is Father's home" and /or "Father is home."

HOME. AT LAST. THE END.

"Where" we find means "where to end." Returning to read the
second poem of the book, "The Temper," "The temper is frag-
ile / as apparently it wants to be," I would read to say that it
wants to end at last.

Seeking the way toward "wisdom's fine ending"—here, surely,
I am right that Creeley remembers Olson's warning and, with a
will that confronts Olson's will, Creeley addresses "places of
fabulous intent," the, "mirrors of wisdom, quiet." If he so pro-
poses where he is going—"I'll dash off / to it," he says in
"Characteristically," and, in "Xmas Poem: Bolinas," "we'll get
high / and go find it," he proposes a poetry that is at once
projective and deliberate. There is a tension between resignation
and resolution throughout. In reading we return again and again
to the note to re-sign the word, the phrase, to reread the sign.

So, thirty things to declare at Death's customs. "The sea / opens
below you, / west." To go west. "It sounds out." Out there, I
hear, the way out. And in the poem "As We Sit": "a long /
stretch . . . before us" . . . "the road goes out to the channel."

"Hear // the ocean under / the road's edge"; it steadily erodes the way we go. The poem "In The Fall" picks up the proposition of the temper's wanting to be fragile, where now let us read it as "needing to be" as well as "wishing to be"—it is what we took it to be in need of, it needs in order to be. The "green growth" of "Post Cards" 5 comes to rest as "Hanging leaves / hang on" in the fall.

The promise that "These things are not / without an ending." They end in order to be.

IV

And we the people of this time called "ours." . . .

LINDA W. WAGNER

Creeley's Late Poems: Contexts

When I started writing about Creeley and his work a dozen years ago, it was largely to defend his short-line poetics, his ultrapersonal subjects, his interest in language and language theory. In 1977, after the publication of *Thirty Things* and *Away,* the need seems to remain nearly the same; the reading context, however, has changed so radically that justifying Creeley's structure and subject matter on grounds of his personal preference is begging the question.

Wittgenstein. Wittgenstein's *Zettel* and the notion of reality and self-perception. What *is* this self the poet—trapped in the poverty of contemporary poetics (thankfully Frank O'Hara could write about paintings once in a while)—must use as content, theme, albatross? Wittgenstein. Wittgenstein's *Philosophical Investigation* and the notion of *knowing,* and then, subsequently or simultaneously, *saying:* the trap, the freedom, of language-games:

78. Compare *knowing* and *saying:*
         how many feet high Mont Blanc is—
         how the word "game" is used—
         how a clarinet sounds.
     If you are surprised that one can know something and not be able to say it, you are perhaps thinking of a case like the first. Certainly not of one like the third.[1]

From *boundary 2* 6, no. 3; 7, no. 1 (Spring/Fall 1978): 301–8. Reprinted in *American Modern: Essays in Fiction and Poetry* (Port Washington, N.Y.: National University Publications/Kennikat Press, 1980), 178–86, 262. Reprinted by permission.

Comparing Wittgenstein's cryptic numbered observations with Creeley's recent poems gives the reader the same sense of enigma, of closed system; the verbal notes seem intended to be provocative, perverse, incomplete—but incomplete only until one recognizes the language-game.

TWO

Light weighs
light, to the hand,
to the eye.

Feel it
in two places.[2]

In this poem about knowing, tactile and sensual—or at least partly about knowing—Creeley rests on an underlying system of images: visual perception as an index to sensitivity, compassion, is common in Creeley's poetics. In "Characteristically," also from *Thirty Things,* the poet plays more openly with the language-game premise, that language is refuge as well as key. (Wittgenstein: "The *truth* of my statements is the test of my understanding of these statements. // That is to say: if I make certain false statements, it becomes uncertain whether I understand them. // What counts as an adequate test of a statement belongs to logic. It belongs to the description of the language-game.[3] . . . This possibility of satisfying oneself is part of the language-game. Is one of its essential features."[4])

CHARACTERISTICALLY

Characteristically and other words,
places of fabulous intent,
mirrors of wisdom, quiet
mirrors of wisdom. Help

the one you think needs it.
Say a prayer to yourself.

•

Echoes preponderantly
backwards. Is alone.

•

I'll dash off
to it.[5]

Poems that speak primarily about the poet's problems of
identifying and describing, poems that are epistemological both
in content and method, have been Creeley's trademark through-
out his career. He has, from the beginning, been involved with
knowing, perceiving; and the linguistic problems connected
with that perceiving. His early fascination with the poetry of
Wallace Stevens—that most experimental of all the modern
poets in terms of his own language-games—suggested the direc-
tion for Creeley's own personal poetics. And for all the parallels
his better-known poems appeared to have with the writing of
William Carlos Williams, Creeley's interest was either the later
Williams (particularly "The Desert Music," which gropes to-
ward a definition of poetic language, among other things) or
with the dimension of language and its use in Williams's early
poems. In a 1964 letter, Creeley made the distinction between
idiomatic and *colloquial* in Williams's poetic vocabulary: "They do
echo a 'spoken' sense of sequence, rather than a 'literary' one—
but the individual words . . . are often in no sense 'colloquial.'
More frequently, the vocabulary itself, in Williams, . . . all key
terms seem not 'colloquial'; yet the emphasis is an instance
clearly of spoken 'term.' "[6] What Williams was able to achieve
puzzled Creeley, at times; and he resented the gloss of inexact
critical terminology which created similarities when there might
well have been more important differences.

One of the fallacies of that same kind of criticism is that in
naming Creeley a "Black-Mountain" poet, in grouping his
work with that of such different poets as Robert Duncan, Denise
Levertov, Charles Olson, and even, at times, such Beat poets as

Allen Ginsberg and Phil Whalen, many crucial observations about his poetry and his poetics have been forestalled.

One central approach to Creeley's work, all of his work, should have been epistemological. Wittgenstein's premises of knowledge imperfect till trapped in language, and language imperfect trapped as it is in its own game patterns—these were the bases for what I would call Creeley's "hesitation" stance toward both speaking and expressing meaning. On its most practical level, this hesitancy shows up as short lines in the poems, extremely fragmented syntax, a start-stop rhythm that does accurately reflect Creeley's own normal speech pattern. In the 1950s, when poets were fighting for the right to re-create their natural if idiosyncratic speech patterns, readers saw the extremely short lines as illustration of that fight for freedom, and felt no need to look beyond the fact that sentence flow was, often, strangely interrupted. That Creeley's speech rhythm was unlike that of most contemporary poets was accepted as a given: form and the freedom from traditional prescriptions were so involving in themselves that no further justification was necessary.

Students of poetry in the 1950s and the early 1960s were so excited about formalistic concerns—those years being the apex of the craft consciousness that started a half century earlier, with Ezra Pound's "Make it new" blazoned across the literary world—that those considerations obscured the more traditional interest in content, message, saying. But when this generation of poets ran head on into the later 1960s readers, for whom content was all, whether in protest against racism, sexism, Vietnam, or the elitism of innovative poetry, there was no longer any common bond poetically. If, as most critics were saying, if Creeley's poetry was important because it illustrated an individualistic breath measure and poetic line—and only that—then why should a generation of readers who had shaped their lives to individualism be impressed? The poetic freedoms of the 1950s were only intellectual backwash to the children of the 1960s.

The currency of Creeley's poetry is not, of course, in its line division; and it has never been. It lies instead in the reason for his verbally tentative approach toward expression; and in his attitudes toward language. Existentialist in his increasingly noticeable insistence on the need for syntactic individuality, Creeley continues the direction of his early writing in *A Day Book, Pieces, Away,* and *Thirty Things*—to the bewilderment of readers who had been urged to read his work twenty years before for what were, at best, peripheral reasons. It had all been clearly established in the 1963 novel, *The Island,* the fiction in which John could no longer find even his wife, much less his rationale for loving her, his work, his purpose, his identity:

> He couldn't find her. He could barely see the path, and managed to keep on it only because he had used it so often, going to the sea. What was supposed to be the point of it all, then. . . . He could not feel anything any more . . .[7]

The way to some sort of self-knowledge has usually been thought to be immediate sensory perception (Wittgenstein: " 'I know that this is a hand.'—And what is a hand?—'Well, *this,* for example.' "[8]). Creeley's novel strips its antihero of every means of achieving self-understanding, and leaves him thinking his wife dead—in her very presence. Misreading all physical clues, John comes to only the bleakest and most limited kinds of understanding—i.e., that he does not understand. When Creeley later writes about *The Island,* he uses the term "narrative" as being more accurate than "fiction":

> It [narrative] comes from a root having to do with "to know"—which is useful, and hence the act of, to make known.[9]

The 1972 *A Day Book* extends the same kinds of premises, the use of immediate experience, usually portrayed in prose, set against more philosophical, questioning sections that jar the reader's expectations. If Williams's "No ideas but in things" was Creeley's rationale, he was doing a great many embroideries on the initial object line: these red wheelbarrows are alternately swathed in star-dotted gauze or draped in curtains of heavy black velvet, as this typical entry illustrates:

Going to sleep. Waking up. Moving. Waking with stomach ache, sudden premonition of death—probably echo of the past weeks and fear of one's own "time." What would it be like. Nothing much—certainly nothing you can live in. Aunt's apparent tiredness. Doctor's sense, she didn't want to try to continue living. Better—she knew what she didn't want to do anymore. Arrangements within self, rapport with the surrounding. Keep it moving. Can *thinking* be prior to action, *is* an action, etc. Never felt one would or could think of something previous to its "circumstances" and/or recognition. Couldn't somehow "get ahead" of it. Always in situation of "seeing it" now that "it's there."[10]

"So explain myself, to myself . . ." the day book goes on, and it becomes clear, that the connecting thread that loops throughout the book is this questioning of what seems to be self-knowledge, the pragmatic American "Know thyself" seen as not only difficult but probably impossible. And from the vantage point of the day book approach, Creeley has been moving in a more fragmentary mode of expression in the last poem collections—toward the same kind of goal. The titles of the books suggest this far-from-optimistic progression: from *Words* to *Pieces* to *Thirty Things,* an admission of the power of the nonverbal (the book built, as printed, in conjunction with the Bobbie Creeley illustrations, of which there are also thirty), and finally to the nonverbal stance of *Away.*

The progression in the choice of titles also suggests that Creeley's concern with language and its range of implication, its paradigm for expression of meaning/meanings, has changed. Once convinced that there were words to say whatever he needed to express, as in the powerful poems to his daughters and Bobbie in *For Love,* Creeley seems, in the late poems, to be less sure of that equivalent kind of relationship. "I'll never get it right enough, / will never stop trying. . . . All the negatives in existence / don't change anything anyway. . . ."[11] Words may not be able to express the things—whatever that concrete noun has to do with the emotional states that most poetry works with—so well as the poet had intended, but perhaps the nature of words is to be beyond that kind of expression, to become entities in themselves rather than equivalents. What appears to be happening in the later poems, language used as fact, as object in itself, rather than language as reduction of feeling into grammar, is suggested in Creeley's remarks in the recent *APR* interview. He begins by describing a conversation with Samuel Beckett, who was saying "his wish would be to realize one word that would be autonomous, that would depend upon no other situation either in existence or in creation for its actuality. It would be in some ways like 'Om,' but it would be initial, it would not be created out of some other possibility." Creeley continues,

> this you get to in Wittgenstein's . . . he has a lecture on religion in which he speaks of the impulse of language to go to nonsense, to where it shall survive totally apart from any other reality. A wall against which we all beat our heads, knowing we'll never pass that limit, but that which we nonetheless still try to do, to move into a situation of pure creation. . . .[12]

He admits in that interview to being fascinated by the possibility of getting "one or two syllables to create a spectrum of event or happening that would otherwise be as long as two thousand pages."

The late poems:

> Falls
> always. . . .
>
> ("Up in the Air")

> Every day
> in a little way
> things are done.
>
> Every morning there is
> a day. Every day
> there is a day. . . .
>
> ("Every Day")

Raining here
in little pieces
of rain.
Wet, brother,

behind the ears,
I love your hands.
And you too,
rain. . . .

("Funny")

Approached linguistically, with the reader concentrating on literal meaning, these seemingly fragmentary segments are less than impressive. One already senses, however, even in this loaded group of examples, Creeley's wry sense of language, of humor, of repetition (the *rains*, the *heres*, the *rooms*, the insistence on place, on person in place); the pattern starts to make sense. We fall into Creeley's sense of language—rather, his sense of language begins to absorb us. We accept his conventions of meaning, and the result of reading through a collection like *Away* is the conviction that this is a unified book, that the poems are once again built around the central themes of family; the loss of love—either in the loss of Bobbie and her love, or that of his mother through death; and the rebirth of his love for his children. Familiar Creeley themes: no poet working today relies so entirely on his intimate observations about his intimacies. The amazing point is that Creeley continues to pull it off, interesting us, convincing us that his private concerns are ways of understanding our own perhaps very different personal lives and minds. Seeing Creeley's face bared to bone in that mirror of language, his own language, makes us look hurriedly for our own reflections; or, as the epigraph from Wittgenstein reads,

"One can own a mirror; does one then own the reflection that can be seen in it?"

The image recurs throughout *Away:* in "Circles," the love poem to the lost lover, "If I wanted / to know myself, / I'd look

at you. // When I loved / what I was, / it was that reflection."
Never simplistic, however, the poet continues,

> Color so changing here,
> sky lightens, water
>
> greens, blues.
> Never far from you,
>
> no true elsewhere.
> My hands stay with me.

The immediate, the true; however obscured all other realities
may be, the knowledge that yes, one's hands are still intact—the
pose of the searcher, the observer, hands in lap, eyes intent: this
is the pose Creeley's poetry suggests. "I don't love / to prove
it—love / to know it." The real, the actual, but how to fix that
actuality in words. The most poignant poem in the book is
Creeley's "For My Mother: Genevieve Jules Creeley," and in
that long poem, he cries, "Mother, I / love you—for // what-
ever that / means, / meant—more // than I know, body / gave
me my / own, generous, // inexorable place / of you. . . ."
Finding the sensual satisfaction of place, of person, abandoning
words, though the human consciousness must still use them, but
the poetic consciousness less often Stein-like, Creeley faces the
dilemma repeatedly of working the medium defined by the sim-
plest of human thought processes—the reduction absurd that
there could ever be *any* word equivalent to any human feeling.
Anger, love, peace, sorrow—his poems have traced the modula-
tions in his reactions to the syntactic mystery for twenty years.
That he has moved away from those problems, into a purer state
of word equivalency, may be the change between the poems of
For Love and *Away;* but the change is not radical. Reading Witt-
genstein and Gertrude Stein and Wallace Stevens before coming
to Creeley might not be redundant preparation; accepting his
recent work in the spirit of excitement that rereading it never
fails to create might be a more appropriate exercise. After all, he
has said it very clearly:

I'm telling you a
story to let myself
think about it. All

day I've been
here, and yesterday.
The months, years,

enclose me as
this thing with arms
and legs. And if

it *is* time
to talk about it,
who knows better

than I?

NOTES

1. Ludwig Wittgenstein, *Philosophical Investigations,* trans. G. E. M. Anscombe (Oxford: Basil Blackwell, 1953), 36e.

2. Robert Creeley, "Two," in *Thirty Things* (Los Angeles: Black Sparrow Press, 1974), 59.

3. Ludwig Wittgenstein, *On Certainty,* trans. Denis Paul and G. E. M. Anscombe (Oxford: Basil Blackwell, 1969), 84, 12e.

4. Ibid., 7, 2e.

5. Creeley, *Thirty Things,* 17.

6. Robert Creeley to author, Placitas, New Mexico, May 29, 1964.

7. Robert Creeley, *The Island* (New York: Charles Scribner's Sons, 1963), 185.

8. Wittgenstein, *On Certainty,* 275, 35e.

9. Creeley to author, 1964.

10. Robert Creeley, *A Day Book* (New York: Charles Scribner's Sons, 1972), unnumbered.

11. Robert Creeley, *Away* (Santa Barbara: Black Sparrow Press, 1976), 56, 11. All subsequent unidentified quotations are from poems from this collection.

12. Terry R. Bacon, "How He Knows When to Stop: Creeley on Closure; A Conversation with the Poet," *American Poetry Review* 5, no. 6 (Oct., 1976): 7.

CHRISTOPHER LAMBERT

From "Possibilities of Conclusion"

Robert Creeley has been walking the same, if steadily shortening, tightrope for some time. Balanced on what Louis Martz has called the "taut edge of poetic existence,"[1] his poetry displays an irritating kind of tunnel vision, each successive volume only acting to further narrow the field of his attention. Under such ever-increasing magnification, it might even be fair to say that Creeley's is a poetry of the microscope. As the volumes slide past, more and more his language and ever-diminishing subject matter assume a ritualistic character, recurrent and closed. When coupled with the disturbing wariness of completion in his later volumes, the poem trapped in the act of *being* the poem, his verse approaches a state of covert solipsism or private incantation. Perhaps the extreme was reached in his collection *Thirty Things,* with the poem "A Loop,"

> No
> one
> thing
>
> anyone does

which Creeley conceives of as a Mobius twist in language, an endless repetition. A poem like this goes nowhere, has nowhere to go except back upon itself; here the piece of rope upon which he performs his tricks is at its shortest. Happily, with his latest volume, *Later,* he has again given himself more room to maneuver. Since two volumes of critical attention, Cynthia Edelberg's

Review of *Later* from *Parnassus* 9, no. 2 (Fall/Winter 1981): 255–66. Reprinted by permission.

Robert Creeley's Poetry: A Critical Introduction and *Was That a Real Poem & Other Essays* (a collection of Creeley's own criticism), have been published recently, one must at least applaud Creeley's timing.

If we recall William Carlos Williams's instruction that a poet thinks with his poem, Creeley's has always been a poetry of *occasion*. He has consistently refused to allow intellection to predetermine the poem. Even as early as 1964, in his essay "A Sense of Measure," he is at pains to "make understood I do not feel the usual sense of *subject* in poetry to be of much use. . . . I feel that subject is at best a material of the poem, and that poems finally derive from some deeper complex of activity."[2] As to what this constitutes Creeley is less than precise, as if he wants to sustain a deliberate mystification of the specifics of his poetic process. Edelberg's new book (which marks something of a milestone by lending Creeley's poetry academic credibility) comprehensively explores a linear progress of development in his verse, moving from a state of limited intellection through a successive and intentional series of "refinements" to a state which she calls "home," an aphorism for its essential privacy.[3] Nevertheless, Creeley militates against a poetry of vague outpourings of emotion. By subjecting his verse to a continual process of concentraton, the extreme brevity of his poetic line acts as a tonal regulator; in the end, his poetry has something of the character of the miniaturist. At times, it is almost as if this method is too exclusive and delicate for the harsh vagaries of the world outside.

Unlike the more conspicuous concerns of his Black Mountain colleagues (Robert Duncan's attempt to "transform American literature into a viable language"[4] or Edward Dorn's fascination with "geography" and political motivation), Creeley's poetry has a distinctly personal cast—the reader often little more than a spectator of the poet's interior life. His poems rigorously inhabit this closed world. Often the very act of thinking is, in Edelberg's words, "a self-sufficient occasion."[5]

> In my head I am
> walking but I am not
> in my head, where

is there to walk,
not thought of, is
the road itself more

than seen. I think
it might be, feel
as my feet do, and

continue, and
at least reach, slowly,
one end of my intention.

("Walking")

A poem such as this is almost hermetically sealed, too much like a conundrum. For Creeley, the focus of attention remains stubbornly singular, the scale always localized; he offers neither the poetic range of Duncan, Dorn, and Levertov nor their varied interests. His is an elaborately egocentric poetry. And it is precisely this collision of the private with the public requirements of language and audience that determines Creeley's characteristic poetic posture, the tightrope walker. Sadly, it is a stance that only intermittently recognizes the difficulties it presents for the reader.

Caught as he is in this balancing act, Creeley cannot afford Olson's expansiveness. Whereas Olson employs an open form (resulting in sprawling, scattered clusters of breath units, usually of variant length), Creeley employs an intricate control of lineation and structure to sustain the intrinsic fragility of his expression. In his poetry articulation is the intent.

Poetry seems to me to be written momently—that is, it occupies a moment of time. . . . I seem to be given to work in some intense moment of whatever possibility, and if I manage to gain the articulation necessary *in* that moment, then happily there is the poem.[6]

The limited field described, the stress upon precision, and the simultaneity of creation and presentation act as indices within which his poetry operates. The result is an intuitive, one might say instinctual structure; by way of example he cites the analogy of driving, the road only becoming itself in the moment of one's attention. Alternatively, in the preface to his collection of short stories *The Gold Diggers* he describes the process as, "I begin where I can and end when I see the whole thing returning." One must be glad that at least Creeley knows what he is doing; like Ali Baba, only he knows the password.

Having stipulated that it is only the "quality of the articulation" that determines a poem's permanence, Creeley winnows his language down to its most fundamental, while attempting to ensure that the resultant spareness of his phrasing in no way vitiates the poem's internal mechanics. The demands on his control are considerable. Even in his latest volume, a number of poems seem exasperatingly thin.

> What'd you throw it on the floor for?
> Who the hell you think you are
>
> come in here
> push me around
>
> ("Riddle")

There is nothing more than posturing, barely the framework of a poem. So much has been whittled away that what remains is only runic. Similarly, the complexity of syntax regularly demonstrated by his poetry underlines his need to sustain a language that is hard, clear, and unadorned; what Creeley is after is an authority in language akin to Pound's. When augmented by his seemingly willful confusion of punctuation, it is a need that is not always fulfilled.

> Weather's a funny
> factor, like once
>
> day breaks, storm's
> lifted, or come,
>
> faces, eyes,
> like clouds drift

over this world,
are all there is

of whatever there is.
("Eye O' the Storm")

Under such pressure, Creeley's poetry constantly skirts the danger of becoming too elliptical.

Nevertheless, precisely this progressive method of reduction accounts for the strengths of Creeley's verse. His poems do not "mean" in any prosaic sense; numerous critics have noted that his work is almost impervious to paraphrase. Ed Dorn, for example, describes his poetry as of "a molecular constituency."[7] Michael Hamburger, commenting on "his almost total avoidance of metaphor," characterizes him as a poet of the "deep image."[8] Certainly Creeley's best poems do linger on the tongue, complete units precisely because of their austerity, their phrasing as fresh now as at first reading.

Cast in the perpetual present tense, Creeley's work has a fragmented, epiphanal quality about it. This is even true of the mosaiclike structure of his first collection, *For Love*. Obsessed by the failure of love (the autobiographical element explicit), he exposes his personal crisis of isolation to progressively more minute examination, imitating in miniature his actual emotional dislocation. But as the volume proceeds, he queries even such limited intellection, viewing it by the close with suspicion:

The poem supreme, addressed to
emptiness—this is the courage

necessary. This is something
quite different.
(from "The Dishonest Mailmen")

It is one of the consistent confusions of Creeley that his poetry intends this kind of selflessness through an obsessive, one might say neurotic, focus upon himself. As Edelberg defines it, "Creeley's compelling need to sort out the confusions of his own life

takes precedence over his compelling need to present a re-
strained, contemplative demeanor to the world."[9]

As this examination continues in *Words* and *Pieces,* Creeley's
efforts at reduction become more ruthless. He pays less attention
"to some final code of significance"[10] and more to the con-
tingencies of articulation. In *Words* one can see a movement
away from the more ostensible therapeutic concerns of *For Love,*
a movement that registers a growing distrust of the abstract
limitations of language as it relates to emotion.

> He pushes behind the words
> which, awkward, catch
> and turn him to a disturbed
> and fumbling man.
>
> (from "Waiting")

No longer concerned with simply evoking emotion as it pertains
to his personal crisis, in *Words* Creeley attempts to achieve a
precise equivalence of particular states of emotion:

> Locate *I*
> *love you* some-
> where in
>
> teeth and
> eyes, bite . . .
>
> (from "The Language")

Creeley wants a language that he can taste, touch, and mold,
"words as substantial as the material of wood."[11] What follows
is an increasingly sparse vocabulary, as if by circumscribing lan-
guage he will succeed in making it more definite; more often
than not the economy merely causes greater syntactical compli-
cations.

In *Pieces* this movement takes another direction altogether. A
long, rambling (and in the end, self-indulgent) sequence dedi-
cated to Louis Zukofsky (for reasons best known to Creeley
himself), the volume is a jumble of titled and untitled poems,

drafts, fragments, and snippets of prose. In it, Creeley tries to simulate his notion of the poem as process:

> CAN FEEL IT in the pushing,
> not letting myself relax
> for any reason, hanging on.
>
> •
>
> Thinking—and coincident
> experience of the situation.
>
> "I think he'll hit me."
> He does. Etc.
>
> •
>
> Reflector/ -ive/ -ed.

The parts mean to have a relatedness and coherence of their own, the broken lines, fragments, and sudden shifts of form to convey by themselves much more than their semantic meaning. Forced by Creeley's failure to connect the elements together into some kind of sequence for himself, the reader becomes an unwilling translator. Such involution sets severe (and often unrewarding) problems for the reader.

In volumes like *A Day Book* and *Thirty Things*, Creeley intensifies this descent into a language so incestuous as to refuse the possibility of interpretation; neither the journalistic format of the former nor the latent obscurity of the latter escapes the confines of private reference. What, for example, is one supposed to make of a poem like "Alice"?

> The apple in
> her eye.

This is nothing more than a cryptic fragment, focused so narrowly and under such strain as process that any attempt at decoding it is futile. The reduction in poems like these has become so extreme as to reach a level of self-absorption. Lost is the hardness and lyricism that distinguishes his best poetry.

> Stone,
> like stillness,
> around you my
> mind sits, it is
>
> a proper form
> for
> it, like
> stone, like
>
> compression itself,
> fixed fast,
> grey,
> without a sound.
>
> ("After Mallarmé," from *For Love*)

In these volumes Creeley's persistent dissection of experience has resulted in an almost complete breakdown of syntax and diction. Often, he just whines. If we accept Jerome Mazzaro's definition of Creeley's poetry as "a long monologue of self-definitions,"[12] we must assume that Creeley has begun to talk exclusively to himself.

Accordingly, with a sigh of relief we see that his latest book, *Later,* represents a dramatic return to the possibilities of articulation. While not sacrificing the laconic mode of his best writing, Creeley has undergone something of a transformation in this volume. The tone of desperation and neurotic self-abuse evident in his earlier verse is replaced by one of acceptance—"What, younger, felt / was possible, now knows / is not . . ."—like the quiet of Williams's later verse. If nothing else, Creeley seems to have grown old gracefully. Similarly, throughout the book he adopts a slightly more open, meditative structure that recalls the Williams of *Pictures From Brueghel*. The poems in *Later* are less compressed and occupy a more resonant terrain.

I'll not write again
things a young man
thinks, not the words
of that feeling.

There is no world
except felt, no
one there but
must be here also.

If that time was
echoing, a vindication
apparent, if flesh
and bone coincided—

let the body be.
See faces float
over the horizon let
the day end.

("After")

The phrasing and execution here have the same kind of quiet complexity that distinguishes Eliot's *Four Quartets*. But its smoothness in no way invalidates its subtlety, just as its compactness does not alter its concision. With the years upon him, Creeley has returned to lyricism.

But there is more to it than merely the progress of age (Creeley is fifty-six), for the poems do not register a simple submission to decay. Rather they stress particular aspects of growth, an assurance implied by the volume's title. Creeley has moved from the agitation and discontinuity of *A Day Book* and *Thirty Things* to a state of mind that betokens a kind of wisdom.

Knowing what
knowing is,

think less
of your life as labor.

> Pain's increase,
> thought's random torture,
>
> grow with intent.
> Simply live
> ("On a Theme by Lawrence, Hearing Purcell")

Poems like this do not indicate a giving up but an opening out from the deliberately narrowed world of his preceding poetry. The elevated, almost metaphysical tone and diction of the first seven lines permit the affirmative declaration of the close, "Simply live."

Perhaps more noticeable than anything else, *Later* relaxes the defiance which gives so much of Creeley's earlier writing the semblance of a battlescape, words hard won. In its place, for the first time his poems begin to have a reflexive quality, a movement *through* a range of experience; he no longer rails at each turn but now pauses to collect and digest. Even his most obsessive concerns are given an uncharacteristic clarity.

> There are words voluptuous
> as the flesh
> in its moisture,
> its warmth.
>
> Tangible, they tell
> the reassurances,
> the comforts,
> of being human.
>
> Not to speak them
> makes abstract
> all desire
> and its death at last.
>
> ("Love")

No longer must he rout and plunder language; he has finally allowed it to be concrete.

> The small
> spaces of existence,
> sudden
>
> smell of burning
> leaves makes
> place in time
>
> these days
> (these days)
> passing,
>
> common
> to one
> and all.
>
> ("Later [3]")

The thematic concerns remain the same (love, loneliness, emotional dislocation), but the tone is less self-conscious, the language direct. Unlike Williams, who developed the looser structure and melody of his triadic line, Creeley maintains his rigorous control. But the balance has been altered; he has retreated from the constraints of solipsism, and the reader is no longer a distant observer.

Rarely do the poems in *Later* display the destructive frenzy of his earlier verse. Whereas up to this volume he luxuriated in the inconclusive, now he can't "let it all / fail, fall apart. . . ." ("Spring in San Feliu"). He finally offers the possibility of conclusion.

> In testament
> to a willingness
>
> to *live,* I,
> Robert Creeley,
>
> being of sound body
> and mind, admit

to other preoccupations—
with the future, with

the past. But now—
but now the wonder of life is

that *it is* at all,
this sticky sentimental

warm enclosure,
feels place in the physical

with others,
lets mind wander

to wondering thought,
then lets go of itself,

finds a home
on earth.

("Later [10]")

Creeley has at last found a tonality consonant with the drive of
his poetic attentions. The dignity of this personal testament (as
with many poems in the volume) has none of the persistent
ambiguity with which one has come to associate his work. Nor
is there the disruptive, sterile distance that results from his in-
tense reliance upon style. Creeley has brought his microscope
into focus, so that these poems have a greater internal coherence
and a more definite correspondence to general experience. Sim-
ply one might say that Creeley has discovered a perspective.

When we'd first come,
our thought

was to help him. . . .

Was I scared
old friend
would be broken

by world
all his life
had lived in,

or that art,
his luck,
had gone sour?

My fear
is my own. . . .
(from "Corn Close: for Basil Bunting")

But if Creeley's poetry has had a transfusion here, become
fluid again, he has not entirely escaped certain cloying features
of style and practice. He continues, if not accelerates, his irritat-
ing habit of name-dropping, a practice which pushes the reader
outside the poem in order to fully understand it. Poems like
"Reflections" and "For John Chamberlain," with lines like
"Let's sit in a bar and cry again. / Fuck it! Let's go out on your
boat . . . ," illustrate all too clearly the preciousness which
M. L. Rosenthal finds so distressing a feature of his work, what
he calls his "tendency to regard as quintessential poetry any
twist of phrase that happens into his mind."[13] "News of the
World," by contrast, suffers from an extended irony that, nei-
ther tough nor hard-edged enough, is simply sloppy. Nonethe-
less, such deficiencies are more than counterbalanced by the
excellences of the volume; if one has followed Creeley through
each frustrating phase of his poetic career, *Later* comes as some-
thing very near a triumph.

NOTES

1. Louis L. Martz, "Recent Poetry: The End of an Era," *Yale Re-
view* 59, no. 2 (Dec., 1969): 256–61. [Excerpt reprinted in this collec-
tion.]

2. Robert Creeley, *Was That a Real Poem and Other Essays,* edited by
Donald Allen (Bolinas, Calif.: Four Seasons Foundation, 1979), 13–14.

3. Cynthia Edelberg's book (*Robert Creeley's Poetry: A Critical Intro-
duction* [Albuquerque: University of New Mexico Press, 1978]), the first
book-length critical analysis of his poems, is concerned with his vol-

umes from *For Love* through *In London*. She declares in the foreword that her interpretations do "not claim to be definitive; rather, the hope here is simply to contribute to a fuller understanding of a highly significant body of poetry." [Her chapter on *In London* is reprinted in this collection.]

4. Creeley, *Was That a Real Poem and Other Essays,* 77.

5. Edelberg, *Robert Creeley's Poetry,* 56.

6. Linda W. Wagner, "An Interview with Robert Creeley," in *The Poetics of the New American Poetry,* edited by Donald Allen and Warren Tallman (New York: Grove Press, 1973), 281.

7. Edward Dorn, *Views,* edited by Donald Allen (San Francisco: Four Seasons Foundation, 1980), 118.

8. Michael Hamburger, *The Truth of Poetry* (New York: Harcourt, Brace and World, 1969), 286.

9. Edelberg, *Robert Creeley's Poetry,* x.

10. Ibid., 64.

11. Ibid., 169.

12. Jerome Mazzaro, "Integrities," *Kenyon Review* 32 (1970): 165.

13. M. L. Rosenthal, "Problems of Robert Creeley," *Parnassus* 2 (Fall/Winter 1973): 205. [Reprinted in this collection.]

FRED MORAMARCO

Pieces of a Mirror: Robert Creeley's Later Poetry

One of the most consistent characteristics of Robert Creeley's earlier poetry—and I use the word "earlier" to describe the work done through the mid-seventies—has been its grounding in the immediacy of a present moment. His has been an empirical poetry of attention concentrated on an unfolding experience. Characteristically, the reader is plunged into the middle of an ongoing event, offered a snatch of conversation or a bit of internal monologue, which recreates the feeling of a fleeting moment, a sudden awareness, or a traumatic episode. Creeley was a leader in the generational shift that veered away from memory, history, and tradition as primary poetic sources and gave new importance to the ongoing experiences of an individual's life. Along with Ginsberg, Ferlinghetti, O'Hara, Blackburn, Snyder, and other poets whose work became prominent in the fifties and sixties, he developed a new poetics of experience and awakened a sense of new rhythmical possibilities for the spoken word. The unforgettable sound of his voice reading poetry typified Olson's famous dictum that poetry needed to put into itself "the breathing of the man who writes."[1]

Creeley sharpened and developed his style throughout the sixties and seventies in a series of books that seemed almost designed to exemplify the principles of projective verse. These principles insisted that contemporary poetry divert its attention from the traditional tools of the poet—standard forms, metaphors, poetic diction, imagery, and so on—and concentrate in-

Previously unpublished. This essay is a slightly revised version of a lecture delivered at the 1984 MLA Convention.

335

stead on the outward structure of poetic movement, the self-generating form of the poem that took shape as the process of creating it was under way. Attention to experience on the one hand and attention to composition on the other were the twin poles of his poetry. He writes, in a poem called "Waiting," of how the poet "pushes behind the words" struggling to bring poems into being, giving his emotions and experiences the formal contours that embody their meaning. Without the transformative aspects of poetry—its ability to distill and crystallize the flux of experience—life seems "a dull / space of hanging actions."

For Creeley poetry has always been both useful and necessary. By discovering appropriate forms for the transitory emotional states he needs to write about, he has always used poetry to take measure of both the world around him and the state of his being at any particular moment. *Measure* in Creeley's lexicon means much more than poetic meter and rhythm; it is a standard of valuation and judgment. To develop a sense of measure is to develop a sense of worth. "Measure . . . is my testament," he wrote in 1964. "What uses me is what I use and in that complex measure is the issue. I cannot cut down trees with my bare hand, which is measure of both tree and hand. In that way I feel that poetry, in the very subtlety of its relation to image and rhythm, offers an intensely various record of such facts. It is equally one of them."[2] This sense of measure, which includes taking stock, assessing value, and discovering those things one values most, is what links Creeley's earlier and later work.

In his two most recent collections, *Later* (1979) and *Mirrors* (1983), the poetry seems to shift into a new phase characterized by a greater emphasis on memory, a new sense of life's discrete phases, and an intense preoccupation with aging. As Creeley approaches age sixty these seem appropriate enough concerns, but some readers have felt disoriented by the sense of pastness that emerges in these poems as an alternative to the "here and now" attentiveness of the earlier work.[3] The poems in *Later,* as the title unflinchingly announces, face directly the fact that the later phase of Creeley's life and career has arrived. He realizes that

> I'll not write again
> things a young man
> thinks, not the words
> of that feeling

Creeley remains attuned to the present in these poems, but the words that convey present feelings both incorporate and reflect upon the past. These words continue to measure a life. Although memory is the source of many of the poems in both books, Creeley, following his mentor William Carlos Williams, is after the thing itself, not merely a current memory of the thing. He seems intent on recovering those "pieces" (a favorite Creeley word) of a past and ongoing life that can provide us with a representative image of that life. Each poem offers us a small piece of Creeley's reflective mirror of words. In poem after poem there are echoes of Pound's "dove sta memora" ("where is memory"), that major theme of the Pisan Cantos, which Pound wrote at age sixty, determined to perpetuate the memories of those things that meant most to him. "What thou lov'st well remains," he wrote in Canto 81's most famous lines,

> the rest is dross
> What thou lov'st well shall not be reft from thee
> What thou lov'st well is thy true heritage. . . .

And

> Pull down thy vanity, it is not man
> Made courage, or made order, or made grace,
> Pull down thy vanity, I say pull down

Creeley concludes a poem called "Song" in *Mirrors* with strikingly similar sentiments:

> . . . All vanity, all mind flies
> but love remains, love, nor dies
> even without me. Never dies.

These are the poems of a man taking leave of vanity and searching for his true heritage.

Certainly a major part of that heritage is the excitement and energy of the Black Mountain–Beat Generation days when poetry seemed much more central to American life and culture than it does today. Compared to the "oldtime density" he evokes in a poem called "Place," the contemporary literary landscape often appears empty and alien. "I feel faint here," he writes,

> too far off, too
> enclosed in myself,
> can't make love a way out.
>
> I need the oldtime density,
> the dirt, the cold,
> the noise through the floor—
> my love in company.

The surety of purpose reflected in the poetry of the earlier period has given way to a sense of limits and uncertainty. "Myself," the first poem in *Later*, announces this theme:

> What, younger, felt
> was possible, now knows
> is not—but still
> not changed enough—
>
> . . . .
>
> I want, if older,
> still to know
> why, human, men
> and women are
>
> so torn, so lost,
> why hopes cannot
> find better world
> than this.

This futile but deeply human quest captures the spirit of Creeley's later work. It embodies a commonly shared realization: one becomes older but still knows very little about essential aspects of life, particularly the mysteries and complexities of human relationships. As Alan Williamson has noticed about the quality of many of the poems in *Later,* "In general, the stronger the note of elegiac bafflement and rage (the past utterly gone, the compensating wisdom not forthcoming), the better the writing."[4] This is a brave theme for a mature poet to embrace because it leaves him vulnerable to the charge of having learned little from his experience. Creeley's candid admission that maturity has not always brought wisdom, and that he is sometimes less, not more certain of what he believes and values, is the subject of one of the best poems in *Later,* "Prayer to Hermes." Here he evokes the weakness that accompanies a loss of confident assurance in one's beliefs:

> What I understand
> of this life,
> what was right
> in it, what was wrong,
>
> I have forgotten
> in these days
> of physical change.
> I see the ways
>
> of knowing, of
> securing, life grow
> ridiculous. A weakness,
> a tormenting, relieving weakness
>
> comes to me.

But even in this confession of weakness, Creeley demonstrates his strength as a poet, his mastery of subtle vocal and linguistic patterns. In the first stanza, the assonance of "I," "life," "right," and the soft alliteration of "what," "what was," and "what was wrong" underscore the weariness the lines convey; in the second stanza the linking of "these days" and "see the ways" separated by the intrusive presence of "physical change" upsets the rhythmical pattern of the poem in the same way that actual physical change upsets the comfortable assumptions of youth; and in the third stanza the linking of end and internal rhymes ("knowing," "grow") and the repetition of the word "weakness" as the stanza grows weak with caesurae and unstressed end syllables—all demonstrate the Creeley style at its apex.

In *Mirrors* the commitment to identifying and reconstructing those past events that have shaped the fullness of his present life deepens. The epigraph to the collection is a quotation from Francis Bacon: "In Mirrours, there is the like Angle of Incidence, from the Object to the Glasse, and from the Glasse to the Eye." Poetry in this sense is the word mirror that deflects the experience of the past into our awareness in the present. For Creeley's later work it is the verbal space where past and present intersect.

A poem called "Memory, 1930" illustrates this conjunction. Creeley reaches into his store of semiconscious early childhood memories to illuminate the moment he became aware his father was dying. Since he experienced this trauma at age four, he was obviously too young to comprehend the impact it would have on his entire life. Here he presents it as a major fissure in his early life viewed from an angle of incidence over fifty years later. "My sister's / recollection of what happened won't / serve me," he writes, and then creates a picture of himself as a child, witnessing what appears as a nearly surreal scene:

> I sit, intent, fat,
>
> the youngest of the suddenly
> disjunct family, whose father is
>
> being then driven in an ambulance
> across the lawn, in the snow, to die.

The slowness of the final line with its two caesurae causes the image of the departing ambulance to disappear as if in slow motion. It is as if Creeley, who has written about the death of his father more obliquely in earlier work, can now bring that momentous event clearly into focus to observe the impact it had on his young self, who sits intently observing its occurrence. On some deep level the youngster registers the image, then buries it, to be exhumed a half-century later. The older Creeley watches the young Creeley watching his father being driven away in an ambulance to die.

This poem and others in *Mirrors* reveal how integral a part of ourselves our memories become with each passing year. As we age, we accumulate more experience and thus more memory, becoming more complex personalities. Sometimes we take on the mannerisms of those close to us and reexperience the situations of our pasts. In "Mother's Voice," Creeley not only still hears his mother's voice after her death, but realizes that its very timbre and rhythms have become a part of his own voice:

> In these few years
> since her death I hear
> mother's voice say
> under my own, I won't
>
> want any more of that.
> My cheekbones resonate
> with her emphasis.

This theme of the present incorporating the past is developed figuratively and symbolically in "Prospect," one of the most memorable and resonant poems in *Mirrors*. It is a completely atypical Creeley poem, and because it utilizes conventional elements of poetry—symbolism, metaphor, and imagery—in a surprisingly typical manner, it is not likely to be looked upon with favor by admirers of the earlier work, who sometimes prefer deconstructing such qualities into their component phonemes. It is, of all things, a nature poem, and conveys something of its author's psychological state. I think it takes no deep looking into the poem to see the landscape as emblematic of the state of Creeley's life at the time he wrote it, recently invigorated by a new marriage and the birth of a new child:

Green's the predominant color here,
but in tones so various, and muted

by the flatness of sky and water,
the oak trunks, the undershade back of the lawns,

it seems a subtle echo of itself.
It is the color of life itself,

it used to be. Not blood red,
or sun yellow—but this green,

echoing hills, echoing meadows,
childhood summer's blowsiness, a youngness

one remembers hopefully forever.

There is a nice ambiguity in that "hopefully." One remembers such a landscape as charged with hope, and one will hopefully continue to remember it. It is, in its current manifestation, a landscape filled with echoes and repetitions. Green, traditionally the color of life and vitality, dominates, but in various and muted tones that make it seem "a subtle echo of itself." This is not the "oldtime density" of actual youth, because it lacks the passion and energy of that stage of life ("not blood red, / or sun yellow"), but is instead the reflective, contemplative landscape of maturity:

It is thoughtful, provokes here

quiet reflections, settles the self
down to waiting now apart

from time, which is done,
this green space, faintly painful.

That final phrase surprises, coming at the end of an otherwise tranquil and nearly celebratory poem. It implies that although embarking on a new life creates the illusion that we can exist in an Edenic landscape apart from time, in reality we carry our pasts into whatever new present we inhabit. "Fáintlў páinfûl," with its echoing first syllable rhyme, is exactly right to convey the contrary feelings of relief and regret the poem ultimately leaves us with—relief that such transitions are not more painful, regret that there is any pain at all.

But pain, in its various manifestations, has been one of the most constant elements in Creeley's work, and this late poetry continues to search for words to express it with sensitivity and exactness, and without the sometimes maudlin excesses of "confessional verse." Though these poems are more rooted in memory than the earlier work, they remain committed to taking measure of a life—to getting things exactly right. Measure continues to be Creeley's testament, and as we look into the mirror of his later poems we see not only his aging, but our own.

NOTES

1. Charles Olson, "Projective Verse," reprinted in *The New American Poetry,* edited by Donald Allen (New York: Grove Press, 1960), 386.

2. Robert Creeley, *A Sense of Measure* (London: Calder and Boyars, 1972), 34.

3. See especially Clayton Eshleman, "With Love for the Muse in Charlie Parker Tempo," *L.A. Times Book Review,* Mar. 4, 1984, 3, and Robert Peters, "Review of *Later,*" *Library Journal,* Sept. 1, 1979, 1703.

4. Allen Williamson, "Later," *New York Times Book Review,* Mar. 9, 1980, 8.

CREELEY AND THE VISUAL ARTS

From "Robert Creeley on Art and Poetry: An Interview with Kevin Power"

Introduction

The following conversation with Robert Creeley took place in Buffalo in 1976. My hope was to cover the range of his various involvements with painters—an ample undertaking that, if it was to be anything like complete, would have to include mention of Laubiès, the Abstract Expressionists (especially Kline, Guston, Pollock, and de Kooning), Rice, Altoon, Chamberlain, Marisol, Indiana, Kitaj, Dine, Okamura, Bobbie. My intention was to throw some light on those shared intuitions and impulses that link poetry and painting, especially those concerns that revolve around a shared vocabulary of *process, gesture, energy, field,* and notions of when a work begins and finishes.

Action Painting and Projective Verse are parallel languages, major pushes in the definition of what it means to be "American," a locating of that particular idiom. They grew, I believe, under the shadow of existentialism but totally rejected its abstract language and its physical paralysis. Whereas the European felt himself a prisoner both in terms of space and culture, the American reaction was to smash the door down and drive on West.

Faith was placed in the instant, in the capacity to confront what was happening. In a period of moral crisis and uncertain

From *Niagara Magazine,* no. 9 (Fall 1978): unpaged. Reprinted by permission. I have selected passages from the interview that disclose Creeley's relationships with the artists important to him and the correspondences between their art and his poetry.—ED.

values the artist trusted only the immediate experience. The event was both form and unity. You couldn't guarantee it would be "interesting" but you could leave an authentic record of its intensity. None of us can ask more than to be fully *present* in what we're doing. We know it's a possibility that's always there but one that so often keeps on slipping through our fingers. We blame the other for failures that are our own, and try again to work out from our own mistakes. That's why so much of this work is, as de Kooning puts it, personal biography. Yet a language of gesture is constantly endangered by the self's willingness to imitate itself, to repeat itself without the risk.

Creeley explores the nature of human event. The poems in *For Love* leave, as O'Hara writes of Kline's work, the event of his passage. They register presence, the shape we give to a particular moment, phrase, or action. And presence is, indeed, a key concern for Creeley and he opens his *Presences: A Text for Marisol* with the following quotation from Donald Sutherland: "Classicism is based on presence. It does not consider that it has come or that it will go away, it merely proposes to be there where it is." Pollock's desire to be "in" his paintings was, of course, a similar insistence. At root they're both talking of the quality of life, the way we fashion our various meanings, the way we strip ourselves. One of the paradoxes of Marisol's work is the way she shows that the masks we hide behind, irrespective of whether they be comfortable, aggressive or defensive, are as much ourselves as the particular mask we hold to.

Creeley's realized that there's no conflict between figurative and abstract. Each age carries its own face, and there comes a moment when it's imperative for the artist to define it. "If anything stands presently in need of definition, like they say," he writes in his introduction to the latest Kitaj exhibition, "more demandingly than the word, *person,* I don't myself know what it is or can be. Whether the preoccupations be social, political, psychological, legal, economic or biological, there seems no commonly satisfying resolution of meaning, either in or among the concepts variously." And Kitaj's work has, like Creeley's own work, brought intelligence and feeling to bear on that complex of human motive and desire, on those intensities of confidence, lostness, vulnerability and giving that are most completely ourselves. "*I* am human, I am restless, unsure, insistently questioning as to how *you* are feeling, what it is *you* know, and what do *they* mean. In Kitaj's art there is such a driven amplitude of attention, so many articulate layers of information and care. The axes of possible directions at times seem infinite—as if one might "go anywhere"—and yet the preoccupation seems to me always rooted in the fact of the human: the singular, the communal, the one, the many, in the places of its history, in the presence of our lives." We are one and we are of the many. Both Kitaj and Creeley, sometimes with anguish, sometimes with joy, are opening up the magnificent complexity of what "ofness" is.

Kevin Power
Paris, December, 1977

Kevin Power: How did your interest in poetry begin?

Robert Creeley: In college I had the respectable interests of someone in the liberal arts in the forties. I remember that before I really had any information about the Abstract Expressionists, I was particularly fascinated by Klee's *Notebooks,* where he would talk about taking a line for a walk, or the kind of thing that John Wieners picks up on. ["Poem for Painters," in *The Hotel Wentley Poems* (Corinth Books).] I mean his use of a black grid, using and then drawing a line in such a way that the line became the viable process of the registration rather than the temporary position upon the surface. I think, early on, the whole imagination of art interested me, but what particularly moved me was the idea of a subject, or something . . . you focused on . . . as a subject and then saw that it didn't realize what you had in mind.

By the time I'd finished college I still had the kind of liberally educated person's inclination. A lot of my friends at that point were art historians, like Bill Lieberman and Jake Bean. Sadly, I didn't know Frank O'Hara when I was at college. But it's really when I get to France that I begin to feel closely involved, especially with a painter called René Laubiès to whom I was introduced through Pound.

Power: The man who was to do the cover on your first book for the Divers Press, one of the Ecole de Paris painters.

Creeley: Yes. There's also a friend whom I had previous to that time, when we were living outside of Aix, named Ashley Bryan. He was a painter but he was primarily a friend and his information was not vital to me in any significant way. He was a particularly warm and sweet man.

Power: Laubiès and the Ecole de Paris painters served essentially as an introduction to Abstract Expressionism?

Creeley: Yes, Laubiès was [full of] information [about] people like Hans Hartung and Jacques Villon. It's interesting that the first show of Pollock that I ever saw was in Laubiès's gallery [Galerie Fachetti, Paris], and it was also Laubiès who introduced me to Julien Alvard, who was an interesting critic of the forties and fifties and who becomes a wheeler-dealer of the fifties. It was at Fachetti that I began to see the work that interested me. Sam Francis was showing there and it seems to me that Gene Davis exhibited in that gallery. In other words, what I'm trying to say is that my senses of painting were already latching me into the idea of process. My wife was really habituated to the notion of figure painting and thought of it in that nineteenth-century vocabulary. I suppose she was probably trying to find an emotional alternative to where she was at, as we became more and more at odds with each other emotionally. But, in any case, I was fascinated with the idea of process. Then we moved from France to Mallorca, and after that I went to teach at Black Mountain. Laubiès up to this point had been a very particular friend, although we were still moving in habituated or historically oriented schema of attitudes. But at Black Mountain I literally came into all the energy of and all the interest in the so-called Abstract Expressionists. They were very much a part of that college, although at that point they weren't physically present. A man who was present was Dan Rice who, in no glib sense, was the chosen of Kline, de Kooning and Rothko—he did a lot of work for Rothko. They really thought that he was very probably "it." And another friend that I had at that time who was in some ways even more crucial, just with his thinking, is John Chamberlain. Well, actually, his activities as a sculptor were absolutely decisive to me, and his head is incredible. Then a third friend who is not, quote, "nationally" known but who is a very interesting painter, is Jorge Fick, and he was also important to me. Through their interests I began to be closer to active American painting. Then there's also the fact that Cy Twombly had been at Black Mountain as a student—Olson was interested in him and wrote a note for what was, perhaps, his first exhibition. But I always thought that Olson's take on painting was affectionate and personal, although Jack Tworkov told me once that Charles had given him a lovely talk upon the role of the imagination in the history of Western art. It had made such dazzling sense that Tworkov had managed to arrange for him to give a public talk in Washington and got a handsome fee for him, but when Charles actually talked to the people, Jack said you could no longer make head nor tail of what he was saying. But anyhow these were the ones who were really incisive for me. . . .

Power: Were you quickly able to make use of Abstract Expressionist concepts in poetic terms?

Creeley: Oh, yes, almost immediately. There was a magazine coming out at that time called *Transformation,* published around 1948. That began to be real information. But I'd pick out particularly the relationship with Chamberlain and Altoon, whom I met in fifty-four, and who then came to Mallorca in late fifty-four or early fifty-five.

Power: With Chamberlain, was it the fact that he was defining an American quality and using American materials that interested you?

Creeley: No, not precisely. He has that lovely statement that could be interpreted as a national condition but is, in fact, much more personal, when he replied to someone who asked him why he used derelict automobile body parts, that—well—Michelangelo had a lot of marble in his backyard, and this is what he had in his. But what's more interesting with John's head is how he qualified materials per se—the automobile parts in his sculptures are not, of course, being used because they're parts of automobiles—he loves their industrial color, as did all the Abstract Expressionists in one way or another.

Power: I see that, but it remains on one level a definition of the local. In this case, it's a car that provides the shapes that interest him. It's an attitude that carries reminders of both William Carlos Williams and Olson.

Creeley: Yes, they really revered Williams. One thing that's interesting is that both the older and the younger painters of the forties read the poets. You could go to de Kooning's studio and find the work of all the active young poets. Philip Guston, for example, had read me long before I'd read him, so to speak, or seen his work. He knew my poems very well, not just as a form of flattery, but really knew them.

Power: Did Guston give you any idea as to what interested him about your work?

Creeley: He liked the "After Mallarmé" poem in *For Love*. It turns out that in fact it's not Mallarmé, but Jouve. He'd generously taken me up to the studio to show me the work that was still there. This was in fifty-five, just before the first show at Janis. He was very good to me in a very old-fashioned sense. He really befriended me. For example, he contributed a drawing to a book that got lost by the printer called *The Dress*. He was to have done the frontispiece, which was really very generous. But, in any case, his taking me up to his studio to show me the work that was still there opened up the chance of discussing various things. He loved the reification of the mind, like processes of thinking, and thought a lot about it. His work at that time reflects this in some way. Anyway, he quoted me this poem—he quoted it in French and then translated it literally—and it stuck in my head very distinctly. We'd also been talking about Mallarmé, and when I got back to the place where I was living I remember writing it down as a poem—not verbatim as what he'd said, but my reconstruction of what we'd been talking about. He's a very literate man, is Philip Guston—really involved with reading and writing.

Power: Would it be a fair analogy to suggest that your poems, as the Guston Canvas, have a multiplicity of focusing?

Creeley: Yes, it's an emotional field with a lot of associational "bleeping."

Power: One in which you could peak at various points?

Creeley: Yes, you could pick up an emotional center and let it make this crazy extension overlay where it isn't primarily linear.

Power: More like clusters of energy?

Creeley: Yes, as in Guston's paintings of the fifties.

Power: In *For Love* you seem to have two kinds of poems—one kind pushing through toward a decision, like Kline's work; the other climaxing at various points and staying clear of a central meaning. I guess I'm forcing the analogy a bit there?

Creeley: Well, equally with Kline I loved the fact that it was like a so-called epiphanal moment of consciousness. It was an instant resolution. It wasn't the accumulation of decisions, although no doubt it was also that, but it was predominantly one center of intensive emotional nexus or node.

Power: Were you tapping energy in a similar fashion?

Creeley: For a long time I think I worked in a factually parallel way; I really depended upon some emotional crisis, or some drive of that order, to locate myself. I used the vocabulary of Pollock: "When I'm in my painting . . ."

Power: Would you say there's a necessity, in fact, to exhaust the moment of possibility; that the process of the poem and painting represent this exhaustion of possibility? Was this a responsibility in any way?

Creeley: Not responsibility, just habit. I thought that the literary vocabulary of that time was overloaded with the terminology of the New Critics and ideas concerning the poem "bien fait," et cetera. The same thing went for Robert Duncan, I think, and his relationship to that group of friends on the West Coast, that whole group around Clyfford Still—Diebenkorn, Ed Corbett, Hassel Smith. In the whole extension of that group he found another vocabulary of energy that was really far more attractive than the professional literary situation either permitted or recognized. All of this was a central influence and then Olson, of course, really gave us the key to the vocabulary with his idea of composition by *field,* as opposed to some structure that has some end in view and works to accomplish it.

353

Power: But that was, of course, already evident in Abstract Expressionism with their treatment of the field.

Creeley: Yes, absolutely. The first show I saw was Kline's in the foyer of the Living Theater down on the Lower East Side. It was quite incredible. There was a beautiful moment that I remember. It was an incredible small space with very narrow hallways, it couldn't have been more than four feet. I was following this kind of charming thirtyish matron with a lovely fur coat, and at one point she's left one of these areas and she's now moved into this hallway. She turns to look at the painting and she literally bounced. I mean, she went "whaam." That was a lovely thing to see, that thing just hit her. It was that physical energy that really moved her. Happily, I knew these people not as rich and famous, since in a sense they never became that. I remember de Kooning taking a roll of bills out of his pocket to pay for a drink. It was astounding, but it was just what he had in his pocket, and there had been fifty cents there a few days ago, and now he had this great wad of notes. His life-style never changed that much.

Power: You seem to share with de Kooning this concern for material and the idea of woman not just simply as a theme, but as a source of action?

Creeley: Well, we all revered William Carlos Williams and all of these men really came up variously through his terms: Chamberlain, Dan Rice, John Altoon, all came up this way. We were all like idealist Americans, we had this very typical American idealism about the sense of what life could be if it humanly were permitted to be. We all had an intrinsic respect for and love of physicality. We were all very intimidated by the English discretion, although Francis Bacon was certainly doing fine work at that time, but not much was heard about him. I remember sitting in a lovely conversation with Guston where he's speaking of Courbet. He's talking about this moment in a particular painting when everything is just moving, like going in to eat dinner or something, and then there's this moment, like they say, when the painter truly located it. Everything is movement and grace, and it's just that moment that is so dear to Guston.

Kline could speak of Turner, I think, in much the same way. All of this comes up in that interview with Frank O'Hara.[1] So there was no kind of raw savage Americanism, but they were understandably hostile to the School of Paris. Altoon's characterization of the School of Paris after the war was that they were just polishing rocks, no substance, just polishing to the point of obliterating any of its energy.

Power: Would it be fair to say that you shared with de Kooning a situation which was basically unstable, nervous, and ambiguous?

Creeley: In a way, but not on any precise level. In the fifties I had a beautiful, unexpected response from him. He was in a depressed state of mind, so in mid-afternoon he took a walk along the East River. He intended to jump in the river, apparently, but he started stopping for drinks somewhere around Tenth Street and he never made it. One time I was talking with Kline and Fielding Dawson, whose senses of the painters and the various relationships I really like. I mean, his *An Emotional Memoir of Franz Kline*[2] really hit me. A lot of people think, well, what do we learn about Kline? I feel that what we learn is the emotional and factual significance these people had for us. In any case, we were out on the street taking some of Franz's canvases to be stretched. The company was myself, Nancy, Franz, and Fielding. Franz and Fielding were ahead of us, with Nancy and myself behind. Nancy was the sister of Bill's lady, so to speak, the mother of his daughter. I mean Bill de Kooning's. We got separated at an intersection, a light changed, and they were about half a block ahead. Then suddenly Nancy spotted Bill de Kooning moseying along the street, and in a very beautiful matter-of-fact voice said to me: "Here's ten dollars, now go into that liquor store across the street, buy a bottle of Jack Daniels, or whatever, go to Bill and say that Nancy says that she will meet him in one hour or two at his studio and that you're to go up with him and have a drink and wait for her there. Otherwise he's going to do himself in or something." I bought the bottle and then reported to de Kooning that I'd been sent as an emissary to have a drink with him. He was sort of amused, so we went back to his place and drank for a while, until he kind of pleasantly passed out. I remember there was one moment when I was getting his legs up onto the bed when I suddenly looked up and realized that he was watching me, amused, and then he went to sleep. The whole place was very shipshape, very modest, like a working man's place, but all in order. So I sat there for at least four hours, and frankly, as a kid, I checked out everything I could find. I didn't go through his mail or anything, but I looked at every activity that was there. I was fascinated by the process of his painting, which was to do an initial series of sketches, almost to work out a possible design for the activity. He'd blocked in the areas on one of the canvasses he was working on with pastels; that is to say, he'd blocked in the areas he hadn't yet painted. He kept an activity of color groups like a formal pattern. So that what was surprising to me was not some notion of working up to a place, call it, but the incredibly methodical process whereby he worked himself to the points of decision. Instead of just saying, "What'll I paint today?" there was an incredible forestructure of the whole activity. Obviously in that way he was unlike Kline.

Power: And unlike you, since you also wouldn't be able to work from this kind of forestructure, would you?

Creeley: No. That was really the European pattern, that first you began to conjecture, and then to consider the structure possible within that conjecture, then to test it, modify it, et cetera, but the whole pattern had already been basically decided.

Power: The pattern of corrections would be the liberating impulse?

Creeley: Right.

Power: I think it's Thomas Hess who remarks that where de Kooning paints a shoulder, you could also see a Tenth Street café, so that there remains this active presence of the immediate experience, even within what you might call a planned structure. That seems analogous to your method of describing a nervous or uptight situation, and one that may be intensely personal, in the textures of your immediate street language. In other words, there's a similar play between personal meaning and street usage?

Creeley: Yes, but I've no strict method. De Kooning was a very methodical painter. He really worked on it. So that the painting was not a description of activity. It was fascinating to see how, with all that forethought, the energy didn't disperse in that situation of preoccupation. But, apparently, in the move from one step to another there was sufficient volatile circumstance to give him play, whereas Kline's painting is like sketches of the possibility of working directly. Guston's studio intrigued me because there were just masses of paint everywhere. I've never seen so much paint, globs of it all over the place. It was a strange sort of paradox. Here was this man who was almost—like not dandyish—but still always benign, literate, and rather well-dressed, with paint all around him. Then there was Franz and Bill, who were much more street people, yet insisting on some kind of order. Philip always looked affluent, he could easily have been a professor or something. In one particular painting he was working on there was this red, these incredible masses of jelly red all over the place, and he told me how many tubes, like gallons, he'd used.

Power: Your use of reductive bursts of energy in the poem (not so much ego trips as invitations, you've said of them) are similar to Guston's clusters of energy. Kline said he viewed painting as giving, and I guess both Guston and yourself would agree with that?

Creeley: I think even the last couple of years are an instance of this for Guston. That shift, if I'm not mistaken, can only be made in your head. The three shifts basic to his paintings are all, quote, "mind experiences"; they're mind changes, not changes involved with physical occasion or technique. They're not like Kline's move from figurative to, quote, "abstract," where you simply get the line becoming more and more dominant and taking over other modifications and delineations, like moving back to initial structure.

Power: Would there be any parallel between Kline's use of the line and your own?

Creeley: Yes, probably, but difficult to be precise.

Power: How does existentialism tie in with the attitudes and theories of the Abstract Expressionists?

Creeley: Well, I read everything, but it scared me to death. I was of the generation, you know, that grew up on "The Kafka Problem." We read Kafka's works continually but didn't particularly get involved with the philosophical situation of Heidegger or whoever. I didn't attempt to read Maurice Blanchot, who was then a "heavy" in Paris. Then there was another tie-up in the relationship of Alex Trocchi and Christopher Logue. There was an interesting Japanese painter in that group, but I didn't really know him. I'd seen his work in reproductions.

Power: Sugai?

Creeley: No, the guy who did the splotchy numbers.

Power: Zao-wou-ki?

Creeley: Possibly, but we didn't really approve of him.

Power: But the Abstract Expressionists clearly had a fair sense of existentialism. The lectures at the Club seem to refer fairly consistently to it, and the concept of "alienation" must have offered substantial common ground?

Creeley: But not philosophically. They hadn't codified a social attitude. They felt singular, they felt individuated, but with the possible exception of Guston I don't think they'd have stated it in existential terms.

Power: Motherwell, perhaps?

Creeley: The two I deeply regret not knowing were Joan Mitchell and Grace Hartigan. My two friends in that circumstance, and I'm talking about the time of Black Mountain, were John Chamberlain and Dan Rice, although since then we've moved in very different ways. Chamberlain, however, I consider a friend of my life. Altoon, as I've said, was also very important for me as long as he was alive. He's a very different place and head but he took me into the whole situation of Arshile Gorky and into certain aspects of de Kooning, that for John, with his preoccupation with materials, weren't his direct involvement. John really, if you look at him, sometimes does a take on de Kooning. I have a lovely little collage of his at home which looks like a de Kooning, it has his whole sense of color.

The initial context of those metal pieces is really close to de Kooning's head.

Power: With Altoon you mention that you were surprised at the speed he located the images in his pencil drawings.

Creeley: Yes, he used to watch kids draw and he was fascinated with how they knew where the line should go. Not that they had some particular insight, or superior insight, but how the activity created the image.

Power: What was it that you found relevant in Chamberlain's work?

Creeley: Well, you see, both John and Dan Rice were deeply respectful of de Kooning. He was a true hero for both men, but both of them were, understandably, contemptuous of sitting at his feet. This was no homage to the artist you respect—better to use what he gives you and get off his back than to be sitting night after night at his table, drinking his beer or wine or whatever. John Altoon, when he came to New York, was trained as a commercial artist, and when I first met him was still doing commercial artwork as a means to a livelihood, although he'd already moved into the locus of the Arts Club.[3] John Chamberlain had various reasons, but he was, in any case, almost hostile to Dan. When Chamberlain came to New York he was trained as a hairdresser no less, and he falls back on that, making twenty-five an hour, and he works at that a couple of times a week and provides a situation for himself and for his wife and children. Whereas Dan really went the trip of the "starving artist" much more. I remember the time when he was passing out in the street, surviving thanks to the affection of people like Rauschenberg, who took care of him as artist and friend. He's like the "artist against society." John's attitude to that was, "Fuck it, let's see what one can do to survive." But to answer your question more specifically, I remember one beautiful moment with Chamberlain. We were at his house, and he was then living in New York City, like the whole house was just beautifully abstract. It was a crazy old farmhouse that they were variously remodelling. There was a small barn, and a garage adjacent, which he used as a working place. He was working down on the floor of this garage-barn, and he'd been trying to put together this large piece, and so he had all this metal all over the place. He hasn't welded it yet. It's just been put together, and we're now up on this grid looking down on this kind of small space. John says maybe it should be this way or that way, and there we are just looking at it, when John suddenly moves in this beautiful gesture and just jumps right down into it. He's kicking and hauling the jagged pieces of metal around, and at the same time he's looking up and saying—"How does it look now?" So there's this incredible moment for me when Chamberlain was there *in* his sculpture. I love this quality of his work.

Power: The same would apply to Pollock . . .

Creeley: Right, that same feeling. He thought of it as truly energy. He was very proud of one story apropos of hanging a show in Chicago. A maintenance crew had been assigned to John to help him get the wall pieces up and various things located. They were trying to hang one wall piece, and here's the crew that's been provided for this specific job. They're really shocked, and John's saying to them, "Come on, give me a hand," as they say. But they're just looking and saying, "No way, brother, that thing could kill you," and they literally won't touch it. John was very proud of that, the fact that they were scared of hanging one of his own pieces. As far as I was concerned, it wasn't only his imagination that appealed to me, but his factual interest in the nature of the materials. Sculpture, he'd say, is something that, if it drops on your foot, it'll break it, so you either have to move your foot or the sculpture. He'd also thought about the characteristic adjectives used to describe a piece of sculpture: that it was very heavy, that it rested on a pediment, that it had this material weight. As a result, he said he wanted to use things that would have the adjectival characterization of "fluff" or "glare." He was thinking in a whole alternate vocabulary. He was very parallel to my head in terms of, what are the materials of possible statement. Obviously they're words. But what are the terms used to qualify this activity? What's happening here? What can happen in this nexus of language? We wanted optimum tension, optimum energy state, and optimum use of all that was in it. We didn't want any lagging. I think we were both turned on by Olson's "no leaning on the oars." The situation has to be such that one perception instantly transforms to another, so there's no waiting around. It's a high energy construct. I think that's where we both centered.

Power: A continuous tightness of form?

Creeley: Yes. I remember John would sit in on those sadly taught classes of mine that I gave in Black Mountain. He was kind of checking it out, he wasn't formally involved. There were only five people. He was very charming. I remember I'd have an exercise which was to take some characteristic verb, like *sit—the man sat,* et cetera—just take some harmless noun and attach it to some common verb, and simply think of a sequence of ten contexts in which that activity takes place, then finally transform these to the activity in each case. Nothing heavy, just—*the man sat on the beach, the man sat on the toilet, the man sat on a pie,* et cetera.

Power: An exercise on the nature of basic structures, their capacity for transformation, and the relevance of context—all areas that Chamberlain has largely explored.

Creeley: Yes. We were taking very common events in language and transforming them by situation. John came in with this fantastic list and said, "Here." It just blew my mind, and he would constantly be doing things like that. For example, I saw him a couple of years ago, and he told me he'd collected something like a hundred and fifty clichés that he felt were not so determined by place, time, and social circumstance that they couldn't operate commonly in the world. Thus, depending on their translation, they could be active in the context of another language. They could operate commonly in the world like a cliché of experience. What he wanted to do with the grid of a hundred and fifty clichés, or whatever number he had, was, as he put it, to *wash* them with different informational fields. So he was asking me if I could think of various ways to wash them, as you bathe something in color, just wash them with diverse circumstantial possibilities. Or, another example, when he went to the Rand Corporation—he'd been put in touch with them by the

L.A. County Museum et al.—he issued memos throughout the whole structure asking all the persons working at Rand to note for him what they'd each consider the most interesting answer they'd ever had the occasion to know. He didn't want to know the question, he just wanted to know the *answer*. He had said that the response was nothing, literally no one replied, except for one woman who said that they had far better things to do than answer stupid questions. But you see, I was fascinated by what he was doing. So he said he finally did his own answers and had them printed on plastic sheets that showed through, so that you kept on seeing other answers besides the one you were looking at, so he did create a multidimensional condition of visual "number."

Power: This is close to the condition of your book *Pieces?*

Creeley: Yes, John's head is very close to mine in those respects. When I gave him *Words,* when that came out, and later asked him what he thought of it, he said, "Well, it's all about dimensions." That one sentence really qualifies what the book is all about better than any other criticism I've read of it.

Power: In these poems you also let the individual word explore, so to speak, its own energy in whatever situation it finds itself?

Creeley: Yes, that's also true. . . .

Power: Do you think that action itself has any ontological significance?

Creeley: Yes, there's this insistent respect for, like, "move it," "change the subject," "let's get going."

Power: Would this lead to any cumulative awareness of an improving situation, or is it simply a new situation?

Creeley: Well, if some situation is seemingly intolerable, or has become claustrophobic, then changing it through your own agency at least offers immediate relief. There is that kind of reticence that Phil Whalen beautifully gets to, when he says, "Don't change it, you'll only fuck it up more." Those situations certainly exist, but I really have a personal interest in activating change. Changing it, at least, removes the situation from what seemingly are its limits, or tests them as a real condition. I am a person who tends to have a habit of logical containment, although, thankfully, I keep the poem out of it or apart from it.

Power: That helps clarify why Kline's remark, "I paint what I don't know," was so important for you?

Creeley: Very much so. It was a true reassurance, since I used to feel as a young man that people would say, "What are you doing?" and I'd have this awful sick feeling that I really didn't know what I was doing. To such an extent that many times even when I'd done it, I still didn't know what I was doing. I was very tentative about the effects of it all. I remember one particular occasion in Mallorca when Martin Seymour-Smith and myself met Graves one afternoon. He'd just finished work and was coming down the steps of his house. He looked at us very cheerily and said, "I'm half way through a poem for *The New Yorker*." That blew my mind, I just couldn't think of ever being able to say something like that. I felt righteous about it, I felt confused about it, I felt depressed by it—a great diversity of responses. I felt contempt for it, I felt respect for it. I just didn't know what I felt about it, since it had never occurred to me that you could thus design a poem and write it, and have a particular circumstance in mind. Obviously now I could feel more understanding, but as a person of twenty-five or twenty-six it was just incredible.

Power: Why was it so important for you to write what you didn't know?

Creeley: It was trying to extend, I suppose, the consciousness of being alive or aware, like "missing or testing some proof" as Olson says. It amounts to trying to use the act as a means to exploring the world. . . .

Power: Hans Hoffmann also said that he didn't know what he was doing at the outset of the work, and you've also said at the beginning you fumble around waiting for something to happen. It's the sense of positively latching onto the work that you're after there?

Creeley: Yes, it's not that I don't want to know what I'm doing—I want to know what I'm doing absolutely. I don't necessarily want to know where I'm going, and that, of course, is something different. . . .

Power: You've referred to autobiography as life tracking itself. Is *A Day Book* a text of that idea, and is it consciously indebted to Williams's *Kora in Hell?*

Creeley: Yes, probably. I'm sure it is, absolutely. I didn't consciously choose it as a model, but I sure did as an experience of something: that was the possibility. Chamberlain would like to take *A Day Book* and say, "What else is new in town?" which would, in fact, be a proper answer to its confusions. I like the book, but I can dig what he's saying.

Power: There's some kind of convergence of intent with Robert Indiana's numbers on the cover. Indiana has said that he was interested in the kind of numbers that appear on office calendars, and the kind of rush of events that collected around them. Your days in *A Day Book* are also marked by this same multiplicity of event flashing through them. The day is itself the unifying factor to these fragmented occasions of your presence in it. Or at least the prose seems to belong to such an order?

Creeley: Right, precisely: there's the dilemma of the book. The prose is a sequence of daily writings, which do take place in that order, although there are gaps of a week or two between various segments. But, nevertheless, they do progress in that chronological pattern. The dilemma is, and it was formally a real one, that the first poems in the book are written at the same time as some of the prose, they were concurrent in that fact. But I couldn't break up the condition of the prose to insert those poems, because it would really have disturbed the pattern of the prose. So I had these two sections to fit together, and that was a problem.

Power: You also mention Dieter Rot and say that you were interested in the "me-ness" that he puts into his work.

Creeley: Yes. I don't know a lot about his work, but German friends spoke of him and this particular quality seemed relevant to my own concerns.

Power: Is that analogous to the situation in Samuel Beckett's *Malone Dies,* where the man is lying in his bed surrounded by a pile of unopened packets that, in a way, are his life? He refuses to open these final surprises, but he's intimately bound up with them?

Creeley: Yes, that's there—like Satie, who left packets of clothes and mail unopened.

Power: What is it that interests you about the everyday object: the same kind of significances that one finds in Dine's work, for example?

Creeley: I suppose it's the energy of something before it's been consumed or transformed that interests me. It's this initial energy—it isn't like, don't touch it, or, don't spoil it. But from my own situation I think what I really found attractive in Dieter Rot's circumstance was that he could live somewhere until the accumulation of the event was factually forcing him physically out, and then he would simply seal the apartment or room as an event of his own existence. It's highly analistic. Where I part company with Dieter Rot is in this analism of what he's involved in doing. But I do like the sense of art being the event of the *effects* of having been alive. In that early poem, "The Rites"—"trace of line left by someone"—there's that same sense of its being humanly the event of some factual person's having been there—not egocentrically, but literally, I'm here. You know, in the Second World War it was, "Kilroy was here." . . .

Power: You've said that experience is created by a system, and you cite the distribution of a network of streets and the relationship an individual makes with them. Is the *Marisol* text a similar kind of patterning, but this time, related to a person?

Creeley: Not exactly; I used a pattern that would locate the time dimensions of the writing, by which I mean almost a physical kind of limitation: the number sequence. In other words, there's a somewhat parallel circumstance in terms of what size canvas one painter might choose as a working condition or a context: an initial location of where, and by what means, some event would take place.

Power: In a minimal sense of a system working itself out?

Creeley: Yes, having a phase particular to itself and without reference to the information that might otherwise occur. Some kind of true decision to have a bounded field. Scientists tell me that is a distinction of physics; to have a bounded field, as opposed to an unbounded one.

Power: And was that also a random imposition of order on yourself, i.e., to establish an ordering sequence to work within? It's another kind of "presence"?

Creeley: Yes, sure, when you're writing in a pattern of one page there's one possibility, and with two pages another, and with three pages a third. Each of those durations, or extensions, or whatever you call them, has within its own condition an information. Three pages state something differently than one.

Power: Physically they do something different, like with, say, the use of a large canvas?

Creeley: Yes, physically. It's like using what Chamberlain calls a module, that is, one, or one plus one, or one plus two—that is, it can be extended, but the basic module is one page. You think of it as one page, or as two pages, or as three pages, but the basic module is one, and you keep on returning to it—that's the locus you're using.

Power: And with the *Marisol* text you made it circular, going out and back?

Creeley: It turns out that way, it actually ends on the second. I mean, the sequence is five, there are five situations of three such possibilities. They recur on the fourth circumstance of that sequence, and therefore end on the second.

Power: You say that phasing sticks in your mind. Do you use it here as a way of locating the instances of autobiography?

Creeley: I'm not trying to "objectify" myself, as that would simply end up as a report which would be as subjective as any other, but I am trying to locate situations of experience, particularly in this case my own. But I want to locate them in a context that will be indifferent to them, and one thing about that pattern is that it is utterly indifferent. It isn't a novel, it isn't stories, it isn't personal in the sense that *I* invented the numbers one, two, three.

Power: I was thinking of Reich's explorations of phase patterns where the repetitions in fact become different, so that as you select details from your personal life, that could be called repetitive because you've done them before, yet at the same time you know that on each occasion they're different.

Creeley: It's a very modest or limited situation of that kind, and I wanted it to be, in a funny way, pat: that is, I wanted it to stand pat in its own condition. I didn't want it to be extensive in a way that a novel might be, I wanted it to be very simply located, but at the same time I didn't want its order to be hidden. I mean, given that pattern initially, it will probably be included as an overt part of the technique. I don't think it will have any particular meaning for people, I just want it there as part of the structure. I don't even know that one page will report itself so accurately when it's turned into type, since typewriting and typesetting have a different effect. I don't know that the duration of one page has any constancy. I mean, one page could be a minute, or one page could be a year. The phasing in the act of writing doesn't necessarily come through. It's almost like going back to someone like Charlie Parker, who could make a note have a duration of hours or make it have a duration of a flash, but if someone said, "Gee, that was slow," or, "That was fast," he'd say, "Well, actually, if you measured it with a metronome, for timing, you'd find that it was just one beat."

Power: The structures behind *A Day Book* and *Presences* have, then, a similar intent?

Creeley: Yes, they're part of one whole, so to speak. . . .

Power: You begin the *Marisol* text with a quotation from Donald Sutherland: "Classicism is based on presence. It does not consider that it has come or that it will go away; it merely proposes to be there where it is." Did you feel that has a direct bearing on Marisol's work?

Creeley: I just felt that she's a master of that value. She has a piece called *Sleeping Women*, I think; it's a cluster of women leaning against something, but the impact is incredible—a complete sense of presence.

Power: *The Party* also does that with her thirteen or fourteen masked situations.

Creeley: Right, the first time I was ever in her studio that piece was lying around, largely taking over the studio; this great, happy, dusty, sawdusty kind of place, and there was *The Party* moving back into the bathroom.

Power: Janis has got that piece now. It reminds me of the story about her, also indicative of repeated presences. She gave a talk somewhere with a mask on, and when she was finally persuaded to take her mask off, her face was revealed made up in precisely the same manner.

Creeley: Yes, I remember a lovely incident in San Francisco, and I love this kind of coincidence. I'd hitchhiked into the city with a friend, we were down at Enrico's in North Beach, just sitting at the bar, when literally Marisol walks by, her first time in San Francisco.

Power: Do you feel the American artist is under a pressure to surface everything, to project aggressively? Marisol's work seems to declare: "Well, here's the surface, but that's not it."

Creeley: I think the impulse here is to "get it on" and have the new line made for the Fall. I mean, that's what's incredible about Robert Duncan saying he won't write another book until 1985— that's a wild date to choose. Living with Jess, he was very cognizant of the pressures to have another show. You're doing great, that book did it, do it again. We tend to want it forever at a particular pitch, and that just isn't factually possible. We just don't work that way. We don't physically have the condition. We just don't have it. We're a country so involved with the future that we only look to what's rushing into that factor of experience. At the moment, the past is a qualification we have very little respect for. We're really scared of history as a context.

Power: In the *Marisol* text are the presences, like the Marisol figures, facets of your various concerns, e.g., language per se, the imagination made actual, autobiography, the role of pronouns, et cetera?

Creeley: Yes, *presences,* just dimensions of human presence, occasions of human presence, modes of human presence. I was trying to get hold of different kinds of experiences of presence. It's a situation that lets you ring the changes!

NOTES

1. Frank O'Hara, "Franz Kline Talking," in *Standing Still and Walking in New York* (San Francisco: Grey Fox Press, 1975), 89–94.

2. Fielding Dawson, *An Emotional Memoir of Franz Kline* (New York: Pantheon, 1967).

3. See Dore Ashton's *The New York School* (New York: Viking, 1972), chaps. 13, 14.

WENDY BRABNER

From " 'The Act of Seeing with one's own eyes': Stan Brakhage and Robert Creeley"

Avant-garde filmmaker Stan Brakhage and poet Robert Creeley have been friends for many years—a friendship strengthened by an exchange of dedications, poems, films, and writings, and linked by such common mentors as Walt Whitman, Gertrude Stein, Robert Graves, and Ezra Pound, as well as the mutual friendship of Charles Olson, Robert Duncan, Michael McClure, and Ed Dorn.[1] While these figures have influenced both men, the work of Brakhage and Creeley remains largely autobiographical. Because of this, the forms of their art are constantly evolving, adapting to the forms of their lives. . . .

Through the course of careers that span more than thirty years, Brakhage and Creeley have always seemed to be, as Creeley once remarked of Charles Olson, "looking for a language."[2] This search has taken them through the various modes of expressionism, surrealism, symbolism, and mythmaking; through confrontations with the revelatory limits of love and art; through personal crises; through numerous mentors; and at present, to autobiography as pure form, ironically coming full circle with Creeley's early contention (ca. 1950) that "FORM IS NEVER MORE THAN AN EXTENSION OF CONTENT."[3]

In the sense that the subject of their work is always the artist himself, his thoughts and feelings, the autobiographical impulse that surges through their films and poetry is firmly rooted in

---

From *The Library Chronicle of The University of Texas at Austin*, n.s., no. 17 (1981): 85–103. Reprinted by permission.

romanticism—a path from which they have rarely strayed. Brakhage, in particular, follows Wordsworth's belief that true art is a "spontaneous overflow of powerful feelings." While both Brakhage and Creeley utilize the principles of romanticism in the content of their works, they have searched throughout their careers for a form which will express their inner thoughts and emotions. This search extends beyond their poetry and film-making into their personal lives.

Both Brakhage and Creeley suffered traumatic childhoods, growing up relatively isolated and searching for a community and a means of communication. Creeley's loss of an eye and the death of his father at an early age precipitated feelings of inadequacy: "I didn't have a clue as to what men did, except literally I was a man. . . . I loved to get with people—but I didn't have any sense as to how you do it. I mean I was curiously lost. My father being dead, I didn't know what the forms were."[4] Brakhage, on the other hand, was adopted by a couple who saw him as "just the right baby" to patch up a disintegrating marriage. Sensitive to the tensions of such a marriage, the young Brakhage developed numerous ailments:

I managed, by the time I was two or three, to desensitize my whole skin surface. I stopped my nose with sinus, my ears with infections, my eyes were wacky, my asthma to stop my breathing, and I couldn't go out to play and run off my increasing fat because I had a hernia and wore a truss from early childhood. I became . . . further and further removed from the activities of other children.[5]

Brakhage's parents eventually divorced, and he spent a lonely childhood moving from town to town, which later became a way of life for him, as it did for Creeley. To this day, both artists are "nomads," continually on the move throughout the globe: lecturing, screening films, reading poetry. Both men are energy personified, restless and in constant motion, compulsive talkers and travelers. Michael Rumaker recalls that his first meeting with Creeley (at Black Mountain College) was "like being dropped into the presence of a fierce, impatient bird, strapped down, restricted, in a too tight ribcage of flesh."[6] For both

Creeley and Brakhage, traveling helped to release some of this energy and, as young men, relieved their sense of isolation from the rest of the world. In a letter to Parker Tyler, dated February 28, 1959 (later printed in the "State Meant" section of *Metaphors on Vision*), Brakhage wrote:

> Time and again I've changed location, moved back and forth across this country, which I suppose many people have wondered about. The reason is simple: it's the only private personal key I have for the coffin lid, it's the trick with which I stay alive, a change of scene and a way of life being that "gimmick," if you will, with which I reawaken the self, re-illusion the dreamer, and thus prevent the death of the spirit— all that I hold dear in life.[7]

Meanwhile, through their art Creeley and Brakhage had begun to confront the void—their insecurities, their separation from the rest of the world. Ekbert Faas has written that "the void seems to attract Creeley with the power of a religious mystery,"[8] and in writing to Edward Dahlberg in 1955, Creeley revealed: "I know often I am so pulled by my nature back into myself, that it seems I finally do covet loneliness or propose it as a curious security. Which god knows it is not."[9] That same attraction to the void is present in Stan Brakhage, and his early responses leaned toward explosive doomsayings of insanity and violence.

At first Creeley and Brakhage confronted the void through mythmaking—playing with myth, creating myths about themselves, and utilizing those from the romantic, symbolist, and surrealist traditions. Like the romantics, both men felt that their media had revelatory powers, and like their predecessors, both believed that their ability to fashion poems and films was a "gift" from an unknown source, the "Muse" (compare Creeley's "The Gift" with Brakhage's *The Gift* [1972]). Both depended on their poetry and cinema to *reveal,* to bring them mystically to self-knowledge.

Soon, however, they realized that their art was re-veiling more than it was revealing. Gradually they discarded the forms of mythmaking, just as they had abandoned early forays into expressionism, which both men had tested along with sur-realism, as an autobiographical mode—Creeley in such poems as "The Crow," "A Form of Women," "'You've Tried the World, Try Jesus,'" "The Dream," and "The Warning," and Brakhage in such films as *Unglassed Windows Cast a Terrible Reflection* (1953), *The Way to Shadow Garden* (1954), *Anticipation of the Night* (1958), and *Dog Star Man* (1961–64).

Despite its use of expressionism and surrealism, *Anticipation of the Night* represents a turning point in Brakhage's career. In a letter to Parker Tyler, he wrote:

> I try to anticipate the night always, before it has closed entirely. And my recurring nightmare, the one in which mad dogs pursue me across a swamp at night and eventually tear me to pieces is just this, this change of location, this running. I refuse to be held at bay. The dogs *will* tear me to pieces if ever I'm caught.[10]

Later, Brakhage would write that "possession thru visualization speaks for fear-of-death as motivating force."[11] This was accomplished literally during the filming of *Anticipation of the Night,* where the film reflects his state of mind. Dissatisfied with the meager financial rewards of being a personal filmmaker, despondent over cultural life in the United States, and frustrated in his search for a lasting community and someone to love, suicide was a tempting way out:

> I figured I would hang myself, in a nice 19th-century gesture, at the end of the film with the camera running, leaving a note and asking that it be attached to the end of the film.[12]

At this point in Brakhage's life, he had just broken up with his fiancée, Barbara Moore, the daughter of a wealthy Colorado family. Brakhage's feelings of anguish over this affair mirror Creeley's torment during the slow and painful breakup of his nine-year marriage to Ann MacKinnon. Both men seem to have been looking for a woman to enter their lives as an anchor, a bridge across the void. In Creeley's "A Song," written "for Ann," he reports:

I had wanted a quiet testament
and I had wanted, among other things,
a song.
That was to be
of a like monotony.

(A grace

Simply. Very very quiet.
A murmur of some lost
thrush, though I have never seen one.

Which was you then. Sitting
and so, at peace, so very much this same quiet . . .[13]

Similarly, Brakhage recalls that "something, physically in my-
self, was wrenching out to another being. . . ."[14] By the time
the final scene of *Anticipation of the Night* was shot, events had
changed in Brakhage's life and he had chosen not to commit
suicide—although he had decided to simulate his death by hav-
ing it filmed in silhouette, with the protagonist (played by
Brakhage) always seen in shadow. During the shooting, Brak-
hage was on a chair with a rope around his neck when he said,
"Well that's that!" And absentmindedly stepped off. For-
tunately, a friend pulled him down before he began to strangle.
In retrospect, Brakhage feels that he had to enact a death wish
("a step backward," as he described it in *Metaphors of Vision*) in
order to move forward in his relationship with Jane Collom,
whom he had just married and who acted as camerawoman
during the filming of this scene.

At that point I was not really seeing Jane or what we had, the
strength of our love, and what it could build: she was the
person who received the camera when I said, "Well that's
that!"[15]

For a long time, both Brakhage and Creeley "were not really
seeing" women for what they were. A symbolist attitude to-
ward women recurs frequently in Creeley's early poetry and

Brakhage's early films, accompanied by nightmare visions of sexual tension and frustrations caused by an inability to communicate. In Brakhage's first film, *Interim* (1952), the stylized narrative is largely autobiographical. A young man struggles to communicate with a stranger—a young woman. The camera tilts down a stand of trees to a view of swirling water, mirroring the couple's inner strife; as their hands touch, they look at each other and then look away, removing their hands. The water metaphor is present throughout the film: rising steam suggests sexual tension, and a sudden downpour signals emotional release. For a moment they embrace, but after the rain ends, the young man leaves the woman. Their relationship has been fragmentary (as emphasized by the editing), transitional (the film is set by a depot with trains rushing by), and largely unsatisfying.

Subsequent Brakhage films continue the motifs of sexual tension and the inability to communicate. Women are seen as unapproachable, occasionally portrayed on a pedestal (*Unglassed Windows Cast a Terrible Reflection* and *Daybreak* [1957]), but more often are seen in horrible, twisted, nightmare visions. Sexual frustration is almost inevitably accompanied by violence. In *Unglassed Windows Cast a Terrible Reflection,* two men fight over a woman; one man accidentally beats the other to death and, upon realizing what he has done, "accidently" commits suicide. In *Desistfilm* (1954), an extreme, distorting close-up of a girl's laughing mouth is followed by a close-up of the opening of her blouse. In *The Way to Shadow Garden* (1954), a solitary, nearly insane young man bows to a pelvis-shaped sculpture and offers it a toast. Later, he breaks his shot glass, spraying glass splinters into his eyes. In *In Between* (1955), a frightened man runs through darkness and is confronted by crude painted heads of women, their eyes and lips emphasized in close-ups. Sexual tension in *Reflections on Black* (1955) is characterized by numerous fragmented shots of a young woman intercut with close-ups of a coffee pot on a burner, the hot liquid beginning to bubble out of its spout. The inability to communicate is graphically illustrated in *Whiteye* (1957) by a tracking shot which discloses "I love you" written in reverse on glass window panes and a later shot of a right hand entering the cinematic frame, pen in hand, writing "My love . . ." on paper to the accompaniment of sounds of a foghorn and gunfire; then a left hand reaches into the frame and crumples the paper. If a couple ever *does* get together in these early films, this "normal" kind of love is inevitably distorted or interrupted. For example, in *Desistfilm,* a couple embracing is seen through the distortions of a glass jug, and in *Reflections on Black* a couple making love on a couch is interrupted by an older man who enters the room and glares at them.

Similar responses can be found in Robert Creeley's poetry. Like the filmmaker's, the poet's vision of women was clouded by his concept of the Muse as female. In poems like "The Door" and "Kore," he chases after the muse: "Lady, I follow," " 'O love / where are you / leading / me now?' " But in poems like "The Bed" and "Ballad of the Despairing Husband," Creeley begins to mock the romantic tradition with the bitterest of ironies. Byron's "She Walks in Beauty" is destroyed in "The Bed" with the following lines: "She walks in beauty like a lake / and eats her steak / with fork and knife / and proves a proper wife," and in "Ballad of the Despairing Husband" the rhythms of a sixteenth-century ballad are filled with venom: "Oh come home soon, I write to her. / Go screw yourself, is her answer. / Now what is that, for Christian word? / I hope she feeds on dried goose turd." His poem "The Mirror" foreshadows the poetry of *For Love,* with its awareness of the hopelessness of the romantic position the poet had taken earlier: "It becomes the incredible in which I believe, / that any god is love." In "The Mirror," a mirror image of the later poem "The Operation," the poet blames himself for his loss of innocence. As he looks at the woman "in the first light," he sees "the horrible / incompetence, and dull passive greyness / of myself." In "The Operation," the woman is equally at fault: "Your eyes bulged, the grey / light hung on you, you were hideous," though here the speaker admits that "my involvement is just an old / habitual relationship."

With *For Love,* Creeley articulates with great courage the unavoidable, which is not only the breakup of his first marriage but his loss of innocence and the gradual realization of just what it is that poetry and women can and cannot do. In "The Rhyme," he writes, "I saw her / and behind her there were / flowers, and behind them / nothing." The nothingness is not in the woman, but in the gaping hole left by the destruction of illusion. "The Dishonest Mailmen" describes Creeley's own confrontation (seen as a conflagration) with not only the "they" of the exterior world but the "they" created in the poet's own mind. "Letters," literally pieces of words, are being burned. The terror of facing "emptiness" is magnified by Creeley's tone: casual and petulant like a child's. Ironically, the poet's realization is still rooted in romantic terms, a heroic quest for "the poem supreme":

> They are taking all my letters, and they
> put them into a fire.
>
>   I see the flames, etc.
> But do not care, etc.
>
> They burn everything I have, or what little
> I have. I don't care, etc.
>
> The poem supreme, addressed to
> emptiness—this is the courage
>
> necessary. This is something
> quite different.

This poem points the way toward Creeley's later developments in *Words, Pieces,* and *Thirty Things,* serving a function similar to that which *Anticipation of the Night* served for Brakhage. In both works, poet and filmmaker metaphorically confront their fears and conquer them through some form of violent action. Brakhage symbolically hangs himself at the end of *Anticipation of the Night,* thereby allowing himself to be reborn. In "The Dishonest Mailmen," Creeley acknowledges the "dishonesty" of his earlier poetry, "burning" his past the way an ex-lover burns old love letters as a rite of exorcism. In terms of their use of artistic traditions and of their personal lives, both works represent a break from the past and the beginning of each artist's own voice. Such an understanding of their art could not have occurred without a transformed attitude toward women and the achievement of some form of stability in their own lives. In a letter to Ian Hamilton Finlay, dated November 27, 1961, Creeley wrote of his second marriage:

> In any case I would I think be utterly lonely if it were not for my marriage because my wife not so much bolsters me up, nor simply sympathizes, as allows me somehow the clear sense of being a man I otherwise stumble about trying to find—or did when single god knows.[16]

The intensity of the artists' search for a center in their lives is immediately recognized when one considers that Brakhage married his wife, Jane, a few weeks after he met her, and that two weeks after they met, Creeley married his second wife, Bobbie Louise Hoeck. Bobbie Creeley contributed collages and monoprints to many of her husband's publications, and Stan and Jane Brakhage are almost an entity unto themselves, one speaking for the other, with Brakhage's films signed "By Brakhage," which "should be understood to mean 'by way of Stan and Jane Brakhage.'"[17] But significantly, as late as 1973, Jane saw that Brakhage was unable to create a portrait of her because he was always creating a portrait of himself:

> I've just been doing something like having a baby, or minding the kids, or standing around or something. And he just photographs a woman having a baby, sweeping the floor, or making a bed. It's the making of the bed, not how *Jane* makes the bed or what *Jane* does with it.[18]

By the late 1960s and early 1970s Brakhage and Creeley's use of an almost uncontrolled subjectivity had led them into a dizzying abyss, a void with no exit. They pulled back and tried to take a very "objective" look at the world. For Brakhage, this meant an almost documentary approach to filmmaking in the films of "The Pittsburgh Trilogy." One of the trilogy films, *The Act of Seeing with one's own eyes* (the literal translation of the word *autopsy*), was confined to a coroner's examining room. This film was a shocking confrontation for Brakhage, as critic John du Cane described it: "the great artist coming to beautiful terms with shit death."[19] Essentially a romantic film, it is ironically in a "cleaner" and more objective style. At roughly the same time, in *Words,* Creeley shifted his emphasis from himself to the structure of his poems. Yet neither man could escape from a preoccupation with autobiography and both sought to reconcile this idea of self with the form of their art. They recognized the need for control, yet for both artists this control had to be self-directed, honest, and natural. Creeley and Brakhage found this control in an autobiography of *structure.* In 1974, Creeley explained:

> . . . Writing . . . began to lose its specific edges, its singleness of occurrence, and I worked to be open to the casual, the commonplace, that which collected itself. The world transformed to bits of paper, torn words, "it/it." Its continuity became again physical.[20]

For both men an emphasis on the natural led them to the last of the romantic tenets: the celebration of the commonplace. The filmmaker began making "dailiness films," a record of the daily life and activities of his wife and children, while the poet began writing poems that tended toward very objective views of the activities of everyday existence—something as "banal" as "Thinking light, / whitish blue, / sun's / shadow on / the porch floor."[21] They became interested in recording the passage of time, recording commonplace objects. This new development in their art was firmly linked to the centering of their personal lives. As Brakhage has commented:

> You'd almost think, to read people's biographical statements [about the Brakhages], that since we've moved to this house [their permanent home] that we stopped having any biography, and, in a sense, that's true. We stopped having a series of adventures that could be tabulated. [Since moving to the house,] the *real* thing that has *always* centered my concerns, all my life long, *began*—which is to say, the non-chronologically oriented day-to-day living. And so, I'm not very biographically interesting from that point on because biography is a form that's *so* rooted to the dramatic, to its ups and downs

and clashes. The really great creative new thrust in this century—such a deeply significant, middle-class thrust that I've certainly pitched myself at the center of—is a coming to terms [with] daily living.[22]

And while Creeley has wearily acknowledged that "we will talk of everything sooner or later," he has also stated that

I don't want to write what is only an idea, particularly my own. If the world can't come true in that place [in his writing], flooding all terms of my thought and experience, then it's not enough, either for me or equally, for anyone else. It must somehow be *revelation,* no matter how modest that transformation can sometimes be. Or vast, truly—"the world in a grain of sand."[23]

Brakhage's *The Stars Are Beautiful* (1974) is a study of the link between the commonplace and the cosmic, and yet on another level, parodies such a view. The filmmaker's narration alternates silence and "dailiness" sound—the ambient sounds of Jane and the children at work. His narration, continuing throughout the film, grows more and more outrageous, with visuals emphasizing his more ludicrous comments. Early in the film the camera holds on what looks like a telescopic shot of a planet (but which is actually the head of a nail driven into a wall), while Brakhage is heard portentously intoning in a voice-over: "There's a wall there. A great dark wall with holes in it and behind the wall is an enormous fire of white flames." At one point, Brakhage states: "The black of the sky at night is ashes." As he says this, the camera zip-pans and Brakhage cuts to a grayish black ("ashes") frame. As the camera holds, he continues: "The moon: a bubbling drop of water. This is the same with us, i.e., as the universe burns, so do we. Our heads contain water very much like the sky holds moons. The burning in us keeps the water in our heads boiling and sputtering." As the filmmaker says "sputtering" he cuts back to ambient sound: the fluttering of a bird's wings and conversation. Brakhage continues his consciously ridiculous associations, comparing stars to tea, blotters, sperm, and cigarettes.

The *process* of speech, vision, and thought is central to the idea of revelation in the work of both Creeley and Brakhage. Creeley's poems are improvisations of speech and thought: words tumbling in a brain, musings from the tongue. Similarly, Brakhage experiments with vision, utilizing blinks, blurs, phosphenes, retinal imagery—what he calls "closed-eye vision."[24] He has always dreamed of making films without the barrier of a camera, a direct eye-to-celluloid art, and has boasted that "I am the most thorough documentary filmmaker in the world because I document the act of seeing as well as everything that the light brings me."[25] (In 1963, Brakhage made *Mothlight* by pasting mothwings, flower petals, and leaves between two strips of clear mylar film and running it through a projector.) Both Brakhage and Creeley are also interested in the process of thought, its movement and evolution, going beyond Gertrude Stein's "rose is a rose is a rose" and taking heed of Charles Olson's cry that "one perception must must must MOVE, INSTANTER, ON ANOTHER!"[26]

Even though their techniques vary, both filmmaker and poet have utilized silence as a reflection of their feelings of isolation from the world. Most of Brakhage's films are silent; the absence of sound allows him greater control over the "world" of a film and, symbolically, over the world outside. Brakhage's emphasis on the content of a visual experience usually demands the form of silence (not only the silence on the sound track but the "silence" of black leader that punctuates imagery); Creeley's pauses, ellipses, and large spaces between lines are an extension of a content of silence: the poetry of isolation and reflection. Additionally, both artists make use of silence as a rhythmical structuring device. In a Creeley poem silence is a pause for breath; in a Brakhage film black leader is the blink of an eye.

Warren Tallman, in his "Robert Creeley's RIME-THOUGHT," appears to be the first to have noticed that Creeley's poetry shares certain affinities with film. Comparing the poet's use of punctuation in the short story "Mr. Blue" to the rhythms of experimental film, he writes:

The commas, periods, stresses and pauses break the 54 words in 19 segments, approximately 3 words per segment. Think for a moment of the 16 frames per second in film projection. Then think of experimental films which present not 16 phases of a single image but any number of different images up to 16. By concentrated handling of the projection speed and the sequence of images the film can catch the viewer up in a shifting rhythmic flow of the projection at the same time that the latter observes what is happening on the screen. Similarly, Creeley provides a carefully modulated flow of the telling which catches the reader up at the same time that he follows what is being told.[27]

Creeley's use of such punctuation in his poetry is closely related to experimental film, which is often defined as "film poetry." In a 1978 review of Brakhage's *Western History* (1971) and *Short Films, 1975,* Creeley noted that "film, as poetry, as the language arts more generally, is a serial art. One thing 'comes after' another: words, images."[28] Creeley's poetry shares another link with film in that many of his books are carefully designed to incorporate visual material: photography and photomontage. Often the text and image appear to be a schema for a film— similar to Moholy-Nagy's proposal for a film in the final section of his *Painting, Photography, and Film.* Creeley's *His Idea* (with photos by Elsa Dorfman), a poetry "flip book," is at least superficially similar to Brakhage's *Loving* (1957) and *Short Films, 1975: #9.* Significantly, in *Thirty Things,* Creeley's "But," written "for Stan's birthday," is a poem-as-film loop, accompanied by a Bobbie Creeley monoprint portrait of Brakhage within the frames of a filmstrip.

Such uses of language after the manner of film were indirectly reinforced by Creeley's knowledge of Charles Olson's "Projective Verse." Olson's emphasis on movement, the idea of one perception leading "IMMEDIATELY AND DIRECTLY . . . TO A FURTHER PERCEPTION," parallels film in which one image builds on another (twenty-four frames per second).[29] Creeley's relationship with Olson has been well chronicled; less well known is Brakhage's. An admirer of Olson's poetry and theoretical writings, Brakhage corresponded with Olson, visited him in Gloucester, Massachusetts, and included parts of "Projective Verse" in his apologia, *Metaphors on Vision.* [30] Brakhage may have been attracted to Olson's theories because they corresponded to some of the theories of the great Russian film director Sergei Eisenstein, Brakhage's spiritual mentor. Olson's theories appealed to Brakhage and Creeley because they encompassed both artists' need for freedom and, simultaneously, control. Olson's concept of "open field" allowed for epics like Brakhage's *Dog Star Man,* as well as the intimate, conversational style of Creeley's "I Know a Man." Further, this freedom of form permitted the energies of both men to be transmitted in a relatively unadulterated state. Olson understood that energy must have direction, and his concepts helped to channel the energies of the two artists by emphasizing the need to hone one's media to its smallest components in order to gain control over one's art. Olson thought of the two halves of poetry as

the HEAD, by way of the EAR, to the SYLLABLE
the HEART, by way of the BREATH, to the LINE[31]

Later, Creeley would write ". . . the poet is after . . . the poem in its full impact of speech. . . . Breath anyhow is one means to a solution, I think it is the *only* means."[32] In the case of Brakhage, he may have found Olson's emphasis on syllable and line similar to Eisenstein's emphasis on the shot as montage cell—Olson's method of control akin to cinematic editing. Brakhage has also acknowledged the influence of Louis Zukofsky and, less directly, of Creeley on his editing style. Out of all the poets, Brakhage feels that Zukofsky has influenced his editing the most:

All the others, except Creeley in later books that I've mentioned [post *Words*], didn't learn their lessons. They still have continuity senses that tend to hold things together. . . . They *didn't* learn their lessons, finding their own form, as Zukofsky has, of Gertrude Stein's great discoveries that a word *is* a word. Creeley got to it, along Stein's alley, in his own way, New England way.[33]

By the late 1960s and early 1970s, both Creeley and Brakhage began to "learn their lessons." Olson had pointed the way toward a more natural art: an unhampered energy flow, more exactness, the utilization of the medium's smallest components, an emphasis on the medium of transmission itself, an art attuned to "a most real world." In a letter to Ian Hamilton Finlay, dated November 27, 1966, Creeley commented:

> In New England there is a great pragmatic practicality brought to all terms of so-called reality, including art—"can you do anything with it etc." That was my despair for some time, but I feel most comfortable being trusted, as a "decent man," by the generality of people, and my great love for Olson and his work is very much based on the literal tangibility of that world he derives his own values from—a hand to hand exposure of men and women in a most real world, to my own sense at least. I.e., "He left him naked / the man said / and nakedness / is what one means . . ." Which is where my world comes alive, in theirs, and so on—I would hope.[34]

Olson's statement "MOVE, INSTANTER, ON AN-OTHER!" underscores the questing nature of Brakhage and Creeley's art. In a strangely purposeful but uncharted journey, their art *is* process: one poem or film leading to another. Brakhage formalizes this evolution by grouping certain films together: the five parts of *Dog Star Man,* the thirty *Songs,* the four parts of *Scenes From Under Childhood,* "The Pittsburgh Trilogy," the *Sincerity/Duplicity* series, the Roman Numeral and Arabic Numeral series, et al.[35] In fact, he regards several of his films as "chapters" in "The Book of Film." In much the same way, Creeley organizes his individual poems into volumes. Yet, like the apples of Tantalus, "truth" hangs just out of reach, each new work bringing filmmaker and poet that much closer and simultaneously that much farther away from ultimate knowledge. Brakhage's first film and Creeley's first poem were apples of a different sort; their revelations were the "original sin" that committed both men to the path of poetry and filmmaking. Cast from a fool's paradise, Brakhage and Creeley must continually do battle with "the void" or else be betrayed by revelations that are less than honest. In 1974, Creeley wrote that as he grew older he realized that "lost in some confusion of integrity, I had to tell the truth, however unreal, and persisted towards its realization even though unthinkable."[36] Similarly, Brakhage's serial autobiography of the 1970s, *Sincerity,* came to a temporary halt with the "revelations" of *Duplicity: Reel One* (1978) and *Duplicity II* (1978):

A friend of mine of many years acquaintance showed me the duplicity of myself. And, amidst guilt and anxiety, I came to see that duplicity often shows itself forth in semblance of sincerity. Then a dream informed me that "Sincerity IV," which I had just completed, was such a semblance. The dream ended with the word "Duplicity" scratched white across the closed eyelid . . . I saw that the film in question demonstrated a duplicity of relationship between the Brakhages and animals (Totemism) and environs (especially trees), visiting friends (Robert Creeley, Ed Dorn, Donald Sutherland, Angelo Di-Benedetto and Jerome Hill among them) and people-at-large. . . . Accordingly, I changed the title to "Duplicity."[37]

Interestingly enough, thirteen years earlier, Creeley had noted that "This issue of sincerity itself, however, can be a kind of refuge of fools."[38]

As John Donne has written, "Who are a little wise, the best fools be." With the advent of Brakhage and Creeley's middle years, their works have lost the terrible straining intensity of youth, gaining a calmer, more peaceful, more "foolish wisdom." *Later,* the title of Creeley's most recent collection of poetry, seems aptly to describe this phase in his life. On one hand, it *is* "later" in his life, and on the other, it seems to sum up a casual attitude toward life—an offhand "Oh yes, later I'll get to that." In "Desultory Days," a poem from the same collection, the loner who sat apart from the rest of the world is now transformed into the fool on the hill: "Ah friends, before I die, / I want to sit awhile / upon this old world's knee, / yon charming hill, you see, / and dig the ambient breezes, / make of life / such gentle passing pleasure!"

Charles Olson's question, then, "In what sense is / what happens before the eye / so very different from / what actually goes on within . . . ," is one that Stan Brakhage and Robert Creeley have tried to answer throughout the course of their careers. Their lives and art have been an unending search for an integration of self into worlds both cosmic and commonplace, an attempt to demonstrate that the world outside and the world within are "two souls therefore, which are one."

NOTES

1. In a letter to Louis Zukofsky dated April 30, 1962, Creeley wrote: "One thing happened at least in Denver and/or Boulder. . . . I met a very pleasant young film maker, Stan Brakhage" (from the letters of Louis Zukofsky at Human Research Center [HRC], University of Texas at Austin Library, Austin, Texas). In 1976 Brakhage recalled that he and his wife related to Robert and Bobbie Creeley "because they were a family *and* they were a quarreling couple. That's why we were involved with each other, but then I was also involved with his poetry, of course" (from an interview by Wendy Brabner and Gerald R. Barrett with Stan Brakhage, Newark, Delaware, 1976).

2. "Robert Creeley in Conversation with Charles Tomlinson," in *Contexts of Poetry: Interviews 1961–1971,* edited by Donald Allen (Bolinas, Calif.: Four Seasons Foundation, 1973), 20.

3. Charles Olson, *Selected Writings,* edited by Robert Creeley (New York: New Directions, 1966), 16.

4. "Lewis McAdams and Robert Creeley," in *Contexts of Poetry,* 148.

5. Brabner-Barrett interview.

6. Michael Rumaker, "Robert Creeley at Black Mountain," *boundary 2* (Spring/Fall 1978): 143. [Excerpts from this essay are reprinted in this collection.]

7. From the letters of Parker Tyler at HRC.

8. Ekbert Faas, "Robert Creeley," in *Toward a New American Poetics: Essays and Interviews* (Santa Barbara, Calif.: Black Sparrow Press, 1978), 154.

9. From the letters of Edward Dahlberg at HRC.

10. From the letters of Parker Tyler at HRC, Feb. 28, 1959.

11. Stan Brakhage, *Metaphors on Vision/Film Culture No. 30,* edited by P. Adams Sitney (Fall 1963), unnumbered.

12. Ibid.

13. Robert Creeley, *For Love* (New York: Charles Scribner's Sons, 1962), 18.

14. Brakhage, *Metaphors.*

15. Ibid.

16. From the letters of Robert Creeley at HRC.

17. Brakhage, *Metaphors*. This later came to include the Brakhage children.

18. Hollis Frampton, "Stan and Jane Brakhage, Talking," *Artforum* 11, no. 5 (Jan., 1973): 77.

19. John du Cane, "Real Film Hits London," *Time Out*, Aug. 31, 1973.

20. Robert Creeley, *Was That a Real Poem or Did You Just Make It Up Yourself* (Santa Barbara: Black Sparrow, 1976), unnumbered.

21. Robert Creeley, "Maybe," in *Hello: A Journal* (London: Marion Boyars, 1978), 16.

22. Brabner-Barrett interview.

23. Creeley, *Was That a Real Poem or Did You Just Make It Up Yourself*. See Brakhage's comments on *The Text of Light* (1974) in his *The Seen* (San Francisco: Zephyrus Image, 1975).

24. Brakhage, *Metaphors*. Brakhage writes that "closed-eye vision" is a combination of "eye-nerve action and reaction. . . . The commonest type . . . what we get when we close our eyes in daylight and watch the moving of shapes and forms through the red pattern of the eyelid."

25. Frampton, "Stan and Jane Brakhage," 79.

26. Olson, *Selected Writings*, 17.

27. Warren Tallman, "Robert Creeley's RIMETHOUGHT," in *Three Essays on Creeley* (Toronto: Coach House Press, 1973), unnumbered.

28. Robert Creeley, "Three Films," in *Was That a Real Poem and Other Essays* (Bolinas, Calif.: Four Seasons Foundation, 1979), 124.

29. Olson, *Selected Writings*, 17.

30. Brakhage's correspondence with Olson is at the University of Connecticut at Storrs.

31. Olson, *Selected Writings*, 19.

32. Robert Creeley, "A Note on Poetry," in *A Quick Graph: Collected Notes and Essays* (San Francisco: Four Seasons Foundation, 1970), 27.

33. Brabner-Barrett interview.

34. From the letters of Robert Creeley at HRC.

35. Creeley has also published seril works, including *Numbers* (New York: Poets Press, 1968), $1°2°3°4°5°6°7°8°9°0$ (Berkeley: Shambala, 1971), and *A Day Book* (New York: Charles Scribner's Sons, 1972).

36. Creeley, *Was That a Real Poem or Did You Just Make It Up Yourself*.

37. From Brakhage's description of the *Duplicity* films, intended for publication in *Filmmakers Cooperative Catalog No. 7*.

38. "Linda W. Wagner: A Colloquy with Robert Creeley," in *Contexts of Poetry*, 80.

A SENSE OF INCREMENT:
THE COLLECTED POEMS

ROBERT HASS

Creeley: His Metric

Someone tells the story that when Robert Creeley was at Harvard in the forties and began reading William Carlos Williams at a time when there was no professor to tell one how to read William Carlos Williams, he simply assumed that all of Williams's lines were end-stopped, so that when he began to write his own poems in the one genuinely original verbal music in the English language in the second half of the twentieth century, it was with a patient sense of apprenticeship. Which of course all writing is, so the story has a wonderful rightness, though I doubt it is true. Creeley is a very subtle and conscious artist; he saw something in that work that no one else had seen.

When Williams broke his lines in odd places, when he wrote

> It's all in
> the sound. A song.
> Seldom a song. It should
>
> be a song—made of
> particulars, wasps,
> a gentian—something
> immediate, open
>
> scissors, a lady's
> eyes . . .

Hass's review of *The Collected Poems of Robert Creeley, 1945–1975* first appeared in the *Threepenny Review*, no. 16 (Winter 1984): 5–6. Reprinted in *Twentieth Century Pleasures: Prose on Poetry* (New York: Ecco Press, 1984), 150–60. Copyright © 1984 by Robert Hass. Reprinted by permission.

391

it is reasonably certain that those line breaks in awkward places where words are most riveted together were intended to speed up the movement. The break between *in* and *the* was so unnatural that it hurried you from one line to the next and, in doing so, imitated the swiftness of perception. At the same time, it roughened the poem visually, gave it the kind of ungainliness that Williams found beautiful. When he wanted a slow, grave line, he gave you the elements of the perception in neat, syntactical units with natural pauses at the line end:

> Or the tree's leaves
>
> that are not the tree
> but mass to shape it

Creeley, the young man reading those poems in the time of the ascendancy of Eliot's prose, of a reawakened interest in the tetrameters of the old man Yeats, knew what everyone knows, that in a line of poetry the last position is emphatic, and whether by cunning or mistake, he read Williams accordingly, giving each line a full pause at the end. Try reading Williams that way, with a full stop at the end of the line. It syncopates the rhythm and throws an odd emphasis on the last word in the line:

> It's all *in*
> the sound. A *song.*
> Seldom a song. It *should*
>
> be a song—made *of*
> particulars, *wasps,*
> a gentian—*some*thing
> immediate, *open*
>
> scissors, a *lady's*
> eyes . . .

What becomes visible is the strangeness of the struggle to articulate the fact of the sentence. Creeley was reading about how to make a song, all right, but with a completely new and equal attention to the operation the mind has to perform in order to do so.

It was a while before the rest of the world would be similarly struck. I remember when it happened to me, partly because I had just heard Creeley read at a poetry festival in England. I was lying on a beach in Cornwall in the early spring; it was unseasonably hot and, in the variability of that weather, one large dark cloud which seemed to be coming straight out of France passed over us and let fall two or three minutes of gentle snow. One of my friends, who was in London studying to be an analyst, had been reading to us from another new arrival to the Anglo-American shore, Jacques Lacan's *Ecrits*. Lacan seemed to be proposing that because the resolution of the Oedipus complex and the acquisition of language occurred around the same time, they were the same thing. The *non* of you-can't-have-your-mother and the *nom* of the father and his access to mastery of the world through symbols were identical, so that the laws of language were the very form of consciousness and they carried its freight of loss and guilt and symbolic power. The idea was fascinating—it made the simplest of language gestures explosive and puzzling—and very French—the bourgeois gentilhomme discovering this time that prose spoke him—but not really funny; all the spiritual loneliness of the twentieth century was in it.

It *should*

be a song, made of
particulars, *wasps,*
a gentian, *some*thing
immediate . . .

Should be, *of* particulars: the disjunctions make us feel, if not understand, the almost unformed, prehensile yearning that lurks inside every preposition. Inside, I found myself thinking, the prepositional disposition of the human mind and its fictions of location.

My wife was trying to learn to do group therapy from a Greek psychiatrist at a hospital near Cambridge. Her training thus far had consisted of listening to him trying to get the middle-class English trainees to say *I* instead of *one*. "*I* feel, *I* feel, *I* feel," he would scream in frustration. And an unruffled student replied, "But sometimes one means *one*, doesn't one?" It had seemed an amusing story about English reticence, but Lacan made you wonder if the American *I* was any more personal, any less a matter of pure acculturation. Creeley had written:

> As soon as
> I speak, I
> speaks. It
>
> wants to
> be free but
> impassive lies
>
> in the direction
> of its
> words . . .

It, Bruno Bettelheim has reminded us, is what Freud called the unconscious. Lacan seemed to be saying that all of language and all of the cultural assumptions that we inherit when we acquire language are the *I*, by virtue of which *it* had become inaccessible. I remember feeling disoriented by the idea. My friend, for reasons I still don't understand, seemed delighted. The weather passed over, heading west, and we were in sun again. "Freak snow," somebody said, "The guy is freak snow."

This explains something about Creeley's popularity in the sixties, which had puzzled me. How could a poet whom I found so austere and demanding attract such a wide and enthusiastic audience? I had sat with his poems so long before they yielded their meaning that it was dismaying to go into a college lounge jammed with people sitting on the floor, nodding their heads in profound sympathy and agreement with some poem they had only heard once. They weren't faking; the answer had to lie elsewhere, in the difference between what Susan Sontag has usefully called erotics and hermeneutics.

At the State University of New York at Buffalo, in the salad days of that amazing institution, I got a clue one day during a massive seminar on popular culture. The year must have been 1969; the room was packed with students and faculty dressed, as the style was, to their archetypes: Indians, buffalo hunters, yogin, metaphysical hoboes, rednecks, lumberjacks, Mandingo princes, lions, tigers, hawks, and bears. Everything the American middle class had repressed lounged in that room listening to speaker after speaker with beatific attention. Which took some doing. I remember in particular a graduate student from the Progressive Labor Party who read an exceedingly long essay on the parallels between Bob Dylan's career and the growth of political theory in the New Left. "John Wesley Harding," I think, corresponded to a reawakening of working-class consciousness among students and intellectuals. When he finished, Edgar Friedenburg, the sociologist, rose to speak. He is a dapper man and he wore a light gray suit with a striped broadcloth Brooks Brothers shirt. His glasses sat low on his nose, his hair was tousled, and he looked amused. He only managed one sentence: "I have been reflecting this afternoon that we are patient beings, and that, though popular culture deserves our most urgent attention, it requires from us a good deal less credence and more clearwater." Some of the audience laughed; and a student in front stood up, jabbed a finger forward, and said, "Friedenburg, it took twenty fucking years of repressive *fucking* education for you to learn to talk like that."

No wonder Creeley packed the halls. His audiences were extraordinarily sensitive to language and they did not distrust it, but they distrusted deeply the *assumption* of it. Beyond the issues in any particular poem, they heard that attitude shared and worked through when Creeley read:

> One more day gone,
> done, found in
> the form of days.
>
> It began, it
> ended—was
> forward, backward,

> slow, fast, a
> sun shone, clouds,
> high in the air I was
>
> for awhile with others,
> then came down
> on the ground again.
>
> No moon. A room in
> a hotel—to begin
> again.

In the assumption of language, people get on airplanes at Kennedy, have good or bad flights, are reminded of various things such a passage might symbolize, land at Heathrow, take a black cab into London, and arrive at a little hotel just off Somethingorother Square, the whole experience thick with names and an inherence of literary and historical associations, all welded together by the grammatical assurance of the experiencing subject. That is not what this poem renders; it is just not that comforted or comforting. It renders, below these twentieth-century pleasures, what the mind must, slowly, in love and fear, perform to locate itself again, previous to any other discourse.

The erotics of language: the stunned, lovely, slow insistence on accuracy that the mind is, in language. I don't know what other rhythms could render this more movingly:

> It began, *it*
> ended—*was*
> forward, backward,
>
> slow, fast, *a*
> sun shone, clouds,
> high in the air I *was*
>
> for awhile with others . . .

"The organization of poetry," Creeley said in an interview in 1965, "has moved to a further articulation in which the rhythmic and sound structure now become not only evident but a primary coherence in the total organization of what's being experienced." And this: ". . . words are returned to an almost primal circumstance, by a technique that makes use of feedback, that is, a repetitive relocation of phrasing where words are returned to an almost objective state of presence so that they *speak* rather than someone speaking through them."

Poetics, for the last seventy years, has assumed the existence of a dialectical tension between conscious and unconscious thought. The system of analogies derived from Lévi-Strauss and Lacan and Derrida seems to assert that consciousness carries with it its own displaced and completely symbolic unconscious, that is, the structures of language by which consciousness is constituted; and this unconscious is to consciousness what language—"the collective, structural, unconscious system of differential relationships which constitute the possibility of any individual speech act"—is to particular acts of speech. This is what Creeley's mode and the attractiveness of his mode have to do with, at least much of the time; it is a poetics which addresses the tension between speaking and being spoken through language; and he makes a brilliant and unnerving music out of it.

It is a truism that the person who believes that consciousness is sufficient and in control is, by definition, out of control. Anyone who thinks of language merely as a tool used to perform a particular speech act is in the same condition. For the student in that audience, Professor Friedenburg's syntax was an illusion of mastery in a world manifestly and wildly out of control. I thought there was in it as well a good deal of resentment toward the forms of mastery that are possible. The confrontation was a stand-off. It interested me because the place where they stopped was precisely Robert Creeley's point of departure: the fact, as Lacan has innocently insisted, that there is in the nature of our use of language "something more meant than what we say."

A more familiar way to talk about this matter is to evoke the exposure scene in *The Wizard of Oz,* where the two visions of language are also two visions of mastery and power in general. I am thinking of the scene in which the wizard, a stern face on a huge screen, booms out his mighty definition of himself: I AM OZ; and Dorothy's little dog Toto, the only creature in the room not scared witless by the impressiveness of it all, trots up to the curtain and pulls it back, revealing a nervous man fiddling desperately at a control panel and speaking into a microphone. Language has such power that poets are always both the image on the screen and the figure at the controls who tries to act as a medium for that powerful projection. Creeley has dealt with this problem by always writing from the point of view of the man behind the curtain. In doing so, he arrived by instinct at terms very like those of the postexistentialist philosophers of consciousness. His own sources are native; he took his hints from the hipster sensibility of the late forties and fifties, from jazz improvisation with its departures from melody out of fascination with the possibilities of the instrument, and from action painting with its similar interest in its own media and its understanding of art and consciousness as acts.

If Lacan and hipster culture seem to have this meeting ground, it is no coincidence. What else is experience in the second half of the twentieth century about, but the sense of a world run by people with insane assurance who manipulate large and unmanageable forces over which they have almost no control? "The unsure egoist," Creeley wrote, "is not good for himself." But if he makes us conscious of the process by which ego comes into being, tries to make some purchase on the experience of its emergence, defines exactly what that purchase is and is not, he may be the writer above all worth listening to. It is also not a coincidence that Creeley wrote the poem of the decade about a world gone out of control and the crazy assumption of control that the ego makes:

> drive, he sd, for
> christ's sake, look
> out where yr going.

To speak about only this issue in Creeley's work is, I know, to leave out almost everything. This beautifully produced book from the University of California Press contains almost seven hundred pages of verse. It is thirty years' work and is full of discoveries and rediscoveries. *For Love,* which must be one of the most widely admired books published since 1945, retains its intimacy and its sting. *Words,* which is central to the issue I've described, is work of painful, sometimes luminous austerity. *Pieces* is, among other things, a meditation on time, on temporality as the condition of consciousness and of art. It is imagistic in method, but its images are to the traditional image what an X-ray is to a photograph. It is also the book that began to irritate critics. It is full of small, wry musings like this:

> Thinking—and coincident
> experience of the situation.
>
> "I think he'll hit me."
> He does. Etc.

and

> People
> were walking
> by

He wants that *by* to suggest all of time even as it catches the comedy of the fact that people go for walks partly to walk *by* things, to do a leisurely imitation of mortality, to, as Creeley would say, etc. These small, quick dances of the mind do not always work, but for me at least they are never without interest. There is a lot here that is playful, verbal equivalents of those Jim Dine drawings which try to discover the difference between pencil scribbles and pubic hair. The exhilaration of them, of this body of work, is the sense of an artist for whom the rhythms of any articulation are a possible poetry. "Who comes," he says elsewhere, "comes on time." Also, "What do you want with the phone / if you won't answer it." What else have I left out? He is a love poet above all. And a poet of dark wit and irritability and friendship. Sometimes his poems can rip you open and then turn ironically aside. The worst reproach that can be made against his work is that some of it seems begun by Francis Bacon and finished by David Hockney. That can be dismaying, but the root of the impulse is also his great strength; it is a loathing for eloquence as a form of delusion and self-importance. If you go to Creeley as you go to some other poets, for love of the social power or the transforming grandeur of language, you are likely to find him either frightening or incomprehensible. His way has been to take the ordinary, threadbare phrases and sentences by which we locate ourselves and to put them under the immense pressure of the rhythms of poetry and to make out of that what dance or music there can be. In the end, his tradition is the New England one of Puritan self-examination which extends from Edward Taylor through Emily Dickinson to Robert Lowell. None of these writers is his own particular master, and he departs from them in making the impulses of his own speech the object of scrutiny. In any case, he is a master, one of the handful at work in America in any art.

THOM GUNN

Small Persistent Difficulties

Popular though Robert Creeley's poetry has become in recent years, its language has never fitted in with the official current notions of the poetic. For example, the verbs do not work harder than, say, the adjectives; there is as little metaphor as in the most straightforward prose; and the diction throughout tends to be general, unsuited to the sensory effects we prize nowadays. So much for the orthodoxies of the twentieth century, Creeley might remark, but I am left trying to reconcile my conviction that poetry does work primarily through the vigour of its language with my experience that *his* poetry does speak to me, and to many others, in a way that is powerful and persuasive.

How does his language work, then? In commenting on the neutrality of Creeley's diction, one poet has evoked the name of Waller, and another has compared his pared-down antirhetorical flatness to the plain style of an early Elizabethan like Barnabe Googe. Nor do you have to go far to pick up Renaissance echoes: here is a poem from about 1960 called "For Friendship":

> For friendship
> make a chain that holds,
> to be bound to
> others, two by two,
>
> a walk, a garland,
> handed by hands
> that cannot move
> unless they hold.

Review of *The Collected Poems of Robert Creeley, 1945–1975* from *Times Literary Supplement*, Nov. 4, 1983, 1226. Reprinted by permission.

Neither Waller nor Googe are inappropriate names to connect with this sweet-natured and sweet-sounding generalization, in which the complete neutrality of language exposes a density of definition, and if the sheer melody of Waller is not achieved (or even aimed at), it is in a sense glanced at by the tetrameters, which Creeley both creates and at the same time carefully rejects in the lineation of the first stanza. The rejection of regularity, minute though it is here, already points to a great difference between Creeley's and any Renaissance practice. The poem reminisces about iambs but it has its own slightly shifted rhythm, which is sustained not by a tradition but by the varying pace of the singular voice.

If Creeley has come to dislike simile, finally, as "always a displacement of what *is* happening," he has come also to dislike all regularization, because it does something like the same thing. In a recent interview he said about Charles Tomlinson's use of the triadic line, which was invented late in life by William Carlos Williams, that Tomlinson was "missing where the initiating impulse is in Williams." It is all-important for him then to be true to what *is* happening, to stick to the initiating impulse, to keep from what he sees as the dead predictabilities of a systematized rhythm or language. Throughout his career I notice the recurring term *stumbling* for his poetic procedure, most recently in the "Prayer to Hermes" (from *Later,* not included in *The Collected Poems*), in which he addresses the god,

> My luck
> is your gift,
> my melodious
> breath, my stumbling.

If one stumbles, led or pushed by impulse, one stumbles into the unforeseen, the accidental. Even so, the accidental may have its patterns. In a poem of more than twenty years ago, "For Love," he says:

> Let me stumble into
> not the confession but
> the obsession I begin with
> now. . . .

A confession may be for once only, but an obsession recurs. However, it recurs as something felt afresh and with its original force: to adopt Lawrentian terms, you might say that it rises up again as a renewal and not a repetition. The poetics of impulse and renewed accident is closer to Lawrence's "poetry of the present" ("flexible to every breath," said Lawrence) than to the sententiae, or perhaps cynical epigrams, of Googe's beautiful poem "Of Money."

It was Creeley who made the famous remark that form is never more than an extension of content, and in so far as the accidents of composition are embodied in the surviving poem, his remark is constantly illustrated, for he apparently does not tidy up the odd, the peculiar, or the awkward. His suggestive or at times puzzling strangeness is directly opposed to the calculations behind those kinds of rhetoric of which he has so much dread. There is for example the disconcerting language of the last lines of "The Whip": "for which act // I think to say this / wrongly," where because the reference of "this" is unclear and the locution "I think to" unusual, the whole poem is called in question: thus the characteristics of the style enter the content of the poem, as they always must.

Easy as Creeley's poetry looks at first glance, then, much of it is to be grasped only with the closest attention. *The Collected Poems* is a formidable volume to read straight through: even though it stops short at 1975, thus omitting two later books, it is 678 agreeably printed pages long. You are lucky in fact if you have had the opportunities to read most of the work as it came out in the original collections over the last thirty years.

But certain general impressions strike me at once about his career as a whole. The first is that the style goes through only quite minor changes from beginning to end. I find more of the wonderful comedy early on, and the most recent poetry of all (I am thinking of *Later*) has been hospitable to some dreadfully soft emotion about growing old, but essentially the poetry is still written with the same plain, terse language and the same sure command over the verse movement. The next general tendency is that there *are* changes in the organization of the poems volume by volume. The early poems are complete in themselves, independent of each other, however much they may share themes. In the collections of the 1970s, however—*Pieces* and *In London,* for example—poem leads into poem, group leads into group, and the book rather than the individual poem becomes the meaningful unit. There is also in these books far more fragmentary material included—what you might plausibly call notebook jottings, some of them interesting in connection with the rest of the work or with our thinking about Creeley, some of them less so. The poetics of accident may permit a stumble of this sort, entitled "Kid":

> "What are you doing?"
> Writing some stuff.
>
> "You a poet?"
> Now and then.

Form here is only too clearly an extension of content. I can afford to comment with a certain acerbity because my admiration is so great elsewhere: I want to warn the new reader who dips into the enormous book and pulls out this kind of thing before coming to the good writing. But it would be a mistake for any critic to train his big guns on such minimal poems; there are a large number of them, exercises, notations, experiments, jokes, but after all, there is a certain proportion of deadness present in the complete collected works of any poet.

In one sense, though, "Kid" *is* a characteristic poem, for its very modesty. It is an epigram, of sorts. Creeley is at once to be differentiated from his old associates Olson and Duncan by the kind of poem he wants to write. Where their ambitions were epic, expansive, inclusive, drawing upon whole libraries of external material, his were doggedly narrower, drawing almost entirely on the irregular pulse of the personal. This is not to say that he aims at the "lyric," even though he has entitled many a poem "Song," for with him it is the speaking voice that matters, not singing or lyring but stumbling, with all the appearance of improvisation, tentatively and unevenly moving forward, but with a singular gift of "melodious breath," a gift for the true-sounding measure that Williams himself once praised. (Before you accuse Creeley of speaking in cliché about his lines taking "the beat from the breath," you should remember that it was he and Olson who originated the phrase; it is not their fault that others stiffened it into platitude.) And his narrow subject matter, that field of energy through which he stumbles, is the intensely apprehended detail of the heterosexual private life.

The feeling in his best poetry is fresh and clean; as though it is discovering itself just as it gets written. Creeley takes nothing for granted, and if his doing so makes for the wonderful unexpected funniness of "I Know a Man," and for the hilarious lines in his serious troubadour poem "The Door," and for the frankness of "Something," the poem about the pee-shy lover, it is also responsible for a depressed awareness of vulnerability like that illustrated in the note about going through New York in a taxi where he records his "continual sense of small . . . persistent difficulties." The vulnerability exposed in Creeley's poetry is almost constant. But nobody has ever pretended that stumbling was a fluid motion; it is, precisely, an encountering of small persistent difficulties in moving ahead, and if the phrase about New York describes one of the main subjects of his poetry it of course can be taken to refer to the style as well. Finally you could say that his strength arises from his constant perception of weakness. If he is the most heterosexual of poets he is also the least macho.

One situation you can find again and again in Creeley is that of the speaker in bed, either alone or not, uneasily lapsing in and out of sleep, in and out of dream. It occurs for example in a well-known poem, "The World," which starts:

> I wanted so ably
> to reassure you, I wanted
> the man you took to be me,
>
> to comfort you, and got
> up, and went to the window,
> pushed back, as you asked me to,
>
> the curtain, to see
> the outline of the trees
> in the night outside.

To hear a reading by Creeley at his best is to be aware of the importance he gives to line-endings. He makes a point of pausing on them *always,* whether there is punctuation or not; his free verse line is thus always preserved as an audibly identified unit. The result is a kind of eloquent stammering; there is a sense of small persistent difficulties all right, but of each being overcome in turn, while it occurs—the voice hesitates, and then plunges forward. You can see how such a reading suits the above lines, with what kind of obstinate holding-on it must stumble forward, even past the interruption, the almost pushed-in qualification of "as you asked me to," and finally getting there, to the end of the sentence, having thus *felt* its way through the poem's opening. The movement forward in these lines is certainly as much part of the meaning as the language itself, which as usual is plain in the extreme. Plain yet not always obvious: "ably" makes a point of much subtlety about the kind of firm flexibility he would have if he were the man she took him to be. And that third line, a breath-unit in itself, implies a large and complicated statement about assumptions and appearances. I want to go on to quote the rest of the poem, taking it in two more parts, not only because it is one of Creeley's best but because once you have come to terms with it you have made an entry into all of his work by discovering the comprehensiveness of packed life beneath the apparently simple and prosaic surface. It is a bare scene indeed: nothing much, nothing physical anyway, has been seen with clarity, nothing much has been done. An outline of trees is visible, that is all, because a curtain has been pushed back. But an outline of certain feelings has also been suggested, and that gives us something to go on when we embark on the long second sentence:

> The light, love,
> the light we felt then,
> greyly, was it, that
>
> came in, on us, not
> merely my hands or yours,
> or a wetness so comfortable,

but in the dark then
as you slept, the grey
figure came so close

and leaned over,
between us, as you
slept, restless, and

my own face had to
see it, and be seen by it,
the man it was, your

grey lost tired bewildered
brother, unused, untaken—
hated by love, and dead,

but not dead, for an
instant, saw me, myself
the intruder, as he was not.

It is a sentence so thick with comma-enclosed qualifications, because so much is happening simultaneously, that you can easily lose yourself in it. But the remedy is in the voice: it is even truer of Creeley than of most poets that the way to understand him is to learn how to read him aloud. From testing one reading against another you can "feel out" what it is "we felt" that ties the first part of the sentence together. We felt not merely each other's hands, not merely the wetness (of orgasm, it must be), but the grey light which in dream vision congeals to the ghost of the dead brother. Such exploration of the voice shows the density of the sentence to be wonderfully justified: it is not sensory writing in the usual way, not like Tennyson or Hart Crane, but it is as if, rather, Creeley goes directly to the organs that do the sensing. Synaesthesia occurs casually and as a matter of course. And the greyness when it comes the third time has become a quality of being—for the grey brother who lived in some limbo, where he still momentarily persists, was "unused, untaken": his greyness, his indefiniteness was such that "the world" had no use for him at all, it did not even exploit him. The reading voice (mine, yours, not necessarily Creeley's) continues, interrupting itself, but resuming, into a further change. The ghost intruder for an instant looks on me, the speaker, as the intruder in the bed. That is the man *he* takes me to be. By comparison with him even I seem "able"—competent, fluent, potent—belonging as I do to the world of the living. The pathos is far-reaching.

> I tried to say, it is
> all right, she is
> happy, you are no longer
>
> needed. I said,
> he is dead, and he
> went as you shifted
>
> and woke, at first afraid,
> then knew by my own knowing
> what had happened—
>
> and the light then
> of the sun coming
> for another morning
> in the world.

The last line would perhaps be weak if "the world," though not referred to as such before this, had not picked up so much weight of meaning during the poem as a whole. The world here is the real world with its common-sense light contrasting to the grey light of the love-making and the ghost: but wasn't it also the place that produced the brother, that rejected him so thoroughly before his death? The reassurance of the new day is tempered by the implication that we are creating our own ghosts of deprivation and despair as we go about our lives.

The poem is characteristic of Creeley at his best. He has gone beyond, or behind, the classic twentieth-century split between image and discourse: he does not attempt sharpness of physical image, and the discursive part of the poetry is more aptly termed "assertion" (the word used of it by Robert Pinsky, the poet who compared him to Googe). Though "The World" takes a narrative form it is like many of Creeley's nonnarrative poems, in that the real course it follows is that of the mind, wandering, but at the same time trying to focus in on its own wandering and to map a small part of its course accurately and honestly, however idiosyncratic that course may seem to be—idiosyncratic in its pace, in its syntax, even in its subject matter. In attuning our voices to that mind, in paying our full attention to the way it moves and shifts, we become part of its own attentiveness and can share in "the exactitude of his emotion."

It is by that sharing that the apparent idiosyncrasy ceases to be such, that is ceases to be special or unique. Creeley himself has the best comment here, on the opening page of the introduction to his Penguin selection from Whitman: "It is, paradoxically, the personal which makes the common in so far as it recognizes the existence of the many in the one. In my own joy or despair, I am brought to that which others have also experienced."

Robert Creeley's Continuum

But for the size of this book, I would not believe that Robert Creeley is fifty-seven now. "All that was in print is here," Mr. Creeley says in his preface: everything printed in book or magazine or broadside during a thirty-year span "like some ultimate family reunion!" There is "a sense of increment, of accumulation," he writes. He's pleased by the three decades' continuum:

> One thing
> done, the
> rest follows.

> •

> Not from not
> but in in.

> •

> Here here
> here. Here.

That is one kind of Creeley poem, so minimal it's barely there. In its place in a sequence called *Pieces* it has a context: a sexual dream. But one could apply it to the entire *Collected Poems*. It's not a bad motto.

At the other extreme, his fullest kind of poem is like this one, "Air: 'The Love of a Woman' ":

Review of *The Collected Poems of Robert Creeley, 1945–1975* from the *New York Times Book Review*, Aug. 7, 1983, 13. Reprinted by permission.

The love of a woman
is the possibility which
surrounds her as hair
her head, as the love of her

follows and describes
her. But what if
they die, then there is
still the aura

left, left sadly, but
hovers in the air, surely,
where this had taken place?
Then sing, of her, of whom

it will be said, he
sang of her, it was the
song he made which made her
happy, so she lived.

There's no arguing with that, with its lovely chiming sounds:
"her," "hair," "aura," "air" and the responding "he," "the,"
"made/made." Its delicacy of sound harks to the sixteenth cen-
tury, when "air" had the firm connotation of a tune. But a word
like "possibility," a phrase like "had taken place"—those cut it
off from the past. They are elements Campion wouldn't have
put into a lyric: no one save a contemporary of ours, who's shed
all fear of being thought naively accurate. (Blake does it some-
times, but by inadvertence.)

Turning the pages, you may wonder at first if he knows
which his good poems are (a reason to throw in all of them?).
After a while it doesn't matter; Mr. Creeley's effort has not been
to achieve the anthology piece, the isolated stand-alone wonder
like Carew's "Ask me no more . . ." or Waller's "Go, lovely
rose." The elusive continuity of the limpid forward movement
of the mind, like rippling water reflecting, has been his lifelong
fascination. Let the splendid poem occur every now and then—
as it does.

And let no one pretend that uttering simple words is not an odd occupation. This is called "The Problem":

> He can say, I am
> watching a boat tug
> at its mooring, a small
>
> rowboat. It is almost
> three in the
> afternoon. Myself
>
> and my wife are
> sitting on the porch
> of a house in Grand-
>
> Case, Saint Martin,
> French West Indies—
> and he says it.

The point, of course, is that the words convey no information to anyone present. Why he speaks them, then, is "The Problem"— not so distant as it seems from the problem of why anybody writes a simple lyric. For the more "universal" it is, the less it can tell us.

But we take pleasure in words that tell us nothing, pleasure in their shapes and sounds, and also in recognizing that we are not alone and that someone else knows it. The philosopher Ludwig Wittgenstein would have been astonished by none of this, but it nudges into terrain where he was rigorous.

Here we have Mr. Creeley's other twentieth-century note: the acknowledgment of a problematic aura that attends the simplest utterances. Sometimes he'll make a mere four- or five-word "poem," a poem by typographic courtesy, transparently banal, as if defying words to be uninteresting (unproblematic). In those moments he's closest to the most rabbinical of his masters, the late Louis Zukofsky, who looked up *a* and *the* in every dictionary and could be held by their rigors at 3 A.M.

Or (rarely) he'll be anecdotal, as in "The Teachings":

of my grandmother
who at over eighty
went west from West Acton,
to see a long lost son named
Archie—by Greyhound, my
other uncle, Hap, got the *Globe*
to photograph her, and us—
came back from Riverside, California,
where Archie was—he'd left
at eighteen—and he'd tried,
she told us, to teach her
religion, "at her age"—"as
much a fool as ever"—and
she never spoke of him again.

Or he'll imitate a master—here Pound:

Crashing sound, the woods
move. Leaves fluttering,
birds making chatter—
your body sans error.

But again and again he'll risk all on pure openness. Here is "A
Picture":

A little
house with
small
windows,

a gentle
fall of the
ground to
a small

stream. The trees
are both close
and green, a tall
sense of enclosure.

There is a sky
of blue
and a faint sun
through clouds.

    "There is a sky / of blue"; that is all the content. But phrased and arranged, set into lines that obey no perceptible law, it is, mysteriously, triumphantly, poetry.

Bibliography

Collected Works

All That Is Lovely in Men. Asheville, N.C.: Jonathan Williams, 1955. [Poems with fourteen drawings by Dan Rice.]

Away. Santa Barbara: Black Sparrow Press, 1976. [Poems with thirteen illustrations by Bobbie Creeley.]

Backwards. Knotting, England: Sceptre Press, [1975]. [Poems.]

A Calendar 1984. West Branch, Iowa: Toothpaste Press, 1983. [Poems.]

Charles Olson and Robert Creeley: The Complete Correspondence. Edited by George Butterick. 6 vols. Santa Barbara: Black Sparrow Press, 1980–85.

The Charm: Early and Uncollected Poems. [Mt. Horeb, Wis.]: Perishable Press, 1967 [not finished and bound until 1968]; San Francisco: Four Seasons Foundation, 1969 [expanded edition]; London: Calder and Boyars, 1971 [first English edition].

The Collected Poems of Robert Creeley, 1945–1975. Berkeley: University of California Press, 1982.

The Collected Prose of Robert Creeley. New York and London: Marion Boyars, 1984.

Contexts of Poetry: Interviews 1961–1971. Edited by Donald Allen. Bolinas, Calif.: Four Seasons Foundation, 1973.

The Creative. Sparrow 6. Los Angeles: Black Sparrow Press, 1973. [Lecture first given as part of the Milton S. Eisenhower Symposium 1972 at Johns Hopkins University under the title: "Creativity: The Moving Force of Society?"]

A Day Book. Berlin: Graphis, 1972 [thirteen plates by R. B. Kitaj]; New York: Charles Scribner's Sons, 1972. [Expanded edition including substantial selection of poetry "In London."]

Divisions and Other Early Poems. [Mt. Horeb, Wis.]: Perishable Press, 1968.

The Door: Selected Poems. [Dusseldorf/München, W.Ger.: S Press, 1975]. [Audiocassette.]

Echoes. West Branch, Iowa: Toothpaste Press, 1982. [Poems.]

Ferrini and Others. Gloucester, Mass.: Vincent Ferrini, 1953. [Poems.]

The Finger. Los Angeles: Black Sparrow Press, 1968. [Long poem with four collages by Bobbie Creeley.]

The Finger: Poems 1966–1969. London: Calder and Boyars, 1970.

5 Numbers. New York: Poets Press, 1968. [First half of poem sequence "Numbers."]

For Love: Poems 1950–1960. New York: Charles Scribner's Sons, 1962.

A Form of Women. New York: Jargon Books in association with Corinth Books, 1959. [Poems.]

The Gold Diggers. Palma de Mallorca: Divers Press, 1954. [Stories.]

The Gold Diggers and Other Stories. London: John Calder, 1965; New York: Charles Scribner's Sons, 1965.

Hello. [Christchurch, New Zealand]: Hawk Press, 1976. [Verse journal collected later as the New Zealand section of *Hello: A Journal, February 29–May 3, 1976.*]

Hello: A Journal, February 29–May 3, 1976. New York: New Directions, 1978; London: Marion Boyars, 1978. [Poems.]

His Idea. [Toronto]: Coach House Press, 1973. [Poems with seven photographs by Elsa Dorfman.]

If You. San Francisco: Porpoise Bookshop, 1956. [Poems with four illustrations by Fielding Dawson.]

The Immoral Proposition. Karlsruhe-Durlach, W.Ger.: Jonathan Williams, 1953. [Poems with seven drawings by René Laubiès.]

In London. Bolinas, Calif.: Angel Hair Books, 1970. [Poems.]

Inside Out. Sparrow 14. Los Angeles: Black Sparrow Press, 1973. [Lecture first given as part of the Buffalo Conference on Autobiography in the Independent American Cinema 1973 at the Center for Media, State University of New York at Buffalo.]

The Island. New York: Charles Scribner's Sons, 1963; London: John Calder, 1964. [Novel.]

The Kind of Act Of. Palma de Mallorca: Divers Press, 1953. [Poems.]

Later. New York: New Directions, 1979; London: Marion Boyars, 1980. [Poems.]

Later: A Poem. West Branch, Iowa: Toothpaste Press, 1978. [Poem sequence "Later," 1–10.]

Le Fou. Columbus, Ohio: Golden Goose Press, 1952. [Poems with one drawing by Ashley Bryan.]

Listen. Los Angeles: Black Sparrow Press, 1972. [Radio play with eight monoprints by Bobbie Creeley.]

Mabel: A Story. Paris: Editions de l'Atelier Crommelynck, 1977. [Includes twelve etchings by Jim Dine.]

Mabel: A Story and Other Prose. London: Marion Boyars, 1976.

Mazatlan: Sea. San Francisco: Poets Press, 1969. [Poems.]

Memory Gardens. New York: New Directions, [1986]. [Poems.]

Mirrors. New York: New Directions, [1983]. [Poems.]

Mother's Voice. [Santa Barbara]: Am Here Books/Immediate Editions, [1981]. [Poems.]

Numbers. Stuttgart: Edition Domberger; Dusseldorf: Galerie Schmela, 1968. [Poem sequence in English and German with ten colored serigraphs by Robert Indiana.]

$1°2°3°4°5°6°7°8°9°0.$ Berkeley: Shambala; San Francisco: Mudra, 1971. [Long poem with illustrations by Arthur Okamura.]

Pieces. Los Angeles: Black Sparrow Press, 1968 [poems with eight collages by Bobbie Creeley]; New York: Charles Scribner's Sons, 1969 [not merely an expanded version of the Black Sparrow Press edition but Creeley's third book of collected poems published in the U.S.].

Poems 1950–1965. London: Calder and Boyars, 1966.

Presences: A Text for Marisol. New York: Scribners, [1976]. [Prose with sixty-one photographs of Marisol's sculptures.]

A Quick Graph: Collected Notes and Essays. Edited by Donald Allen. San Francisco: Four Seasons Foundation, 1970.

Robert Creeley Reads. London: Turret Books/Calder and Boyars, 1967. [Booklet with recording of Creeley reading poems.]

St. Martin's. Los Angeles: Black Sparrow Press, 1971. [Poems with eight monoprints by Bobbie Creeley.]

Selected Poems. New York: Charles Scribner's Sons, [1976].

A Sense of Measure. [London]: Calder and Boyars, [1972]. [Notes, essays, interviews.]

A Snarling Garland of Xmas Verses. By Anonymous. [Palma de Mallorca: Divers Press, 1954].

Thirty Things. Los Angeles: Black Sparrow Press, 1974. [Poems with thirty-one monoprints by Bobbie Creeley.]

Was That a Real Poem and Other Essays. Edited by Donald Allen with a Chronology by Mary Novik. Bolinas, Calif.: Four Seasons Foundation, 1979.

Was That a Real Poem or Did You Just Make It Up Yourself. Sparrow 40. [Santa Barbara]: Black Sparrow Press, 1976. [Essay.]

The Whip. Worcester, England: Migrant Books, 1957. [Poems with one drawing by Kirsten Hoeck.]

Words. Rochester, Mich.: [Perishable Press], 1965 [poems]; New York: Charles Scribner's Sons, 1967 [not merely an expanded version of the Perishable Press edition but Creeley's second book of collected poems published in the U.S.].

Editions

Black Mountain Review 1954–1957. New York: AMS Press, 1969. [Reprint of the original magazine, volumes 1–3, issued in Black Mountain, N.C. Introduction added.]

Mayan Letters, by Charles Olson. Palma de Mallorca: Divers Press, 1953; London: Jonathan Cape, 1968. [Preface by Robert Creeley.]

New American Story. Edited with Donald M. Allen. New York: Grove Press, 1965.

The New Writing in the U.S.A. Edited with Donald Allen. Harmondsworth, England: Penguin, 1967. [Introduction by Robert Creeley.]

Selected Writings of Charles Olson. New York: New Directions, 1966. [Introduction by Robert Creeley.]

Whitman: Selected Poems. Harmondsworth, England: Penguin, 1973. [Introduction by Robert Creeley.]

Selected Secondary Material

[*An asterisk indicates that the work, or a portion of it, appears in this volume.*]

Alexander, Michael. "William Carlos Williams and Robert Creeley." *Agenda* 4, nos. 3–4 (Summer 1966): 56–67.

Allen, Donald, and Warren Tallman, eds. *The Poetics of the New American Poetry.* New York: Grove Press, 1973.

Altieri, Charles. "The Unsure Egoist: Robert Creeley and the Theme of Nothingness." *Contemporary Literature* 13 (Spring 1972): 162–85.

———. "Placing Creeley's Recent Work: A Poetics of Conjecture." *boundary 2* 6, no. 3; 7, no. 1 (Spring/Fall 1978): 513–39.

———. *Self and Sensibility in Contemporary American Poetry.* Cambridge: Cambridge University Press, 1984.

André, Michael. "Two Weeks with Creeley in Texas." *Chicago Review* 24, no. 2 (1972): 81–86.

Atapi, Zsolt, James Campbell, and Carl Snyder. "Robert Creeley: An Interview." *Atropos* 1, no. 1 (Spring 1978): 24–30.

Bacon, Terry R. "How He Knows How to Stop: Creeley on Closure." *American Poetry Review* 5, no. 6 (Nov.–Dec., 1976): 5–7. [Interview.]

Banks, Russell. "Notes on Creeley's *Pieces*." *Lillabulero,* no. 8 (Winter 1970): 88–91.*

Bartlett, Lee. "Creeley's 'I Know a Man.'" *Explicator* 41, no. 1 (Fall 1982): 53–54.

Basil, Robert. "Creeley Teaches in Buffalo." In *Robert Creeley: The Poet's Workshop,* edited by Carroll F. Terrell, 301–9. Orono: National Poetry Foundation, University of Maine at Orono, 1984.

Bawer, Bruce. Review of *Mirrors. Poetry* 144, no. 6 (Sept., 1984): 345–46.

Bellman, Samuel Irving. Review of *The Collected Poems of Robert Creeley, 1945–1975. Western American Literature* 19, no. 2 (Aug., 1984): 142–44.

Bernstein, Charles. "Hearing 'Here': Robert Creeley's Poetics of Duration." *Sagetrieb* 1, no. 3 (Winter 1982): 87–95.

Beum, Robert. "Five Poets." *Poetry* 92, no. 6 (Sept., 1958): 387–88. [Review of *If You.*]*

Bowen, C. [Carl Harrison-Ford]. "A Continuity, A Place—The Poetry of Robert Creeley." *Poetry Magazine* (Australia) 18, no. 5 (Oct., 1970): 3–9.

Brabner, Wendy. "'The Act of Seeing with one's own eyes': Stan Brakhage and Robert Creeley." *Library Chronicle of the University of Texas at Austin,* n.s., no. 17 (1981): 85–103.*

Bromige, David. "Creeley's *For Love:* Two Responses." *Northwest Review* 6, no. 3 (Summer 1963): 110–22. [*See also* John William Corrington.]

Brownjohn, Alan. "Some Notes on Larkin and Creeley." *Migrant,* no. 6 (May, 1960): 16–19.

Butterick, George F. "Robert Creeley and the Tradition." *Sagetrieb* 1, no. 3 (Winter 1982): 119–34.*

Cameron, Allen Barry. "'Love Comes Quietly': The Poetry of Robert Creeley." *Chicago Review* 19, no. 2 (1967): 92–103.

Campbell, James. "Musing from the Mountains." *Times Literary Supplement,* May 30, 1980, 620. [Review of *Was That a Real Poem and Other Essays.*]

Carroll, Paul. "Country of Love." *Nation,* Aug. 25, 1962, 77–78. [Review of *For Love.*]

———. *The Poem in Its Skin.* Chicago: Big Table/Follett Publishing Co., 1968.

Carruth, Hayden. "A Secular Lover." *New York Times Book Review,* May 1, 1977, 58–59. [Review of *Selected Poems.*]

Charters, Samuel. *Some Poems/Poets: Studies in American Underground Poetry Since 1945.* Berkeley: Oyez, 1971.

Chung, Ling. "Predicaments in Robert Creeley's *Words.*" *Concerning Poetry* 2, no. 2 (Fall 1969): 32–35.

Clark, Tom. " 'Desperate Perhaps, and Even Foolish, / But God Knows Useful': Creeley and the Experience of Space." *boundary 2* 6, no. 3; 7, no. 1 (Spring/Fall 1978): 453–56.

Collins, Douglas. "Notes on Robert Creeley." *Lillabulero* 2 (Winter 1968): 27–40.

Conniff, Brian. "The Lyricism of This World." In *Robert Creeley: The Poet's Workshop,* edited by Carroll F. Terrell, 289–300. Orono: National Poetry Foundation, University of Maine at Orono, 1984.

Constable, John. "The Power of Robert Creeley." *Cambridge Review* 89, no. 2129 (1966): 27–29.

Cook, Albert. "Reflections on Creeley." *boundary 2* 6, no. 3; 7, no. 1 (Spring/Fall 1978): 353–62.

———. "The Construct of Image: Olson and Creeley." *Sagetrieb* 1, no. 3 (Winter 1982): 135–39.

Cookson, William. Review of *Poems 1950–1965. Agenda* 4, nos. 5–6 (Autumn 1966): 64–66.

Cooley, Peter. Review of *Pieces. North American Review* 255, no. 2 (Summer 1970): 74–76.*

Corman, Cid. "A Requisite Commitment." *Poetry* 83, no. 6 (Mar., 1954): 340–42. [Review of *The Kind of Act Of.*]*

———. " 'For Love' Of." *Kulchur* 2, no. 8 (Winter 1962): 49–64.*

———. *At Their Word.* Santa Barbara: Black Sparrow Press, 1978.

Corrington, John William. "Creeley's *For Love:* Two Responses." *Northwest Review* 6, no. 3 (Summer 1963): 106–10. [*See also* David Bromige.]*

Cox, Kenneth. "Address and Posture in the Poetry of Robert Creeley." *Cambridge Quarterly* 4, no. 3 (Summer 1969): 237–43. Reprinted as "Address and Posture in the Early Poetry of Robert Creeley." *boundary 2* 6, no. 3; 7, no. 1 (Spring/Fall 1978): 241–46.*

Crunk [Robert Bly]. "The Work of Robert Creeley." *Fifties,* no. 2 (1959): 10–21.*

Davidson, Michael. "The Presence of the Present: Morality and the Problem of Value in Robert Creeley's Recent Prose." *boundary 2* 6, no. 3; 7, no. 1 (Spring/Fall 1978): 545–64.

Davison, Peter. "The New Poetry." *Atlantic Monthly,* Nov., 1962, 85–86. [Review of *For Love.*]

———. "New Poetry: The Generation of the Twenties." *Atlantic Monthly,* Feb., 1968, 141–42. [Review of *Words.*]

419

Dawson, Fielding. "On Creeley's Third Change." *Athanor* 4 (1973): 57–58.

Dickey, William. "Reticences of Pattern." *Poetry* 101, no. 6 (Mar., 1963): 421–24. [Review of *For Love*.]

Diehl, Paul. "The Literal Activity of Robert Creeley." *boundary 2* 6, no. 3; 7, no. 1 (Spring/Fall 1978): 335–46.

Dorn, Edward. Review of *Pieces*. *Caterpillar*, no. 10 (Jan., 1970): 248–50.

———. "Of Robert Creeley." *boundary 2* 6, no. 3; 7, no. 1 (Spring/Fall 1978): 447–48.

———. *Views*. Edited by Donald Allen. San Francisco: Four Seasons Foundation, 1980.

Duberman, Martin. *Black Mountain: An Exploration in Community*. New York: E. P. Dutton, 1972.

Duddy, Thomas A. "On Robert Creeley." *Stony Brook*, no. 3/4 (1969): 385–87. [Review of *Words*.]

Duncan, Robert. "*For Love* by Robert Creeley." *New Mexico Quarterly* 32, nos. 3–4 (Autumn–Winter 1962–63): 119–24. Reprinted with changes made by author as "After *For Love*." *boundary 2* 6, no. 3; 7, no. 1 (Spring/Fall 1978): 233–39.*

———. "A Reading of *Thirty Things*." *boundary 2* 6, no. 3; 7, no. 1 (Spring/Fall 1978): 293–99.*

Eckman, Frederick. "Six Poets, Young or Unknown." *Poetry* 89, no. 1 (Oct., 1956): 60–62. [Review of *All That Is Lovely in Men*.]

———. *Cobras and Cockle Shells: Modes in Recent American Poetry*. Flushing, N.Y.: Felix Stefanile/Sparrow Magazine, 1958.

Edelberg, Cynthia Dubin. *Robert Creeley's Poetry: A Critical Introduction*. Albuquerque: University of New Mexico Press, 1978. [Chapter 4, "In London," is reprinted in this volume.]*

———. "Creeley's Orphan Lines: The Rhythmic Character of the Sequences." *Sagetrieb* 1, no. 3 (Winter 1982): 143–62.

Eggins, Heather. "A Place, a Habit, and a Heart: The Theme of Place in the Poetry of Robert Creeley." *Poetry Review* 71, no. 4 (Dec., 1981): 60–62.

Ehrenpreis, Irvin. "A World of Sensible Particulars." *Times Literary Supplement*, Aug. 7, 1970, 871. [Review of *The Charm*.]*

Enright, D. J. "Manner Over Matter." *New Statesman*, Aug. 6, 1965, 187–88. [Review of *The Gold Diggers*.]

Eshleman, Clayton. "With Love for the Muse in Charlie Parker Tempo." *Los Angeles Times Book Review*, Mar. 4, 1984, 3, 7. [Review of *The Collected Poems of Robert Creeley, 1945–1975* and *Mirrors*.]

Faas, Ekbert, ed. *Towards a New American Poetics: Essays and Interviews*. Santa Barbara: Black Sparrow Press, 1977.

———. "Layton and Creeley: Chronicle of a Literary Friendship." In *Robert Creeley: The Poet's Workshop*, edited by Carroll F. Terrell, 249–73. Orono: National Poetry Foundation, University of Maine at Orono, 1984.

Feld, Ross. "The Fate of Doing Nothing Right." *Parnassus* 12, no. 1 (Fall/Winter 1984): 95–122.

Fles, John. "The Root." *Kulchur* 1, no. 1 (Spring 1960): 39–42.

Flint, R. W. Review of *The Island*. *New York Review of Books*, Nov. 14, 1963, 10.

Ford, Arthur. *Robert Creeley*. Boston: G. K. Hall, 1978. [Chapter 3, *"Words,"* is reprinted in this volume.]*

Franks, David. Review of *The Gold Diggers*. *Whe're*, no. 1 (Summer 1966): 94–96.

Fraser, George Sutherland. Review of *Words*. *Partisan Review* 35, no. 3 (Summer 1968): 467–75.

Fredman, Stephen. *Poet's Prose: The Crisis in American Verse*. Cambridge: Cambridge University Press, 1983.

Freeman, J. P. Review of *The Gold Diggers*. *Cambridge Quarterly* 2, no. 4 (Autumn 1967): 414–20.*

Fuller, John. Review of *Poems 1950–1965*. *London Magazine*, n.s., 6, no. 8 (Nov., 1966): 107–8.

Funsten, Kenneth. Review of *The Collected Poems of Robert Creeley, 1945–1975*. *Los Angeles Times Book Review*, Apr. 17, 1983, 8.

Gerber, Philip L. "From the Forest of Language: A Conversation with Robert Creeley." *Athanor* 4 (1973): 7–15.

Ginsberg, Allen. "On Creeley's Ear Mind." *boundary 2* 6, no. 3; 7, no. 1 (Spring/Fall 1978): 443–44.

Grenier, Robert. "A Packet for Robert Creeley." *boundary 2* 6, no. 3; 7, no. 1 (Spring/Fall 1978): 421–29.

Guillory, Daniel L. "Robert Creeley and the Surprise of Zen." *Unicorn* 3, no. 1 (1973): 18–21.

Gunn, Thom. "Small Persistent Difficulties." *Times Literary Supplement*, Nov. 4, 1983, 1226. [Review of *The Collected Poems of Robert Creeley, 1945–1975*.]*

Hall, Donald. "Other Voices, Other Tones." *Atlantic Monthly*, Oct., 1977, 103–4. [Review of *Selected Poems*.]

Hamburger, Michael. *The Truth of Poetry*. New York: Harcourt, Brace and World, 1969.

Hamilton, Ian Finley. *A Poetry Chronicle*. New York: Harper and Row, 1973.

Hammond, John G. "Solipsism and the Sexual Imagination in Robert Creeley's Fiction." *Critique* 16, no. 3 (1975): 59–69.

Hass, Robert. "Creeley: His Metric." In *Twentieth Century Pleasures: Prose on Poetry*, 150–60. New York: Ecco Press, 1984.*

Hassan, Ihab. *Contemporary American Literature: 1945–1972*. New York: Frederick Ungar Publishing Co., 1973.

Hayman, Ronald. "From Hart Crane to Gary Snyder." *Encounter* 32, no. 2 (Feb., 1969): 77–78. [Review of *Poems 1950–1965*.]

Heller, Michael. "A Note on *Words*: To Break with Insistence." *Sagetrieb* 1, no. 3 (Winter 1982): 171–74.

Hicks, Granville. "Three Tales Told Out of School." *Saturday Review*, Nov. 9, 1963, 39–40. [Review of *The Island*.]

———. "The Poets in Prose." *Saturday Review*, Dec. 11, 1965, 31–32. [Review of *The Gold Diggers*.]

Hoffman, Frederick J. *Patterns of Commitment in American Literature*. Edited by Marston La France. Toronto: University of Toronto Press, 1967.

Howard, Richard. "'I Begin Where I Can, and End When I See the Whole Thing Returning.'" In *Alone With America: Essays on the Art of Poetry in the United States Since 1950*, 65–74. New York: Atheneum, 1971.*

Hughes, Daniel. "American Poetry 1969: From B to Z." *Massachusetts Review* 11, no. 4 (Autumn 1970): 652–55. [Review of *Pieces*.]

Jackson, Richard. "Projecting the Literal World." In *Acts of Mind: Conversations with Contemporary Poets*, 164–71. University, Ala.: University of Alabama Press, 1983. [Interview.]

Johnson, Lee A. "Robert Creeley: A Checklist 1946–1970." *Twentieth Century Literature* 17, no. 3 (July, 1971): 181–98.

Jones, LeRoi. Review of *A Form of Women*. *Kulchur* 1, no. 3 (Spring–Summer 1961): 81–83.

Junkins, Donald. "Creeley and Rexroth: No Simple Poets." *Massachusetts Review* 9, no. 3 (Summer 1968): 598–601. [Review of *Words*.]

Kaufman, Robert F. "The Poetry of Robert Creeley." *Thoth* 2, no. 2 (Winter 1971): 28–36.

Keller, Emily. "An Interview by Emily Keller." *American Poetry Review* 12, no. 3 (May/June 1983): 24–28.

Keller, Karl. Review of *The Collected Poems of Robert Creeley, 1945–1975*. *Los Angeles Times Book Review*, Oct. 30, 1983, 12.

Keller, Lynn. "Lessons from William Carlos Williams: Robert Creeley's Early Poetry." *Modern Language Quarterly* 43, no. 4 (Dec., 1982): 369–94.

Kenner, Hugh. "More Than Pretty Music." *National Review*, Nov. 19, 1960, 320–21. [Review of *A Form of Women*.]*

———. "Robert Creeley's Continuum." *New York Times Book Review*, Aug. 7, 1983, 13. [Review of *The Collected Poems of Robert Creeley, 1945–1975*.]*

———. "Poeticize or Bust." *Harper's Magazine*, Sept. 1983, 67–68. [Review of *The Collected Poems of Robert Creeley, 1945–1975*.]

Kern, Robert. "Composition as Recognition: Robert Creeley and Postmodern Poetics." *boundary 2* 6, no. 3; 7, no. 1 (Spring/Fall 1978): 211–30.

Kessler, Jascha. Review of *The Collected Poems of Robert Creeley, 1945–1975*. Radio broadcast on KUSC-FM, Los Angeles, Mar. 23, 1983.

Knief, William. "An Interview with Robert Creeley." *Cottonwood Review* 1, no. 4 (1968): 3–20.

Kunitz, Stanley. "Frost, Williams, and Company." *Harper's Magazine*, Oct., 1962, 103, 108. [Review of *For Love*.]

Lambert, Christopher. "Possibilities of Conclusion." *Parnassus* 9, no. 2 (Fall/Winter 1981): 255–66. [Review of *Later*.]*

Lawlor, William T. "Creeley's 'I Know a Man': A Metaphysical Conceit." *Iowa Review* 15, no. 2 (Spring–Summer 1985): 173–75.

Leed, Jacob. "Robert Creeley and *The Lititz Review*: A Recollection with Letters." *Journal of Modern Literature* 5, no. 2 (Apr., 1976): 243–59.

Levertov, Denise. Review of *Pieces*. *Caterpillar*, no. 10 (Jan., 1970): 246–48.*

———. *The Poet in the World*. New York: New Directions, 1973.

McGann, Jerome. "Poetry and Truth." *Poetry* 117, no. 3 (Dec., 1970): 200–203. [Review of *Pieces*.]

McGuire, Jerry. "No Boundaries: Robert Creeley as Post-Modern Man." *Sagetrieb* 1, no. 3 (Winter 1982): 97–118.

Mackey, Nathaniel. "*The Gold Diggers:* Projective Prose." *boundary 2* 6, no. 3; 7, no. 1 (Spring/Fall 1978): 469–87.

Malkoff, Karl. *Crowell's Handbook of Contemporary American Poetry*. New York: Thomas Y. Crowell Co., 1973.

Mandell, Ann. *Measures: Robert Creeley's Poetry*. Toronto: Coach House Press, 1974.

Mariani, Paul. "'Fire of a Very Real Order': Creeley and Williams." *boundary 2* 6, no. 3; 7, no. 1 (Spring/Fall 1978): 173–90.

———. *A Usable Past: Essays on Modern and Contemporary Poetry*. Amherst: University of Massachusetts Press, 1984. [Reprints "'Fire of a Very Real Order': Creeley and Williams."]

Martone, John. Review of *Mirrors. World Literature Today* 58, no. 4 (Autumn 1984): 600.

Martz, Louis L. "Recent Poetry: The End of an Era." *Yale Review* 59, no. 2 (Dec., 1969): 256–61. [Review of *Pieces*.]*

Maslow, Ellen. "A Discussion of Several of Creeley's Poems." *Kulchur* 5, no. 20 (Winter 1964–65): 66–71.

Mazzaro, Jerome. "Integrities." *Kenyon Review* 32, no. 1 (1970): 163–65.

———. "Robert Creeley, the Domestic Muse, and Post-Modernism." *Athanor* 4 (1973): 16–33.

Mesch, Harald. "Robert Creeley's Epistemopathic Path." *Sagetrieb* 1, no. 3 (Winter 1982): 57–85.

Messing, Gordon M. "The Linguistic Analysis of Some Contemporary Nonformal Poetry." *Language and Style* 2, no. 4 (Fall 1969): 325–28.

Milner, Philip. "Life at All Its Points: An Interview with Robert Creeley." *Antigonish Review,* no. 26 (Summer 1976): 36–47.

Moon, Samuel. "Creeley as Narrator." *Poetry* 108, no. 5 (Aug., 1966): 341–42. [Review of *The Gold Diggers*.]

———. "The Springs of Action: A Psychological Portrait of Robert Creeley (Part I: *The Whip*)." *boundary 2* 6, no. 3; 7, no. 1 (Spring/Fall 1978): 247–62.

Morgan, Edwin. "One: Two: Three." *Times Literary Supplement,* Oct. 15, 1976, 1307. [Review of *Mabel: A Story and Other Prose*.]

Murray, Timothy. "The Robert Creeley Collection at Washington University, St. Louis, Missouri." *Sagetrieb* 1, no. 3 (Winter 1982): 191–94.

Murray, Timothy, and Stephen Boardway. "Year by Year Bibliography of Robert Creeley." In *Robert Creeley: The Poet's Workshop,* edited by Carroll F. Terrell, 313–74. Orono: National Poetry Foundation, University of Maine at Orono, 1984.

Navero, William. "Robert Creeley: Close. In the Mind. Some Times. Some What." *boundary 2* 6, no. 3; 7, no. 1 (Spring/Fall 1978): 347–52.

Novik, Mary. "A Creeley Chronology." *Athanor* 4 (Spring 1973): 67–75.

———. *Robert Creeley: An Inventory, 1945–1970*. Kent, Ohio: Kent State University Press, 1973.

Oates, Joyce Carol. Review of *Selected Poems. New Republic*, Dec. 18, 1976, 26–28.

Oberg. Arthur. "Robert Creeley: And the Power to Tell *Is* Glory." *Ohio Review* 18, no. 1 (Winter 1977): 79–97.

———. *Modern American Lyric: Lowell, Berryman, Creeley, and Plath*. New Brunswick, N.J.: Rutgers University Press, 1978. [Reprints parts of "Robert Creeley: And the Power to Tell *Is* Glory."]

Olson, Charles. "Introduction to Robert Creeley." In *Human Universe and Other Essays*, edited by Donald Allen. New York: Grove Press, 1967.*

Oppenheimer, Joel. "The Inner Tightrope: An Appreciation of Robert Creeley." *Lillabulero*, no. 8 (Winter 1970): 51–53.

Ossman, David. *The Sullen Art*. New York: Corinth Books, 1963.

Paul, Sherman. "A Letter on Rosenthal's 'Problems of Robert Creeley.'" *boundary 2* 3, no. 3 (Spring 1975): 748–60.

———. "Gripping, Pushing, Moving." *Parnassus* 9, no. 2 (Fall/Winter 1981): 269–76. [Review of *Charles Olson and Robert Creeley: The Complete Correspondence*, vols. 1–2.]*

———. *The Lost America of Love: Rereading Robert Creeley, Edward Dorn, and Robert Duncan*. Baton Rouge: Louisiana State University Press, 1981.

Perloff, Marjorie. "Four Times Five: Robert Creeley's *The Island*." *boundary 2* 6, no. 3; 7, no. 1 (Spring/Fall 1978): 491–507.

Peters, Robert. "Robert Creeley's *For Love* Revisited." In *The Great American Poetry Bake-Off*, 29–35. Metuchen, N.J.: Scarecrow Press, 1979.*

Potts, Charles. "*Pieces:* The Decline of Creeley." *West Coast Review* 5, no. 4 (Apr., 1977): 3–5.

Pound, Ezra. "Selections from Ezra Pound's Letters to Robert Creeley: March 1950–October 1951." *Agenda* 4, no. 2 (Oct.–Nov., 1965): 14–21.

Power, Kevin. "Robert Creeley on Art and Poetry: An Interview with Robert Creeley." *Niagara Magazine*, no. 9 (Fall 1978): unpaged.*

Prunty, Wyatt. "Emaciated Poetry." *Sewanee Review* 93, no. 1 (Winter 1985): 78–94.

Quartermain, Peter. "Robert Creeley: What Counts." *boundary 2* 6, no. 3; 7, no. 1 (Spring/Fall 1978): 329–34.

Rajnath. "Poetry, Language, and Reality: Some Notes on the Poetry of Robert Creeley." *Indian Journal of American Studies* 14, no. 1 (Jan., 1984): 33–42.

Rasula, Jed. "Placing *Pieces*." *Sagetrieb* 1, no. 3 (Winter 1982): 163–69.

Rexroth, Kenneth. "Bearded Barbarians or Real Bards?" *New York Times Book Review*, Feb. 12, 1961, 44.*

Ricks, Christopher. Review of *A Day Book. New York Times Book Review*, Jan. 7, 1973, 5, 22.

Rosenthal, M. L. "In Exquisite Chaos." *Nation*, Nov. 1, 1958, 327.

———. *The New Poets: American and British Poetry Since World War II*. New York: Oxford University Press, 1967.

———. "Problems of Robert Creeley." *Parnassus* 2, no. 1 (Fall/Winter 1973): 205–14.*

———. "Poets in Search of Self." *New York Times Book Review*, Sept. 23, 1984, 34. [Review of *The Collected Prose of Robert Creeley*.]

Rumaker, Michael. "Robert Creeley at Black Mountain." *boundary 2* 6, no. 3; 7, no. 1 (Spring/Fall 1978): 137–70.*

Saroyan, Aram. "An Extension of Content." *Poetry* 104, no. 1 (Apr., 1964): 45–47.

Savery, Pancho. "'The Characteristics of Speech': 56 Things for Robert Creeley." In *Robert Creeley: The Poet's Workshop,* edited by Carroll F. Terrell, 223–48. Orono: National Poetry Foundation, University of Maine at Orono, 1984.

Sheppard, Robert. "Stories: Being an Information, An Interview." *Sagetrieb* 1, no. 3 (Winter 1982): 35–56. [Interview.]

Simpson, Louis. Review of *Words. Harper's Magazine,* Aug., 1967, 89–90.

Sorrentino, Gilbert. "Black Mountaineering." *Poetry* 116, no. 2 (May, 1970): 110–20.*

———. *Something Said.* San Francisco: North Point Press, 1984.

Spanos, William V. "Talking with Robert Creeley." *boundary 2* 6, no. 3; 7, no. 1 (Spring/Fall 1978): 11–74. [Interview.]

Stepanchev, Stephen. *American Poetry Since 1945: A Critical Survey.* New York: Harper and Row, 1967.

Stitt, Peter. "Tradition and the Innovative Godzilla." *Georgia Review* 39, no. 3 (Fall 1985): 643–44. [Review of *The Collected Poems of Robert Creeley, 1945–1975.*]

Stratton, Dirk. "If It Is: Robert Creeley's 'If You.'" *Sagetrieb* 3, no. 1 (Spring 1984): 105–9.

Sward, Robert S. Review of *For Love. Chelsea* 12 (Sept., 1962): 146–52.

Sylvester, William. "Robert Creeley's Poetics: I know that I hear you." *boundary 2* 6, no. 3; 7, no. 1 (Spring/Fall 1978): 193–210.

———. "Creeley, Duncan, Zukofsky 1968—Melody Moves the Light." *Sagetrieb* 2, no. 1 (Spring 1983): 97–104.

———. "Is That a Real Statue or Did Marisol Just Make It Up?: Affinities with Creeley's *Presences.*" In *Robert Creeley: The Poet's Workshop,* edited by Carroll F. Terrell, 275–87. Orono: National Poetry Foundation, University of Maine at Orono, 1984.

Tallman, Warren. *Three Essays on Creeley.* Toronto: Coach House Press in association with Beaver Kosmos, 1973.

———. "Sunny Side Up: A Note on Robert Creeley." *Athanor* 4 (Spring 1973): 64–66.

———. "Haw: A Dream for Robert Creeley." *boundary 2* 6, no. 3; 7, no. 1 (Spring/Fall 1978): 461–64.

Terrell, Carroll F. "A Visit to an Idol." In *William Carlos Williams: Man and Poet,* edited by Carroll F. Terrell, 41–46. Orono: National Poetry Foundation, University of Maine at Orono, 1983. [Interview with Creeley.]

———. "Dove Sta Memoria." In *Robert Creeley: The Poet's Workshop,* edited by Carroll F. Terrell, 199–222. Orono: National Poetry Foundation, University of Maine at Orono, 1984. [Interview.]

———, ed. *Robert Creeley: The Poet's Workshop.* Orono: National Poetry Foundation, University of Maine at Orono, 1984.

Thompson, Frank H., Jr. Review of *The Island. Prairie Schooner* 38, no. 4 (Winter 1964–65): 365–66.

425

Thompson, John. "An Alphabet of Poets." *New York Review of Books,* Aug. 1, 1968, 35. [Review of *Words.*]*

Tillinghast, Richard. "Yesterday's Avant-Garde." *Nation,* Nov. 19, 1983, 501–4. [Review of *The Collected Poems of Robert Creeley, 1945–1975.*]

Turner, Alberta. "The Same Skin, but Even More at Home in It." *Field,* no. 30 (Spring 1984): 75–82. [Review of *Mirrors.*]

Vernon, John. "The Cry of Its Occasion: Robert Creeley." *boundary 2* 6, no. 3; 7, no. 1 (Spring/Fall 1978): 309–27.

von Hallberg, Robert. "Robert Creeley and the Pleasures of System." *boundary 2* 6, no. 3; 7, no. 1 (Spring/Fall 1978): 365–79.*

———. *American Poetry and Culture 1945–1980.* Cambridge, Mass.: Harvard University Press, 1985. [Incorporates "Robert Creeley and the Pleasures of System" in Chapter 2, "Robert Creeley and John Ashberry: Systems."]

Wagner, Linda W. "The Poet as Novelist: Creeley's Novel." *Critique* 3, no. 1 (Spring 1964): 119–22. [Review of *The Island.*]*

———. Review of *The Gold Diggers. Studies in Short Fiction* 3, no. 4 (Summer 1966): 465–66.*

———. *American Modern: Essays in Fiction and Poetry.* Port Washington, N.Y.: National University Publications/Kennikat Press, 1980. [Includes "Creeley's Late Poems: Contexts," reprinted in this volume.]*

———. "'Oh, Pioneers!' One Sense of Creeley's 'Place.'" In *Robert Creeley: The Poet's Workshop,* edited by Carroll F. Terrell, 175–81. Orono: National Poetry Foundation, University of Maine at Orono, 1984.

Weatherhead, A. Kingsley. *The Edge of the Image.* Seattle and London: University of Washington Press, 1967.

Whittemore, Reed. "*Pieces* by Robert Creeley." *New Republic,* Oct. 11, 1969, 25–26.*

Will, Frederic. "To Take Place and to 'Take Heart.'" *Poetry* 111, no. 4 (Jan., 1968): 256–58. [Review of *Words.*]*

Williamson, Allen. "Music to Your Ears." *New York Times Book Review,* Mar. 9, 1980, 8. [Review of *Later.*]

Wilson, John. "Modernism's Narrowing." *Iowa Review* 13, nos. 3–4 (Spring 1982): 233–45. [Review of *The Collected Poems of Robert Creeley, 1945–1975.*]

Zukofsky, Louis. "'What I Come To Do Is Partial.'" *Poetry* 92, no. 2 (May, 1958): 110–12. [Review of *The Whip.*]*

POETS ON POETRY   Donald Hall, General Editor

Poets on Poetry collects critical books by contemporary poets,
gathering together the articles, interviews, and book reviews
by which they have articulated the poetics of a new generation.